Центру „Великобритания“, [...]
в день представления этой книги
с благодарностью всем, кто способ-
ствовал им осуществлял публикацию книги
в этой прекрасной стране
Лондон
8·VI·94   Никита Забалуцкий.

The Life of Zabolotsky

with best wishes
to the Centre —

Robin Milner-Gulland

Good luck in looking
East!

Colin Dearne

The Life of Zabolotsky

Nikita Zabolotsky

Edited by
R. R. Milner-Gulland

Translated by
R. R. Milner-Gulland and C. G. Bearne

University of Wales Press
Cardiff
1994

9180

British Library Cataloguing-in-Publication Data.
A catalogue record for this book is available from the British Library.

ISBN 0-7083-1262-4

Jacket design by Design Principle, Cardiff
Printed in Great Britain by the Cromwell Press, Melksham, Wiltshire

Contents

Illustrations

Introduction

WHO WAS Zabolotsky? Why should his biography concern us?

Nikolay Zabolotsky was a Russian writer who was born in April 1903 and died from a heart attack in October 1958. Personally unostentatious, he seems to have aspired above all to live a quiet family life and work as a professional poet (probably a more achievable ambition in twentieth-century Russia than most Western countries, but still no highroad to fame or fortune). To a large extent he realized these aspirations, which though worthy may seem humdrum. There are three factors, however, that lift him and his life completely out of the ordinary, impart a remarkable overall drama to his life-story, and make the appearance of a full-scale account of it an event likely to be of interest not just to specialists in modern Russian poetry and culture, but to all those interested in literature and the literary process on the one hand, and in the traumas of twentieth-century – specifically Soviet – history and politics on the other.

First comes the poetry that Zabolotsky produced. It (or what survives of it) is not much in quantity: his original works will easily fit within a single volume. Yet it is not only entirely distinctive: it shows great and puzzling variety. Several voices, apparently quite unlike each other, are heard at different times in his work: behind them one senses a strong but elusive and largely concealed poetic personality. The 'middle period' works (1930–40s), in particular, have a special resonance in the late twentieth century in their exploration of 'green', ecological themes. Zabolotsky's work is not only strange and compelling in itself, but mysterious in its origins, impulses and underlying significances.

The second factor is the time through which he lived. Born well before the Revolution, he got his education during the post-revolutionary turmoil, began to write seriously and to be published in the ambiguous period of NEP (the 'New Economic Policy', 1921–8), achieved a little fame then and in the 1930s, and eventually lived to witness the 'thaw' under Khrushchov. Before that, however, he was unexpectedly and disastrously caught up in the Stalin 'Terror' of the late 1930s. Arrested in 1938, he spent six and a half years in prison and two more in exile. Though such a fate was shared by all too many of his compatriots, Zabolotsky's case was perhaps unique, in that he was an already established writer who endured the tribulations of prison camp and survived to re-establish himself in literature and (as was only revealed long afterwards) to tell the tale. As this volume for the first time makes clear, the whole terrible episode is well-documented, and the possibility of reconstructing his prison life – in many ways typical, in others exceptional – with considerable detail gives Zabolotsky's biography remarkable historical as well as human importance.

The third factor that makes his life extraordinary is closely related to the two already mentioned. It is Zabolotsky's sense of mission. This is the life-story of an unobtrusive, courteous and fastidious man, uninterested in politics, of clerkly demeanour (as many new acquaintances remarked), the antithesis of the inspired Bohemian, who was driven from early in childhood till his last day by the overwhelming sense of what he could do and what it was his responsibility to do in poetry. It is a story of an innate, unconquerable stubbornness that jeopardized his life and probably saved it too. Nothing in his early circumstances or upbringing, incidentally, seems to offer us any simple explanation for his heroically obstinate genius: he grew up in a family of peasant origins in what even for Russia was the exceptionally provincial and out-of-the-way province of Vyatka in the north-eastern forests, where he received an adequate but unremarkable education, subsequently becoming an indigent student in post-revolutionary Petrograd. Thereafter his life-story presents the riddle of a personality both ordinary and extraordinary, with its unsought confrontations with historical and political circumstances, its frustrations and triumphs, in a way that sets up universal resonances.

Zabolotsky's biography would be impoverished, of course, were it to focus too narrowly on its subject alone. Solitary and individualistic as in many ways he was, he none the less has a place, and an important one, on the cultural map of twentieth-century Russia. He scarcely took part in what is thought of as 'literary life', but the small number of writers, artists and thinkers who were close to him – largely unknown till long after their deaths – were not only of great importance in the unfolding of his talent, but are nowadays recognized as highly significant in modern Russian culture, carrying forward the achievements of the modern 'heroic age' of the arts in the first decades of this century, developing them (against formidable odds) in new and startling ways, and speaking with undimmed immediacy to a new end-of-century generation. Members of this circle of friends – notably Daniil Kharms and Aleksandr Vvedensky – set up the literary and artistic group *Oberiu* in the late 1920s, whose manifesto Zabolotsky largely wrote. They had plenty of enthusiasm for communicating with the public, and for a couple of years managed to do so through anarchic theatricalized events and public readings – but the gradual strangling of cultural pluralism during the Soviet 1930s consigned them to obscurity and worse. Among them only Zabolotsky, who managed to publish a small volume of poems in an edition of 1,200 copies, achieved some measure of fame (or – given the shock the volume caused – notoriety). Zabolotsky was not averse to public recognition in itself (indeed was sometimes naïvely appreciative of such small signs of it as he received) but abhorred any striving after it. Another writer, Vera Ketlinskaya, recalled after his death a conversation in which – still in his twenties – Zabolotsky 'talked about the secret essence of literary creativity, of how such work demands the whole of a person with nothing left over, how he must abandon all side issues – in particular the thirst for money and success – and of how a writer cannot have an easy life. This conversation was a turning-point in my career'. Zabolotsky's uncompromising and self-abnegating sense of mission puts him in the company of an interesting, characteristically Russian series of visionaries – each of whom he particularly admired – who repudiated worldly success, lived ascetically and mixed philosophical, artistic and didactic impulses in their work: from Grigory Skovoroda, the eighteenth-century religious poet and teacher, through Lev Tolstoy, Nikolay Fyodorov (the eccentric religious philosopher, admired by Tolstoy), the twentieth-century visionary poet Velimir Khlebnikov, the artist Vladimir Tatlin, to the ascetic painter Pavel Filonov, with whom Zabolotsky took lessons in the 1920s, and the scientist Konstantin Tsiolkovsky (with whom he corresponded).

All this may give a picture of grim-faced dedication and joylessness, of a personality admirable, no doubt, but not particularly sociable or appealing. Yet such a conclusion would be remote from the truth. Zabolotsky (like some of the visionaries just listed) had a strong vein of humour in his rather enigmatic make-up: it expressed itself in his life and his writing sometimes with uncomplicated jollity, sometimes with understated Chekhovian subtlety, often grotesquely and fantastically, sometimes through parody or biting wit. The impromptu epigrams and parodies that he traded with his friends would in themselves be enough to merit him a place in the company of the funniest poets of the twentieth century (alas, all too few of these verses survive). But more broadly – or perhaps profoundly – verbal wit underlies most of his early (to the public, often disorientating or shocking) poems and has a greater place in his later, apparently straightforward and monologic, poetry than is at first evident. If his work is often challenging to the reader, it can be refreshing and inspiriting too.

Anglophone readers of poetry will probably be well aware that Russian literature experienced a remarkable poetic flowering in the twentieth century. Even in Stalin's time writers such as Blok, Mayakovsky, Yesenin, Pasternak and Akhmatova were translated and discussed in the West; since 1960 the trickle of translations has become a torrent, with the discovery of new generations of 'thaw' and subsequently 'dissident' poets, and the rediscovery of such major talents as Tsvetayeva and Mandelshtam to add to the roll-call of earlier achievement. Zabolotsky has so far had only a modest place in this process: apart from a slim but admirable Cape edition, long out of print, translations have been scattered and haphazard, studies of him sparse (see our Bibliography). This neglect has basically reflected the situation in the Soviet Union, at any rate in his lifetime, when he was to a large extent neglected, viewed with suspicion, semi-suppressed or wilfully misunderstood. Yet since his too-early death in 1958 his name (as with those of his few close colleagues) has become one to conjure with and his reputation has steadily grown. That fame did not come earlier is partly an accident of his generation. The poets just named, all some ten to fifteen years older than him, embarked on their careers before the Revolution, and unlike Zabolotsky had a substantial body of work published before the Soviet government began seriously to interfere with literature in the 1930s. When with Khrushchov's 'thaw' there was a relaxation of publication policy again, Zabolotsky had only a couple more years to live. The years that should have witnessed his maturity, around the age of forty, were of course lost to literature as he struggled for survival in prison-camps and exile.

More importantly, perhaps, Zabolotsky was always a loner. In his youth he underwent, and then threw off, the influence of each of the poets mentioned above (though he retained great respect for Mandelshtam, and later developed it for Pasternak). With his humble provincial background he was remote from the sophisticated Petersburg or Moscow intelligentsia in which most of the more famous poets developed their talents. By the time he acquired an individual voice and began to be published – the later 1920s – he seemed a lonely (and scarcely prominent) eccentric, had considerable difficulty getting into print, and when noticed at all was generally an object of attack, not only from Soviet critics but also from as prominent an *emigré* as the poet Khodasevich. Later of course – from about 1960 – he began to be discussed more widely and gradually came to be regarded as on a footing with the great figures of the Russian poetic 'silver age'. Yet still he was subject to serious misunderstandings. Soviet critics generally could not, or would not, openly recognize the alarming and subversive subtexts in (particularly) his early work – Soviet editions indeed usually ignored the latter's very existence – while Western commentators, knowing both his 'difficult' early poems and his 'accessible' late work seemed baffled as to how to bridge the gap between them. Thus an ill-informed critic (R. Poggioli, in what is still a standard textbook) would write '. . . there resounded the mischievous and whimsical voice of Nikolai Zabolotsky, who was, however, first reprimanded into silence, then tamed into that parrotry which seems to be the supreme law of Soviet art' ('reprimanded into silence' is a remarkable euphemism for imprisonment!). Even a sympathetic and intelligent commentator (Helen Muchnic) concluded that 'unlike Akhmatova or Mandelstam, Zabolotsky is moved by nothing other than the desire to write . . . That is why it was possible for him to change his style without being untrue to his poetic self'. Yet in recent years, above all since his natural-philosophical works of the 1930s–1940s have become better known, it has become apparent that Zabolotsky was, on the contrary, a great poet of ideas, one who was constantly renewing himself while retaining his inner consistency: he is a poet of metamorphosis and regeneration not only in his themes, but in his very practice as a writer.

All this means that a detailed and authoritative biography of Zabolotsky, balancing 'inner' development with 'outer' events in his life, informed by deep knowledge of the poems, has long been needed. Nikita Zabolotsky, the poet's son, has unique qualifications for the task. Born in 1932, he is old enough to remember his father before his arrest (and to have known friends of his early years such as Daniil Kharms); as well as his own knowledge, however, he has crucially been able to draw on the memories and archival materials of his mother, the poet's widow Yekaterina Vasilyevna (still happily with us). Nikita Zabolotsky was a professional biologist – following his father's interests and grandfather's vocation – until devoting himself to the study of his father's life and work. Written during the period of *glasnost,* this biography has also been able, for example, to profit by the opening-up of KGB records and by the recollections of survivors from the days of the cultural polemics and Stalinist repressions that so affected the course of the poet's life – no longer inhibited by the taboos and constraints of decades. Indeed, new archival discoveries have led to several important modifications of this English-language version since the Russian text was completed in 1991. Post-Soviet chaos in the Russian publishing world, however, has meant the continual post-ponement of the volume's appearance in its original form, and this English version is its first publication in any language.

Beyond its unmatched insight into a writer's world, Nikita Zabolotsky's work makes a considerable contribution to the historio-graphy of twentieth-century Russia. He is a sober, judicious and sharp-minded historian with a gift for re-creating the volatile atmosphere of the period – so remote yet so recent – through which his father lived. In particular, of course, the account of Zabolotsky's arrest, imprisonment and exile in 1938–46 is a unique record. In general terms we are familiar with the scale of the arrests and repressions from writers such as Robert Conquest; from Solzhenitsyn's *Gulag Archipelago* we have a wealth of anecdotal detail about prison-camp existence. Zabolotsky's record – told through letters, recollections, memoirs and official documents – lets us follow one case minutely, from arrest and interrogation, through most varied stages and circumstances, some very harsh, some relatively benign, to ultimate release. It admits us to the psychological world of the victim and those close to him, and ties his experiences to the shadowy politics of the wider world. In particular we witness the mechanics of denunciation, the personal acrimonies involved, the strange world of pseudo-legality in which mass arrests and arbitrary sentences were carried out, the capricious factors that could lead to downfall or salvation for the individual, the rationalizations with which people came to terms with incredible happenings, the frequent stubborn courage both of those arrested and those who were not – which sometimes, if not very often, brought good results.

For reasons of speed it was decided that this translation would be a co-operative endeavour. I must thank my collaborators, Alex Anderson (who drafted most of chapter 1) and Colin Bearne (who did part of chapter 1 as well as chapters 3, 5 and 6) for their prompt efforts. I myself translated chapters 2, 4, a section of 6 and many shorter passages, together with Appendix I, as well as revising the text generally, and preparing editorial matter. I am happy to acknowledge that in questions of editorial approach and narrative style I have been influenced by a valued mentor, the late Max Hayward: his translations of Nadezhda Mandelshtam's two volumes of memoirs seem to me a yardstick for a presentation of such modern Russian works that will be both scholarly and generally accessible. Thanks are due to Gerry Smith, Donald Rayfield, George Hyde and Nikita Zabolotsky for help of various kinds; to Daniel Weissbort and the other translators for permission to reproduce some of their translations of Zabolotsky's poetry in Appendix II; and in particular to Ned Thomas and the University of Wales Press for their faith in the significance of Nikolay Zabolotsky and his biography.

Robin Milner-Gulland
University of Sussex

Note on Transliteration, Names and Verse Translation

There is no single agreed system of transliteration from Russian into English (partly because of the vagaries of English spelling and pronunciation, partly because of the varied purposes – scholarly and popular – transliteration has to serve). We have chosen to use the popular system set out (for example) at the beginning of each of the three volumes of the *Cambridge Companion to Russian Studies* (CUP) which has been found in practice to give anglophone readers a fair idea of the original Russian pronunciation. In a few cases where a Western spelling has become firmly established we use it rather than a strict transliteration (Chagall; Meyerhold; Crimea; Dnieper and so on). 'Soft' and 'hard' signs are omitted in names.

Russian personal names have three elements: (1) the first or proper name (*imya*); (2) the patronymic (*otchestvo*), derived from one's father's first name with the termination –ovich, –evich or –ich (masculine), –ovna, –evna, –ichna (feminine); (3) the surname, generally ending in –ov, –ev, –yn, –in or –sky (masculine), –ova, –eva, –yna, –ina, –skaya (feminine). 'Familiar' forms of first names are common (for example 'Kolya' from Nikolay; 'Katya', 'Katenka' etc. from Yekaterina). It is usual and polite to address or refer to people by first name and patronymic alone.

Both 'familiar' names and patronymics tend to confuse non-specialist readers. In this version we have made sparing use of both: instead we have followed such admirable modern translators of Russian literature as Max Hayward and Ronald Hingley in preferring to stick with either a standard first name or a surname unless there is a particular reason to do otherwise. Thus Zabolotsky's wife, Yekaterina Vasilyevna Zabolotskaya (née Klykova), is referred to by the name Yekaterina. However Nikolay Zabolotsky himself is normally referred to as 'Z' in the main text (following the usage 'M' in Nadezhda Mandelshtam's two volumes of memoirs).

The many passages of verse quoted in the original text of this volume set special translation problems that have had to be solved in an *ad hoc* way in each situation. Since they are mostly introduced to make biographical points, they have normally been translated 'prosaically' (sometimes abbreviated). In the hope of making good the inevitable distortion to Zabolotsky's image as a poet occasioned by this 'prosaic' approach, we include in Appendix II a small anthology of his work in poetic translations by various hands. It should also be mentioned that I have taken the liberty of rendering two examples of humorous domestic verse in Chapter 6 into a free English doggerel equivalent. The poem which concludes the main text, 'Testament', is also given in a poetic rendering.

R.R.M.G.

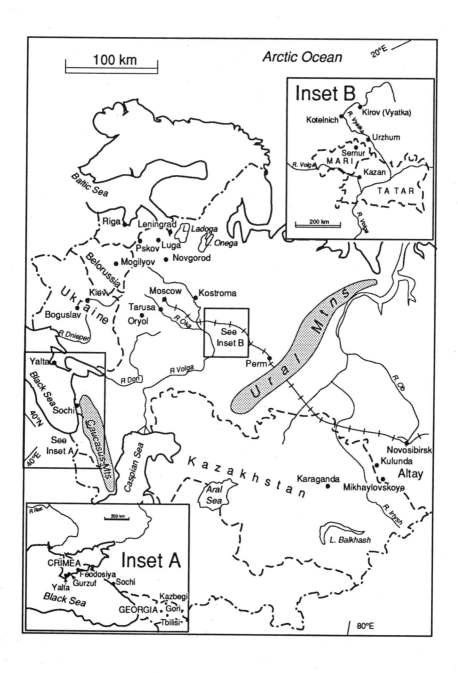

The former USSR, showing places of importance in Zabolotsky's life: the west.

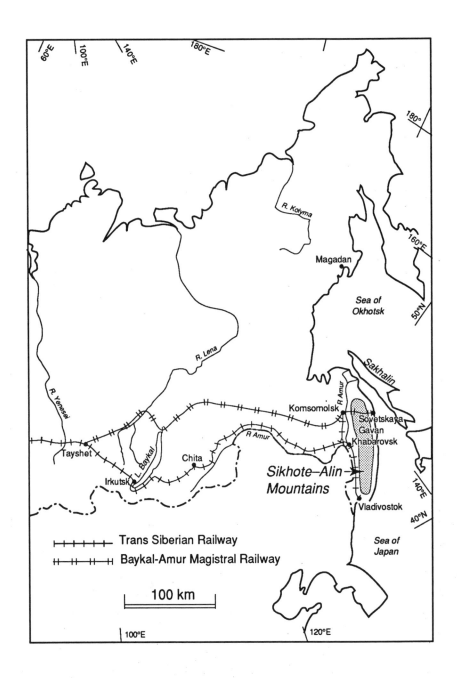

The former USSR: the Far East.

Epigraph

[From lecture-notes by Nikolay Zabolotsky, 1957]

I am a human being, a fragment of the world, one of its offspring. I am Nature's thought and reason. I am a particle of human society, one of its units. With my assistance both Nature and humanity will transform themselves, are perfecting and bettering themselves. But just as reason has not yet attained to all the secrets of the microcosmos, so in the sphere of the macrocosmos it is as yet only a talented child making its first astonishing discoveries.

As a poet I live in a world of bewitching mysteries. They surround me on all sides. Plant life in all its multiformity – this herb, these flowers, these trees – is a mighty realm of primordial life, the basis of all that lives: plants are my brethren, they nourish me with their substance and their breath; all of them live side by side with me. How could I ever renounce my kinship with them? The mutability of the landscape produced by vegetation, the conjunction of the foliage and branches, the play of sunlight on the fruits of the earth are the smile on the face of a friend linked with me in a blood relationship.

The tongue-tied animal kingdom, the human eyes of horses and dogs, the childlike babble of birds, the heroic roar of the beasts all remind me of my yesterdays. Can I forget them?

A multitude of human faces, each of which is a living mirror of inner life, the most subtle instrument of a soul full of secrets: what could be more alluring than continually observing them, interrelating with them, enjoying their fellowship?

Invisible to the eye are the noble structures of thought that like energized phantoms loom over the world of humanity, inspire me and fortify my belief in humankind. The efforts of the better part of mankind – already doing battle with human ills, with the lunacy of internecine wars, with the enslavement of one person by another, courageously penetrating the secret places of nature and bringing about its transformation – these signal a new and superior stage in the life of the world. The complex, polymorphous world with its delights and sorrows, tragedies and farces surrounds me, and I myself am one of its active particles. My activity consists in my skill with words.

Journeying in this world of bewitching mysteries, the genuine artist strips objects and phenomena of their everyday coverings and speaks to the reader: 'Those things that you have become used to seeing daily, over whose surfaces your habituated and indifferent gaze slides, are really far from ordinary, far from everyday, but full of inexplicable delight, of great internal content, and in that sense mysterious. Now I remove the veil from your eyes: look at the world, work within it and be joyful that you are human!'

A poet works with all his being simultaneously: with reason, heart, soul and muscles. He works with all his organism, and the more harmoniously integrated this work, the higher its quality. For thought to triumph he embodies it in images. For language to work he draws forth from it all its musical might. Thought – Image – Music: that is the ideal trinity towards which the poet strives.

The Shaping of the Self

I

ON THE HIGH bank of the River Vyatka in the Urzhum district of Vyatka province there once stood a picturesque village called Krasnaya Gora. Not far off one could make out the remains of a fortress built in ancient times by river sailors, so-called *ushkuyniki*.

These folk were something between mercenaries and pirates – fitted out by Novgorodian nobles and merchants in the fourteenth and fifteenth centuries for the task of seizing northern and eastern trading domains from the central Russian princedoms. Sailing down the Volga, Kama and Vyatka rivers on great flat-bottomed boats, they boldly engaged in combat with local militias and Tatar detachments, pillaging riverside settlements as they went. After Novgorod lost its independence*, the raids of the river sailors gradually tailed off and some of them settled in the territories they had subdued. It is within the realms of possibility that descendants of these headstrong envoys from the territory of Novgorod were still living in Krasnaya Gora as the nineteenth century dawned.

It was here in 1830, in the family of the peasant Yakov, that the grandfather of the poet Nikolay Alekseyevich Zabolotsky – Agafon Yakovlevich Zabolotsky – was born. Agafon entered the army at an early age and lost touch with his peasant roots during the course of many years of military service. He served not far from home, and at the time of the Crimean War he was stationed in the district capital, the town of Urzhum. When the Vyatka militia was mobilized by imperial edict in 1855 under the leadership of General Lanskoy, Agafon Zabolotsky was drafted into the ranks of the general's own Urzhum levies. He took part in the training of militiamen and set off with an Urzhum force to relieve the besieged city of Sevastopol. However the journey took them too long and by the time the militia had got as far as

* Novgorod was absorbed into Muscovy in the 1470s [Ed.].

1

the environs of Vladimir or Kursk, Sevastopol had already fallen. They were ordered to return home.

Agafon completed his service in Urzhum as a non-commissioned officer of the local military command. On coming out of the army he began work as a forest warden and bought his own house – thus joining the ranks of the middle classes.

Agafon Yakovlevich was still a fully able-bodied man when, at the age of fifty-seven, he died suddenly from a stroke. Z never saw his grandfather alive, but his grandmother outlived her husband by many years and retained a firm place in the poet's memory as a quiet, kind old lady.

Aleksey Agafonovich, the father of the poet, was born in Urzhum in 1864. Upon graduating from the Kazan agricultural college he received the title of agronomist and became the first educated man in the long line of Z's peasant forebears. It was around 1890 that local administrative bodies known as the *zemstvos* began to assume a much more lively role in Russia. The newly educated classes, represented by doctors, teachers and agronomists, were playing an ever greater part in local government and the range of issues with which provincial and district councils could concern themselves was expanding. The growth and development of agriculture in Russia at that time was a major focus of their work. In an attempt to promote agriculture and animal-husbandry, experimental demonstration farms and agricultural exhibitions were set up, where the latest agricultural machinery and equipment, more productive plant strains, new cattle breeds, fertilizers, and scientific methods of combating weeds and pests were demonstrated. Attempts were made to get the peasantry interested in all these innovations, and a demand was created for competent agronomists who were familiar with peasant ways and able to communicate with the peasant farmers on their own level. Aleksey Agafonovich Zabolotsky was just such a man. As soon as he finished agricultural college he began work on one of the *zemstvo* demonstration farms, on the outskirts of Kazan. A firm and reliable person, he took his work seriously and very soon made his mark in his allotted task. He always felt a bond of kinship with the peasantry and envisaged his calling to be to relieve and lighten their hard and sometimes thankless burden of labour. As he saw it, the science of agronomy would transform the life of the peasantry, and he spared no energy in trying to overcome the centuries-old unenlightened conservatism of Russian peasant attitudes.

Aleksey worked in the Kazan provincial *zemstvo* for about twenty years in all; first as an agronomist, then as director of the demonstration farm. His work went well, and this made the troubles which came his way in 1909 all the harder to take. What exactly took place remains unclear to this day: perhaps he rubbed the *zemstvo* authorities up the wrong way or slipped up in his work somewhere. Whatever it was, he was obliged to quit his post and he found himself without work. By the time he was forced to leave the farm at Kazan, Aleksey already had a large family. He had married late, after a short courtship and engagement – probably in 1902, when he was about thirty-eight years old. What happened was that one of the agricultural farm's employees received a visit from his sister, a young teacher from the town of Nolinsk called Lidiya Andreyevna Dyakonova. One of six children of a lowly postal official, she had lived from a very tender age as an orphan, in the care of her eldest sister. She left grammar school in Vyatka with a silver medal of excellence to her credit and in 1897 undertook a year's teacher training. She went to live in Nolinsk with her uncle, who was a doctor, and took up teaching. But she fell ill and lost her voice. It was at this point that she came to see her brother on the farm. There she met Aleksey – by now a middle-aged man – and soon afterwards they got married.

It would hardly be true to claim that married life was a carefree and totally happy experience for them: they had widely diverging personalities. Middle-aged, a stickler for order in all things, Aleksey had grown up in a family with strict ways and he most probably stuck to these ways when ordering his own family affairs. His predilection for science and books made him less attentive to matters of religion. He was always engrossed in his practical work on the farm and preferred to give the 'higher things' of life a miss. Lidiya Andreyevna had a very different nature. When she got married she was little more than twenty years old. She was straightforward, enthusiastic and loved poetry. Full of all sorts of half-formed dreams of putting herself at the service of the people, she wanted to move to a city, to the centre of social life. It soon dawned on her that all these daydreams of youth would have to be jettisoned. Her life was completely filled up with family concerns, her husband and her children. She held Aleksey in high esteem and for a long time continued to use the formal mode of address when speaking to him. However, the dissimilarity in their characters and views on life, together with Aleksey's ever more pronounced failure to keep himself in check, often led to rows. Whenever he raised his voice and demanded order in his family it seemed to his dowry-less wife that her husband was scolding her for her poverty. She would feel insulted, burst into tears and complain about her lot in life.

On 24 April 1903 (by the old Russian calendar, which was thirteen days behind the present day one) the first child was born to the Zabolotsky family – a son named Nikolay: the future poet. He was baptized in the church of St Barbara in Kazan. The baptismal certificate, which was given out later, read:

> Aleksey Agafonovich Zabolotsky, from the town of Urzhum in Vyatka province, member of the lower middle class, and his lawful wife Lidiya Andreyevna, both members of the Russian Orthodox Church, their son Nikolay born on 24 April, baptized on the 25 . . .

When Aleksey lost his job in 1909 there were already four children in the family: Nikolay, Vera (born in 1905), Mariya (1907), and Aleksey (1909). In order to support his wife and children the out-of-work agronomist had to take the first job that came his way. He became an insurance agent in Kukmor, a remote settlement in Kazan province, and he moved there together with his family. Aleksey could not adjust to the loss of the job he enjoyed so much; he gradually became depressed and, uncharacteristically for him, even took to drink. He made trips to the *zemstvo* authorities to plead for work in his area of expertise. This gloomy period in the life of the family did not last too long – about a year in fact – but increasingly frequent arguments between his parents and a sense of things going badly in the household left their imprint on the eldest son's memory.

In 1910 Aleksey at last got a promise of a job from the *zemstvo* of his own native Urzhum district, as an agronomist on a demonstration farm in the village of Sernur, sixty kilometres to the south-west of Urzhum. The family moved there in the summer or autumn, and from January 1911 Aleksey was officially taken on to the staff of the Yepifanyev farm at Sernur as an agronomist.

Sernur and the Yepifanyev farm are worth describing in a little more detail, for it was precisely in these places that the formation of Z's poetic nature began. It was here that the seven-year-old boy felt for the first time the joy of getting to know the surrounding world of nature. This was where he would grasp the meaning of his father's work, realize the nature of peasant toil and folk wisdom, discover the splendid world of books and first sense his calling.

The village of Sernur was the centre of a *volost*, the smallest administrative division of Tsarist Russia, and lay roughly halfway between Kazan and Vyatka in Vyatka province (nowadays it is a regional centre of the Mari Autonomous Republic). A well-built church towered up in the centre of the settlement, together with the brick-built houses of merchants and priests. A wide market square separated these buildings from the stone edifice of the *volost* administration and the wooden structures of the *zemstvo* hospital, which were surrounded by a fence. There were adjoining villages on either side of the settlement by the names of Nurbel and Nizovka, forming together an almost continuous long main street lined with little houses set in lush gardens. At the *volost* administration building this road was intersected by another, sloping down towards a small river and a bridge that marked where the road to Urzhum began. Beyond the bridge, among the trees, could be seen the green roof of the large two-storeyed log building that housed the local primary school. Young Nikolay started to attend lessons here from the autumn of 1910.

The little river flowed along behind the peasant cottages and gardens that lined the Nurbel–Sernur–Nizovka thoroughfare. It was split up by weirs in several places, thus forming a series of ponds, along the banks of which grew weeping willows. Two water wheels worked here, driving millstones. The white tree trunks of an ancient birch grove reared behind the school, not far from the Zabolotskys' house. Beyond the ponds, the river and the ancient birch grove, and to the right of the Urzhum road, were the lands of the agricultural farm: a large orchard, market gardens, cattle-sheds, fallow fields and cattle pastures. Blending in with copses tailing off into the distance, the ponds, groves, gardens, fields and meadows resounded with bird-song, opening up a truly beautiful world for young Nikolay to explore. When he was grown up he recalled: '. . . the magical countryside around Sernur has never died in my soul and has cast its reflection on much of my poetry.'

Aleksey often travelled out to the fields and the villages to inspect crops. He lectured at peasant gatherings about the benefits of multi-field crop rotation and other methods that would enable the peasants to reap more from the land. The man whom the peasants saw was a tall, smart and distinguished fellow of middling years with a head of black hair and a light red beard, combed into two wedges. He dressed in a light coat and wore clean shiny boots. He talked in a slightly muffled voice with a noticeable Vyatka accent. The peasants listened with interest, scratched the backs of their heads and mused. They were more concerned with their everyday worries and they grumbled about their poverty, the requisitions that were made of them, the unfair division of common land, and the exactions of the village headman. But the stubborn agronomist did not try to bring the peasants round with words alone. He showed his methods at work. On his farm the peasants were able to see with their own eyes the benefits of the new agricultural ways. They could compare fertilized with unfertilized plots of land; the primitive three-field crop rotation with the nine-field method. There they could evaluate different sorts of fertilizer and new plant strains, and there was a chance to see agricultural machinery in action. One of the rooms in the Zabolotskys' house in Sernur was equipped as a small laboratory. Local peasant farmers often came round to be shown by Aleksey how to determine the germinating capacity of seeds, the quality of the soil, and what mineral fertilizers looked like. He would also take the opportunity to talk about the surprising qualities exhibited by plants, the various factors that affected the wheat harvest, the uses of poultry and how to combat weeds. Despite the peasants' conservatism, Aleksey succeeded in getting almost everybody in his area to switch over from the three-field to the nine-field system by the time of the Revolution, as well as bringing in several other handy new agricultural methods. Z, the agronomist's eldest son, paid great attention to his father's talks with the peasants, and when he grew a little older his father helped him to rig up a laboratory for himself in the store-room of the house at Sernur. Z's younger brother Aleksey, who at this time was still very young (his family nickname was Lelya), used to watch with awe the magical chemical transformations which his elder brother demonstrated for him in his store-room laboratory. Much later in adulthood Aleksey Alekseyevich wrote to his elder brother:

> Apart from the passion for poetry, the only thing that comes back to me from early childhood is your chemistry activities. Do you remember how you used to try to do clever things with those retorts and test-tubes? The first time I ever remember seeing the usual chemicals like sulphur, vitriol and so on was in your hands. And then that hobby got overtaken by another – the magazine *The Rascal* . . . those far-away, sweet days of childhood!

When Nikolay got a little older his father sometimes took him on trips around the villages and fields in his area. Perhaps the ageing agronomist was exhibiting a secret hope that he could instil an interest in agriculture in his eldest son and make an agronomist out of him too – his successor. Zabolotsky senior knew that one life was not enough to accomplish all that he had set out to do: to transform the antiquated peasant landholdings into something like model farms. Nikolay encountered a lot of new things during these trips. He saw how the peasants lived and laboured, and started to understand what his father was striving to get the work-weary and sceptical peasant to see.

In fact, the boy was surrounded by peasant life in Sernur too. Piles of logs used to be left lying around in the middle of the village, waiting to be used in building work, and young Nikolay especially liked to listen to the conversations of the peasants who would gather there in the evenings. The peasant men talked about superstitions and the ancient

6

and arcane books kept by the Old Believers of the neighbouring village. They recalled tales told by their grandfathers and swapped local news and gossip. The agronomist's son would sit up for hours with the peasant men on such evenings, listening in on their conversation and getting home late for bed.

At that time the local Maris still held to their pagan beliefs and customs. The birch groves around Sernur were considered holy and so on feast-days believers and shamans assembled there to perform their pagan rites. Bonfires were lit, sacrifices were made to the gods, there was dancing to tambourines and spells were cast. The birch groves were linked with legends about good and evil souls, and magical powers trapped in plants and animals. It was hardly surprising that local children would be filled with superstitious dread when passing underneath the branches of these aged holy birches. Russian Orthodox priests struggled against paganism by seeking to adapt to the old ways of the Maris. Sometimes they did it by holding Christian services in these selfsame birch groves. Now the groves have gone – they were chopped down at the beginning of the 1930s because of their association with religious cults.

Shamans were still to be found here and there even during the period when the Zabolotskys lived in Sernur. During his trips with his father Z witnessed the unforgettable sight of a Mari shaman performing an incantation. Years later he remembered this heathen prayer in the heat of a discussion about the place of unintelligible, arbitrary language in poetry and exclaimed: 'Now that was the real thing!' The pagan ethos of nature worship, anthropomorphism and deification of plants, animals, rivers and boulders went hand in hand with the way a child first perceives the surrounding world of nature. Together with his father's agronomic activities, all this conditioned the future poet's interest in natural science and natural philosophy.

Z judged that his father's education, moral attitudes and work placed him about halfway between the peasantry and the intelligentsia. Nevertheless, it seems that he was closer to the rural intelligentsia of that time than he was to anything else. He shunned the more well-to-do people in the village – the merchants and priests – yet it seems that he did not mix easily with people of his own status either. His acquaintances included work-colleagues from the farm, elderly peasants, neighbours: in short, people with whom he could chat unhurriedly about life in general, local history, the local countryside, the latest gossip and peasant business.

Zabolotsky the agronomist loved nothing more than to while away his leisure hours philosophizing on abstract themes; discussing the wise ways of nature, human attempts to understand the universe and distant star systems. Neighbours would drop in, people from his home town would come visiting, and one of those discussions young Nikolay so loved to hear would start rolling. 'There's nothing in this world quite as simple as it seems', his father would say, as he downed a beer. 'Set against all the universes that exist, we are like tiny insects. And are we even capable of understanding how this universe fits together?'

Aleksey also got involved in good works. The first year of his work on the farm at Sernur proved to be a terrible one: the peasant farms in the area were laid low by a bad harvest and famine set in. The peasants had to be helped somehow. The Mari writer and local historian K. K. Vasin has provided a written account of what was done:

> A. Zabolotsky, his teacher friends and the postal workers decided to open a free canteen for children in the village. They collected money amongst themselves, but as none of them was particularly well off, the money turned out to be too little. So Zabolotsky wrote to the opera singer Shalyapin* in St Petersburg, for Shalyapin had been born in Vyatka province. Zabolotsky asked him as a fellow Vyatka man to help a good cause. Shalyapin responded to the request, sent some money, and the canteen was opened.

The story was also noted in *The Urzhum District Zemstvo Assembly Magazine*. In fact this magazine made several mentions of Zabolotsky senior's *zemstvo* activities. It was not for nothing that Lidiya Andreyevna used to say proudly of her husband: 'Everyone in the region respects Aleksey Agafonovich. They hold his opinions in high regard in the *zemstvo* too.'

Aleksey was possessed of the peasant's congenital respect for learning and books. From 1900 onwards he subscribed to the popular magazine *Niva* and collected and bound the magazine's literary supplements. Sometimes he would buy other literary publications, and books on agronomy and biology too. His book cabinet held the works of Pushkin, Lermontov, Turgenev, Goncharov, Dostoyevsky, Lev Tolstoy, Derzhavin, Karamzin, Tyutchev, Fet, Aleksey Tolstoy, Nikitin, Koltsov, Shakespeare, Hugo, Hamsun . . . Seven-year-old Nikolay would approach his father's books with due caution, spend a long time looking them over, and read for the umpteenth time the little notice that had been placed behind the glass of the cabinet: 'Dear friend! Love and respect books. Books are the fruit of the human mind. Care for them – do not tear them or leave marks on them. Books are hard to write. For many people books are as essential as bread.'

* Often spelt Chaliapine [Ed.].

The boy used to sit down by the cabinet and dwell in seclusion on every phrase of the little notice which had been cut out of a calendar. Then he would get a book out and absorb himself in reading. Lidiya loved books too and often read the poems of Pushkin, Nekrasov, Aleksey Tolstoy and Koltsov to the children. Recalling his childhood, Z wrote:

> It was there, in front of the book cabinet with its message of universal panacea taken from a calendar, that I chose a profession for myself once and for all time and became a writer, while not yet fully understanding the real implications this great event held for me.

The boy's literary bent exhibited itself ever more clearly with each passing year. He wrote poems and compiled his own poetry album, in which he wrote out his favourite Pushkin and Lermontov poems, along with his own juvenile verses. He read them to his little sisters and his brother. One of the album poems began with the words: 'In mighty Sernur a terrible thunderclap resounded . . .', followed in ballad spirit by:

> The dragon flies down,
> And gobbles up everyone else –
> Giving himself a treat.
> And I alone remain!

Z had soon read all the books from his father's cabinet that were within his reach. It is very likely that the family also used the *zemstvo* library, where one could borrow cheap editions of the Russian classics, along with adventures and study books. In a letter he wrote in the 1940s Z rather proudly recalled that by the time he was twelve he already 'knew Russian literature pretty well'.

Many of Z's early childhood impressions made a permanent imprint on his soul. His recollections were joyful and poetic ones such as Christmas, with a decorated Christmas tree in the house, the stove alight, steam belching from its open doors. The boys would appear, frozen and covered in hoar frost, asking, 'Can we sing some hymns?' They would burst into song, 'Your Nativity, Christ our God . . .' And then Christmas presents. Z remembered how

> one day in winter, during a biting cold spell, a miracle-working icon was brought into the village and my friend Vanya Mamayev, a Mari boy, went from house to house with the monks from morning to night, carrying a church lamp on a long pole, and wearing only a thin layer of outer garments. The poor thing half froze to death, and for his torment he received the reward of a varnished little picture of St Nicholas the Miracle Worker. I envied his good fortune with the very blackest envy.

Life in Sernur was particularly free and easy in summer. Z often went fishing, either with his father or his younger brother (this was a pastime the mature poet would have nothing to do with). He loved to play croquet – for a time the whole family was hooked on it. Later on he fell in love with football.

In 1912 Russia celebrated the hundredth anniversary of the Battle of Borodino. Children were taught about the war of 1812 at school, people read books about the heroes of Borodino, and a roaring trade was done in postcards showing representations of the battle scenes and generals of the war. 'Weighed down with paper medals and wooden sabres, we charged across the neighbouring gardens, our lances lowered for attack, and engaged in ferocious combat with thickets of nettles, which represented for us Napoleon's army,' recalled Z. 'I was always Platov, the Ataman of the Cossack forces, and never agreed to take more senior roles, because Platov represented for me the classic figure of Russian heroism, daring and mettle.'

The Zabolotskys displayed great enthusiasm for singing. Often when the whole family was gathered at home father would pick up his guitar and sing, either by himself or with Lidiya Andreyevna – or for that matter with the children too. Aleksey had a good voice and was said to be an excellent guitar player. It was thanks to this that when he was young he and his guitar were always welcome guests at the houses of relations or neighbours on feast-day evenings. The family sang Russian and Ukrainian songs, and sometimes even Mari songs – albeit garbling the words. Lidiya would perform something from 'Askold's Grave', and sing 'The wind swirls' and 'There stands a high mountain'. Everyone sang 'The storm hides the sky with darkness', 'Stars, my little stars' and 'Venerable lime tree' together. Having got himself into a good mood Aleksey would give a jaunty guitar solo and then, screwing up his eyes, burst into impassioned song: 'Hey you birdies of mine, you dear old notes of mine! Good new notes, twenty-five rouble notes . . .'

The children inherited a love of music and a good ear. Z learned to play the guitar from his father and knew a lot of songs and ballads. Later on he took to singing not just among his friends, but at school concerts and amateur performances.

But there were also bitter moments. His father's unrestrained, even despotic, character often had a painful effect on the life of the entire family. Lidiya would also insist, as far as she was able, on having her own way, and sometimes she laughed at him behind his back because of his penchant for talking about 'eternity and perpetuity', as Aleksey's philosophical discourses were called in the family.

A third son, Aleksandr, was born to the Zabolotskys during the year the family moved to Sernur (at that time the two daughters, Vera and Mariya, were five and three respectively). In the summer of 1912 the family was hit by a terrible misfortune: little Aleksandr died. Later, in 1914 and 1918, two more daughters were born: Natalya and Yelena. With so many children to care for, money was getting a bit tight. Aleksey's salary as an agronomist was severely stretched by the need to feed, clothe and educate them all.

Weighed down by domestic worries, Lidiya aged prematurely. The care of the children became the anchor of her life, and she gave herself up entirely to coping with the everyday chores. The principles of conscientiousness and fair play were instilled in all the children. Their father's activities and their mother's tales about people who did good works imbued the children with the notion that life was inconceivable without service to society or firm moral ideals. The children were brought up to believe that people live not just for themselves, but to fulfil a certain duty to those around them.

II

When Z completed primary school in Sernur at the age of ten, his parents decided to send him off to secondary school in Urzhum. Aleksey's native town of Urzhum was located on the hilly banks of the Urzhumka river and had around 8,000 inhabitants. Most of the houses were wooden structures, but the main streets boasted stone or brick buildings. There were about twenty craftsmen's shops and several small factories, including a vodka and spirits distillery, a cheese and milk dairy, a tanner's and a sawmill. Along the River Vyatka, about seven kilometres out of town, there was a wharf, used by merchants for shipping out timber and other local goods.

The sights of Urzhum in those days consisted of the 'Temperance Society' – a town club where the local merchants gathered and made merry; five or six churches; the long wooden edifice of the 'Auditorium' Theatre; the *zemstvo* administration, the military office, the Potapov Hotel, a very solid-looking prison located on the market square, a chemist's, the barracks of the local garrison, and a fire brigade which came complete with its own band. The amateur dramatics society put on performances at the 'Auditorium' and films starring Vera Kholodnaya and Mozhukhin ran at the 'Furore' cinema. There was an excellent music school and a couple of good libraries. In addition there was the stout brick-built secondary school building, constructed in 1912 by the Vyatka provincial *zemstvo*. It was here that Lidiya brought her eldest son to sit the school entrance exams in the summer of 1913.

Z recalled this important event of his young life in his prose sketch 'Early Years':

> The examinations were held in a vast hall. Parents crowded anxiously outside the hall's glass doorway. As my mother was leading me into this sanctuary of learning I heard someone in the crowd say: 'Well, that one will pass. Look at him – what a forehead!' Indeed, everything did go well at first. I gave good answers in the orally tested subjects – Russian language, divinity and arithmetic. But my written arithmetic let me down: I got something muddled and tried long and hard to understand what. I despaired of getting the question right, and I am sorry to say that I rather feebly broke down in tears at my desk. Luckily, a teacher chose to glance over my shoulder at my answer paper. Grinning, he poked his finger at the spot where I had made the mistake. I immediately saw it and then everything slotted into place. When the list of accepted candidates came out my surname was on it.
>
> I was overjoyed beyond all imagining! My world expanded a thousandfold, for insignificant little Urzhum appeared to me as a colossus of a city, brimful of wonders. The High Street, with its magnificent red brick cathedral, was stupendous! Piano music drifted down from the open windows of a merchant's house – I was captivated, never having heard the like before. And then there was the orchestra in the municipal gardens, the policemen standing on the corners, and shops stuffed with extraordinarily expensive and wonderful things! And those sweet schoolgirls in their brown frocks and white pinafores, every one of them a beauty! I was so embarrassed and timid in the face of their tender charms that I hardly dared raise my eyes to look at them. Not for nothing had I already been writing poetry for three years, reading famous poets and picking things up from them left, right and centre!

The secondary school offered an admirable standard of education. The Vyatka *zemstvo* was one of the most progressive in Russia and did not skimp on equipping the school. On the whole, the lessons were given by very competent and liberal-minded teachers. Z remembered many of them all his life.

Mathematics and art were regarded as most important subjects and while Z never could summon up much enthusiasm for mathematics, he demonstrated talent in painting and drawing, being able both to sketch with a pencil and paint in water-colours and oils. In the drawing classes the benches were arranged in a circle so that everybody could see the model. Each pupil had an easel. Plaster copies of the sculptures of antiquity stood along the walls. Reproductions of Old Masters, both Russian and foreign, were shown during the lessons. Z recalled that:

'We had our own well-known local artists, and generally painting was a subject that everyone took an interest in.' This widespread interest certainly did not bypass Z, and his best friend at school, a modest and impressionable lad named Misha Ivanov, painted exceedingly well and later tried to get into art school in Moscow. The art teacher, Fyodor Loginovich Larionov, enjoyed particular popularity with his pupils, not only for the interesting way in which he conducted his lessons, but also for his distinguished looks and enthusiasm for music and the theatre. He came from a poor Chuvash family but was given a grant by the provincial *zemstvo* on account of his exceptional abilities, and graduated from Kazan art school. He arrived in Urzhum in 1902 to take up art teaching, and ended up devoting more than sixty years of his life to fostering culture and the arts in the town. Not long before Z started at the secondary school Larionov had put on a production of Glinka's opera *A Life for the Tsar*. It ran both at the school and at the 'Auditorium'. The roles were filled by teachers, doctors, court and *zemstvo* officials and their wives. The art teacher himself sang the part of Ivan Susanin. Soon after that he staged Verdi's *Aida*. In so doing he made a huge impression on the young future poet. Z had this to say about it:

> It was in my first school year that by dint of the efforts of the teachers, the local intelligentsia and the elder pupils there was a staging of *Aida* – the whole thing. Granted the accompaniment was just a piano, and the props and so on were a bit limited, but the amazing thing is that it was staged at all!

History became one of young Z's favourite subjects. The history teacher, V. P. Spassky, loved to ask his pupils, 'What occupies the highest place in the state?' When they chanted in response, 'The Tsar', he would narrow his eyes cunningly and say, 'No. The law stands above all'. He obliged everyone to write down his explanations in their exercise books, and instilled a deep understanding of his subject, enabling his pupils to see the kernel of an issue.

Z took an interest in natural science and chemistry. The way natural science was taught made it particularly enthralling: for instance, everyone was gripped by the arguments surrounding Darwinism, and pupils enjoyed the right to back either the scientific viewpoint or to adhere to the literal interpretation of the word of God. Divinity was also taught, of course, but it never generated much enthusiasm among the pupils. The natural science teacher, N. V. Praksin, was a well-educated and widely read man. He was a great fan of Chekhov's tales, and he would read them aloud in class whenever the time came to break up for the school holidays. The intonations he came up with were so killingly funny that his readings would reduce both the whole class and himself to helpless laughter. That was Z's first acquaintance with Chekhov. For a long time afterwards he imagined Chekhov just as a humorist.

The chemistry room was the scene of fascinating experiments. The teacher would pour lilac- and green-coloured mixtures together to produce a liquid of transparent appearance. Getting carried away himself, he would shout: 'Look, you might think it's water in the test tube, but in fact there's God only knows what mixed together in there!' During the holidays Z repeated some of these experiments in the store-room at Sernur.

The teaching of German was taken very seriously. French was taught too, but not so well or thoroughly. Z further improved his German during his higher education, and his knowledge of the language stayed with him. When still quite young he read Goethe's *Faust* in the original.

Young Z also shone in the gymnasium. He remembered how 'we performed on gymnastics open days, dressed in special striped shirts of three colours, and the whole town would turn out to admire our performance.'

In the junior classes the teaching of literature left a lot to be desired. Only when Z reached the age of twelve or thirteen did the situation change for the better. A new teacher, Nina Aleksandrovna Rufina, arrived from Moscow. She was to play a significant role in consolidating the poetic aspirations of the young Z.

For the first four years of secondary school Nikolay lived away from his parents as a boarder. They paid thirteen roubles a month for his upkeep and care. His father often travelled to Urzhum on business and to attend meetings of the *zemstvo* administration. He would stay a day or two at the Potapov Hotel and invite his son round. Z remembered these meetings for the 'luxury' in which Aleksey tended to indulge when in Urzhum. He treated his son to caviar, cured sturgeon and cheese – delicacies usually beyond the family's means. Z's father used to take his son home for the holidays. For travelling he had the use of a coachman and a pair of horses from work, harnessed either to an unsprung carriage or to a Cossack sleigh. The hours spent journeying across this wonderful region's winter and spring landscapes of fields and woods were simply unforgettable. With lessons over and done with, home and freedom lay ahead. In summer this meant going fishing and playing games with his brother and sisters. In winter the Christmas tree, skating . . . And whatever the time of year, there would be books, poetry,

14

journeys with father, chemistry in the store-room and many other wonders which could only be experienced at home.

The year 1914 saw the outbreak of the First World War. At first, with the Russian army conducting successful offensives in East Prussia, everyone was obsessed with following the fortunes of the front line by means of moving and re-positioning little flags on maps. But when it came to moving the little flags backwards – and sometimes very far back – the maps were soon abandoned. Although the war was being fought far away in western Russia its effects were felt in Urzhum, with the sound of women's laments and the drunken cries of new conscripts issuing from the recruiting office. Despite everything, it was impossible for the schoolboys not to envy their elder co-pupils, who, having passed out of the officers' training college, came wearing their epaulettes and ceremonial sabres to bid farewell to their teachers before being sent off to the front. In May 1915 one of them was killed. His name was Koshkin, and his body was brought back to Urzhum in a lead coffin. The whole training college turned out for his funeral, which was accompanied by a band and solemn speeches. For his part, Z wrote a 'highly patriotic poem' entitled 'On the Death of Koshkin', and for a long time afterwards considered it to be the very epitome of elegant wordcraft.

The Zabolotsky children were not inclined to deep religious feelings, but nevertheless Z, with his musical and dreamy nature, could not resist the fascination of the evening church services:

> Those quiet all-night services in a dimly lit church, flickering with little points of light, drew one involuntarily into a state of thoughtfulness and sweet sadness. The choir was splendid, and when the girls' voices sang 'Glory to God on High' or 'Quiet World' a lump came to my throat, and as children do, I believed in something high and merciful existing up above, which would probably help me to achieve real human happiness.

Many young people in Urzhum were enthusiastic about literature in general, and poetry in particular. They composed poetry themselves, they read their favourite poets, and the girls copied poems into albums. In 1916, when Z was eleven years old, he met and quickly made friends with Misha Kasyanov, a boy of twelve who, together with a group of friends, was thinking of publishing his own literary magazine. They knew that Z wrote verse, and it was for this reason that he was invited onto the magazine, despite being a whole year younger than the rest of them. In his reminiscences about Z, Kasyanov described his encounter with him at the first meeting of the magazine's editorial group. This very early account is most valuable for the picture it gives us of Z's appearance and character at that time:

> The lad . . . had a bit of a forehead, was slightly shy, but he looked at you very firmly . . . Nikolay started to compose verse from the age of eleven or twelve [the poet himself claimed to have started at the age of seven. N.Z.]. He himself felt that 'this is for life. I can already tell.' He said something like this to me: 'You know what, Misha. I've got an aunt. She writes poems too. She says, "If someone starts writing verse, then he'll keep doing it until the day he dies."' When I first got to know him, Nikolay was a tow-haired child, as meek as a mouse. He never got into fights and remained taciturn, as if guarding something within himself. He talked either with a bare minimum of gestures, or none at all. You did not see him waving his arms about like the rest of us did. He spoke dispassionately, but in a positive, firm way. It was only later, when he was a young man, that I saw him exhibit passion and animation in arguments . . . Running parallel with his seriousness and his philosophical disposition, right from his tender years, Nikolay always had something merry in his nature, and sometimes a sharp strain of mischief.

A shared love of poetry and joint appearances in amateur concerts and shows brought Z and his new friend close together. Misha Kasyanov came from the village of Shurma in the Urzhum district, where he was brought up in the family of his aunt, a village schoolteacher, and her husband, a private tutor. He attended primary school in Shurma and then, like Z, was sent to the Urzhum secondary school. Kasyanov lodged with the family of an excise official called Polner. There were three children in the family, one of whom – Boris – studied in Kasyanov's class. The other two were daughters. One of them, Leonilla, later married Z's friend from secondary school, Sboyev. The mother was an educated and energetic woman who gave piano lessons, and the children's aunt, Emiliya – whose married name was Samartseva – was a teacher in a girls' grammar school. On feast-days lots of young people gathered at the Polner house for games, charades, folk and other dances. Aunt Emiliya would join in the fun and organize the games, whilst Mrs Polner would accompany on the piano. Z took part in these domestic performances. An operetta entitled *Pavel Ivanov* in which Z played the lead role was performed several times at these theatrical evenings. Musically, he was quite talented. At the school's evening concerts he not only recited poetry, but sang ballads, accompanying himself on the guitar. He played the balalaika too. In spring 1917 the art teacher Larionov staged Gogol's play *The Government Inspector*. The mayor was played by Z's classmate Pyotr

Lifanov. He was a bit older and taller than the other boys and had a deep voice just right for the role. Judge Lyapkin-Tyapkin was played by Kasyanov, and Z took the part of the school supervisor Khlopov. The young poet's performance was more than just a bit of school dramatics: it was a real introduction to theatre – for the production became the talk of the town and was so successful that it was quickly transferred from the school stage to the 'Auditorium'. Experience of making public appearances and knowing how to deport himself on stage were to come in very handy later on in life: and these skills were picked up in Urzhum, thanks to the growing enthusiasm of young people there for theatre, music and poetry.

When 1917 arrived, little Urzhum came to life under the pressure of revolutionary events. Kasyanov later recalled:

> At school we organized a 'Pupils' Union'. Mikhail Bykov was elected as chairman. The union's representatives got the right to sit in on the school's holy of holies – the sessions of the Teachers' Council. Standards of discipline fell quite noticeably, and work standards were not that great either. To give an outlet to the seething energies of the young, which were getting out of hand in the secondary school, and later in the girls' school too, they organized special evenings devoted to literature and singing.

As usual, Z spent the 1917 summer holiday at home in Sernur. It was an unsettled time. All the foundations of the old order were disintegrating and the struggle for a new life was seizing hold of the furthest corners of the country. Revolutionary-minded soldiers started returning to Sernur from the front, full of determination to settle scores with any structures of the old Russia still holding out in their native region. After the February Revolution peasants' committees and 'Committees against Poverty' began to spring up. The Sernur peasants did not, for their part, hold to any particular political line. So it was that although Aleksey's work colleague at the demonstration farm, Ivan Milyutin, actively preached revolutionary ideas and recruited several Sernur peasants into underground political activity, he and his friends had no clear political direction. As K. Vasin puts it:

> They read Bolshevik literature, and Social Revolutionary and Anarchist pamphlets with equal fervour and enthusiasm. They had a special liking for publications of a broad democratic orientation. They demanded the convocation of the Constituent Assembly, and that land be shared out equally among the peasantry.

Aleksey took no part in the political struggle, and tried to keep away from the stormy events of the times. He was wary of the February

Revolution, and took a wait-and-see attitude regarding it. However, some of the farmworkers disliked their agronomist's demanding nature and took a decision to proclaim him an enemy of the people. Some with anarchic inclinations took advantage of the unfolding situation in the village to search the Zabolotsky home. The rifle-toting soldier who directed the search for the arms and provisions supposedly concealed by his agronomist father made a big impression on Z. Naturally, nothing of the kind was found, but nevertheless, as one can imagine, Aleksey's relations with the local authorities and with the farmworkers became tense in the wake of the search.

In autumn 1917, on the eve of the October Revolution, the entire Zabolotsky family moved house from Sernur to Urzhum. Several factors dictated the move. It appears that the atmosphere surrounding Aleksey in Sernur had reached such a pitch of unpleasantness that it was becoming impossible for him to continue his work on the farm. Yet in Urzhum he was well known and had hopes of being offered a job. Moreover, one by one the children had all moved to Urzhum to attend school there, and Lidiya was keen to follow them.

After moving they lived at first with some distant relatives by the name of Perevozchikov. Aleksey was quickly appointed to head an Urzhum farm which had acquired a herd of pedigree cattle confiscated from wealthy landowners after the October Revolution. The family was provided with a home, which contained a laboratory for the agronomist. Aleksey got his experiments going again: on plots of land, in the plant nursery, and in the apiary. In 1919, when Kolchak's White Army was threatening to break through in the direction of Urzhum, he evacuated the pedigree herd to remote villages. While there he contracted typhus and for a long time could not get well again. Once recovered, he took up the reins at the Urzhum state farm and gave a lot of his time to educational and voluntary activities. In the 1920s he founded a local museum in Urzhum, donating to it his own collection, which had been gathered during his trips around the villages of the Urzhum district. The exhibits included ancient manuscripts written on thick parchment-like paper, pieces of medieval chainmail, a mammoth's tooth, and a herbarium of local flora . . . Zabolotsky senior composed tables and diagrams for the museum, giving a breakdown of the region's plant life and the structure of its agriculture. Z's brother, Aleksey, remembers how he prepared a poster for the museum on the instructions of his father, featuring the headline: 'Our birds – the harm and the good they do.'

Little by little, society began to recognize Aleksey Zabolotsky's achievements in the sphere of agronomy. He was honoured as a Hero of

Labour in 1923, and a touching tribute sent by the town's trade unions has been preserved among Z's papers.

Aleksey's devotion to his calling, his relationship with the natural world and with the peasantry, his congenital inquisitiveness, and the breadth of his interests all affected his eldest son's way of looking at the world. According to his brother, Z always showed a sense of gratitude when remembering his father:

> In our family we often made father's love of philosophizing a butt of laughter, but I can't recall Nikolay ever making a joke on that subject. He always loved his father and deeply respected him. Even after the war he wrote in one of his letters to me that he was greatly indebted to father, for to a large extent his own creative powers had been inherited from him . . . It goes without saying that we all owe a lot to our mother too, for her gentleness, kindness and sincerity. More than anything else, she concerned herself that we should grow up as good, fair and kind people.

The Zabolotskys' house in Urzhum stood between the farm where Aleksey worked and the town's new cemetery. A small plot of land around the house was painstakingly cultivated by its owner. There was a room in the attic. This became the preserve of Nikolay, who had already matured into a young man. His literary-minded friends such as Mikhail Kasyanov, Nikolay Sboyev and Mikhail Ivanov often came visiting. They smoked cheap tobacco, talked about life, daydreamed, read their own and other people's verses, argued about the new government, about philosophy, and especially about poetry. They never tired of picking over poems which they had only just written, and they were never able to decide whether they were good or bad. Kasyanov wrote a valuable description of their poetic pursuits at that time:

> At that time we were under the influence of the Symbolist poets, first and foremost Blok and Bely. I also liked Fyodor Sologub – very much, in fact. I read poems of his which had already become stage favourites, like 'The Swing' and 'When I Swam in the Stormy Sea', at Saturday gatherings. Nikolay taught me to understand the expressive brevity, precision and emotional richness of Anna Akhmatova, of whom he was a great admirer. By 1919 we had already graduated beyond Balmont and Igor Severyanin. At that point we still did not know much about Mayakovsky. Only in the summer of 1920 did the book *Everything composed by Vladimir Mayakovsky* finally make it to Urzhum.

Very few of the many juvenile poems written by Z in Urzhum have survived. Kasyanov was able to remember part of a poem Z dedicated to him:

> In the twilight the sunset gilds the metal bars.
> The surf roars and someone groans,
> And somewhere someone is burying somebody,
> And a tired cobbler hammers in the nails.
> Yet a knight errant,
> The spitting image of the Syracuse tyrant,
> With a disdainful, narrow ironic smile
> Totally alone, totally alone . . .

The poem's first line was connected with the following episode from the young poet's life. During the summer holidays in 1918 Z got a job as secretary to the village soviet in one of the villages on the outskirts of Urzhum. Groups of bandits and White Army detachments were lurking outside the town. Units of Latvian riflemen were dispatched to Urzhum to get rid of them. One day the bandits succeeded in robbing the Urzhum treasury and made off in the direction of Kazan. In pursuit of one of the raiders, the Latvian riflemen swept into the village where Z was working and started to interrogate the employees of the village soviet. It turned out that the young secretary had indeed seen the fugitive, but of course had no idea that he was supposed to arrest him or tell somebody in town about him. The upshot was that Z himself was arrested and sent to prison in Urzhum. His confinement did not last long – he was released after a few days. Hence the line about the metal bars gilded by the setting sun. It was long remembered in the family how Lidiya took parcels to her son in prison.

Along with the breaking up of the old order came a change in the country's intellectual life. Despite Urzhum's distance from the main cultural centres of Russia there was nevertheless a palpable sense in this small town of young people's eagerness to get in touch with the new breezes blowing through literature. The influx of members of the intelligentsia fleeing from famine in the capital in 1918 and 1919 had a catalytic effect on the town's cultural life. In his memoir 'Early Years' Z wrote proudly of Urzhum that these people had found there 'a fertile soil for work and understanding, and general admiration'. They included musicians, artists and teachers. Two young teachers from Moscow undoubtedly exerted an influence on the young literary enthusiasts, and on Z in particular. One of them, Nina Rufina, became his class's literature teacher. When this slim, blue-eyed, young woman gave a lesson no one could remain unmoved by her inspired yet rigorous delivery. Rufina both loved and knew a lot about poetry. She played the violin and led a literature circle at the school, doing so in an interesting way and encouraging two of its members – Z and Mikhail Kasyanov – in their pursuit of poetry. The other teacher was Yekaterina Levitskaya.

She taught natural science at the town school. She, too, took her subject very seriously and later moved to a scientific post at a biology institute in the capital. Both these teachers lived in the same flat – which became a meeting-place for the town's young literary enthusiasts. Z and Mikhail often went there together. They read and discussed their own verses, planned literary evenings, and talked about literature, philosophy and new developments in natural science.

Without a doubt Rufina and Levitskaya sensed that young Z had a talent and advised him to read more, to write poems, to work on his style and, most important of all, not to let himself get into a rut in the provinces, but to go and study in one of the big cities. Z convinced himself that he could become a real poet only if he got a good education, moreover in the capital, for that was where the sources of modern literature had their origin. It seems that even then he understood that it was obligatory for a poet to be a thoroughly cultured and educated person, and that any talent had to be complemented by knowledge and rooted in knowledge – and would only then assume a sharply defined shape, informed by his own way of looking at the world. A poet had to have his own personality, and that was up to him to create himself. A child's dreams began to solidify into a real-life plan. And a great aim demanded decisive action.

But in the mean time fifteen-year-old Z and his nervy, frail friend Misha Ivanov, the lover of painting, contented themselves with taking boat trips up the River Urzhumka, starting from the weir and water-wheel and rowing far out of town to the place known as 'The Rocks'. They caught fish and divulged their most intimate secrets to each other. Both of them were in love, both intended to devote their lives to art, and both were full of the bravest hopes.

The poems which Z read to his friend were dominated by themes of rivers, birch trees, young love, and premonitions of an unusual life to come. But jocular, ironic motifs showed through too. Behind his mask of seriousness Z could slip quietly into parody. In 1918 he wrote a long tongue-in-cheek poem about life in Urzhum and called it the 'Urzhumiad'. His friends Nikolay Sboyev, Boris Polner, Mikhail Kasyanov and several schoolgirls of his acquaintance were all depicted in the poem. To Sboyev, a stickler for old patriarchal ways and for living in seamless harmony with nature, Z dedicated the following lines:

> Take a look at this one going by –
> That's the philosopher Sboyev Nikolay,
> He damns culture in its entirety:
> American locks,

> The various mixtures from the apothecary,
> Test tubes, bottles, powders in a box . . .

In 1919 Z carefully copied his poems into a self-made book which he entitled *Urzhum*. According to the poet's wife:

> Z kept the handwritten collection *Urzhum* until 1938. He had stitched the little book together himself. It was a bit narrower than an exercise book, about two centimetres thick. . . I recall that there were a lot of poems about nature – about birches covered in hoar-frost, glittering snow, starry skies. The poem 'On the Death of Koshkin', which is mentioned in 'Early Years', was there too.

In this way Z started the habit of gathering his work into manuscript or typescript collections, so that he could plan future published editions of his poetry. He gradually came round to the view that the final goal of a poet's life should be to establish a complete *œuvre*, which could take a worthy place in Russia's literary heritage, rather than just to write individual poems.

Between 1918 and 1920 the house of the music teacher and local patron of the arts L. E. Shekhovtsova was a popular meeting-place for all sorts of different people in Urzhum – representatives of the district government, visiting artists, and young people who were attracted to music and poetry. Z and his friends were among Shekhovtsova's visitors. Sboyev performed his vocal numbers, Grisha Kuklin recited poetry to musical accompaniment, and Z sang ballads in his young bass voice. For example, he sang the ballad 'Three young page-boys left their native shore forever . . .', and his poem 'Bathers' Melody' was on one occasion set to music for him by his hostess.

Meanwhile his intention of going to study in the capital crystallized. Z and Kasyanov decided to enrol in the history and literature faculty of Moscow University. Z's parents no doubt approved of the decision, but the family was barely making ends meet. Equipping their eldest son to go to Moscow and paying for his upkeep there was out of the question – especially considering that his father was now in bad health as a result of typhus. Z was faced with having to support himself. We have already seen how in the summer of 1918 he worked in a village soviet. The following summer he got a job in one of Urzhum's administrative establishments.

It seems that by the age of sixteen Z was already a fully independent young man, who had precisely determined his great goal in life. To achieve this goal he was prepared to quit his native region and his relatively comfortable life in the provinces in order to study, work, and get literary recognition.

In spring 1920 there was a leaving ceremony at the United Labour Secondary School, as it was now called. For Z and his classmates the years of childhood and schooling had come to a close. Under the greenery of the birches of the old cemetery by the Mitrofanyev church the young poet read out his latest verses to his friends:

> I am a proud pilot, preparing to set sail,
> Preparing to sail to other shores.
> The wind hisses impudently at me in rhyme,
> The far distance is coloured by a midnight frigate.
> I shall sail and underneath life's cupola
> Whisper to God: 'Hello brother!'

These distinctly immature verses give a good sense of the young optimism of Z as he stepped out in life, full of hopes. And in the final analysis it was hardly important that he had got the pilot muddled with the captain, as Kasyanov told him. Perhaps he truly felt himself to be as yet merely a pilot – a master of his little Urzhum haven, who had suddenly taken it into his head to sail to distant shores.

When the academic year came to an end the two teachers, Rufina (who later married and took the name Dulova) and Levitskaya, left Urzhum. Z and Mikhail soon received a letter from them, with their Moscow addresses and clear directions on how to find them in the big city. Rufina and Levitskaya promised to help them to get fixed up in Moscow and to prepare for the university entrance exams. A decision was made not to put things off until then, but to travel straight away. Kasyanov went to Shurma to bid farewell to his family and friends. Meanwhile, in the house on the Urzhum farm they were baking rusks and getting things ready for Z's impending journey. They even wanted to make him a suit, so that he would look thoroughly presentable in the city. Material was obtained, but there was no thread. Z wrote to his aunt in Vyatka:

Aunt Emiliya! I have a big favour to ask of you: please buy me a spool of black thread No.40 or 50 at the market. I think that the money I am enclosing should be enough. We have got the cloth here, and I simply have to make myself a suit before going to Moscow. But there is no thread anywhere in the town. The thread can probably be forwarded via comrade Shchelkanov from the regional youth committee. 18 June 1920.

History is silent on whether or not the suit was made, but the letter does show that Aunt Emiliya was already aware of the coming trip to

23

Moscow. That implies that the decision was the subject of thorough discussion in the family, involving the Vyatka relatives. Pyotr Shchelkanov, mentioned in the letter, was a leading figure in Vyatka Communist Youth and literary circles. How exactly Z struck up an acquaintance with him is unclear.

So the time to bid farewell to family, to Urzhum, and to childhood had come. All the necessary documents, clothes and provisions were gathered and packed, and in midsummer 1920 Z, Mikhail Kasyanov and another schoolfriend by the name of Arkady Zhmakin set off for Moscow. Kasyanov recalled the journey:

> We travelled up the River Vyatka to Kotelnich, where we squeezed aboard a train. We had a dreadfully uncomfortable time of it. Crumpled and squashed, we found ourselves on the platform between carriages and next to a passenger car filled almost beyond bursting point. We later managed to get into the corridor next to the toilet. And that is where we stayed, together with our three big bags of rusks and other less bulky belongings. The journey from Kotelnich to Moscow took us around four days of insufferable heat, stuffiness and crampedness. Somehow one of our bags of dried bread was swiped during the night, which had the effect of sharply reducing our resources and later made an impact on our Moscow rations. At last we arrived in Moscow and found ourselves in Kalanchovskaya Square . . .

III

Unable to jam themselves into a packed tram on the railway station square, the three friends set off on foot. They walked to Prechistenka Street, where the women teacher-friends who had promised the two young poets their support lived in one of the narrow lanes. They walked for a long time, asking the way from passers-by and gazing curiously at the buildings and endless streets. All around them a complex, unfamiliar life was going on. They could hardly wait to discover it and to become part of its beckoning enigma.

We can get a notion of the capital at that time from these lines written by Marina Tsvetayeva in March 1921 in a letter to M. A. Voloshin in the Crimea:

> There are a billion poets in Moscow now, and a new trend every day. The latest is the *nichevoki* – the nothingists. I recite in a café. Moscow is on rations, earnestly businesslike, living from day to day – its fences have been removed, it is dirty, the domes of the Kremlin are black, with crows sitting on them; everyone on the streets is dressed in khaki, and you

cannot move for studio-clubs: theatre and dancing are devouring everything. But it is free. You can live here, skimming the surface: just trying to ignore the scarcities.

The young men from Urzhum were to encounter every aspect of Moscow life mentioned in the letter. Naturally they would have preferred to see the 'billion poets', to get acquainted with the new trends in poetry, and to go to the theatre, but to start with their time and thoughts were seized in the vice-like grip of rationed, 'businesslike', 'day to day' Moscow.

Rufina and Levitskaya got a room for the boys in Tyoply Lane, but it came with the condition that they were obliged to provide the landlady with fuel for the forthcoming winter. Together with the workers of some establishment they had to go to the woods outside Moscow to make a stockpile of firewood. The stockpilers were entitled to half of the six cubic metres which they had sawn up in the course of a week's work, but Z and Mikhail were inexperienced in such wordly affairs and were tricked out of their share of the firewood. The feckless woodcutters quickly moved into another flat, which they had luckily found in the same apartment block. It belonged to an ex-trader who was at risk of having some of his living space requisitioned. To avoid losing one of his rooms in this way he installed the two young men in it. Like so many other inhabitants of the city, they heated the apartment that winter by dismantling and burning nearby fences. It was no surprise to see that by the end of winter there was barely a wooden fence left in the whole of Moscow.

But the biggest problem of all was food. They had eaten the last of the provisions they had brought from home before the university entrance exams had even started, and now their only hope was to receive a state ration. Apparently the ration cards given out to students of the History and Literature Faculty were next to useless. Someone advised them to try for the 'militarized' medical faculty, where the medical students were getting a ration that was colossal by the standards of the time: a pound of bread a day (admittedly they gave it out only once a month, but all the same one got twelve kilograms at one go), sugar, butter, herring or Caspian roach, and for that matter the student refectory had potato and cabbage soup and a potato-and-beetroot main course for lunch. Holding out against the temptation of such an allowance was hopeless, so the two friends decided with their customary youthful optimism to study in two faculties at once – their preferred Faculty of History and Literature at the First Moscow University and the Medical Faculty at the Second University. They

25

passed the exams without any problems and were accepted into both faculties. But they soon found out that studying in two places at once was not quite as simple as they had supposed. All their time was consumed by compulsory medical classes and regular tests on their medical studies, none of which could be skipped because medical students who fell behind had their allowance stopped. The end result was that their studies at the Faculty of History and Literature were hopelessly neglected. Z was distressed at having to make such a forced departure from his intended plan, but he hoped he would last out until better times when he could make up what he had missed.

The days were swallowed up by lessons and worldly concerns. On their way to university in the morning the two friends stopped off at the Soviet tea-room in Khamovniki Lane, where for an affordable price they could get some boiling water, a small teapot of carrot tea and a spoonful of jam. They brought their ration bread with them and breakfasted there. Then they attended lectures or studied in the bone museum, the anatomy theatre or the chemistry laboratory. But hunger would soon distract their thoughts away from science and force them to think about lunch or about the next ration allowance. After queuing and receiving their monthly ration, they held feasts which Kasyanov remembered as moments of incomparable pleasure:

> After receiving all these blessings we did not waste a minute and hared off to the tea-shop (this time to the university tea-shop), cut the bread, spread butter over it, poured sugar on top, and washed it all down with hot water. Since then no fancy cakes have ever been able to give me such wild pleasure as those ration-day feasts.

Understandably, after these bursts of extravagance what remained of the ration barely stretched to cover a fortnight, or three weeks at the very most, so after that the young men were obliged to follow the advice of their own anthem: 'Hey, stand up straight, toughen up!'

Every day the two friends could hardly wait for the arrival of evening, when they could get down to what interested them most. They did exercises in verse composition at home and tried to supplement their literary knowledge in the library. Sometimes they called on their acquaintances, the two teachers, but as the latter were in the habit of giving lessons in the evenings somewhere else, they were rarely to be found at home. But the most magnetic attractions were literary evenings and the theatre. Z and Kasyanov went to hear Valery Bryusov and Vladimir Mayakovsky at the Polytechnic Museum, along with the proletarian poets V. Kirillov, M. Gerasimov and A. Gastev. They attended lectures and debates. On one of these evenings Mayakovsky was on top form, recited a lot, and an ecstatic audience would not let him leave the stage. Before reading out his recently written poem 'The story of how Godmother talked about Wrangel without the slightest sense', the poet said: 'This one hasn't appeared in print because it's censored, but you'll see for yourselves what a very good poem it is.' On another occasion they heard the poem '150,000,000' recited by the author. 'Z was not much taken with Mayakovsky', recalled Kasyanov. 'But he could not resist his energy and vigour, which shone through when he was reciting, and specially when he was arguing with his opponents. On those occasions Z joined in the general applause and even shouted out his approval. But as soon as the reading finished he would revert to his usual cool attitude to Mayakovsky.'

Although Z was influenced by Mayakovsky as a personality he could not take his poetry to heart and when the Polytechnic Museum recitations were over he would joke about the hypnotic effect which the poet had both on the audience and upon himself. One day, after a debate, Mayakovsky came to be standing next to the two young men from Urzhum on an impossibly crowded staircase, and in the crush he accidentally trod on Mikhail's foot. Kasyanov wrote that:

> Z took the mickey out of me for a long time on that score, advising me to donate my foot to a museum. During our get-togethers with Nina and Yekaterina he was forever repeating the same old joke – seizing my leg, raising it aloft for everyone to see and exclaiming, 'Look, what a foot!'

Even more interesting was going to the 'Domino', the poets' café at No.18 Tverskaya Street. One could see Tsvetayeva's entire 'billion' Moscow poets there. One could look them over, listen to their conversations, their arguments and, of course, their poems. At that time, the 'Domino' was in effect serving as a club for the All-Russian Union of Poets – Vladimir Mayakovsky, Valery Bryusov, Andrey Bely, Marina Tsvetayeva, Sergey Yesenin, Boris Pasternak, Vasily Kamensky and many others frequented it. The café was the favourite meeting-place of the Imaginists, led by Shershenevich. Z and Kasyanov used to arrive early, while the buffet still had yoghurt and, if they were lucky, cheap buckwheat. Having fortified themselves, they went on into the small variety hall, where people would already be gathering and readings and literary discussions would be beginning.

The young men feasted their attention on everything that took place in the 'Domino', but conducted themselves timidly. They could not bring themselves to enter into arguments or to get acquainted with the poets, and they certainly did not dare to show anyone their own – as they acknowledged – immature poems. It was only when they got home late at night that they started loudly swapping impressions and declaiming their own and other people's verses. Mikhail was full of admiration for Shershenevich, but Z argued that Shershenevich wrote mediocre poetry. He had a greater liking for Yesenin, and indeed sometimes imitated his style in the poems which he wrote at the time. There were occasions on the deserted streets when they were stopped and had their documents scrutinized by night patrols. Muggers, on the other hand, took no interest in them.

Going to the theatre was too expensive a pleasure, so they bought tickets only rarely. More often they were able to get into the auditorium without tickets, but only at the start of the second act. Z was specially attracted to the so-called First Theatre of the Russian Soviet Republic, which at that time was already under the direction of Meyerhold. His production of Verhaeren's play *Les Aubes*, which the young Urzhumites saw in the middle of November 1920, made a big impression. It was on that very same day that news broke of the Red Army's capture of Perekop and of the expulsion of Wrangel's White Army from the Crimea, and so in the play's final act, instead of launching into his expected monologue, the actor read out a fresh war report which told of the collapse of the last enemy front of the Civil War. The auditorium reacted with stormy applause.

It can be presumed that the young Urzhumites made visits to the Museum of Modern Western Art, and to the Shchukin and Morozov galleries – where they could acquaint themselves with the wonderful collections of Impressionists, Post-Impressionists and recent art. They sometimes went to study in the library of the Rumyantsev Museum.*

Z and Kasyanov spent New Year's Eve 1921 somewhere in the Zamoskvorechye region of Moscow with their friends Rufina and Levitskaya. With the onset of the new year, food became an even bigger problem. Rations were reduced and sugar and butter disappeared altogether. Eventually the medical students' bigger ration was abolished. The daily bread ration took a headlong plunge – half a pound, a quarter, and then an eighth (fifty grammes a day). The only food in ready supply consisted of frozen apples and saccharine, but that was not going to save the situation. Having already eaten through the proceeds of selling some of their clothes at the Smolensk market, the two friends were faced with the real threat of starvation. Z decided to leave the university. He saw no sense in staying on at a faculty for which he had no further use merely in order to starve. Leaving his first year of studies uncompleted, he returned to Urzhum towards the end of

*Subsequently the Lenin Library [Ed.].

February or in March 1921. Kasyanov had by this time developed a real enthusiasm for medicine and stayed on to complete his course of studies and exams, making do with the meagre food he was able to obtain with the help of his landlord.

The difficult time that he had endured in Moscow was not a complete waste for the seventeen-year-old Z. His experience of living independently in the city had toughened him up, he had come into contact with the capital's literary circles, and at the Medical Institute he had acquired knowledge of the fundamentals of chemistry, physiology and anatomy, which he would use later on to aid the formation of his own views on the universe. But nevertheless he recognized that his enforced return to Urzhum was a failure, even a defeat, on the way to his goal.

The district capital that had once so enthused him now appeared small and provincial to Z. The streets looked empty, the buildings old and insignificant. The inhabitants were living poorly under the combined pressure of the onset of famine and of Spanish influenza. After such a long absence from home Z was specially aware of changes that had occurred within his family. His father still could not shake off the effects of that severe bout of typhus. He was often ill and was only just managing to keep up with the requirements of his job on the state farm. He was no longer the powerful and strong head of the household that Z used to know. Z's sisters had matured appreciably and become more independent in their actions. The family's strict, patriarchal way of life was a thing of the past. Six months after returning Z wrote, 'The situation at home is bad. Father is ill and the state farm is rudderless.'

In the spring the whole family dug up the earth on the allotment that had once belonged to grandfather and on the plots round the house. They waited for their harvest of potatoes, peas and vegetables all summer; feeding themselves through the winter would be unthinkable without it. Z was unenthusiastic about helping around the house and spent most of the time sitting in his attic room, reading, studying and writing poetry. From this vantage point he and his younger brother were, to their horror, able to see carts making their way to the cemetery bearing the bodies of the victims of famine, typhoid and Spanish influenza. They were not even in coffins, but were carried along in the carts, barely covered by a white blanket.

In July, Z's schoolfriend Boris Polner dropped by and showed a letter in verse which he had received from Kasyanov, who was now planning to come home to Shurma for a well-earned rest after having passed his exams. Z sent off a similar verse letter to Kasyanov, telling him what was going on in his life and about his plans for the future. He wrote too that he intended to travel to Moscow again to study. The most likely interpretation of what he wrote is that he intended to enrol at VLKhI – the Higher Literary-Artistic Institute, which had just been founded by Valery Bryusov. Z was attracted to the Bryusov institute because it was specifically orientated towards the very thing to which he had decided to dedicate his life.

These plans apparently met with a frosty reception at home. His parents were annoyed and upset that he paid so little heed to the practical needs of the family. They reproached him for what they saw as his egotism, callousness and rudeness, and suggested that at such a difficult time it might well be appropriate for him to train for a more practical profession – one that would earn a crust to support the family. It is possible that these exchanges did have an effect on Z. He conferred with his former classmate Rezvykh, who was home for the summer holidays having completed his first year at the Petrograd Pedagogical Institute, and decided that he too would enrol there, and forgo the Literary Institute. He did not intend to become a teacher, but as a qualification it certainly would not do him any harm, and it represented a useful compromise with the wishes of his parents.

Kasyanov came to Urzhum at the beginning of August to see his old schoolfriends. He recounted how he had starved in Moscow that spring and on the journey back to Shurma, and how his uncle failed to recognize the ragged scarecrow that he had become, assumed him to be a wandering beggar, and shouted at him: 'You'll get nothing from us!' Everyone laughed, although the story did not carry a very cheerful message – especially for those who were soon to set off for the city again to study.

A whole group of them set out for Petrograd together – Z, Rezvykh, Polner, Zhmakin. Kasyanov and Z were going to be studying in different cities and their ways now parted for many years. In Moscow Kasyanov got down to medicine very seriously, graduated from the medical faculty and in time became a leading specialist in anatomical pathology and forensic medicine.

And so it was that in mid August 1921 Lidiya once again equipped her son for a long and difficult journey, though this time there was no bread to dry, and even the potatoes were not yet ready, so there was barely enough food for Z to take with him. It was fortunate that the Zabolotsky family had been able to get three food ration packs and a pair of boots and trousers for Z from the American charity organization ARA, which had recently opened a branch in the area in response to the famine in the Volga region. For everything else the young man would have to look to his own resources. Nevertheless he set off in a buoyant mood – he was given strength by a sense of allegiance to his overriding goal. The expectation of new impressions, discoveries and successes filled his heart with a great joy. A few months later he wrote to Kasyanov:

A person is a quite stupendously uninteresting being if he has no aims, and if he does not, consequently, bring about changes inside himself in order to reach his goal.

In summer 1921 Petrograd looked almost as empty as Urzhum had done when Z had left it. In comparison with pre-revolutionary times the population of the former capital had fallen by over half. Most businesses and shops were not working and there was no smoke billowing from the factory chimneys. There were catastrophic shortages of food, fuel and raw materials. People had nowhere to hurry to and there was no transport for them anyway. Cars, horsecabs and drays had almost completely disappeared from the streets – there was no petrol and the horses had been slaughtered and eaten a couple of years previously. It was only the odd tram that still squealed and thundered as it threaded its way round the corners and the stops, taking on passengers who had been waiting an age for it to appear. Contemporaries recalled that at this time the city was surprisingly beautiful, stunning in its unfamiliar motionlessness. Neither the dereliction of the city's economy, the peeling façades of the buildings, nor the boarded-up windows could dispel the grandeur and harmony of the palaces, streets, squares run wild, rivers and canals of Petersburg as it slid into the past.

One of the witnesses of this unexpected beauty, the poet Vladislav Khodasevich, described the atmosphere of the becalmed city in his essay 'House of the Arts':

Life trickled on in its own way in this magnificent, yet strange city. In the administrative sense Petersburg became provincial. Trade came to a halt, as it did everywhere else. The factories hardly worked at all. The air was clear and smelled of the sea. The bureaucrats and administrators, the traders and merchants, and the factory hands either left town or simply adopted a lower profile. But, for all that, scholarly, literary, theatrical and artistic life flowered with unprecedented clarity. The Bolsheviks were already trying to control it, but so far they were inexpert in doing so; thus its last days were lived out in full creative vigour. Cold and hunger did not detract from the vigour; if anything, they underpinned it. A poet correctly wrote in those days:

I am at ease with hunger,
And merry from inspiration.

31

Having barely set foot on the streets of Petrograd, Z was immediately struck by this beauty of the famous city in its desolation and he felt the beating of its literary pulse. He read the news of the funeral of one of his favourite poets, Aleksandr Blok, on a notice of mourning. The ceremony had taken place on 10 August – not long before Z's arrival – and these notices had not yet been removed from the city's central streets. Later, the little group from Urzhum heard about Blok's last evening appearance at the Bolshoy Drama Theatre, which had taken place on 25 April and attracted around 1,500 of the poet's admirers.

Yet at first Z had more pressing priorities than getting involved in the city's cultural life. He had to take entrance exams and think about what he was going to eat. The dean of the faculty, Vasily Alekseyevich Desnitsky, personally examined everyone hoping to enrol for language and literature. He was one of the founders of Soviet literary studies, and a friend of Maksim Gorky. He quickly discovered that the young man from Urzhum's knowledge was very haphazard – closer to the interests of a novice poet than to the requirements of an entrant into higher education. Many years later Z wrote about this, their first, meeting in a letter to the then seventy-year-old professor:

> I remember very well how you first examined me when you accepted me into the institute in August 1921, when notices telling of memorial evenings for Blok were posted on walls all about town; how I shamelessly muddled Pugachov with Stenka Razin, yet knew all the Symbolists off pat right up to Ellis; and how you told me then that I had some decent grey matter in my head, and that if it could be said that there was anything definite inside – then it was my undoubted wish to study. Really and truly, it was then that the fate of this lad from Vyatka was decided; that fate was decided by you and you made a decision that was both humane and right.

In fact Z's fate was put to the test several times in the following years during so-called 'purges' of the institute, when the social background of its students was scrutinized and representatives of the wealthy classes expelled. According to the rules in operation in those times the agronomist's son was also considered to be 'one of them'. It was thanks only to the intercession of the Dean of the Socio-Economic Faculty, Desnitsky, that Z was able to retain his place at the institute and receive a higher education.

In the 1920s a lot of able young people gravitated to Moscow and Petrograd from the provinces, hoping to get an education and settle down there. Students from out of town were housed in hostels or vacant flats, often together with others from their native region. It was for this reason that Z, Rezvykh and Polner, who were all studying at the Pedagogical Institute, ended up living together in one room in a student hostel on Kamenno-ostrovsky Prospect with Zhmakin, who studied at the Technological Institute. It was impossible to survive on the meagre state ration allowance, and once again – as in Moscow – hunger became a serious obstacle on the road to knowledge.

The only way for Z to survive was to get a part-time job. It was just at this time that the results of Soviet Russia's first trade agreements with Great Britain, Norway, Germany and several other countries started to flow in. Steamers began to sail into Petrograd loaded with machinery, construction materials, coal, flour, sugar, tinned food and parcels from the ARA. The ships could not be kept waiting, so student brigades were formed to assist the professional dockers, who were unable to unload fast enough by themselves. Z joined one of the brigades. On appointed days he and his colleagues from the institute lugged heavy sacks and packing cases out of ships' holds on their backs – often at a run – from early in the morning until late in the evening. Not everyone could cope with the pace, but Z – despite being emaciated from malnourishment – was still strong enough and did not let his brigade down. It was annoying, though, that this manual work was wearing out his valuable American boots. Tired to the point of exhaustion, the students walked back from the port along deserted streets, happy that they had got through the working day and that they would get good wages. In addition to money, which was becoming increasingly useless, their pay came in the form of food. Z told Kasyanov in a letter that for working at the port,

> I shall soon receive provisions (lard, flour, sugar, fish etc.) worth about one to one and a half million in all. I also earned about 400,000 stockpiling firewood. I think I might just be able to spruce myself up a bit with all that – my clothes are so worn out and I am so thin that a lot of people at the institute have difficulty in recognizing me these days. On the food front Arkady, Rezvykh and I (Boris could not bear it and scuttled back to Urzhum) have so far distinguished three periods in our lives: I. the potato period, II. the floury period, and now III., the fatty period. The changeovers from one to the next are signposted by stomach upsets. Life is more or less bearable now, but the cold interferes with studying. I have just started attending lectures and I am beginning to get stuck into the remote original civilizations of mankind – the Sumerian and Hamitic epochs etc. etc. The magazine business is not working out at all.
>
> They have increased the ration, adding: 1lb of bread, 4lb of groats, 5lb of herring, 1 of butter, 1 of sugar and so on. I am not starving any more.

Now at last, having earned what he needed to stay alive, Z could get down to his books in earnest. He decided not to confine himself to his set course of studies at the institute, and drew up a plan of independent study for himself, taking in the study of the theory of versification and a reading programme that would help him find his way around the various literary and philosophical trends. He borrowed books and got advice about what to read on the themes that interested him from fellow students and from his teachers. Hardly any books were being published in these years, but the shelves of the second-hand bookshops held a wide choice, and represented an irresistible attraction for Z. For instance, in one of his letters to Kasyanov we read: 'Today I went to Nevsky Prospect, dropped into a bookshop – I could not stop myself – and blew virtually all the money I had left . . . But Mikhail, you cannot even imagine how happy I am and what books I have bought!' And the letter continues with a list of these books: 'D. G. Gintsburg's *On Russian Verse Composition, Versification* by N. G. Shebuyev, *Experiments in Metrics and Rhythm Systems, Euphony and Harmony, Strophe and Forms* by V. Bryusov, several poetry collections and magazines.' The eighteen-year-old youth was not reading for the sake of indulgence, but was trying as quickly as possible to eliminate gaps in his knowledge and absorb information which would help him to perfect his verse-making skills. His character was such as to demand constant and tangible progress towards his goal. 'I really want to get down to work on rhythm; to work until it hurts; but circumstances do not permit it. I am not writing very much.'

From time to time he was consumed by daydreams of earthly love and a wish for someone with whom to share his hopes and doubts, but there were no friends to hand who could compare with Kasyanov, so he wrote to him in Moscow. He pined over his unrequited love for Ira, a girl from Urzhum:

Oh, how sweet and supple she is, this Ira . . . How I love her and how I hate her. But you, Mikhail, I just love – I swear to God. And it's funny that I do love you – as if she never loved you! Oh Mikhail, Mikhail, we have let our sweet, tender, beautiful Ira slip through our fingers. Well, it seems it was God's will that I was never going to be able to touch her, but what stopped you then, old scatter-brains?

At the same time he felt oppressed by his inability to understand the thrust of current events: 'My country, morals, religion, modernity, revolution – these oppressive questions hang over the soul like a huge weight.' And, 'So many losses – Aleksandr Blok has died, Andrey Bely has left Russia, Nikolay Gumilyov has been executed.'

The young man found it difficult to reconcile the noble ideals of the Revolution with the tragedy of the recently finished civil war and the policy of 'tightening the screws' being pursued during the years of War Communism. He knew from his father of the peasantry's calamitous position as a result of the forcible and almost total confiscation of their grain by the requisition squads sent into the countryside by the central government. On the train to Petrograd he heard talk of a poor harvest, of famine along the Volga, of peasant rebellions. Rumours of discontent among the working classes and of the recently suppressed mutiny at the Kronstadt naval base also reached his ears. The New Economic Policy (NEP) adopted at the Tenth Congress of the Russian Communist Party had not by the winter of 1921–2 achieved any tangible effect. The future seemed uncertain. A whole welter of concerns – the people's suffering; the seemingly senseless destruction of the old way of life; the heavy toll being taken out of him by his efforts to break through to his cherished goal; famine; 'purges'; the execution by firing squad of one of his favourite poets – all these things troubled Z and he wrote to Kasyanov:

It is senseless to cry and complain – to be a Nadson of our times, but somehow these black lines pour out all by themselves:

> In the funereal whistling of revolutions
> Do you see the bloody fingers?
> Thoughts moan, songs writhe –
> Do you hear?
> We – tired of contemplation,
> Of things not logically completed –
> Throw untitled songs into the world,
> Grief drawing out our measures.
> The world has taken away all our wishes,
> All our tears, and hate, and breath,
> And the mud of re-soled heels
> Tramples the suffering of a dear face.

Accursed, yes – accursed life! I am entangled in its grey, viscous threads, as if ensnared – and how do I get out?

Yet when he considered what had happened, Z became more and more convinced that he had to live and work in the real world, in the midst of this turning-point in history. He believed that he should ignore the unavoidable difficulties and find a place in the world and contribute to that range of values which he had still to define for himself. It was therefore very important at the outset to make no mistakes in choosing his path and identifying those basic markers that would help him to move forward. Z had already studied and rejected as inapplicable to his own inner development the poetry of Nadson, Severyanin, Balmont, Akhmatova, Mayakovsky, the teachings of Tolstoy and Nietzsche and any religious views. There already were, however, teachers on whom he *could* rely. An enormous impression was wrought on him by Osip Mandelshtam's collection of poems, *Stone*:

> I feel an irresistible attraction to the poetry of Osip Mandelshtam (*Stone*). I so much want to take on trust his words:
>
>> – There is an unshakeable rock of values . . . –
>> – And I thought: I must not act the poet . . . –
>
> And I am not acting the poet. At least I do not want to do so. I'm beginning to sense a somehow different relationship to poetry, an attraction to deep, meditative verses, to strong meaningful images.

Among the thinkers of the past Z singled out one great German poet: 'The divine Goethe hides the sky from me with his opaque dome, and through it I cannot see God.' Through Goethe's ideas of natural philosophy there opened up anew for him the great treasury of nature, the significance of which for the formation of his world-view Z had felt since his childhood years. Thus gradually Z acquired what was to become for him an 'unshakeable rock of values'.

The characteristic features of student life in the 1920s were a sense of independence, the opportunity and ability to argue one's own point of view in discussions and seminars, and a breadth of interests. There was not that self-imposed isolation of specialists that arose later. Those in the humanities communicated readily with biologists, physicists and mathematicians. The writer Gennady Gor, at the time studying in Leningrad, recalled:

> Amongst my neighbours were a physicist, a biologist and an ethnographer. At the University there was no Iron Curtain dividing 'physicists' from 'lyricists'. Those in the literature faculty would look in on lectures by Ukhtomsky, Filipchenko, Khvolson [professors of physiology, genetics, physics – N.Z.], while the biologists and physicists would come to meetings of the University literary group.

It is likely that a similar mixing of students from the various faculties also took place in the Pedagogical Institute. Towards the end of 1921 they all attended lectures organized there in aid of famine relief, and given by outstanding academics: by the literary expert V. A. Desnitsky on foreign literature, the historian N. A. Rozhkov on the theory of knowledge, the botanist and future president of the Academy of Sciences V. L. Komarov on natural science and ethics. The founder of the university genetics department Filipchenko, referred to by Gor, was a gifted popularizer of the sciences and often lectured to doctors and teachers, speaking in the student residences. In 1923 and 1926 there appeared two editions of his book *Evolutionary Ideas in Biology*, in which, among other precursors of Darwin, he mentions Z's favourite, Goethe. Discussions of the theory of relativity, the sensitivity of plants and the development of genetics were interspersed with arguments about Meyerhold's theatre, about the paintings of Chagall and Malevich, and about new tendencies in literature. Such an atmosphere of interpenetration between the humanities and the natural sciences corresponded well with Z's constant striving towards a holistic perception of the surrounding world.

Z also applied himself energetically to the institute's programme of study. He listened with great attention to lectures on the history of art by the famous archaeologist and art historian Professor D. V. Bubrikh, and tried never to miss seminars by Desnitsky who was very popular among the students. The most active students of the Pedagogical Institute and Leningrad University would go to listen to lectures in the then existing Institute of Art History. The lecturers there included V. M. Zhirmunsky, Yury Tynyanov, Viktor Shklovsky, L. V. Shcherba, Boris Eykhenbaum and other outstanding academics. It is difficult to imagine that Z, who had been so interested in literary studies in his student years, did not attend these lectures, at least selectively. In his autobiography he wrote, 'I was considered a capable student, and at one time I had thought of devoting myself wholly to scholarship; my attachment to poetry turned out to be stronger, and any thoughts of a scholarly career were left behind.'

Special mention must be made of Z's participation in the Institute's literary society called the 'Workshop of the Word'. Right at the beginning of his first-year studies he confided to Kasyanov, 'We are proposing to set up a small circle of poets, and it looks as though there might be the opportunity to get into print.' The circle was made up of students and those younger lecturers who took part in student life. Immediately after the circle had been set up, most probably at the end of the first semester, Z became an active member and initially tried to play a leading role in it. He was looking for like-minded colleagues with whom he could have in-depth discussions on everything to do with writing and literature. It was very important for him to test how his poems would be received and how his ideas on poetry would be evaluated. From his first months at the Institute he had read his verse at student evenings although admittedly without significant success. 'The audience reacts with amazement and somewhat hesitant applause.' He tried to make friends with some of the students but did not encounter a sympathetic response. 'There are lots of good people in the Institute, but they're not up to much.' And now it seemed to him that in the 'Workshop of the Word' he would find sympathetic interest in his literary quest.

The members of the Society decided to produce a literary journal, to start with in typewritten form. A lecturer at the Institute, L. Spokoyny, became the editor, the secretary was D. Osipov, and the members of the editorial board were N. Braun, A. Korablyova, Z and the lecturer V. Molyakov. It is tempting to think that it was Z himself who suggested the journal's title – *Mysl'* (*Idea*). As early as this he was already convinced that at the basis of poetry, and in general of all literature, there had to be a definite authorial idea – 'a strong meaningful image', and it would not be at all surprising if it was he who had insisted that the organ of the 'Workshop of the Word' should be called *Idea*. The first and only issue of the journal appeared in March 1922 and consisted of a booklet of twenty-two pages of closely typed text. But even such a humble production demanded no mean effort from the editors. They had to get money for the paper, for re-typing and for other requirements. For example, in the society's cash book there is the following entry: 'Issued to D. Osipov for the tram (two journeys) to obtain permission – 12000.' Thus to publish a journal of three to five copies special permission had to be obtained from outside the Institute, and a ticket for the tram was far from cheap. The cash that was needed was acquired, basically, from a collection made at Professor Rozhkov's lectures for which a charge was made, and from the Institute authorities.

The journal opened with an address from the editorial board to the readers, in which it was said, in particular: 'The main aim of our journal is to awaken the slumbering creative forces of the student body. The free expression of student opinion, the polishing and sharpening of their ideas: that is the point of its existence.' To judge by the sentiments of this wording, the author or active co-author could have been Z, who had joined the editorial board. The journal contained his theoretical article 'On the Essence of Symbolism', three poems ('Heavenly Seville', 'A grey ibis called from the papyrus', 'Heart-Wasteland'), and a report on a student theatrical evening. The article on symbolism is of note because it gives us some idea of the eighteen-year-old's literary interests and reveals the point of departure for his views on the most important categories in poetry. In the article our attention is caught by the very way the question is posed: 'I am attempting to characterize Symbolism within the sphere of its intrinsic philosophical values.' The young poet was clearly interested by problems of world-view as the foundation for any kind of poetic endeavour and as the basis of the search for his own path. His article is a concise survey, yet it is not a compilation, not a recasting of other peoples' views, but a conscious attempt to extract a useful lesson from those who had gone before him.

Above all he directed his attention to the form of cognition which the Symbolists used, concentrating in the work on the achievements of gnosiology 'from Plato's time to the epoch of Hartmann'. The Symbolists attracted him with their active interpretation of the external phenomena of life, their striving to see inner hidden connections between everyday objects and phenomena. 'The poet is above all a contemplator,' writes Z, understanding by contemplation 'a certain active intercourse between the subject and the world around him'. A photographic depiction of the world cannot be fruitful for poetry: 'The theory of naïve realism is the theory of an idle philistine.' Only a depiction of the world processed by the thought mechanism of the artist is fruitful. 'In this way there is achieved a difference not in what is experienced but in the experiencing,' he writes. (Thirty years later Z was to copy out from Delacroix's *Diary*: 'That which is new is contained in the creating spirit and not in the nature which is depicted.') By their example the Symbolists confirmed the fundamental role of the interaction of the personality of the writer with the surrounding world and this convinced Z of the justice of his conclusion that the path to creativity lay through the self-education of the individual and the subjection of the whole of his nature to poetry. The young seeker had realized what Khodasevich was to write somewhat later:

> The Symbolists were unwilling to separate the writer from the man, the literary biography from the personal. Symbolism did not want to be merely an artistic school, a literary tendency. It constantly struggled to become a creative method of living, and in that lay its deepest, perhaps intangible truth, but in essence the whole of its history passed in the striving towards this truth. (From *The End of Renate.*)

This was the important lesson of Symbolism and Z wanted to make use of it. But he could not respond positively to the Symbolists' efforts merely to turn objective existence into a symbol, behind which were concealed their own creative constructions and imaginings. He rejected an art that was simply 'locked into the creation of its own world'. In the article he maintained:

> The mysterious world which appeared to the Symbolists was far from objective. It carried within it the sharp imprint of the author's individuality. Such was El Dorado for Edgar Allen Poe, 'The inscrutable land of my birth' for Bely, the 'Star Mair' for Fyodor Sologub. The

inspired revelations of worlds were not the voice of nature, but the visions of the individual striving towards it with all the force of poetic attraction. This is how I explain the decline of real Symbolism.

The first-year student's article bore witness to his erudition, and his deeply interested approach to questions of culture. We can assume that his attitude to the courses at the Institute was just as purposeful as it was to the books which came into his hands and to the opinions of his colleagues. Throughout his student years he was consistently establishing for himself a position that would enable him to reflect the real world, glittering with unique experience and independent thought. It was for this very reason that he studied earlier literary schools and avidly absorbed that knowledge without which he could not, as he wrote, manage in his efforts to work out 'original positions and literary forms'.

In his search for like-minded colleagues Z could not fail to turn his attention to his fellow first-year student, a member of the literary association and a future outstanding Leningrad poet, Nikolay Braun. At the outset the careers of both poets had much in common. Braun, like Z, had grown up in the countryside, in Tula province, in a family of educated village people. In his childhood he immersed himself in the world of nature and folk-songs, and grew to love poetry. He was a student at the *Gymnasium* in Oryol where he became interested in painting, amateur dramatics and writing poetry. In 1919 he came to Petrograd looking for wider artistic horizons. There he lived in poverty, getting by with casual work, until in 1921 he became a professional actor and at the same time enrolled in the Herzen Pedagogical Institute.

Young people who arrived in the city from the provinces had an especially acute feeling of the need to come to terms with the contrasts in their life. Their pre-revolutionary childhood had given way to their post-revolutionary youth; from being surrounded by woods and fields they had ended up in a huge city where, removed from the parental loving care they had known, they were faced with the prospect of building their future on their own. The country and the city, nature and civilization, the people and culture, the building of a new society – all these were for them not remote philosophical concepts but part of everyday life. Such themes were probably more than once discussed at the meetings of the literary society, where Braun read from a poem of 1920: 'I am leaving the city, I am sick. The city has crushed me with its weight of steel.'

The journal *Mysl'* included one poem each by Z and Braun on the subject of their attitudes to their past. They both grieved for the humble, but settled and secure, life with their parents, for their former closeness to nature and the fascination of their childhood. But they could not help understanding that it had gone forever and that now the realization of all their ideas and dreams was linked with the city and with the new times, whatever they might be. A poem of Z's already contained in its title a definite image – 'Heart-Wasteland'. A wasteland is an abandoned, uncultivated space, normally overgrown with rank grass and weeds. That was the way the poet viewed his own being.

In the poem, two logically connected themes are woven together – the bitter feeling of the unavoidable break in the world of departing adolescence, depicted in the image of a river, and the awareness of the need to reconstruct and bring to perfection a maturing personality. With desperation the poet observes the unfinished construction of his spiritual being, his heart-wasteland, still filled with childlike vulnerability and chaos of feelings. He orders himself to 'freeze the heart-wasteland' and foretells the inevitable departure of his original perception of the world. Z's reason had already sketched the outlines of self-perfection, of the refashioning of the 'wasteland', and this programme of personality construction demanded will, discipline, and, as he considered, a rejection of the fond memories and impressions of his youth. He associated his coming to maturity with the throwing off or freezing over of something dear to him from his provincial child-hood, and of lighting a sacred pyre on its shore to illuminate life with a new light of meaning. Yet the whole being of someone still almost a boy resisted this coldness, this hardening, this rationalism, and he was forced to admit to himself that he could not completely reject the directness and frankness of earlier years. But at the same time he punished himself for lacking single-mindedness, for being soft and incapable of following his own 'cold' programme to the letter.

With time, the principle of will would emerge victorious in this inner struggle with himself: Z would learn how to drive his intimate feelings – frankness, spiritual warmth, tenderness – into the depths of his soul. There in the depths they would not perish but ripen in anticipation, sometimes displaying themselves in life and in poems, even against the poet's will. This intentional suppression of the lyrical voice and at the same time the urge to express the poet's individuality preconditioned the direction of the search for those same 'original positions and literary forms' that had been discussed in the article on Symbolism.

Nikolay Braun explored this theme of the past quite differently. His poems were clearer, more mellifluous, more poetic, but less independent – in their essence they gravitated towards Igor Severyanin's triolets or the sentimental romance. And this was no accident; Braun at this time

41

set great store by the musicality of poetry, which seemed to him more important than originality or content. Z understood matters differently: he tried to subjugate the word to the idea. His poems were still incomplete in form, but there could be felt in them a searching, a striving towards complex imagery, a psychological tautness. He was clearly trying to follow Mandelshtam's advice not to 'act the poet', but this path turned out to be a lonely one during his student years.

The literary youth of the Pedagogical Institute was more in sympathy with Braun. Artistic effect, a superficial imagery and a tendency to decadence were all in fashion. They treated Z somewhat condescendingly as a 'coarse, unlikeable semi-peasant'.

The occasional person tried to offer him patronage and set him on the right path, which of course antagonized a young man with such an acutely developed sense of his own worth and feeling of pride. He took to avoiding expressing his views openly and followed the advice given in the letter to Kasyanov: 'If you discover something in yourself, don't reveal it to anyone – seem whatever you like to other people, but don't let them get their hands on your heart.'

Gradually Z's active participation in the 'Workshop of the Word' began to drop off. As a result, in February 1923 when the *Priboy* publishing house began to issue a city-wide literary and socio-political journal *Krasny Student* (*Red Student*), and the young literature students at the Institute began to join in, Z was not among them. Neither did his relations with Braun become any closer. Z began to react more and more sceptically to his poetry and, according to Stepanov, he is on record as saying more than once at the beginning of the 1930s: 'He's only fit to deliver milk churns,' most probably a reference to Braun's exclusive attention to the sound of poetry. Nor did Z form any close friendships with other members of the literary association – future writers such as Vagner, Komissarova and Sorokin.

It would be wrong, however, to think that Z was generally without close friends, that he was unsociable and given to perpetual gloomy self-examination. Naturally, he was extremely firm-principled about his views on poetry, but he often showed flashes of restrained happiness and good humour behind his stolid behaviour. In the later stages of his course he got to know the future literary figure Konstantin Bogolyubov. He also formed a friendship with a fellow student from the same year, Anya Klyuyeva, and set about courting her friend Katya Yefimova. He wrote comic verses to Anya and dedicated to Katya a long, serious poem 'Love', which he later destroyed.

Life in the city had undergone a change. After the good harvest of 1922 and the establishment of the New Economic Policy, food supplies had become significantly easier, trade had developed and economic activity had sprung into being. All the same, life as a student was hard – the money scarcely covered a meagre diet and the bare necessities of life. Part-time work had to be done and, when he was completely broke, money had to be borrowed from colleagues. Whether Z went back home to Urzhum during his student years, or used all his vacations for paid work, we do not know.

In 1923 as a result of prolonged bad diet Z suffered an acute attack of scurvy – he spent some time in hospital and afterwards because of the pain in his leg walked with a limp for some time. The seventeen-year-old Katya Klykova, who was at that time starting her first year at the Herzen Institute, recalls how her future husband was first pointed out to her – a serious young man, leaning on a walking stick and immersed in deep discussion with his colleagues – 'Look at that one there – with the stick – Nikolay Zabolotsky – the poet'.

Z's graduation certificate attests that he had completed the full course of the Department of Language and Literature of the Socio-Economic Faculty at the Herzen Pedagogical Institute in December 1925. But in fact at this time his teaching practice requirement was still outstanding and he did not fulfil it until the spring of 1926. For that reason, the certificate of completion of the course at the Institute was not issued to him until somewhat later – in October 1927 after he had done his military service. In his autobiography he wrote: 'In 1925 I finished at the Institute. I had under my belt a voluminous notebook of bad verses; my other belongings could easily have been packed into a small basket.'

The Oberiuty

I

AFTER graduating from the Institute, Z continued to live in the student hostel on Red Dawn Street, hoping that he would not be thrown out before his approaching call-up into the army. The deferment of military service to which students were entitled would run out in September 1926, and he had to use the remaining time to get a firm foothold in literary circles, and to achieve some success, however limited, as a poet. It was hard to find temporary work and he had no regular income.

Z and two of his student friends – N. P. Rezvykh from Urzhum and A. M. Blokhin from Tver – lived in an attic room in the hostel. In the autumn of 1925 they had been joined by Nikolay Sboyev from Urzhum, who had also decided to try and settle in the capital. It was Sboyev who described the beggarly existence of the 'four youths' somewhere on the seventh floor of a student hostel:

> They lived in poverty; they had in their possession only a few mass-produced objects: a primus stove, a teapot, a kettle to heat up something to drink, some bottles to keep paraffin. Individually they had brought a few objects from home – wicker baskets (woven from willow), folding penknives and some crockery. Rezvykh had a pocket watch, the only luxury item among them.
>
> Our room had about ten square metres of floor space, but the ceiling sloped because of the roof and there was not much air. The window gave sufficient light, and there was a splendid view out of it: beyond the Great Nevka* we could admire part of the Vyborg Side as far as the Polytechnic Institute and Sosnovka. The central heating worked well enough, but even so when there was a north wind the water in the teapot would freeze. Our 'everyday nourishment' was black bread washed down with hot water. But on lucky days there would also be some hot food – kasha (buckwheat porridge) with butter or boiled cod. Cod like that is not to be found nowadays – not with such an aroma: from one

* One of the branches of the River Neva in its delta [Ed.].

little cod fish there would be a smell that went right round the passages and rooms of the top floor. Quite often there were days when none of us had any money at all: the more phlegmatic of us would languish on their beds, while others would gather up what strength they still had to trudge through the city in search of any work – but work there was none. With luck one might get a job on the streets clearing snow from the tramlines when there was a heavy fall, or loading and unloading firewood; I sometimes managed to 'work' as a walk-on actor at the People's House (one rouble a time), and also as a model at the Academy of Arts, the art school on Herzen Street, or at the Artists' Society – but all this was chance casual work, hired 'at the door'.

On one of the hungry days Rezvykh got up gloomily, without a word, and disappeared. The poor fellow could not take it any more and sold his watch (inherited from his father): we ate the food he brought back in silence.

Despite the impoverished and hungry life, the four young people did not despair; Z would read his new poems to his friends and bring along collections of poetry and the works of poets who interested him, copied out by hand. Everything that was read out underwent finicky criticism. They swapped jokes, epigrams, funny drawings and caricatures of each other. They loved singing popular songs. Sboyev recollects:

All of them had good voices and the results were pretty good, particularly when they sang church music. I must say at once that none of the young people were inclined towards religious experience, except for me. Zabolotsky once even tried to talk me out of my religious inclinations, producing the practical argument that an atheistic, scientific world-view was beyond the reach of mockery, whereas a believer could easily have his feelings hurt.

One day in the summer or autumn of 1925, Z announced to his friends that he faced the awesome task of reading his verse at the Leningrad Union of Poets. An audience of poets and poetry-lovers assembled in a small reading-room of the Union's building on the Fontanka. At the end of the evening the secretary of the Union, M. A. Froman, introduced the unfamiliar figure of a young man who attracted attention because he did not resemble the accepted figure of a poet. Neatly dressed, ruddy-cheeked, somewhat shy, he read, it seems, only one poem in a clear, self-confident voice. There was thin, polite applause, but two people clapped longer and more enthusiastically than the others. The evening ended and these two got up, went over to the new boy and congratulated him. They introduced themselves as Daniil Kharms and Aleksandr Vvedensky. 'We're young poets too: I'm twenty, he's twenty-one. We're looking for new paths in poetry and are interested in good poets who are just setting out. Your poem struck me as completely novel and I was quite shaken!', said Kharms. Vvedensky chuckled condescendingly, but supported his friend: 'I hadn't heard any worthwhile poems for a long time. I've been lucky today – it was worth waiting for. It's a funny thing: you look like a low-grade clerk and write such daring verse. Appearances are always deceptive. Let's get to know each other better.'

Late as it was, all three went off to Nadezhdinskaya Street, where Kharms lived with his parents, the Yuvachovs. There they talked for a long time about poetry, read verse and drank cheap sweet wine. It emerged that they all revered Velimir Khlebnikov and that a certain similarity in their evaluation of contemporary poets united them. Z was not worried by the obscurity and absence of logic in his new acquaintances' work, for behind their unusual combinations of words he sensed a genuinely experimental poetry, somehow close to his own searchings – without superficial beautification or sentiment: a poetry characterized by a separation between poetic and personal experience, by multiple significances, clever verbal inventions and rhythms, irony and ingenious fantasy. He was admittedly perplexed that these strange poems, particularly those of Vvedensky, lacked a foundation of meaning, a tangible thematic structure. Nevertheless in what related to form he could agree with them, and at their very first meeting a mutual trust and concern were established.

His closeness to Kharms and Vvedensky helped Z to join the stream of avant-garde art that for a time determined his creative progress and enriched his poetry with new devices taken not only from literature but also from art.

Up to the mid 1920s the poetry and painting of the Russian avant-garde largely went hand in hand, and one of those who inspired this interaction was the artist and theoretician Kazimir Malevich. Founder of Suprematism in painting and author of an article 'On poetry' (1919), he called for freedom from objectivity and anecdotalism, and affirmed colour and sound as the fundamental materials of art. In 1923 he headed a unique scholarly institution for the study of the laws of creativity: the Museum of Artistic Culture, which the following year was transformed into the State Institute of Artistic Culture, *Ginkhuk* for short. Several talented artists, theatre people and poets came to work at the Institute, among them P. N. Filonov, P. A. Mansurov, V. Ye. Tatlin, V. Yermolayeva and L. A. Yudin. All were gifted, bold, gripped by new ideas and ready to labour unceasingly for them. Sometimes the subjects under research were rather esoteric. Thus the artist Mansurov studied the influence of forms created by living nature on form in art.

The poet and outstanding theatre director Igor Terentyev together with the very young Aleksandr Vvedensky read out meaningless lists of words to the artists, who had to represent them through painting. Then they would try to discover the associational correspondences between verbal and pictorial transrationality.

Another person who worked in *Ginkhuk* was the founder of the Petrograd group of Transrationalists, the poet A. Tufanov, who largely accepted Malevich's ideas. Working as a proof-corrector in the *Priboy* publishing house, Tufanov began to write verse which he called 'alliterational', since ordinary words were replaced by meaningless phonemes. In his pamphlet *To Transrationality* (1924) he proclaimed that the highest type of poetry was the so-called 'spontaneous lyric', which, he thought, continued and completed the poetry of the Futurists, replacing the signifying or abstract word with pure sound. What resulted was phonetic transrationality, sound-music.

In Tufanov's flat a group of semi-professional Transrationalist poets would meet: Yevgeny Vigilyansky, a teacher; Igor Markov, an engineer; Matveyev, an accountant. At the beginning of 1925 there appeared among them the young Daniil Kharms and in his wake Aleksandr Vvedensky, who had quarrelled with somebody in *Ginkhuk*. These two kept together and did not go along with the more systematic Transrationalists. At their suggestion the group started calling itself the 'Left Flank', while Kharms and Vvedensky kept for themselves the neologistic appellation *Chinari,** underlining their autonomy in the company of the Transrationalists. The 'Left Flank' arranged a few readings in student and factory clubs, but in its initial form it did not last long, and fell apart at the beginning of 1926. Only the *Chinari* Kharms and Vvedensky continued to be close, and soon afterwards, together with the poets Z and Bakhterev, resurrected 'Left Flank' with new membership and new literary aims.

Kharms had an unforgettable appearance, emphasized by his unusual clothes. He had a pale, thinnish face, a bow-tie or cravat, trousers with bands at the knees, woollen gaiters or leather leggings, curious headgear, often changed, or a black headband. In his mouth he had a pipe, in his hand a walking-stick. He was not very talkative, but was pleasantly eccentric, courteous in an old-fashioned way; he had a fine sonorous voice and a calmly self-confident manner. In his actions as in his writings he obeyed some kind of internal rules rather than those generally accepted. His poems followed his tendency towards the

---

* Presumably derived from *chinit* 'to devise' or 'to mend'; perhaps also *chin* 'rank' [Ed.].

paradoxical, extraordinary and irrational. But Kharms also knew and often valued those tendencies in art that differed from his own experiments. His broad knowledge and inner tact were always appreciated by those who talked to him.

Aleksandr Ivanovich Vvedensky was a quite different personality. He made no attempt to distinguish himself or astonish the public through his appearance and clothing. With his handsome, faintly pock-marked face, dressed in a well-made and well-ironed suit, self-confident and theatrical, he was a success in company, particularly with women. Sometimes he was haughty and arrogant. If he did not like the person he was talking to, he would converse like a condescending *maître,* without removing his cigarette from his mouth. As a schoolboy he was fond of theatre and took part in school plays. He was a natural gambler, and when he had any spare cash would visit the Vladimirsky Club.

His poems were not intended to make sense, but their abstract associativeness was achieved not by the meaningless combination of phonemes or by word-invention – rather through strange combinations of normally comprehensible words. He considered himself 'the authority of senselessness' and at the same time the enemy of Transrationality, meaning by that the exclusion of normal vocabulary from poetry.

In our own day Kharms and Vvedensky have become famous as initiators of a literature and theatre of the absurd, and as remarkable children's writers. At that time, in the mid 1920s, they were taking their first, though fully confident, steps in the literary world.

Z was glad that he had at last found fellow spirits who liked his work and understood his thoughts about poetry. From autumn 1925 he and the *Chinari* used to spend time at the home of Tamara Meyer, ex-schoolfriend and future wife of Vvedensky, a charming young woman with a sensitivity for poetry, to whom the friends dedicated mostly jocular poems and missives. There he got to know some more young writers: the future author of popular scientific and historical children's books, L. S. Lipavsky (alias Savelyev), the musician and philosopher Ya. S. Druskin and N. M. Oleynikov, recently arrived from the Donbass.* Of all these people Z struck up particularly friendly relations with Kharms and, from the beginning of the 1930s, with Oleynikov.

At the end of the summer of 1926 Kharms and Vvedensky were commissioned to write a play for the experimental theatre called *Radix* that then existed as part of the theatrical division of the Institute of the History of Art. Both loved theatre, direct contact with the spectators

* Industrial region near the River Donets in Ukraine [Ed.].

and stage effects, and they excitedly started putting together an unusual play called *Mummy All in Watches*. Simultaneously they joined the *Radix* creative group and took part in the rehearsals, in which the play was essentially re-created anew with the help of the whole group. The play was put on in the White Hall of the Institute of Artistic Culture on St Isaac's Square – the same place where three years previously the artist Tatlin had produced a grand spectacle: the innovative production of Khlebnikov's dramatic poem *Zangezi*.

Z too started going to the *Radix* rehearsals at *Ginkhuk*. He liked the participants' enthusiasm and the bold operation of their boundless fantasy. Anyone in the hall could propose ideas: the production team, the playwrights, the *Lenfilm* actors who were taking part, amateurs and professionals from theatrical studios, artists who looked in on the rehearsals. Z was captivated by this atmosphere of collective endeavour, and he also joined in discussion of the action, thought of new approaches and even proposed new characters. As a result of this collective endeavour everything imaginable got into the production – the recital of abstract poems, the appearance of unexpected characters, murders and resurrections, tricks, dances, mobile décor and modern French music.

For the rest of his life Z considered that was how theatre should be: possessing magicality, circus-like atmosphere, masquerade, bold scenic anti-naturalism. Realistic, run-of-the-mill theatre, such as that established subsequently on the Soviet stage, seemed to him tedious and remote from the proper nature of theatre as an art-form.

The organizers of *Radix* never guessed that their theatre, like *Ginkhuk* itself, would soon be closed down, and they worried about its future repertory. The future theatrical scholar Sergey Tsimbal wrote a play *Gold-dust*, while the young writer Doyvber Levin devised a comedy about the Greek poet Theocritos. Z too was asked to consider a play. Testimony to his intention is given by one of the *Radix* initiators, the then eighteen-year-old art history student Igor Bakhterev. He recollects in his memoirs:

> Zabolotsky too promised to write a play, and talked about a novel theatre of masks. Against smooth coloured backdrops monologues would be spoken and actors representing animals, plants and objects would conduct dialogues. Among them there were people too: they didn't need masks.

Thus at the very beginning of his independent creative life Z was considering the interaction of all existing things, and the nature of the connections between people, animals and plants. In the same year he wrote a poem about this, and three years later began to write natural-philosophical poems using static dialogue and the introduction of such characters as Soldier, Ancestors, Cows, Horse, Tractor-driver, Plough, Wolf and Forester.

Years later, at the end of his life, Z was to remember the idea of his play for *Radix*, and say:

> I'd have liked to write a play in which the characters would have been people, stones, animals, plants, thoughts and atoms. The action would have taken place in the most varied locations – from interplanetary space to living cells. But anyhow, such a play wasn't going to be put on, so there was no point in writing it.

As a result of contact with *Ginkhuk*, Z got to know leaders of the Russian avant-garde who either worked there or were close to it: Malevich and Filonov; also talented experimental artists such as Mansurov, Yudin, Yermolayeva, Yu. Vasnetsov and V. Sterligov. As a contemporary confirms, the *Chinari* and Z could simply drop in on Malevich or Mansurov for an evening cup of tea. But it was his acquaintance with Pavel Filonov, the great artistic innovator, moral hero and thinker, that had particular significance for the poet.

In 1925 Filonov set up his workshop-school of Analytic Art in the Academy of Arts, bringing together a large group of his pupils. Instruction was given not only to professionals but also to amateurs, to whom the teacher explained the principles of his method and fairly quickly taught the elements of his art, the comprehension of what he termed *sdelannost,* 'madeness'. There is evidence that Z was one of these amateur pupils.

Several of Z's drawings from that period have been preserved and there is a noticeable suggestion of Filonov's style about them, in particular in a pencil self-portrait dated 1925 and a drawing of Sboyev. Thus it is quite probable that acquaintance with Filonov preceded the visits to *Ginkhuk*; and later, coming to comprehend Filonov's work, Z attempted to draw in his style. One of Z's literary friends, D. Maksimov, described the room into which he moved after the hostel:

> The walls were hung with coloured pictures showing figures of some kind of weird hominids. Zabolotsky did not hide the fact that these were his own works in which he openly imitated Filonov. He explained to me that Filonov was his favourite artist and that he was in personal contact with him.

Most of Filonov's works were kept in his studio, which he was happy to open even to unknown visitors. Z was often there, looking at paintings and drawings, chatting with the owner, watching him at work. Here is how he described one such visit, early in 1928, to his friend I. M. Sinelnikov:

> The room was cold. A little stove was smoking, with a tin teapot on it. The artist blew on his frozen fingers and got back to his paint brush. He was saying how some rich Americans had turned up. They'd suggested he should go to America or at least sell some pictures there. He answered them, 'I'm a Russian artist and my pictures belong to Russia'.

None of the artists who interested Z – not Chagall, not Kandinsky, not Malevich – aroused such excitement or such a feeling of common purpose as he got from looking at Filonov's pictures. His paintings and drawings steeped the poet's whole being in just the kind of world that he was attempting to create in his imagination and his verse. At the very first meeting poet and artist could not have failed to recognize each other as kindred spirits, and Filonov naturally detected in his visitor a grateful recipient of his ideas.

In the studio Z may have seen the picture 'Animals' (painted in 1925–6) with its elongated, mythical beasts with skewed, suffering, human-like faces, doomed and crushed amid the city buildings. In Filonov's drawings of 1922–6 animals were intermingled with quasi-dehumanized people; stumps of figures and trees deformed by urban existence poked up; coarse, maddened human visages and torsos intermingled with abstract planes and shapes. On one of these drawings can be made out street signs: 'Beer and love', 'Happy Masha's Pub'. As he showed his works the artist would explain that modern civilization with its urbanization, technocracy and worship of material goods diminishes the high destiny of humankind and transforms it into a sort of symbiosis of man and beast. The drama of the contemporary city resided in the degradation of the human impulse, making people faceless and despiritualized, implanting bestial souls in them. Z told the artist that he was working out a similar theme in poetry. But in his opinion animals and plants carried within them precisely that natural impulse that humanity was losing as it resettled itself in the strong embrace of the city, and separated itself from nature. It was no fault of the animals that the embryo of human thinking was not implanted in them; but humanity would not be worthy of its high destiny if it allowed bestial chaos to overwhelm it. In the future everybody would have to be different.

Filonov could show Z pictures from his cycle 'Entry into Universal Flowering' and other paintings on which his conceptions of a future world of harmony were imprinted. In the paintings 'Draymen',

'Cowherds' and 'Peasant Family', Z recognized the embodiment of his own concepts of the future equality of humans and animals. Looking at the faces of cows, horses, wolves and comparing them with faces of people depicted alongside them, he could mentally recite lines from his 1926 poem 'The Face of the Horse':*

> Animals do not sleep. In darkness of the night
> They stand above the world like a stone wall.
> . . . The horse's face is more splendid and more wise.
> He hears the speed of leaves and stones
> Attentively! He knows the animal cry
> And in the ancient grave the nightingale-roar
> . . . And if man were to see
> The horse's magic face,
> He would tear out his powerless tongue
> And give it to the horse. In truth the horse
> Is worthy to possess a magic tongue.

Filonov was happy to speak about his methods and principles in art, believing that they were to some extent universal and therefore useful to the young poet. In June 1928 he set them out in a letter to a novice artist, Vera Sholpo, and subsequently considered the letter a sort of methodological aid for his School of Analytic Art. Much of Filonov's instructional document coincides with principles that Z had already absorbed.

In his letter to Sholpo, Filonov wrote, 'Don't work like a student but like a master'. He called for every atom of a picture to be forcefully worked over with maximal analytic tension of the mind, so as to create 'to the best of your capabilities'. From 1926, Z attempted to behave in just such a way: he did not wish to be a pupil or a poetic 'beginner' – he wanted to be a 'master' since he respected professionalism and devotion to one's work.

Another principle of the artist was equally close to Z's heart: 'Don't set out from the general, from structure – that's charlatanism – but work from the particular to the general, following the formula "the general is produced from particulars, developed to the highest degree".' Working up details and attentiveness to the word were always characteristic of Z. In small things he strove to see an all-embracing principle, beyond individual incidents a general rule.

Finally there is a basic principle of 'analytic art' that is closely related to Z's creative method: its teaching on 'the seeing eye' and 'the knowing eye'. Filonov's letter to Sholpo reads:

* Full translation on pp. 343–4.

All existing tendencies should be consigned to hell, so that you can act as a naturalist experimenter (as in precise scientific papers). Here's what you should take as the basis of doctrine about content: the 'seeing eye' sees only the surface of things (objects), and even then only from a certain angle and within limits . . ., but the 'knowing eye' sees the object objectively, that is exhaustively. The 'seeing eye' sees nothing beyond colour and form . . . But the 'knowing eye' speaks to the experimental master not about that alone: it says that in every atom forming a periphery, in every atom of the surface itself a series of transfigurative transformational processes is going on, and the master depicts these and many other phenomena through an 'invented form' for any necessary occasion.

How well this 'doctrine about content' chimes in with the thoughts that Z expressed when still a first-year student in his article on Symbolism! It is hardly surprising that he counted his acquaintance with Filonov both important and fruitful, despite its being limited to fairly few meetings and conversations. Z knew how to evaluate people, knew whose ideas and work could be incorporated into his conceptual system and thus could enrich and strengthen it. In addition, painterly methods were close to Z's heart from the beginning and he used them successfully in verse-composition. Ten years later, when he was speaking to a doctor about his psychological peculiarities, he particularly noted his excessively developed visual imagination. That way of seeing the world through an artist's eyes and thinking in spatial images to a large degree influenced the formation of his own poetic method. A clear conception of the disposition of objects in relation to each other, of spatial distortions, of the choice of metaphors on the principle of form and colour, the depiction of 'still life' – all this shows that his interest in, particularly, modernist art was far from trivial.

By 1926 the period of learning, of searching and of self-formation had come to an end and Z suddenly reached maturity: he began to work 'as a master' – confidently, expressively and fruitfully. Aware of this maturity, he began to try out his method on varied subject-matter. In May–June 1926 he wrote the programmatic poem *Disciplina Clericalis*. In this 'spiritual regulation' he sets out his position: every elemental thing, every individual phenomenon conceals within itself the unfathomable complexity of the universe – 'movements and thunderings, not yet perceptible to the eye'. The poet exclaims: 'And these are not boards of wood, but sisters, not plants but brothers. Where is thy hand, O Death, show it!' In these words we see the departure-point for Z's future natural-philosophical ideas about metamorphosis and immortality.

In the same year he wrote two difficult polyphonic poems on historical subjects ('Insurrection', 'The Duel'), a poem about football, and the psychological landscape poem 'The Sea'. But the most successful poems of 1926 were two on urban subjects, 'White Night' and 'Red Bavaria' (later renamed 'Evening Bar'), and two of a natural-philosophical character, 'The Face of the Horse' and 'Trees' ('In our dwelling places . . .'). The first two open a series of brilliant grotesques, the works most characteristic of Z in 1926–8, marking the beginning of his public fame. 'The Face of the Horse' and 'Trees' are distinct in content and form from the 'urban' poems, and open up another direction in his work – one that was temporarily hidden but from 1929 became fundamental for him.

These five poems were the first that Z recognized as worthy of his talent, and he always included them in projected manuscript collections of his works.

II

One day, at the beginning of autumn 1926, Z had a visitor in the hostel on Red Dawn Street, the ever-serious and mysterious Daniil Kharms. Squeezing into the small attic room, he solemnly announced that he had to speak about an important matter on which the fate of their common literary existence would depend.

> A few days ago I was at the Art History Institute for a poetry-reading, so as to see how the young people are doing. One of them was interesting – I think you'd have seen him at *Radix*. He's Igor Bakhterev, a student, fond of theatre, likes drawing, understands music. I took his notebook of verse off him and showed it to Vvedensky – he reckons there's something there, too . . . Anyhow that means we've got several poets who think the same sort of way. Why don't we revive 'Left Flank' with a different membership? You, me, Vvedensky, Bakhterev and maybe one or two more. How about it?

Z was interested and answered:

> We ought to think about it seriously. You yourself know that any organization needs a definite framework, and I wouldn't be able to tie myself down with any artistic obligations. Nor would you, anyhow. But that doesn't mean to say that we can't remain individuals and at the same time discover what unites us and strengthens us. That's what's wanted – to define clearly how we're different and why we want to join up into a separate literary group. It's a sensible idea – but I'm going to

have to think about it, and you and Vvedensky must, too. And show Igor my latest poems so he knows who he's dealing with.

All four agreed to meet a couple of days later, and Z gave Kharms two recently composed poems: 'Red Bavaria' and another that has since been lost, 'Autumnal Poem'. Bakhterev testifies that both were written out in calligraphic script and decorated with illuminations in the manner of Filonov. Alas, these manuscripts, like much material in Bakhterev's archive, perished in the Second World War.

In May 1926 Z joined the Leningrad Union of Poets, but that did not exclude his participation in any other literary grouping that suited his tastes and idiosyncrasies. He decided to take up Kharms's idea and organize a circle of writers to uphold their common interests and get their work known. They met on a prearranged day at the flat which Kharms shared with his parents. Z responded favourably to Bakhterev's poems and to those of his drawings that were hanging in Kharms's room, and began to speak about how he conceived of the revitalized 'Left Flank'.

'We must retain our freedom and not get in each others' way. That means we don't need a leader and we don't need rules.'

'But we've got to have something that brings us together!' Kharms objected.

'Of course: let's see what does. First of all we don't accept boring naturalism. We all want to learn from Velimir Khlebnikov. We reject transrational poetry like Tufanov's. We try to see concrete objects and phenomena as the basis of our poetry, so that in them and through them all the variety of life can show itself. But we each see these objects in a different way, and each of us has his own arsenal of expressive means. For example I can't accept Vvedensky's methods – though he does use words that exist on the level of sense, his verse has evident nonsense in it, bordering on transrationality. But we're not a monastery where all the monks have to look the same. We're masters, not apprentices, artists, not daubers.'

Vvedensky warmly supported the principle of the members' independence, but denied that his method of writing would inevitably lead to a dead-end. Kharms, for his part, announced that he was thinking over some ideas that could reconcile Z and Vvedensky. In his opinion meaningless orderings of words could also reveal a certain concealed but objectively existing sense of real things. Despite the friends' differences, 'Left Flank' became a new Leningrad literary group.

Nevertheless, Z straight away deemed it necessary to clarify his differences with Vvedensky, the 'authority of senselessness'. On 26 September, just as 'Left Flank' was being set up, he wrote Vvedensky an open letter which he then circulated to its members and their close friends. He ended it thus:

> Your verses do not grow on the same soil as ours. They do not speak of the life that goes on beyond the limits of our observations and experience – they have no compositional core.
>
> An avalanche of stones whistles by and strange sounds are heard – issuing from the void: it is the reflection of nonexistent worlds. Thus a blind master sits and whittles away at his fantastic art. We have been bewitched and frozen to the spot – the earth recedes from our feet and trumpets in the distance. And next morning we shall awaken on the same earthly beds and shall say to ourselves: 'The old chap was wrong after all.'

The open letter to Vvedensky demonstrates not only Z's exceptional sense of principle in matters of poetry, but also his own creative purposes – those that he had at the beginning of his mature work and at the start of his closest period of alliance with the *Chinari*. It is worth noting that he already then knew what he could make use of from their experience (alogical metaphor, based on new associations) and where he deviated from them on principle.

Soon after the founding meeting, the new 'Left Flank' was joined by an already established poet and student of the visual section of the Institute of Art History, Konstantin Vaginov. He was twenty-seven, had already been published, had joined a group called 'Islanders' at the beginning of the 1920s and from that time had been a friend of Nikolay Tikhonov. His poems were unlike those of Kharms and, particularly, Vvedensky in their logical ordering, and were remote from grotesquerie and experimentalism, although they showed a certain 'mistiness and vibrancy', lending them their own brand of warmth and originality.

Vaginov's culture, modesty, good nature and charm predisposed Z towards him. However their respect for each other's poetry did not lead to close friendship. Although he took part in the 'Left Flank' public appearances Vaginov stood somewhat apart from its other members. Later the story-writer Boris (Doyvber) Levin also joined the group.

One of their first tasks was to put their work before the reader. To this end they wanted to issue collective volumes and arrange poetry-readings. As it turned out, in Bakhterev's words, 'volumes were dreamt up, but not one saw the light of day (money was needed, and there was none), while innumerable performances actually happened – with or without discussions'. They took these encounters with the public very seriously and professionally, reflecting the experience of the rehearsals with *Radix*. Those present at the 'Left Flank' evenings did not merely listen to partly incomprehensible poems, but took part in a kind of demonstration of creative theatre. Even before the readings began the imagination was stirred by posters with inscriptions such as 'Poems aren't pies, we aren't herrings' or 'Art is a cupboard . . .' There were surprising and problematic light and sound effects – for example the evening would open with a deafening explosion from a toy pistol – and there were also Kharms's unusual clothing and behaviour, the painted faces of the poets and the appearance on stage of objects of inexplicable purpose. Among the participants from the first performances onwards were a conjuror, Pastukhov, a classical ballerina, Militsa Popova, and some of the actors from the *Radix* studio. This sort of theatricalization gave a carnivalistic atmosphere to meetings with these poets.

At first Z, like the others, thought up varied and surprising stage effects of this kind. Thus he sometimes went on stage balancing on the flat of his hand a favourite wooden stand-up toy, with cheeks ruddy as his own, which he had from a Christmas tree. But he felt it more important to establish what effect was produced on the listeners by his poetry and not by the accompanying gimmicks, since he (like Vaginov) was less inclined than the others to 'orchestrate' his appearances. Subsequently when he agreed to various tricks of theatricalization it was a question of yielding to the general spirit of the evening rather than following his own inclinations.

The poetry of the 'Left Flank' sounded subtle, and its novelty excited the audience. When Z went up on stage and recited his energetic, expressive poetry, it was as if the magic stage-act had been transferred from external effects into the content of the verse, and, holding their breath, the spectators listened to such lines as: 'Look, it's no dance, no fancy-dress ball / here night irrelevantly follows night, / here wine-slurred laughter soars / like a parrot up in flight . . .'

Literary performances often ended with discussion of the poems that had been read. Speakers from the floor often abused the young poets, but they did also acknowledge their talent and the general atmosphere of excited carnivalism.

At the beginning of November 1926, Z was called up into the 59th Rifle Regiment of the 20th Foot Division for a year's military service. Naturally he was sad that he had to interrupt the literary work that had begun so well, but he was not unduly despondent. It is possible he was even glad to exchange a hungry, insecure life in a cold and cramped attic room for the advantages of a soldier's life – sufficient food, state-provided clothing, a warm barracks. In notes for his autobiography Z wrote: 'Military service was no bed of roses, but it was well-organized, disciplined and there was enough to eat.' Evidently good order and service discipline even seemed attractive to him. He was to serve on the spot, in Leningrad, in a unit stationed on the edge of the Vyborg quarter, with a section consisting of short-term conscripts mostly drawn from the Leningrad intelligentsia.

Onerous field instruction began from the very first day. His barrack companions remembered how on the first evening after lights-out the reflective bass voice of Z rang forth: 'Well then, 364 days left', provoking friendly laughter from the other recruits. Soon there came a chance to use his talents as a writer and artist: Z became editor of the unit wall-newspaper. Possibly the artist V. Sterligov and the poet Ye. Vigilyansky, active members of *Radix*, who knew the 'Left Flank' well and were serving in the same unit, worked on the wall-newspaper too. In his autobiography Z wrote proudly that it was considered the best in the whole region.

The other 'Left Flank' members did not forget their comrade: they visited the Vyborg quarter barracks to see Z, Vigilyansky and Sterligov. 'Left Flank' organized poetry readings in the unit twice during the winter of 1926–7. After the first of these readings Z found enthusiasts for his talent among the soldiers.

The regimental doctor was glad to fix him a place in the medical section when he needed to screw up all his concentration to write a new poem that had dawned in his mind. On 4 November he composed 'The Sea', on 25 January 'Etching', on 30 January 'The Circassian Woman' and on 26 February, while on night-guard duty beside the regimental banner, Z composed his poem 'The Sentry' which his comrades then copied out and read.

In April 1927, in his army barracks, Z wrote what was really his first poem on an everyday social theme, 'New Life'. It was a time when it was becoming ever more obvious that certain groups in society were busy feathering their own nests while paying lip-service to public service and to the ideals of the Revolution. These people well understood what career advantages were opened up by joining the Party and becoming malleable material for Stalin to turn into his loyal *nomenklatura*. A multitude of new-style bureaucrats of variable calibre strove to attain power and personal prosperity. Z was deeply averse to such hypocrisy and opportunism, as to any other falsity in human behaviour. With a certain inner bitterness he satirized the egotistic philistine who would hasten to acquire superficial revolutionary forms of behaviour in order to improve his position.

The deformation of the 'new life', the way it was becoming

interwoven with the selfish activities of the quickly maturing 'young folk', prepared to do anything, became the subject of the poem 'New Life', in which we read the lines:

> the young chap's foot is getting broader,
> steel is thickening his arm,
> and lo! he's sitting in a great big flat,
> dangling a fiancée by the sleeve . . .
> But hereupon some friends drop round,
> the factory sings Hooray! Hooray!
> and the New Life, to do a favour,
> hands out a dish of sturgeon on a plate.
> . . . In staggers the president,
> weaving words of praise for the couple,
> carries in a Vyborg goblet
> military wine and halva;
> and, graciously accepting the red speech,
> Lenin sits on a little table* . . .

Of all the poems of those years 'New Life' was the most socially relevant, though others of his 'urban' poems ('At the Market', 'People's House', 'The Ivanovs') also have a social gloss.

Once a week conscripts could get a pass and have a free day in the city. Z used the opportunity to see his friends, read them his new poems and listen to theirs. Once (on the evening of Saturday 12 March 1927) he called in on Kharms but found him asleep. Thereupon he wrote him two impromptu poems on a large sheet of paper. One was written as if by Daniil Kharms himself: 'My friends came round to visit me. / Alone remained I, lapped in sleep . . .' It ended:

> And I lie here alone, poor wretch,
> my sleepy legs thrown wide,
> before me glows a single bulb,
> my doggerel and boots lie strewn,
> and Kepka wound about my foot
> sleeps like a clockface too.

(Kepka – 'cap' – was the name of Kharms's dog). Beside it was a note: 'Dan, I couldn't bring myself to wake you up – you have a great appetite for sleep. I'm going. Goodbye. Look what I've done. Take note of the poetic advice I've put in a frame. Then tear it up. N.Z.' Kharms did not tear it up: the poems remained with Tamara Meyer, who kept them

---

* In Soviet editions of this poem the reference to 'Ilyich', Lenin, was suppressed (*kulich*, an Easter cake, was substituted) [Ed.].

with other manuscripts. Inside the frame he had put a jocular didactic poem addressed to the *Chinari*, urging them to abandon their doggerel. Underneath the joking surface there were hints of the serious arguments which had arisen between Z and his friends on his days off. In contradiction to Z, who often called upon his friends not to abandon precise thought and real subject matter in art, Kharms said,

> In destroying normal action, the connections between words and their ordinary meanings, we do not destroy reality but on the contrary express it with maximum fullness: we display within it that which cannot be captured by the analytical mind, thinking by means of generally accepted logic. Thus arises a 'naked eye' vision of the real world.

Z paid attention to his friends' arguments and found much that was of use to him in them. He too sought a 'naked eye' vision of the world; he rejected habitual, messy connections, but he understood the concept a little differently from Kharms – not in as other-worldly and mysterious a way. He considered that the emergence of new meanings when words were combined in unusual, alogical juxtapositions was a consequence of the well-known truth that the word in poetry carries a great deal more semantic load than in everyday speech. To push this to the extreme seemed fruitful to him, and like his friends he spoke of 'the principle of semantic collision'.

Vaginov, who also took part in similar discussions, was writing his novel *Goat's Song** at that time. In the words of the book's main character, the 'unknown poet', we can find the friends' argument about semantic collision. The 'unknown poet' says:

> Poetry is a special kind of business . . . It's a fearful and dangerous spectacle: you take a few words, put them together in an unusual way and start sitting over them – one night, then another, then a third – you keep thinking about the juxtaposed words. And then you notice that a hand of meaningfulness reaches out from one word and shakes a similar hand that grows out of another, and a third word reaches out its hand, and you are swallowed up in the new world revealed beyond these words.

Late in 1927 the members of the group decided to compose a manifesto, and entrusted Z with the task of writing its theoretical section. He succeeded in finding formulations that would satisfy himself and all the other members of the group and would also seem convincing to outsiders. Justifying the idea of 'semantic collision', he exclaimed: 'Perhaps you will object that our subject matter is "unreal" or "illogical"? And who said that "everyday life" is obligatory for art?'

* A play on words, since *Tragedy* means *Goat's Song* in Greek [Ed.].

Similarly in a private letter of 1929 he wrote: 'Art isn't life. A special world. It has its own laws and there's no point in our reproaching them for not helping us to make soup.'

Though upholding a more realistic aesthetic, Z none the less valued and absorbed that part of the conceptual world of the *Chinari* that seemed to him fruitful and acceptable for his own practice. All through life he retained an impulse towards a deepened, analytical comprehension of the process of creation and remained unshakeably true to much that he had thought out and absorbed in his youth. At the end of his life, in notes for a projected lecture, he was to write almost in the terms used by Vaginov's 'unknown poet', or those of his manifesto of 1927 (of which at that time he no longer had a copy):

Each word taken individually cannot be viewed as a literary word. It acquires its literary aspect only in conjunction with other words. What sort of conjunctions are these? Above all, of meanings. Word meanings make weddings and marriages. As they flow together these meanings reorganize each other and give birth to transformations of meaning. The atoms of new meanings coalesce into gigantic molecules, which in their turn model the aesthetic image. Conjunctions of images are controlled by poetic thought.

This similarity between the theoretical concepts Z uttered at such different times is all the more astonishing in that their application to his actual working process in the 1920s and the 1950s gave quite different results.

Early in 1927 the Institute of Art History sent an official letter to his military unit requesting that Red Army soldier Z should be given leave to take part in a literary event. People in the Institute were interested in 'Left Flank' and asked its members to read in the Red Room, but this time in an academic way, without theatrical effects. Z was allowed half a day's leave from the barracks for the meeting with teachers and students of the literary section of the Institute. After the poetry-reading there was a discussion in which the literary scholars Yu. Tynyanov, B. Eykhenbaum and V. Zhirmunsky participated. Tynyanov was particularly interested in Z's poems, and later they were often to meet and talk. There is evidence Tynyanov praised Z's poem 'Thoughts of Marriage' (1928), and in 1928 or 1929 gave him a book with the significant dedication 'To the first poet of our times'. After Tynyanov's death Z wrote in a letter: 'Yury Tynyanov was always so attentive to me from when I first set out, and I owed him a lot.' Eykhenbaum, too, at once saw in Z's poems a new and highly promising phenomenon in Russian poetry and spoke of them with great feeling.

That day played a definitive role in Z's literary fate, and gave him yet another friend: his meeting with a young teacher at the Institute, V. A. Kaverin, was the beginning of many years' friendship. 'It wasn't a matter of full-scale, utter frankness of the sort where there are no secrets', Kaverin later wrote,

> There was a certain restraint between us – perhaps because I sensed this quality in him . . . I was too young to comprehend straight away what I now know to have been remarkably characteristic of him: everything that happened with him, around him, with or without his participation, was always and immovably linked with the consciousness that he was a poet. This certainly wasn't a sense of didacticism, an attempt to place himself above others. It was a characteristic that was the moral and aesthetic measure of all that he thought about or did. A sense of high calling was the yardstick of his life.

Thus even during military service Z found opportunities to take part in literary life. He wrote poems, met with his friends, appeared at poetry readings and struck up new acquaintances. He may have taken part in the discussions the 'Left Flank' held with Malevich in the hope of joining up with artists in a new organization – the 'Academy of Left Classics'.

By then *Ginkhuk* had been dissolved, but on its foundations had been constructed a section of the Institute of Art History for the experimental study of artistic culture, directed by Malevich. Kharms told Z that Malevich was interested in their fraternity, and had promised to find space at the Institute for the work of the new union of poets and artists. In March 1927, Kharms noted: 'Our next tasks: 1. To create a firmly based Academy of Left Classics. 2. To devise a manifesto. 3. To join the Press House. 4. To arrange a dance evening so as to raise about 600 roubles for publishing a collection. 5. To edit a collection.'

It is evident that 'Left Flank' expended much effort on attempting to broaden its sphere of activity, to publish its own collection and to turn itself into an officially recognized organization. But by no means everything that had been envisaged was actually achieved.

III

With the arrival of spring it became trickier to keep up contact with his friends – the regiment was transferred from the city barracks to a summer military camp at Krasnoye Selo outside Leningrad. Field tactical exercises, shooting practice and exhausting route-marches began.

During an interval between two expeditions Z received a letter from his old student friend Konstantin Bogolyubov, by now a postgraduate student: he had been a year below Z at the Pedagogical Institute. They were linked by their common love of literature, general view of life and keenness to become writers. They both came from the provinces, had grown up surrounded by nature and found the ugly face of urban life similarly painful. Bogolyubov wrote subtly plotted stories, and loved paradox and fantasy. Both despised sentimental lisping, bourgeois self-satisfaction and the sort of comfortable life that engulfed everything else.

Once Z told Bogolyubov about how his schoolfriend Boris Polner, who had just graduated in economics, had gone to the town of Sarapul on the Kama River, set himself up as an accountant and immediately got married. In the attic room at the hostel their friend's deeds gave rise to jokes and incomprehension. They composed a joint missive to the born-again bourgeois; in it they described the liberated lives of the four devout youths in their narrow cell and even drew a picture of these youths – in long surplices, worshipping an axe suspended in mid-air. The inscription beneath the drawing ran: 'O sacred axe, who hangest in the air, held by no hand, mightily shining!' and added a poem on the same theme.* This mocking and contemptuous attitude to marriage and to a friend's well-being met with Bogolyubov's warm approval: little did he guess that he himself would shortly find a nice girl to marry and call forth the same responses from his student friends.

Back in spring 1926, while Z was still at the Herzen Institute doing teaching practice, there had been a whole student crowd of them together: Kostya Bogolyubov, two girlfriends both in love with him, Katya Shulepova and Katya Klykova, Asya Snetkova whom Bogolyubov fancied and two who were keen on each other, Katya Yefimova and Z. Sometimes other students joined the company; they all had a good time, talked non-stop and read out poems. An atmosphere of young love reigned, together with a foretaste of the working life to come. Gradually Z began to notice he preferred the company of Katya Klykova. However for quite a time they were no more than friends, since everyone knew that Klykova loved Bogolyubov, and Z was involved with Yefimova. Katya Klykova lived with her uncle and aunt in a big flat on Great Pushkarskaya Street, quite near the hostel. Z sometimes visited her and read her the poems of Mandelshtam, Gumilyov, Klyuyev, Vaginov and occasionally Khlebnikov, the classic poets Lomonosov, Derzhavin and Boratynsky, and of course his own verse too.

* A joke based on the idea of an atmosphere so thick from overcrowding that it could suspend an axe [Ed.].

He loved Yesenin's poem 'The nightingale has one fine song . . .', which he read not calmly and solemnly, like other poets, but with a catch in the throat; sometimes he sang it to the guitar. Once he came with Bogolyubov; Katya's uncle, Andrey Ivanovich Klykov, observantly noticing his niece's infatuation, said: 'That Kostya of yours is empty-headed, while that Z, he's his own man, he'll do well.'

Katya Klykova sometimes made the long journey to the squat brick barracks at the furthest edge of the city to visit Z during the winter of 1926–7. Later at the summer army camp, Z had a letter from Bogolyubov in which he announced that he had written an adventure story, 'Endless Earth', and wanted Katya Klykova to read the manuscript. As he was going away from Leningrad he asked that Katya should be given the manuscript to send on to the editorial office of a Moscow journal. This gave Z a pretext to write Katya a letter in which he masked the tender feelings he already sensed towards her in a jocular mode of address imitating someone from a bygone century. That was a 'defamiliarizing' technique he often used in his poems, whether serious or humorous. Its jocular stylistic archaism and its mention of eighteenth-century poets were no accident. At that time Z's interests were by no means limited to contemporary avant-garde movements, but included Old Russian poetry, Derzhavin, Pushkin, Boratynsky and some western poets (Goethe, Pope). Afterwards critics were to note in his poems of 1926–8 not only innovative features, but signs of archaism and classicism.

The well-known literary critic Lidiya Ginsburg, who knew Z well in the 1920s and 1930s and in May 1928 had received from him a humorous poetic missive also in eighteenth-century style, wrote later about the role of tradition in Z's early poems. She affirmed that amid the poet's complex settling of accounts with the 'decayed culture' of the recent past he looked for support in a past that was more remote, in a realignment towards the Russian eighteenth century, and that 'the heritage of eighteenth-century Russia was necessary for Z, but fused with the experience of a twentieth-century poet'.

In autumn 1927 Z took an examination at the end of his military service, achieved the rank of platoon commander and was discharged into the reserve. Although in the next few years he was sometimes called up again for manœuvres and to give instruction to recruits, he was now free and able without hindrance to get down to writing and to arrange his own life.

Late 1927 and the whole of 1928 were happy times for Z. Fate seemed to smile on him: good poems got written, he had some literary earnings, a first collection of poems was accepted by a publishing house, he began to publish slim books for children, the literary group 'Left Flank' received some public recognition. It was good to know he really was a poet, good to be able to live permanently in Leningrad, exciting to experience a growing attachment to Katya Klykova. But when his military service ended he was far from well-placed materially – he had nowhere to live, no money, not even proper clothes. He was lucky to be allowed to keep his Red Army uniform. Nevertheless he had his friends, a firm belief in his own powers and an overwhelming desire to get down to work.

A few days after his army discharge Z, wearing his long soldier's greatcoat, boots with puttees and at the same time a very non-military check cloth cap, turned up at Great Pushkarskaya Street to see Katya Klykova, who remembers his visit:

> Nikolay came along wearing a particularly sly and significant look on his face. When we emerged from the semi-darkness of the lobby-cum-kitchen I saw there were patterns inked onto his cheeks: some kind of trident with a handle at right angles and a diamond shape. He asked me to go for a walk with him. I realized he wanted to give the passers-by a surprise. Arm in arm we solemnly progressed along Bolshoy Prospect, then turned onto the Kamenoostrovsky. Evening was coming on. Not a single passer-by paid any attention to us at all! When we got back I couldn't resist laughing out loud.

Obviously Z wanted to demonstrate Futurist eccentricities, though in general acting up and shocking the public were hardly in his nature and he did not as a rule go in for them.

Katya Klykova had already graduated from the Teacher Training Institute and was working in a primary school. She knew that Z lived his own special inner life and that the most important thing in it was poetry, but after all she too had always loved verse and idolized poets. They met ever more frequently and Z understood he was really in love. This made him contemplate marriage. He considered that on reaching a certain age a man ought to marry – such was the order of life, something not instituted by us and not for us to change. But at the same time he was afraid that marriage would get in the way of his work and ruin the freedom he had at last won. He had often observed that a family man would get stuck in the mud of bourgeois comfort and forget any higher inclinations. He expressed his misgivings in a passage of the poem 'The Ivanovs' written on 29 January 1928 (its first title was 'Street Reflections'):

> Surely I'm not destined to find my place
> where my fiancée waits for me,

> where seats are drawn up in a row,
> where the filing-cabinet's a veritable Ararat,
> entwined with paper doilies,
> where stands the table, and the three-tiered
> samovar clad in iron armour
> roars like a household general?*

But emotion proved stronger than sober reasoning and apprehensiveness; after only a little thought Z decided that the object of his choice was sufficiently sensible and independent, and that her uncle's petty-bourgeois set-up did not affect her. However quite a bit of time was to pass before he decided to propose.

In February 1928 Bogolyubov suddenly got married. He chose a wife whose way of life and interests were quite unlike those of the Institute. Both the Katyas, who adored Bogolyubov, and were each nobly prepared to yield him up to the other, were offended and disillusioned – not so much by his getting married as by the choice their idol made. By the standards of the time it was a luxurious wedding. After the church ceremony there assembled in the bride's flat Bogolyubov's clergyman uncle who had brought him up in the provinces, and a number of smartly dressed women and well-off men, who belonged to the inner circles of the commercial world. There was food of a quality and abundance rare at those times, there were speeches and toasts, songs sung to a guitar. Z was one of the guests and took this luxury as his friend's betrayal of their old ideals. As the guitar strummed amid shouts of 'Bottoms up!' he rose from the table and left.

The same evening he wrote his well-known poem 'Wedding' in which, with obvious exaggeration, he gave a grotesque and colourful picture of a wedding feast, while accusing the groom ('stuck to the bride' and 'forgetting the thunder of hooves') of hypocrisy ('his mobile face . . .'). Few later commentators on Z's work could resist quoting this poem. Nevertheless the picture it gives was certainly not an exact description of his friend's wedding. So when the next morning he called on Bogolyubov and gave him the poem to read, the latter not only took no personal offence, but on the contrary congratulated the poet on his brilliance and invited him to join in the continuing revelry. But Z demurely refused and thereafter decisively broke off not only his friendship but any encounters with Kostya Bogolyubov. They began to meet again only a few years later, when both of them worked in a children's publishing house – but friendship was not re-established.

Meanwhile Z's literary life was beginning to take off. His first

* See the full translation of this poem on pp.348–9.

published work, 'Red Bavaria', appeared in the 1927 Union of Leningrad Poets' collection *Bonfire*; while 'Expedition' came out in *Leningrad Pravda* and 'Football' in the journal *Zvezda* in the same year. These first published poems were an important event in the poet's life and provided a bit of money. Now he could allow himself to rent a small room. In the late autumn of 1927 someone recommended him digs on Konnaya Street which an indigent engineer was letting out in his small flat for a low rent. The narrow corridor led from the entrance to a little room with a single window and a round Dutch stove. It was all very basic: a small working table, two chairs, a stool and an iron bedstead. But after the hostel even this accommodation seemed quite splendid: he could work in solitude and have friends in as he wished.

Konnaya (Horse) Street was located close to the Old Nevsky Prospect and to the characteristically named Fleamarket, Carriage and Ironmongers' Lanes. As D. Maksimov noted, it 'still retained traces of its vanished past: of the coarse rumble of the merchant life of pre-Revolutionary Petersburg'. Not far away was the Horse Market; on Fleamarket Street could be seen warehouses with heavy doors and huge padlocks; carts rattled over the cobblestones, harnessed up to big shaggy cart-horses. Z was much interested in these scenes of city life and transformed them into poetic images.

One result was the poem 'Konnaya Street', which eighteen months later, together with some of his other poems, was sent to the journal *Chudak* (*Eccentric*) with this accompanying note:

Leningrad, 9 June 1929. Dear Comrade Reginin, I can accept your proposed fee (1 rouble 90 kopeks per line of verse). Take a look at 'Konnaya Street' and 'Illness': if either is suitable for *Chudak*, please take it. On receipt of this letter would you kindly let the Leningrad department of *Ogonyok* know of the payment of the sum owing to me for what you take on. Greetings to the editorial board, to Katayev and to Olesha. Yours, N. Zabolotsky.

The journal did not accept 'Konnaya Street' and its text has not survived.

What Z observed at that period also left its mark on 'Wandering Musicians' (August 1928). To get from the street to his entrance-way Z had to pass through two or three successive archways between which there lay inner courtyards with stacks of firewood, rubbish-pits and varied lumber. In the poem this scene was reflected in the lines: 'Around him a system of cats, / a system of buckets, windows, wood / was hanging, multiplying the dim world / into the narrow kingdoms of courtyards.'

In those years out-of-work musicians would often appear in this 'kingdom of courtyards', so as to earn a crust or two of bread with an informal concert. At a time when there were no radios or tape-recorders, and very few had gramophones, people took much delight in such music, especially in romantic or sentimental songs, and gladly threw money to the performers.

> But what was the courtyard? It was a pipe,
> it was a tunnel to those regions
> where warrior-Tamara sleeps
> where my youth pines away,
> where little coins, humming and softening,
> in the unsteady light of a flame,
> fly to the feet of the golden dragon,
> and do a dance, falling into centuries!

How did the poet compose his works? From his student years, when nobody had any personal space in the hostel except his own bed, Z had developed the habit of composing poetry lying on his stomach, writing down the lines in pencil on a sheet of paper on top of a special cardboard box or a file. Sometimes Z put the file away under the bed and drifted off to sleep: when he woke up he would write down some new lines. His mind went on working in the direction he had set himself even when asleep.

The surviving rough draft of the poem 'Beggars at Market' allows us to envisage the successive stages of the creation of a poem. First the poet reconstructed in memory the actual impressions of Leningrad markets in the 1920s and then transferred them onto paper, submitting to his intuition and subconscious, paying no heed to elegance or coherence of text. The lines developed of their own accord under the pencil; one line pulled the next along after it – something emerged on paper that was almost devoid of any evident sense. Then Z clearly defined for himself the basic line of thought and subject of the poem, and correspondingly regularized and clarified the text of the draft. Out of this emerged a coherent, vivid poem of smaller scope, that is known to us as 'At the Market'.*

On the same sheet of paper he added a note explaining the technique of its creation:

On 12 December, a few days after the first draft was written, I made a fair copy of the poem, making substantial changes in the process – see the second variant. Subsequently over the course of two months,

---

* See translation on pp.345–7.

68

thinking about the poem, I also mentally introduced several corrections into the second variant, where they are indicated in ink. N. Z. 1 March 1928.

And yet it was hardly from the intuitivistic, chaotic sketch, entitled 'The Rule of Simplicity', that the poem was made: out of the rough draft only one line was subsequently used.

These drafts, 'Beggars at Market', 'The Rule of Simplicity' and the note of 1 March 1928 are unique surviving documents that allow us to see into Z's creative laboratory. His work combined an intuitive and an analytical method. As if to take issue with the analytical principle of aesthetics, at the end of his life he was to ask:

> What path should a poet take – from the particular to the general or the general to the particular? I think that neither of these paths is right by itself, since naked rationality is incapable of poetic achievements. Neither the analytic nor the synthetic approach on its own is right for the poet. The poet works with all his being, unconsciously uniting these methods.

Sometimes Z would leave Konnaya Street to visit Kharms on Nadezhdinskaya. At one time the friends would meet regularly, on specified days, and would work together – composing verse, drawing, devising manuscripts. They did not allow themselves to talk about anything extraneous.

In truth though, as Bakhterev wrote about Z, it was not always a question of getting down to serious business: 'Nikolay would write humorous verse or copy out his work calligraphically, ornamenting his poetry with entertaining vignettes and illustrations that looked like the work of Filonov's pupils.'

Soon after Z returned from military service there was a 'Left Flank' evening in the Small Hall of the 'Chamber Music Club' on the corner of Nevsky Prospect and Sadovaya Street. Verse and prose were read by Kharms, Vvedensky, Vaginov, Bakhterev and Doyvber Levin. Z was dressed for the performance in his army uniform, and his healthy well-coloured face, restrained manners and round glasses had nothing exotic or bohemian about them, as an eye-witness, D. Maksimov, noted: his was a clear, commanding, major-key reading, with no signs of 'musical self-forgetfulness'. 'Grotesque irrationalism of word-combination seemed to do battle in these poems, in their delivery and their content with clarity of sound, alertness of thought and thematic definition.'

When the readings finished, two friends introduced themselves to the participants – N. M. Oleynikov and Ye. L. Shvarts. As far as we can tell this was Z's first meeting with Shvarts. They quickly became close friends.

Yevgeny Shvarts first came to Petrograd in 1921 as an actor in the Rostov Theatre Company. Two years later he lived for a time at Bakhmut in the Donbass, where his father, a doctor, was working. There he began working on the local paper and made friends with the editorial assistant, Nikolay Oleynikov, an original and remarkable figure. He had grown up in a Cossack settlement on the Don in the family of a well-off tavern-keeper. Breaking off relations with his family, he took part in the Civil War on the Red side, joined the Bolshevik Party in 1920 and at its behest found himself working on a miners' newspaper. Outwardly he resembled a Don Cossack – with curly hair, high cheekbones and deceptively calm, cunning blue eyes. He seldom smiled, but had a mocking, indeed sarcastic manner. His closeness to Shvarts came from their common enthusiasm for literature and liking for witticisms. In the mid 1920s they both came to Leningrad to seek their literary fortunes and were drawn into the orbit of Samuil Marshak, who was energetically engaged in setting up a new children's literature and drawing talented young people, including Oleynikov and Shvarts, into writing for children. In 1927 the new children's journal *Hedgehog*, which was intended to revive the tradition of the earlier *New Robinson Crusoe* (1923–5), had just been proposed. Marshak devoted much attention to this children's journal and tried very hard to build up a collaborative team capable of making it entertaining, original and accessible to a child's apprehension of the world.

After the evening at the Chamber Music Club there was a meeting between the members of 'Left Flank' and representatives of the children's editorial team of Leningrad *Gosizdat* (State Publishing House): an important and thoroughly serious conversation took place between them. Oleynikov and Shvarts suggested that the participants in the reading should try out their talents in children's literature. They persuaded Z, Kharms and Vvedensky that their novel poetic devices, their immediacy of perception and the amusing unpredictability of their bold 'collisions of meaning' would bring brilliant new colour into publications for children. They talked about the new journal *Hedgehog* which was to start appearing the next year, about their getting into print and about the support that Marshak – chief inspiration behind the whole venture – would undoubtedly give the newcomers. In December 1927 Kharms noted that 'Oleynikov and Zhitkov have organized an association of "Writers in Children's Literature". We (Vvedensky, Zabolotsky and I) have been invited'.

Z was interested in this proposal first of all because it gave the possibility of a regular income. He knew that 'adult' poetry would as yet not give him enough to live on, while he rejected any earnings of a non-literary kind insofar as they would deflect him from his proper business. At first though, he wrote, not verse for children, but generally little prose stories, which were published in 1928–9 in *Hedgehog* and even appeared as separate booklets. In 1928 his literary reworking for children of the book *Letters from Africa*, about the work of a Soviet doctor in Africa, also appeared. Nevertheless one of the first, perhaps the very first, of his works for children was indeed a poem, 'The Good Boots', which came out as a separate booklet in 1928 and caused the poet great pleasure; after all it was his first poetic publication. It began in this way:

> In a German village lives a bootmaker,
> He raps with his mallet back and forth,
> There are half a dozen nails in his mouth
> Of various types and various fashions.
> He spits out a nail, knocks it into a boot,
> And at once a new nail jumps into his palm!

Further on in the poem a whole story is recounted about the boy Karlusha, whose feet refused to work until they were shod in good boots. It turned out pretty well, but it seems clear that Z felt that there was something not quite natural to him in this verse, and he went over to prose. In all he wrote more than forty works for children, most often signing them with the pseudonym 'Ya. Miller' or with initials.

IV

While members of 'Left Flank' were carrying on negotiations about working in children's literature, and continuing to meet with artists with a view to joining up into a single group, there arose the hope of their officially becoming part of the *Dom pechati* (Print House). On an autumn day in 1927 the friends who had gathered as usual at Kharms's flat were interrupted in their work by a telephone call from N. P. Baskakov, director of the Leningrad Print House. He and his governing board proposed a meeting to discuss the terms on which 'Left Flank' might become one of the sections of the Print House. They were all much excited by this development – it promised their recognition by the literary world, new possibilities for putting their work before the public, and the hope of publication.

The Print House was located in the luxurious Shuvalov mansion on the Fontanka embankment, and under its roof there came together the most varied artistic tendencies – from the Proletarian writers to the director Terentyev's experimental theatre. Not long before, Gogol's *Inspector General* had been put on with sets by Filonov's pupils. Simultaneously there was a big exhibition in the Print House of the 'Masters of Analytic Art', at which a vast series of pictures was shown under the general title of 'The Fall of Capitalism'. It would appear that the Filonov School intended this title to evoke not the narrow social meaning that was to become customary but a broader concept of the downfall of everything selfish that divided nature and enslaved humanity. Filonov himself took charge of all the work of preparing pictures for the exhibition; later one of his pupils, T. N. Glebova, wrote: 'Working in the Print House was an academy for us. We were seized with enthusiasm and faith in the rightness and uniqueness of our path.' Since Filonov and his School worked in it, the Print House was particularly attractive to Z.

Baskakov was understanding and sympathetic towards the conditions that 'Left Flank' proposed: the new section would stay independent, while the Board would exercise only general control over its activity. On the Board's side there was only one categorical condition – that they should remove the adjective 'Left' from their name. The group's youngest member, Igor Bakhterev, invented the new name: *Oberiu*, a distorted acronym from 'Association of Real Art' (the precise spelling was modified by Kharms). The name 'Left Flank' which had been current for more than a year is nowadays forgotten, and the group of young writers is always referred to as *Oberiu*, its members as *Oberiuty*. With this new name the association lasted till early in 1930, though Z distanced himself from it before then, in late 1928 or early 1929.

The group started to prepare for its new sphere of activity. Baskakov suggested they should write a manifesto article about themselves for publication in the *Print House Advertiser* (*Afishi Doma pechati*) and prepare a major evening performance. In late November they gathered to discuss the following questions (noted down by Kharms): '1. Working out the principles uniting poets and artists. 2. Working out methods of interior work. 3. Working out methods of exterior work. 4. Project for a performance called "Three Left Hours". 5. Costing the performance.'

Now the friends started meeting not in Kharms's flat but in one of the main rooms of the Shuvalov mansion – with soft armchairs, chandeliers, stuccoed ceilings and precious ornamental parquet. After the student hostel, the army barracks and the room on Konnaya Street, the accommodation seemed fabulously luxurious to Z. From all this stucco and gilding, from Filonov's panels and from their magnificent prospects (as it then seemed) his head whirled. The *Oberiuty* discussed how best to broaden the association – to bring in new members and organize new sections. Z was taken with the idea of uniting the various arts – poetry, painting, theatre, cinema – in a single fundamentally new method and common philosophical conception. Notices were hung in the vestibule of the Print House announcing recruitment into *Oberiu* and offering a questionnaire to those interested: Where is your nose located? What is your favourite type of ice cream? And so on. What they valued in the answers were fantasy, imaginativeness and the ability to see what was serious behind the frivolity. V. Kaverin remembered how Kharms came to him once, looked over the room and asked: 'Tell me please, what would you do if a nose were to grow out of your cupboard?' Kaverin calmly answered him: 'Hang my hat on it.' It was this kind of answer that people were expected to give to the questionnaire.

Not many more were recruited – two cinematography students at the Institute of Art History, K. Mints and A. Razumovsky, and (in 1929) the young poet Yury Vladimirov. A theatre group was envisaged; some young artists from the circles of Malevich and Filonov scrutinized *Oberiu* – but discussions with Malevich did not lead anywhere. Oleynikov, Shvarts, Lipavsky and Druskin were close to the *Oberiuty* but did not formally join the association. None the less there arose a feeling of collective activity with a wide range of like-minded people. Many years later, in the 1950s, Z told his son: 'We started out with big intentions and believed in the future. We didn't only have poetry but our own theatre, our own artists, even our music and cinema.'

Yet the *Oberiuty* could not develop as they foresaw, and the blame lies not so much with their own differences as with the change of political circumstances in the country that began as early as 1928 – a change disastrous for the development of those artistic tendencies that went outside the narrow frame of the Russian Association of Proletarian Writers (RAPP) and official ideological demands.

From their collective discussions there resulted the *Oberiu* manifesto printed in the second issue of the *Print House Advertiser* for 1928. In the introduction to the article it stated:

> *Oberiu* is divided into four sections: literature, art, theatre and cinema. The art section is engaged in experimental work, the others can be seen in action at evening performances, at shows and in the press. At the moment *Oberiu* is working on the organization of a musical section.

Two parts of the article – 'The Public Face of *Oberiu*' and 'The Poetry of *Oberiu*' – were written by Z, who believed that a printed proclamation of their association would bring it general attention and make the *Oberiuty* a genuine force in the development of literature. He gave the manuscript of this work to Sboyev, who kept it till it disappeared in the war.

Z wrote that in conditions of revolutionary dislocation in culture and life the proletariat could no longer content itself with the aesthetic methods of earlier schools but that the new naturalistic schools like the Association of Artists of Revolutionary Russia (AKHRR) could lead art into a 'tangle of the most fearful mistakes'. It was hard to find a single way out of the situation, but one should be sought along the pathways of left art. And the *Oberiuty* expressed the conviction that 'only the left path of art will lead onto the road of a new proletarian artistic culture'. In this connection Z was worried by the already perceptible witch-hunts against leftist artistic and theatrical manifestations. He wrote:

> We cannot comprehend why the School of Filonov has been squeezed out of the Academy, why Malevich cannot develop his architectural work in the USSR, why Terentyev's *Inspector General* has been so absurdly cat-called. We cannot comprehend why so-called Left Art, which has no small quantity of achievements and services to its credit, is dismissed as hopeless garbage or, worse, as charlatanism. How much inner dishonesty, how much lack of personal artistic integrity is concealed within this savage approach.

In this difficult situation the *Oberiuty* proclaimed themselves the 'new detachment of left revolutionary art', which was seeking a new apprehension of the world and possessed a universal method for depicting any subject-matter.

All through December 1927 and January 1928 the *Oberiuty* were getting ready for the coming evening performance at the Print House called 'Three Left Hours' – an hour of poetry, an hour of theatre and an hour of cinema. A special poster was printed and a huge billboard put up at the corner of Nevsky Prospect and the Fontanka. The artist L. A. Yudin who designed the poster wrote in his notebook on the eve: 'Tomorrow is the *Oberiu* evening. Can't wait – very much looking forward to it . . . I'm very fond of Z. A pleasant fellow. He's the most reliable of them all.'

On 24 January there was quite a crowd on the Fontanka, curious about the new literary association and the promised programme. The Print House met its audience with jazz and with Filonov's strange pictures.

The big hall was full, with a mixture of writers, artists, young workers and students. Some of Z's student friends were there. The literary part began with a reading of the *Oberiu* manifesto. Then Vaginov read his verse, sadly and monotonously, while a ballerina,

Militsa Popova, silently performed classical movements. Vvedensky, well-dressed as ever, crossed the stage on a tricycle and then read poems that were generally incomprehensible. After him, two stage-hands wheeled out a large polished cupboard upon which the cross-legged Kharms was enthroned. He wore an elaborate hat; there was a green dog drawn on his cheek. He got up and began to recite his poems from the top of the cupboard, winning over the spectators with his splendid diction and expressive intonation. Then he tapped his foot three times and was taken off stage. The very young Igor Bakhterev, when he had finished his reading, fell flat on his back and the stage-hands silently removed him.

Then a big trunk was carried on. Out came Z, who then stood next to the trunk and at once drew attention by his clothing and appearance, so unlike that traditionally associated with a poet: a faded military jacket, soiled boots with puttees, a ruddy countenance, light blue eyes behind glasses, smoothly combed and parted fair hair. In a deep confident voice he recited the poem 'Movement', written six weeks before:

> The cabman sits as on a throne,
> His armour made of cotton-wool,
> And his beard, as on an icon,
> Lies, tinkling with coins.
> Meanwhile his poor horse waves its arms,
> Now stretches like a fish,
> Now once again its eight legs flash
> Upon its glittering belly.

Sensing approval from the hall, he read out a few more of the poems he had composed in the last two years. The audience listened attentively and applauded each poem.

In the second section of the evening there was an unusual spectacle for the audience: a performance of Kharms's *Yelizaveta Bam*, a drama of the absurd with all kinds of stage effects. The musical accompaniment was specially composed by a former classmate of Kharms (and future professor at the Conservatory), Pavel Vulfius. In the third section there was a showing of the experimental film *Meatgrinder*, after which there was supposed to be a debate with the audience. Because it was late at night the administration suggested putting off the discussion till the next evening, but the audience protested – everyone wanted to have their say or hear how others judged the *Oberiu*'s novel approach to art. Bakhterev remembered:

> There was an interval for dancing to jazz, then the audience went back into the hall and the performers sat in two or three rows on the stage.

The experienced Aleksandr Vvedensky chaired the discussion. There was an impartial conversation in which students, salaried functionaries, professional people and a few workers took part. There were sharp divisions of opinion: mostly of course we were ticked off, but politely and appropriately. The poets Zabolotsky and Vaginov stood out.

The young literary scholar N. L. Stepanov was one of those who spoke. He rated Z's poems highly, and confidently announced that a new major poet had arrived. Z was excited – it was an unfamiliar and disturbing experience to hear praise for his talent from outsiders. However he was not to be bowled over by flattery, since he knew the stronger and weaker aspects of his poems better than anyone.

Nikolay Leonidovich Stepanov, like several of the young scholars of that period, was not a Leningrader by origin. As a youth of seventeen or eighteen he came to Petrograd from Poltava, entered the literature faculty of the University and simultaneously got a job in a school for retarded children. After graduating he taught in a school and in workers' continuing education while working at the Pushkin House. He had a fine knowledge and understanding of poetry, and was a particular enthusiast for Khlebnikov: he had begun to prepare the first multivolume edition of his works for publication. At the time he met Z he was working as a postgraduate student at Leningrad University under Boris Eykhenbaum.

Immediately the evening was over Stepanov, with his wife-to-be Lidiya Konstantinovna, went behind the scenes to see Z, introduced himself and again spoke warmly about his poems. He invited Z to visit him and promised to show him unpublished works by Khlebnikov. 'Soon he came to visit me on Bronitskaya Street', Stepanov remembered, 'and we took turns in reading out Khlebnikov: the long poems 'Poet and Watersprite', 'Three Sisters', 'Night Search' . . . Z remembered that evening and subsequently spoke of it several times.' From then on Stepanov became Z's loyal and selfless friend.

After 'Three Left Hours' Z's popularity among poetry lovers noticeably rose. In the same year of 1928 he had two personal poetry-readings – at the Print House and at the Institute of Art History: the auditoria were full of sympathetic young people, the listeners applauded and several times called for poems to be repeated. But there were also listeners for whom they evoked incomprehension, amazement and even laughter. 'At one of the evenings at the Poets' Union', as I. Sinelnikov remembered, 'Nikolay Chukovsky was reduced to tears of mirth. I told Z about this audience reaction and what his attitude to it was. "No problem", he said to soothe me down. "They have a laugh, but all the same a little spark of poetry lodges in the mind . . . Irony is an insurance-policy for verse." '

Some applauded, others laughed, but all admitted that a new step in poetry had been taken, that a new and unquestionably talented poet had appeared. It is worth noting that Z arrived at poetic independence quite naturally and consciously. In this connection Bakhterev tells an interesting story of how the *Oberiu* friends decided on answers to the question 'whom would each choose as a model?'

'Goethe', said Kharms, 'I reckon he's what a real poet is like.'

'Yevlampy Nadkin, when he's chatting round a bonfire with cab-drivers and drunken prostitutes on a frosty night,' said Vvedensky, having in mind a popular character from the humorous journal *Behemoth*.

'David Burliuk, only with two eyes' was Bakhterev's wish – like his hero he was equally drawn to poetry and art. Whereas Z calmly and sincerely confessed 'I want to be like myself.' And that is what he managed to do: he indeed imitated nobody; while some poets just starting began to imitate him – among whom the talented A. I. Gitovich, just arrived from Smolensk, was outstanding.

Once Sinelnikov organized a meeting between Z and a group of students from the Institute of Art History, at which there turned out to be a fair number of his admirers and imitators. At another meeting with a group of poets who had been at Leningrad University the enthusiasm was more restrained. D. I. Maksimov, a member of this group, though he spoke of the fervent affirmation of the corporeal three-dimensional world in Z's poems, nevertheless noted in them a lack of music, of candid beauty, of the 'water of life'.

Z also visited older poets. One evening the company of *Oberiuty* decided to call on N. A. Klyuyev. Vvedensky, who knew him best, was sent ahead to spy out the land and reported back that he had invited them all to tea and doughnuts. As he entered Klyuyev's city flat Z was astonished to see that the room was artfully decorated like a peasant house with plank walls, oaken benches, decorated boxes, an icon-corner, oil lamps and peasant utensils. The bearded host, in a hempen shirt, looking like Father Christmas, kissed them all demonstratively, and in a North-Russian peasant drawl said to Z, 'I've heard all about you, Mikolka* – a fine upstanding rosy-cheeked fellow you are too!'

This sort of bogus and overfamiliar behaviour was something Z found intolerable. And though he admired Klyuyev as a poet, he resolutely rebuffed him and said straight out what he thought about this

---

* Peasant form of 'Nikolka', i.e. Nikolay.

theatrical masquerade: 'I came to see a poet and a colleague, and God knows what I've landed in – some kind of puppet show . . . You're an educated man after all – you write good poems – why on earth all this fooling about?' The host could not stand this: demonstrating the breadth of his knowledge by doing a few high kicks from the French can-can, he announced he was at liberty to do whatever he pleased in his own home, and unceremoniously slung out his guests. Thus ended their personal acquaintanceship, though this did not prevent Z from continuing to find his verse interesting and even reading examples he particularly liked out loud to his circle of friends. In fact there is some evidence that Z visited Klyuyev more than once. As I. I. Markov recalls: 'In Klyuyev's room on Bolshaya Morskaya Street, where old icons stood side-by-side with rare manuscripts, one might meet Nikolay Zabolotsky, Aleksey Chapygin, Aleksandr Prokofyev, Daniil Kharms, Pavel Medvedev.' One may guess that the scene between the two poets described above took place not at their first meeting but at their last.

In 1928 Z got to know N. S. Tikhonov and visited him a couple of times. Sinelnikov recounted how after Z's first visit to Tikhonov he told him, 'It was an interesting evening. Tikhonov showed us some foreign art books. I recited something or other. I spent all evening looking at a book of reproductions of Breughel . . .' Pavel Antokolsky also spoke of meeting Z at Tikhonov's. At the request of the host Z read out some poems, after which Antokolsky's wife, the actress Zoya Bazhenova, exclaimed: 'But that's just like Captain Lebyadkin!' This comparison with the graphomaniac character from Dostoyevsky's *The Devils* might have offended the poet, but as Antokolsky writes, 'he chuckled good-humouredly, looked fixedly at Zoya through his glasses and, quite unembarrassed, said, "I've thought about that too. But what I write isn't parody, it's my vision of things. Furthermore, it's my Petersburg, our generation's Leningrad."' Kaverin, who witnessed this episode, describes it a little differently: 'I remember how at my flat once he met Antokolsky, who said his poems were like Captain Lebyadkin's. He wasn't offended. He thought for a little and said that he rated Lebyadkin higher than many contemporary poets.'

From these two accounts we can reconstruct the sense of Z's answer. He really did consider that his poems were not parody and maybe not even satire – rather his personal vision, his view of the world and in particular of the city. While the comparison with Captain Lebyadkin was of course not particularly pleasant for him he could conceal any displeasure and merely remark that many poets write still worse than the unfortunate captain. In the depths of his soul he valued his talent rather highly, and in the same year he put in a letter to Klykova what he implied behind his answer: 'All the same I know how to write in a way that very few others can.'

V

Z paid a great deal of attention to the look of his own poems. He loved to write them out on good paper with a special pen in his own calligraphy, and to make them up into small collected volumes. One of these, compiled in 1928 and called 'Ararat', survives. In this small exercise book he copied out scarcely more than ten poems of 1926–8, though later a few pages were torn out of it, evidently reflecting the author's scrapping of some of his poems. A book, even a small one, had special significance in Z's eyes. He said to Sinelnikov: 'You have to write not individual poems, but a whole book. Then everything falls into place. You need to respect your own poetry.'

And so the time arrived when Z decided that he had written enough worthwhile poems to compile a thematically and stylistically integrated collection, this time for publication. In or about March 1928 he read Sinelnikov the poem 'The Sentry' and said: 'This is going to be a programmatic poem in the book I'm now getting ready. It'll be called *Columns*. I'm including in this word the concept of discipline and order . . .' Where did this name come from? The 'Ararat' volume contained a poem called 'Column about the Circassian Woman', which might roughly be understood, say, as 'neat column of lines, dedicated to the Circassian Woman'. He then changed the name by dropping the words 'column about', while beginning to call all his poems of that period 'columns'.*

By no means everything that Z had written in 1926–8 was selected for the little book called *Columns*. He gave the most careful thought to its content, which was changed and amplified by new pieces. The latest dated from August ('Wandering Musicians') and September ('Bathers' and 'Immaturity') of 1928. He had reached an agreement on publication with the Leningrad Writers' Co-operative Publishing House earlier, in May or June; he wanted the book to come out 'at the proper season', that is in the autumn, and to be decently designed. He sent a letter on 28 June to L. A. Yudin asking him to be the cover designer – incidentally without relying on any remuneration, since the publishing house was still living on credit and no one was getting paid. 'If you are kind

---

* Some commentators and translators render this word, *stolbtsy*, as 'scrolls': the Russian has both senses [Ed.].

enough not to refuse to do this you will have to regard it as a friendly personal gesture', Z wrote. 'I think your lettering for the big poster "Three Left Hours" would do excellently. The cover should be a very simple bit of lettering with the word *Columns* dominating. Your script is unusual but strong and well-finished. It's got the essence of the thing in it. At first sight there's nothing special about it: take a longer look and there's something completely new revealing itself.'

Z saw the cover as the beginning of the book and wanted it all to be done in a unified style. Firm organization and a quality of unusualness – those were qualities he imparted to his poems. That was how he wished a book to be throughout. However Yudin's design was turned down by the publisher, and *Columns* came out late, with a different cover. The intended unity of style was not realized.

Early in June 1928 Z travelled to Vyatka to visit his relatives. His mother Lidiya had died prematurely, of typhus, in 1926. Soon after her death Aleksey had retired, and the eldest daughter Vera got a job in the town of Vyatka and took her sisters along with her. In 1927 Z's brother Aleksey also moved to Vyatka to complete teacher-training, and their father, already weakened by illness, went there in his children's wake. Z spent little time with his family – a couple of weeks. This was to be his last reunion with his sick father.

During the summer of 1928 Z continued to meet with Katya Klykova – he visited her on Great Pushkarskaya and read his poems. Katya's uncle and aunt often went off to their dacha at Siverskaya, leaving their niece a rouble to get by on for the week, so she half starvd. She gave Z tea and the most basic food. She recalled how once she placed before him a white porcelain dish with a scrubbed carrot floating in some water. Z was delighted – the bright orange carrot was not only tasty but singularly beautiful. Might it not have been then, when he particularly clearly envisaged the living essence of the vegetable world, that he got the first idea for 'Dinner',* written soon after?

Z proposed to Klykova in the autumn. He wrote a letter on 9 November without any of his usual irony and stylization, a rare letter that opened up his inner feelings:

> Dearest One! You have become a person endlessly close to me, and now, when I think about my life and work it is all indissolubly tied up with you. If you are prepared to love me some time I shall do all I can to make you happy. Life would have no sense for me otherwise. Your love is salvation and happiness to me. If only my feeling were to touch your heart! Let's come together and conquer life! We'll have to work and

* Full translation on pp.350–1.

struggle for our futures. So many setbacks ahead, so many disappointments and doubts! But if a person hesitates at such a moment his song is sung. Faith and stubbornness. Work and honour. Let's be together, dear one! Just one look from you is enough to support me – I'll learn to help you too. We'll learn how to move mountains – yes, with these bare hands! How endlessly I love you.

My life is bound up with my art – you know that already. You know about the path a writer has to tread. I have renounced material well-being, 'social position', have separated myself from my family – all for my art. Outside it I'm nothing. What I am you now know. Decide . . .

We'll live first and foremost as friends and comrades. We'll read, study, work and reach others together. The two of us will be better and purer – me, especially. I've got so many failures, deprivations and weaknesses behind me, and now, when I'm close to success, your love will be a pledge for what's good in the future. Formerly I got embittered, but not too much so, got my hands dirty, but not completely, all the same – give me your hand – I'll be firmer than ever.

I'm 24 – already getting on: I've taken a look at life. But I'm not active enough; though incidentally I've become a bit better. There's a lot I can do. I don't know how to get on with many people, I'm not very domesticated, I'm often rude and overbearing – there, you see, lots of sins! Still, I do know how to write like few others; and also I love you with a warmth that a person seldom experiences.

Make your decision! I've opened my heart and I'm not afraid of your answer. But it must be honest. N. Z.

10th. Full of longing. Am writing again. I know I'm loathsome and insignificant. I know I'm getting tangled up in this city, though I'm fighting against it. I know it all. But I still know I can love you doggedly.

12th. No way out for my love. I've come to understand everything, no life without you. I ask for your hand – decide.

The letter was sent off, and met with a favourable response from Katya; but for more than a year the young people tested their feelings, and from time to time they underwent serious strains.

Eventually the proofs of the book *Columns* arrived. Sinelnikov assisted Z in correcting them. When they had finished he said, 'Well, not long till your book comes out. Maybe like Byron you'll wake up and find yourself famous.' 'No', said Z; 'we're living in different times and everything's a good deal more complicated than in Byron's day.' But deep down he hoped the book would not go unnoticed.

Columns contained a mere twenty-two poems, but despite its modest scope and print run (1,200 copies) the book really was noticed by readers and critics alike. Its social resonance was sufficiently remarkable in the literary life of the late 1920s. The impression it made on poetry-lovers and its evaluation in the press came very soon to be diametrically opposed. Here are some contemporaries' reactions to their first reading of it:

D. S. Likhachov (academician, specialist in Old Russian literature and culture, writer): 'In my student years Zabolotsky's *Columns* had an enormous effect on me. I am still extremely fond of it even now.'

P. G. Antokolsky (poet): 'This book appeared in 1929: Zabolotsky was kind enough to send me a copy. I read it with something like burning interest. A feeling of shock, of novelty, of bursting into a realm no one had inhabited before Zabolotsky – those were the predominant feelings. I think very many people felt the same, not just poets.'

B. A. Filippov (literary scholar, USA): 'Writers, the student body of the city and the intellectual classes looked on this book as a sort of revelation. After a month it could not be bought at any price. It was copied out by hand, learnt literally by heart. I myself possessed not only a printed, but a typewritten and a manuscript copy of *Columns*.'

D. Maksimov (university teacher and literary critic): 'These poems were enticing through a kind of organic *strangeness* ('defamiliarization' is hardly the word!), through the unexpressed but hypnotically active 'third sense' contained in them which made the head spin. This 'strangeness' still seems to me a special category not to be accounted for in scholarly poetics. At the time I talked a lot about this with Vigilyansky, a young poet close to the *Oberiuty*.'

S. I. Lipkin (poet): 'I first read *Columns*, on Bagritsky's advice, in the year it appeared – 1929. It struck me, as a young poet, not only by its originality of content, or the tragic quality of an absurdity that was quite unliterary, rather arising from the gap between loftiness and debasement – no, these poems struck me by their classic quality of form, their stern simplicity and the naturalness with which diction moved within the line.'

S. A. Yermolinsky (dramatist): 'I read and remembered his little book *Columns* that appeared in 1929. At the time it dumbfounded people with its mocking, hyperbolic mercilessness of imagery, and its vivid pictures of the NEP bourgeoisie of those years, its old and new ways of life.'

S. A. Bogdanovich (writer, wife of the critic V. A. Gofman): 'I wish only to convey the strength and depth of the impression his poems left and how unexpected they were . . . For us, his contemporaries, he was as if primeval, unique. His subject-matter, his images, his rhymes were all new.'

Eduard Bagritsky and Nikolay Tikhonov were two more poets very favourably impressed. But there were also others who sincerely could not accept the poetry of *Columns*, among them poets whom Z valued very highly: Osip Mandelshtam and the emigré V. F. Khodasevich. Boris Slutsky remembered that to the end of his life Z 'revered Mandelshtam and used to recount with a smile how the latter gave his poems a pasting'.

One of the organizers of the Writers' Co-operative Publishing House, I. A. Gruzdev, sent a few of its books to Maksim Gorky and on 2 June 1929 wrote to him: 'We are working mostly with young writers. Some of them – Brazhnin, Zabolotsky – have already acquired a degree of fame.' A copy of *Columns* was kept in Gorky's personal library. And five years later Konstantin Paustovsky talked with him about the poetry of Svetlov, Z and Pasternak. 'I couldn't resist reading Gorky some favourite lines from these poets', wrote Paustovsky. 'He was unexpectedly touched . . .'

When he got the advance copies of his book, Z made a list of those who ought to be given one, made laconic inscriptions in them and sent off the packages. He sent one copy to Boris Pasternak, who, as Sinelnikov recollects, 'sent back a card with a polite but restrained message of thanks'. He sent a jocular inscription in verse to Oleynikov. A copy was also sent to his mortally ill father in Vyatka; he could only just hold it to read the inscription: 'To my dear father – from a grateful son. N.Z. 12 August, 1929.' In these laconic words were contained both gratitude for the creative faculties he inherited and which were developed in childhood, and also a last farewell message. Soon afterwards his father died.

Z and his friends began to examine the papers and journals with heightened interest, awaiting responses to the publication of *Columns*. Soon reviews began to appear. There was a promising start. The March number of *Zvezda* (*Star*) contained a short article by Stepanov which with astonishing acuity pin-pointed those characteristics of Z's poems that would attract commentators over the decades: generic picturesqueness, a moralizing quality, a Rabelaisian excitement, an epic quality of style, the combination of the sweep of an ode with ironic satire, echoes now of Derzhavin, now of Prutkov* . . . In another note Stepanov counted Z among the leading innovators of the time: 'Speaking of innovators in contemporary literature, I have to mention the names of Olesha, Babel, Ivanov, Shklovsky, Tynyanov, Selvinsky, Zabolotsky and Tikhonov.'

I. L. Feynberg in a short anonymous review (*Oktyabr*, 1929:5) noted

---

* A comic figure invented by A. K. Tolstoy and his cousins in the mid nineteenth century, to whom they attributed homespun parodic or sententious verse [Ed.].

the aesthetic integrity of Z's poetic diction and prophesied: '. . . it is scarcely possible to predict the further course of Z's work, since the "crooked mirror" can hardly remain his only instrument for long.' In *Novy Mir* (1929:6) there was a well-intentioned response from M. Zenkevich. In the journal *On Literary Guard* N. Rykova perceptively wrote that 'the current year has given us the remarkable *Columns* by Zabolotsky, a most interesting poet with a big future'.

But these few well-wishers were soon drowned in the chorus of malevolent vulgarizing critics, who did not wish to get to grips with the text and were ill-disposed towards any true novelty in art. Some of them were sharp-eyed enough to spot how far removed Z's ideas were from the narrow political tasks of the time, and they used his poems as a handy target for 'political unmaskings'.

Z's first book appeared at the beginning of 1929 – a singularly unpropitious time for it. It was the year of the 'great break with the past', a year that saw the violent turn from the NEP policy instituted under Lenin to forced urban industrialization and compulsory rural collectivization. Stalin moved from mere restrictions on the exploitative tendencies of the kulaks* to their liquidation as a class, and put forward the idea that with the coming of socialism the class struggle would inevitably sharpen. In such conditions it was not hard to introduce extreme measures to crush the supposed class enemy.

The Russian Association of Proletarian Writers (RAPP) instantly reacted to the changes of political mood and took advantage of the new situation to crush all literary phonemena that did not fit the Procrustean bed of their own demands. A resolution passed by Leningrad RAPP late in 1929 spoke of class enemies among poets:

> The intensification of class warfare in contemporary poetry is hastening the differentiation of poetic groupings . . .
>
> One must note the appearance of poets who may so far be unaware of it, but have indubitable neo-bourgeois elements in their work (Zabolotsky), and pay the most serious attention to it. (*Rezets*, 1930:1)

Singling out Z for 'the most serious attention' did not bode well for him. With his very first book he had drawn the fire of RAPP and found himself in the thick of the battle as a 'fellow-traveller'. Anatoly Gorelov followed up the attack in the first issue of *Strelka* for 1930:

> Zabolotsky's poems are will-of-the-wisps above graves. When a corpse decomposes it gives off gasses that come through the soil-surface and flare up in a pale blue flame . . . Nikolay Zabolotsky is one of the most

* Rich peasants [Ed.].

reactionary of poets and all the more dangerous in that he is a genuine poet. Zabolotsky's idealistic reactionary world-view is stronger than his voluntary impulses.

P. Neznamov (*Pechat i revolyutsiya*, 1930:4), after calling the poet a clown, a typhus carrier, a sexual psychopath and a cunning stylizer, reaches this conclusion:

> The time has come to look at poetic products politically: is a poet working or not working towards the proletarian revolution, and if he is not, to exclude him. We stand for splendid intolerance. And we find Zabolotsky's poems socially defective.

Articles, sketches and parodies of this kind were henceforth to pursue Z up to the mid 1930s. They had characteristic titles: 'System of Cats', 'Dissolution of Consciousness', 'System of Girls', 'The Sociology of Nonsense', 'Lyric poetry as a weapon in the class war'. Instead of proper criticism which might have helped the poet to see his strong and weak sides, the discussion of *Columns* and his subsequent publications was reduced more and more to abuse, to offensive attacks and to political scare-tactics. About this kind of criticism he bitterly complained: 'It's one thing if they were to say: write about what you like but just leave one subject alone. It's something essentially different when RAPP demands: write about one thing and nothing else.'

Trying not to be down-hearted he wrote out on a sheet of paper the critics' definitions of him: muckshifter-songster, renegade-individualist, sexual psychopath and so on. In his friends' company he would solemnly read out this list, and all of them would cheerily laugh and joke, though they could guess it would soon be no laughing matter.

Did this criticism of *Columns* affect Z's further work? Is his change of poetic voice in 1929–30 linked with this criticism? The biographical facts testify that the complex process of the development of his thinking and his work cannot be reduced to such a simple causal dependence. The changes in the character of his verse are clearly bound up with their subject matter. In the winter of 1928–9 he said to Katya Klykova: 'I've not yet properly learnt how to write poems. When I manage to express my love for you in them, that's when they'll have become genuine poetry.' On the one hand he could affirm: 'I know how to write like few others'; on the other 'I've not yet properly learnt to write poems'. He sensed that his brilliant, grotesque method was not a universal one. It worked for the vivid, stylized portrayal of the city and its environment, but was no good for the expression of frank emotion or of ideas about the greatness and tragic qualities of nature.

Urban subject-matter had been largely worked out, and by 1928 (before publication of *Columns* and the hostile reviews) Z more and more often reflected on a theme that he had temporarily laid aside two years before. In the fifth and eighth numbers of the literary supplement to *Leningrad Pravda* were published the poems 'Hands' and 'Dinner', heralding a new direction in Z's work. In fact 'Dinner' was printed without its very important final stanza, possibly written early in 1929. This stanza directly indicates the thematic connection of 'Dinner' with the poem 'Trees' ('In our dwellings . . .') of 1926:

> If we were to see
> not these squares, not these walls,
> but the warm bowels of the earth,
> heated with vernal lassitude –
> if we were to see in shining rays
> the blessed childhood of plants,
> we should doubtless go down on our knees
> before the simmering pot of vegetables.

Z did just what was said in these lines: he turned his gaze away from 'these squares', 'these walls' and bent his knee before living beings that are linked with humankind by bonds of kinship, and await release by humanity from their age-old sufferings. But the transition from the poetic manner of *Columns* to the following creative period is not as sudden and sharp as it sometimes seems. He felt that it was precisely the milieu of urban philistinism that kindles in the human being an animal, biological element.

So now Z was pondering the future conquest of the element of animality not only in humankind, but in the whole of creation. When he was writing the 1928 poems whose style and subject adhered to the *Columns* manner ('At the Fishmonger's', 'On the Staircase', 'Beginning of Autumn', 'Circus'), he was already thinking of a new large-scale piece dedicated to the interaction of humanity and nature. In January 1929 he began the epic poem 'The Triumph of Agriculture'. A note among his papers allows us to follow the order in which its various sections were composed: at the beginning of 1929, the Prologue and seventh chapter, on 18 February the first chapter, on 3 March the second chapter (all these before the publication of *Columns*), on 29 September the fourth chapter and in 1930 the third, fifth and sixth chapters. From the work's beginning its main axis was mapped out: from chaos to scientific regularity, from egotism to the wisdom of the collective transformation of agriculture and of all nature, from the animal existence of the ancestors to the victory of reason.

The contradictions of urban life became for Z a sort of special example of the imperfection of all being; he wanted to find a way out of this oppressive situation. He considered that everything alive was imbued with a kind of basic consciousness from conception, and he awaited from human reason the end of unthinking exploitation of the vegetable and animal kingdoms, and their incorporation into a rationally ordered life. Humankind's struggle for social justice seemed to him a pledge of the freeing of all nature from primal cruelty, inertia and oppression of the weak by the strong.

Just like *Columns* the long poem 'The Triumph of Agriculture' came out at a most inappropriate moment. Collectivization was in full swing, and thus the topic of the countryside in literature was subjected to strictly defined slogans and clichés. Z's ideas did not fall within this framework. Directed as they were towards the future, they seemed extremely utopian and removed from present-day tasks. The section dealing with 1930 that spoke of the kulak as the basic force of inertia in the country was no help (the 'ancestors' had filled this role in earlier drafts). Critics were looking to find in the poem references to class struggle, to party leadership in the setting up of collective farms, and triumphant reports about the harvest – instead they found animals complaining about their miserable existence, dreams of the scientific organization of all earthly life and of the nurture of animals' reasoning powers.

Z did not, and could not, set himself the goal of reflecting the actual tragedy of forced collectivization; but those who wrote about the poem were as out of touch with reality as they were with Z's natural-philosophical conceptions.

Consequently, when in the October 1929 issue of the journal *Zvezda* the prologue and last chapter of the poem were published, they instantly became the target for devastating RAPP criticism. The poet was not to be forgiven for his independence of thought and the abstract-utopian character of his narrative.

Ensnared in the Thirties

I

ONE DAY in August 1929, as he thought about his forthcoming marriage, Z came to the conclusion that his proposal to Katya Klykova had been a rash move, because a family could take him away from art and make it difficult for him to write. It was also true that when he visited his friends he would meet women he found interesting, and sometimes he got to like them. Although this sort of attraction was never serious, never led to anything, and was essentially light-hearted, he thought it inappropriate for a responsible married man. These reflections led him to the conclusion that he was not ready for such an important step in life, and he sat down and wrote to Katya in decisive terms:

> Katya! You must already have sensed that something is happening to me. Please let me tell you what it is. I do not love you and I cannot marry you. I know that this is outrageous, and in all probability dishonourable, especially after all the publicity I have given to our relationship . . . It's all over. Let's say goodbye and try to forget everything that has happened . . . At the moment I feel very distant from all women. I often think that fate is preparing a life of solitude for me – so that I should be alone with my work, and devote everything to it . . . I shall be happy to meet you at some time in the future – when we shall be just friends. Goodbye. Kolya. P.S. It's awkward if you ring me at *Giz* [State Publishing House]. It's an official institution, and I am only here temporarily. I am not a member of their staff.

Z's true feelings, however, were not reflected by the categorical tone of the letter, which was more of an attempt to convince himself that the decision he had taken was the right one. Within a month, on 29 September, he had written the fourth chapter of 'The Triumph of Agriculture' in which there are easily traceable echoes of his thoughts on family life. The chapter contains a description of the argument between the Ancestors, devoted to the traditional laws of nature, and the Soldier, in revolt against the old world. For the conservative

Ancestors the embodiment of their ideals is the image of a woman bearing children. But the Soldier cannot agree with the idea that the whole point of life is to reproduce your own kind:

> Ancestors, I understand all this,
> But it is important, though, to know –
> Will we not be going backwards
> If all we do is give birth?

'Going back' was what Z feared in his own life. But he was in torment, and after another month had passed he was no longer sure that he had done right in refusing to get married. He wrote again to Katya, this time in very friendly terms. He discussed frankly the way he looked at his own life, explained how he regarded his vocation as a writer, and tried to give a meaning to the poem he had just written, 'The Signs of the Zodiac are Growing Dim'. This letter, and the poem included in it, go some way towards explaining the poet's emotional state. The 'Night Conversations' referred to in the letter is the original title of the second chapter of 'The Triumph of Agriculture' (later changed to 'The Sufferings of the Animals'). This was also the title of the handwritten collection of poems that Z had made at that time.

29th October, 1929. Dear Katya, I got your letter. You ask a lot of questions. Of course, I'm not a teacher of life. I probably shall be sometime, when I've got steadier in myself, but until then I'm not. 'Night Conversations' shows the kind of longing that you and I both feel, and lots of people like us. That's really what it's all about, it's just that it's in verse. I haven't been able to give any answers yet. I don't know them myself, and I freely admit it. I'm in just the same kind of turmoil, and perhaps that's where some of my objective hypocrisy comes from, because at times I find rest and comfort precisely in the very process of writing.

Don't start talking about ladykillers. I least of all am suited to that particular role. Essentially I lead a very solitary life, and no one else has anything to do with it. It's my poetry that matters, not my own self. But I don't begrudge that, it's what I deserve. Art is like being in a monastery, where love is in the abstract. After all, that's the way people regard monks. And despite that monks are still monks, that is, righteous people. Simeon Stylites sits on his column and people come to see him, and when they do, because they are poor people, made to suffer by life, they find comfort in watching him. Art is not life. It is a world of its own. It has its own laws, and it's no good cursing them because they don't help us to make the soup.

When I'm isolated from art I feel incomplete and a sick man. A great many of the men that I know get on a lot better with people than I do. In the whole of my life so far not one woman has been happy with me. When I was at home they used to say that I was selfish and rude. On the other hand I think the feelings people accuse me of lacking have in my case just been diverted and follow a different course.

Of course, work is the saving factor. We must think of something. Teaching does not suit you. You need inventive work, for which you have all the gifts. Then everything will be all right. Can't that old lazybones Desnitsky fix you up with something? He's got influence and connections.

Anyhow, what has happened to you? What are you sick with, and why, and how are you feeling at the moment? Write to me, Katya darling, if you are feeling up to it. I, for my part, feel well disposed (as best I can) towards you – and if nothing comes of it – then what?

Here is my latest poem. Read it if you are bored. I'm getting a bit of praise for it: what do you think? The first two sections should be read in a monotone – as though you are half asleep. The following two sections, about Reason, should be read with feeling, with uplift, almost rhetorically. And the last bit again in a monotone – because it deals with the calming, soothing, and rocking to sleep of someone who is ill. Perhaps these verses will suit your mood as well.

Well, goodbye, don't be sad, and do get better.

N.Z.

I shall be doing military service again until 1 May. In the evenings I shall be teaching territorial servicemen, twice a week. And up to 6 Nov. every evening. Not something to look forward to!

Further on in the letter the poem 'The Signs of the Zodiac are Growing Dim' is quoted. The poem speaks of the revolt of Man's reason:

> In the crowded marketplace of nature,
> in poverty, in mud, and in the dust
> why are you struggling, king of freedom,
> restless dust of the earth?

When the poem was published in 1933 in the journal *Zvezda* these lines, which are so important to an understanding of it, turned out to have been replaced by other less meaningful ones, most likely not at the author's volition. The poet was writing about Reason – the king of freedom and at the same time the dust of the earth – but in his mind were his own personal experiences, and his agonizing quest to come to the right decisions, both in life and in art.

At the end of 1929 the Stepanovs managed to find Z a larger and more comfortable room on Bolshaya Pushkarskaya Street (No. 36, flat 9), and he duly moved there from the rather cramped accommodation on Konnaya Street. His new landlady was a middle-aged woman from the intelligentsia, V. M. Ieromuza. She had been a geography teacher, and in the period before the Revolution she had travelled widely abroad. She rapidly became a loyal friend.

The room had been advertised to let to a single man, and Z sincerely believed that he had no plans to marry in the foreseeable future. Several months after moving to the Pushkarskaya, however, he announced to his friends that he was going to get married. Yevgeny Shvarts remembers that he did so 'gloomily and yet ceremoniously, but at all events with an air of great respectability'. On 25 January 1930, he arrived at the house of Katya's Klykov relatives, collected her and her few meagre possessions, and from that day on they began to live together in Ieromuza's apartment. The latter and her housekeeper, Khristina, came to love the young couple, and easily accepted this breach of the original letting conditions of the room.

The Zabolotskys started welcoming their friends in their Bolshaya Pushkarskaya room. Soon after 25 January Z introduced his wife to Kharms, Shvarts and Oleynikov. Yevgeny Shvarts noted in his diary (not at the time, but recalling it later):

> Z received us with an air of cheerful solemnity. Katerina smiled at us but took no part in our conversations. She reminded me of a schoolgirl from one of Bestuzhev's romantic novels. She wore a black dress, had black eyes, and was extremely slim. She was also very unpretentious and modest. She produced such a favourable impression that for the whole of the long journey home neither Kharms nor Oleynikov said a single word about her. And so we grew accustomed to the fact that Z was married.

On another occasion the Kaverins, the Stepanovs and the Gofmans came round. There was nothing to eat or drink in the house, and while Z went out to buy some beer, Yekaterina did her best to entertain the guests, but she felt embarrassed with her husband's friends, and only with Kaverin's wife, Lidiya Nikolayevna Tynyanova, did she immediately feel comfortable and at ease. One day Vvedensky arrived at their apartment. He was affable and polite, kissed Yekaterina's hand, and generally by his behaviour gave Z to understand that he wished their recent sharp disagreement to be forgotten. Z, for his part, did not want to make peace. He said very little, and was deliberately unwelcoming. Vvedensky did not call again, and Z avoided talking to him when they were being entertained by mutual friends, although at *Detgiz* (the children's publishing house) and in other official places they unavoidably bumped into each other, and on such occasions coldly exchanged greetings.

Z's wife, Yekaterina Vasilyevna Klykova, had lived until the age of eleven at Shuvalovo near Petrograd. Her father, Vasily Ivanovich Klykov, was a descendant of Cossacks who at some time in the past had revolted, been exiled, and had established a settlement of market-gardeners near the town of Maloyaroslavets. In his youth he had worked as a labourer and errand-boy in a distillery. His brother, Andrey Ivanovich, had gained a commercial education by his own efforts, and become a well-to-do broker, a representative of the State Bank on the St Petersburg stock exchange. With his help Vasily Ivanovich had opened up a small general store on the station square of Shuvalovo, but in contrast to his brother he was not imbued with the entrepreneurial spirit – he liked poetry and flowers, and cultivating the kitchen garden as his forefathers had done. The family consisted of four daughters and a son. The mother died when the youngest of them, Katya (Yekaterina), was barely three. Vasily, already ill with tuberculosis, married for a second time. The stepmother, Pelageya Semyonovna, was a woman of severe character, but she took great care in running the household and bringing up the younger children, who loved her dearly. She also played a part in her husband's retail business. Immediately after the Revolution Vasily Klykov had the foresight to wind up the business, and the whole family moved to the town of Lyubim in the Yaroslavl province. The father died here in 1920. In 1923, when the younger children had finished school, the family moved again, this time to Petrograd. Pelageya placed Lida, Olya and Katya in the care of their uncle, Andrey Klykov and his wife, while she remained living on her own. After the Revolution Andrey went on working as a government official and managed to preserve both his apartment in the house he had previously owned on Bolshaya Pushkarskaya and a dacha at Siverskaya. In the period when they lived with their uncle the sisters carried out the duties of concierge and earned some money from casual work. Soon only Katya was left living with her uncle. Between 1923 and 1927 she studied at the Herzen Pedagogical Institute, worked in her spare time as an accountant in an office, and also gave private lessons.

After she married she continued to give lessons in Russian language and literature in a school for backward children in Lesnoye, where she had gone to work when she finished at the Institute. At the same time she was giving arithmetic lessons to the son of the famous physicist, Ya. I. Frenkel. Z thought all this work too much for Katya, and insisted on her leaving the school after the summer, promising to find her more interesting editorial work at the publishing house. But over the summer he got so used to the fact that his wife was putting all her energy into running the house, that he somehow never got round to carrying out his promise. The feeling for domestic order which he had picked up as a child was so much part of him that he was convinced that it was his task to provide for the family and that his wife should look after the house and the children. His feelings for Katya grew deeper all the time, and very soon he found it difficult to imagine life without her.

Several notes have been preserved from the first year of their life together. It was probably in the spring of 1930 that Z wrote to his wife: 'I'm lonely without you around the house. It looks like I've got very used to your being here.' And in another note, somewhat later:

> Katya, darling, I've been invited to meet a very important person. I shall be home around eleven. I've been paid; I've sent 20 roubles home to Vyatka, and given 30 to Vera Mikhailovna (by the telephone). There's 44 on the table. Of that, 3–5 roubles should be given to Khristina. Better make it 5. Please see to it, love. The money is in a wallet. Don't get lonely. There are three sweeties on the table. Have a sleep. I'll call you later.

There is yet another note which relates to a such an occasion: 'Katya, I've gone to see Meyerhold. I've taken a key with me. I may be back late. K.' The meeting in question did not have a sequel, and the acquaintanceship with the great director came to nothing.

In the summer of 1930, when work on 'The Triumph of Agriculture' was finished, the couple took leave from their various jobs, and in July, for the first time in their lives, they went for a holiday, to the Crimea in the south. They stayed on the edge of Feodosiya, in a house right next to the sea, belonging to the relatives of an artist friend from Leningrad. Somewhat to her surprise Yekaterina discovered that it was next to impossible to persuade her husband to go for a walk, or even to go and look at the sea. On the third day of their stay in the Crimea he had got a badly sunburnt back from lying on the beach and was delighted that this now gave him the perfect excuse for staying in the house in his favourite position, lying on his stomach, and reading and writing poetry. This was probably the period at which he wrote the poem 'Man in the Water', which finishes with the lines:

> And on his roasted back,
> laughing at this madman,
> these infusoria
> feasted on the foolish fellow's skin.

There are two other poems thematically related to this one – 'Questions to the Sea' and 'The City under the Sea', written under the influence of Plato. It is remarkable that, with the exception of these sceptical and ironic poems about the sea, not one poem was written about the beauty of the south, either in that year or in the years that followed this first visit to the Crimea. At the time what interested Z was not the external picture of nature, but its inner meaning, the significance of the processes taking place within it, and its relationship to the activities of mankind.

On one occasion the Zabolotskys, together with some friends they had made on the beach, an engineer and his wife, went for a walk to Sudak. After spending the night in a cramped hotel room in Sudak, the Zabolotskys went on to Koktebel to see M. A. Voloshin, whose poetry Z knew and respected. Voloshin probably also knew of Z from his book *Columns*. There was a copy in the library of the celebrated Koktebel house. Maksimilian Voloshin came out to receive his visitors wearing wide, white breeches with tucks at the knees and a long, loose, white shirt. His flowing grey hair was caught up with a gold bangle. He was handsome and affable. He invited them into the house, and after they had talked for a little while, he called his wife, Marya Stepanovna, so that she too could listen to him reading some poems. Voloshin read his poem about the Virgin, and then listened attentively as Z read one of his own poems. This was the only meeting between the two poets.

After the trip to the Crimea the round of everyday life in Leningrad began again. Over the winter of 1930–1 the Zabolotskys had Z's younger sister, twelve-year-old Lyusya (Yelena) staying with them for several months. Yekaterina found her a place at school and tried to train her in a few household duties. The poet's older sister Vera was at that time studying at the Leningrad Medical Institute and made regular visits to Pushkarskaya Street to be with her sister. She was not happy with her brother's way of life – or at all happy with the fact that Lyusya had to sweep the floors and wash the dishes; she was not happy that they had not enrolled her sister in the Pioneers straight away, while her brother's conversations with his friends seemed to her all too outspoken and reprehensible. Vera was an orthodox Komsomol member, who believed absolutely the RAPP articles about her brother's poetry, and condemned him for his 'decadence' and for the 'kulak' poem 'The Triumph of Agriculture'. Because of these sharp disagreements with her brother she removed Lyusya and packed her off to Vyatka to stay with her other sister, Natasha, further away from the 'damaging' influence of her brother. At odd moments Z sent small sums of money to the sisters in Vyatka, but he never met Vera again. When she completed her studies at the Institute she moved to Central Asia, where she worked for many years as a doctor. The two other sisters, Mariya and Natasha, also received a medical training. Lyusya's fate was tragic – at the beginning of the 1940s she committed suicide as the result of an unhappy love affair.

On a summer evening in 1931, Oleynikov, Shvarts and Z, after finishing work at the childrens' publishing section of *Giz*, dropped in, as was their wont, to the 'Kulturnaya' beer-hall on the corner of Nevsky Prospect and the Griboyedov Canal. After they had discussed all the latest literary gossip there was a pause in the conversation. It was interrupted by Z.

'Can anyone tell me why people start a family?'

'So that the human race should be perpetuated, I suppose,' answered Shvarts.

'No, that's not the answer,' Z pronounced significantly. 'It's because nothing starts with us or finishes with us.'

Shvarts thought his friend was about to expound his philosophy – what Shvarts thought of as Z's 'wooden' philosophy – but Oleynikov saw what it was all about at once: the Zabolotskys were expecting a baby.

That summer Z was required to spend six months on a military service course in camp in the little village of Cherekha in the Pskov district. However much he regretted being parted from his work, his friends, and his young wife, he still had to go. Z left his wife in the care of friends, and she lived with the Kaverins and the Stepanovs in the dacha at New Siverskaya, not far from the Mezhensk beach where her uncle's and aunt's dacha was.

Z reached Pskov on 10 July, and on the next day, after a look round the town, he set off for the camp. On the subject of army life he wrote to his wife:

The camp is marvellous. It's on the top of a dry, sandy hill where the pine trees grow thickly. They have tall, bare stems with clumps of foliage at the very top. It's very beautiful and dry. There are two rivers. Today we went for a swim.

I've been in the camp over a week now and my face has gone red from the sun, my nose is peeling, I go swimming every day, I eat like a horse, I run over half a mile at the double, and at night in the tent you'd need an axe if not something sharper to cut the atmosphere. In short, life is going well and I am gradually turning into a real platoon commander. For the moment our exercises are not giving us any particular trouble. I've taken on a social job which suits my talents – I'm producing the company newspaper, *Ilyichovka*. I brought out the first number today, and our lads liked it; I wrote a skit for myself . . . Our days off fly by as voluntary Voroshilov work days – on the 15th, for example, we went to a state farm to weed the beet, and worked until eight in the evening, and on the 20th they say there's going to be an inspection. That will take care of another day.*

My little one, I haven't written to you all this while because we have been on a march. We made three quite longish journeys, we marched and marched, didn't sleep at nights, and several times we had to ford a river. It was pretty tough at times. You get so exhausted that when there's a break you just pitch down under a bush and sleep like a log . . .

In a couple of days' time we shall be dismissing the reliefs that we are working with now . . . I'm fed up with the tent with its mud, I'm fed up with my boots weighing half a ton, and I'm fed up with the damp. We've all got very rough and we long as though it was something from a fairy tale for firm ground under our feet . . . Don't get lonely, my little one. I shall come back and life will return to normal. It won't be very good if I find you worn out and nervy. . .'

In January 1932, exactly two years to the day after they had started living together, the Zabolotskys had a son, and they called him Nikita. Yekaterina was afraid that having a very small baby around would upset the owners of the apartment, and that if they lived together in one room with the child Z would not be able to work at his poetry. As a result she agreed with her uncle Andrey that she and the child would stay in his dacha for a while. Their landlady Vera Mikhaylovna and her housekeeper Khristina, however, had become so attached to the Zabolotskys that for the first few months they would not hear of the little boy being taken away. The good-natured old Estonian Khristina would come into the apartment every day to clean the floor, stop next to the little bed, lean on the side rail, and admire the healthy baby boy. Every time she did so she would pronounce the same phrase: 'He looks and he thinks, what a little doll's arrived!'

In May Yekaterina went off with her son to Luga, where she stayed until the middle of August. On his days off Z would take them some food supplies, and tell his wife how things were going at work. In June he resigned from the editorial staff of *Chizh* and took an editor's job at Soyuzfoto, an organization headed by the prominent literary and Party figure, V. P. Matveyev, with whom Z was on friendly terms. Between one job and the other he had two weeks off, which he spent with his family in Luga. There he used to like going out into the yard and talking to the white cockerel which would answer him with a great show of importance, fixing him first with one beady eye, and then the other. Z would also admire the exuberant growth of rhubarb which covered the yard, and he would go for walks with his little son.

* For a short period in 1930–1 the Soviet authorities abolished the seven-day week and introduced 'continuous production' with, theoretically, a rest-day every fifth day [Ed.].

Materially it was a particularly hard time. Things were becoming more and more expensive, his salary kept being delayed, and some foodstuffs were difficult to get. Even what they were entitled to on the ration cards that were introduced at about that time was not always easy to come by. Z wrote to his wife in Luga: 'When will I be coming? As soon as I get some money . . . It's become very difficult to get money. Nobody has any.' 'I've taken my bread card. I got our sugar for June – 2 kilos 600 grammes. They issued a kilo of cheese, but I couldn't take it because I haven't got any money.'

To add to all these other worries, in the summer of 1932 Z was again mobilized for military service – this time to Belorussia. He had to leave on 11 August. It was necessary to ask Stepanov to help Yekaterina and her baby son to move from Luga to Siverskaya where she was to spend the whole of the winter and the following summer in the dacha belonging to Andrey Klykov. When they were already in Siverskaya Z wrote:

Dear Mummikins, how have you settled in, and how is little Nikita? Live as best you can, my dear ones. If you're short of money, get some from Stepanov.

I've had about 50 roubles from *Yozh*, and now my finances are more in order. I shall be going away with some money. I've managed to get a jar of preserves, 2½ kilos of pearl barley and 2 kilos of cod. I shall leave the barley here, but I'll hand the cod to the Klykovs at no. 52, so that they can bring it to you. I'll take the preserves with me. Counting the one we've got already that will be two jars. Everything's all right . . .

Just in case, I shall leave a warrant for the money from Soyuzfoto (28–29 August) with Oleynikov. He'll take it to number 52 so that it can be sent on to you.

And so Z found himself in Mogilyov. He gazed excitedly at the Dnieper, so rich in connections with Russian history. To his wife he wrote: 'Yesterday we enjoyed a swim in those famous waters.' He took an interested stroll round the market, carefully finding out the prices. It was a period of great hunger. Collectivization and the forced requisition of grain from the peasants had taken their toll. As in Leningrad, milk cost 1 rouble 40 kopecks a litre, butter and lard around 11 roubles a pound. Bread was virtually unavailable and the prices were exorbitant. True, it was good to see a plentiful stock of fresh vegetables, and the supply officers gathered in the town fed their troops primarily on these. Despite his emotional aloofness Z was quite happy mixing with people, and his fellow soldiers always listened to what he had to say. He wrote:

We stayed in a hotel in Oryol where we took a communal room for twelve at 2 roubles a head. They are a good bunch of lads, all platoon supply officers. We soon got on, and we work well together as a collective, and support each other. Everything's neat and tidy and works smoothly. Last night we all went for a walk in the municipal gardens – it's all so provincial and unpretentious that I was reminded of the old times in Urzhum.

On the day following this evening walk they set off for the military encampments near the railhead at Drut. Just as in the previous year there was another round of marches and tactical manœuvres which kept Z away from literature for a whole month. If only he had known at the time how useful this toughening-up through army training and the ability to get on with all sorts of different people, brought together to do their military service, would prove in a few years' time!

Yekaterina and her little boy spent all that autumn and winter and the following summer of 1933 at Siverskaya, while Z paid them regular visits and brought food from the city. In the autumn he went back to town with a whole sack of potatoes.

The Klykovs' dacha was solidly built, with good furniture. There were icons and lamps in the corners of the rooms and metal shutters at the windows. The glassed–in verandah with coloured glazing, the little bath-house in the garden, the outhouses and hay sheds, the little enclosed pump and motor for watering the kitchen garden – all this bore witness to the fact that the owner was well-to-do. The large plot on the high banks of the River Oredezh stood out because of the rich variety of trees and flowers growing there. There was a well-laid-out kitchen garden, a fruit garden and a cottage garden round the house. The upkeep of the whole property required much hard work. In winter the dacha froze, and heating just one room consumed a great deal of wood. A young girl, Irisha, a refugee from the famine-stricken countryside around Pskov, helped to heat up the stoves, carry the water, clear the snow, and do other tasks around the house.

On one occasion in the late autumn, on the evening before a day off, Z arrived at Siverskaya earlier than normal. Yekaterina asked him to take their son for a walk. He normally did not like walking without a goal, but he was always ready for a walk with little Nikita. He took the boy by the hand and walked down the slope, through the back gate of the garden, and out onto the river bank. He stood, in the already freezing air, and gazed long at the dark water, on which thin flakes of transparent ice were floating. It was dark by the time he returned home. His face was radiant and full of triumphant joy. With a special sense of keen interest he told his wife how the river had frozen over in front of his eyes, as though dying, and how this had been like watching the death of a rational being. The impression made had been so strong that he was unable to forget it, and three years later he described it in one of his favourite poems 'The Beginning of Winter':

> The clear and cold beginning of winter
> knocked three times at my door today.
> I got up and went out. Sharp, like metal,
> the winter air enwrapped my heart,
> but I straightened my back, breathed deep,
> and ran easily from the hill to the valley, –
> I ran and I shuddered: the river's terrible face
> suddenly looked at me and pierced my heart . . .*

There are two other poems which are linked to the family's time at Siverskaya. 'Spring in the Forest', written in 1935, is full of echoes of stories Irisha told about her native forests near Pskov, of memories of watching the rooks on the avenue of birches leading up to the dacha, and of the poet's own childhood reminiscences of the hillsides around Urzhum. The stimulus behind the poem 'Morning Song' was an episode later recalled by Yekaterina:

> In the spring of 1933, when my relatives came back to the dacha, we moved into the upper-storey attic rooms. Carrying little Nikita in my arms, I opened wide the large window of the upstairs verandah and called to Nikolay. It was so wonderful! In the garden white and blue lupins were flowering, and from upstairs they looked like candles rising up out of the green, the birds were singing, and the barn rose beyond the vegetable garden.

The whole of this picture is reproduced in the poem 'The Artist's Household', later renamed 'Morning Song'. In the earlier version it began as follows:

> The mighty day had come. The trees had stood erect.
> The leaves had breathed. In the wooden veins
> water had dripped. The square window
> had opened over the bright earth,
> and all those who were in the turret had gathered
> to look at the sky, full of brightness.
> And we too were standing at the window.
> There was my wife in her spring dress,
> and in her arms sat little Nikita,
> all pink and bare and laughing,

* See also pp.337–8.

and his little eyes, full of great purity,
were looking at the sky, where the sun was shining.

The poem is dated 1932, but that is probably a mistake, as everything described in it relates to the beginning of the summer of 1933.

There were other occasions when life at Siverskaya led Yekaterina to have bitter thoughts about her separation from her husband, and about his unjustified coolness towards her. Things were especially difficult in the wintertime, when she sat in the long, empty evenings alone in a cold, snowbound dacha, and thought how few and far between were the letters from Z. Sometimes, when her husband arrived on his day off, she could not contain herself, and complained. He would comfort her, and later put some of his words into a letter:

> I'm really lonely here without you, and sometimes I just feel a very unhappy man. My dear little idiots, your daddy loves you both very much, although he doesn't like to talk about it. I can't stop thinking about what you said to me – that I only loved you properly before, and now it's not the same any more. Of course it's not the same, you silly thing, but that does not mean that it's any less. It just means that it's different – a different kind – after all, it's more than three years since we got married, and there's been plenty of time for deep and constant feelings to be formed. If I should lose you now, what would become of me? I used to believe that art meant everything to me – but now it seems it's only half of what I need. The other half is you and Nikita.
>
> Both halves are dear to me and both halves must exist and support each other.
>
> Pelageya Semyonovna writes that you are still young and should enjoy yourself. Not only enjoy yourself! You should start to have an interest in everything in life again, not just in the child. In the autumn Nikita will be more than eighteen months old, there'll be a flat available – and we shall manage to get it, if we are alive and well. (19 February 1933).

Years later Yekaterina noted down:

Many people have written about Nikolay's difficult character as far as domestic matters were concerned. Whenever I think about this I always repeat to myself his lines:

> And something that had fluttered to me from earth
> I brushed aside unhurriedly with my hand.

If ever Z was immersed in deep thought he was very good at keeping domestic worries at arm's length. This ability to 'brush things aside', gently but firmly, sometimes hurt me. It did not mean that he was cutting himself off from the family, or was not interested in what was going on in it. He took the worries and responsibilities of head of the family seriously. He could not tolerate slovenliness. He did not like digging around in one's emotions. Because he himself was a person with fixed aims in life, he had no sympathy with pointless complaining or with emotional laxity.

In his letter to his wife Z referred to the hope of getting an apartment in the autumn of 1933. In fact a year earlier, despite their lack of money, they had joined a housing co-operative. They had to borrow money from the Kaverins to pay the first subscription. On 15 March 1933, Z wrote to his wife:

> We've absolutely got to pay 350 roubles before the 20th here for the apartment (the one we're going to get), otherwise we lose the right to one altogether. I shall try to arrange it so that the publishing house will pay. And also we've got to get some food from the co-operative. I really don't know what we can do. There's no one we can borrow from – none of them has got any money. And, anyhow, at your end we've got to pay for the firewood and give some money to Irisha . . .

But somehow the money was found for the co-operative, and building went ahead. On the Griboyedov Canal, in the very centre of Leningrad, No. 9, a three-storey house, was having two extra floors added to it, with apartments for writers. True, in the autumn, when the Zabolotskys had hoped to be moving in, the work was still incomplete, and Yekaterina with their son had to move from the dacha once more to Pushkarskaya Street. It was only in the spring of 1934 that the family received its own two-roomed flat on the Griboyedov Canal.

II

For some two and a half years Z worked on children's magazines – in 1930 he was in charge of the supplement department of *Yozh* (*The Hedgehog*), and subsequently, until the middle of 1932, he was editor-in-chief of *Chizh* (*The Finch*). Both magazines were published by the children's section of the State Publishing House for Literature – or, as it was then called, *Giz*. Working at *Giz* was not simply a duty, it was a pleasure, an entertainment even. The editorial offices of the children's magazines acted as a sort of club, which brought together authors, artists, and, of course, the staff of the publishing house. Among the interesting individuals it was possible to meet there were S. Marshak, M. Prishvin, B. Zhitkov, K. Chukovsky, V. Bianki, M. Zoshchenko, M. Yefremov, L. Panteleev, Shvarts, Oleynikov, L. Savelyev (Lipavsky), Kharms and Vvedensky. The 'club' also counted amongst its members

101

established artists such as V. Lebedev, E. Budogosky, V. Yermolayeva, V. Konashevich, B. Malakhovsky, N. Radlov, P. Sokolov, N. Tyrsa and Ye. Charushin. Many of them were in no hurry to leave the editorial building on the Nevsky Prospekt once they had finished work. They would usually gather in groups around the spacious bay-window alcoves. There they would exchange gossip, read poems and epigrams, and outdo each other in wit.

It was frequently Oleynikov who was the centre of attention in such company. In the period 1928–9 he had been the editor-in-chief, and in 1931 he had become editorial manager of *Yozh*. But even during the time when he did not work there he would still enjoy merely coming in to the editorial office. His ironical verse parodies enjoyed special success in the club at the window-bays. S. A. Bogdanovich, one of those who took part in these editorial gatherings, recalls that there were often complete performances of impromptu playlets.

On one occasion, when the noise of the assembled company had abated a little, Oleynikov took a couple of paces away from Shvarts who was standing next to him, and fixed upon him a look of skilfully feigned hatred. They all realized that one of the regular performances was about to begin, and the main participants slipped effortlessly into their roles. Oleynikov changed his angry expression to one of lovelorn sadness, turning to face the desk of the editorial secretary, the attractive Henrietta Davydovna Levitina. In a voice trembling with hurt and agitation he intoned:

> I am in love with Henrietta Davydovna,
> But she, it seems, does not love me.
> To Shvarts she has given a receipt,
> But to me she has given none.

Shvarts, using his training as an actor, smiled the haughty smile of the successful rival, while Henrietta, shrugging her shoulders coquettishly and glancing icily at Oleynikov, began to smile tenderly at Shvarts. Oleynikov's passionate, angry voice went on:

> I hate that damned Shvarts,
> For whom she longs!
> Like some stupid fish she wants to marry him,
> Him with his paltry mind . . .

The last lines of the poem, expressing the lover's plea, – 'Love me, love me. Stop loving him!' – could hardly be heard above the laughter. Just as everyone thought that that was it, Z stepped forward importantly and, turning to Shvarts, produced the crushing improvisation:

Between us, Zhenya, there is a gulf —
You are a tempter of young people,
While I gather up their howls
For my pages of literary edification.

Henrietta Levitina, the wife of V. P. Dombrovsky, an important member of the Cheka, the Commander of the North-Western Frontier Region, and subsequently official of the Leningrad OGPU*, was the constant object of comic rivalry between the poets, who dedicated to her every conceivable kind of improvised love poem. Z also composed a cycle of short poems under the general title 'The Beauty of Grunya (Henrietta)', and these were read to the 'club' on more than one occasion. In contrast with Oleynikov, he chose for himself the role of an eccentric moral mentor who struggles with his passionate feelings and overcomes them by strength of will. The cycle began with the quatrain:

As editor of supplements
I have an eye for beauty,
But as one who knows the wiles of ladies
I keep within the bounds of decency.

This was succeeded by poems with titles such as: 'A Moment of Weakness', 'The Mad Decision', 'Repentance of an Ill-considered Decision' and 'The Return to Useful Life'.

These comic verses were dedicated to various people and written on every possible kind of pretext, but they always purveyed a certain kind of sense, and reflected real situations or human traits. The editorial artist, Genrikh Levin, kept a little oilcloth-covered notebook in which he jotted down all Z's humorous verses. Unfortunately this notebook was lost during the siege of Leningrad.

On a number of occasions the whole editorial gathering was invited back to Henrietta's well-appointed house. The half-starved writers and artists welcomed the opportunity to eat their fill of tasty food and to drink expensive brandy. As a lover of cheese Z was especially attracted by the whole real Dutch cheese, served on a special porcelain dish. After the meal they would remain at the table, improvising verses, listening to foreign records and sometimes dancing.

Their host also sometimes joined their company. He was convivial in a condescending kind of way, pouring them out glasses of brandy and playing the piano. It was hardly likely that any of his wife's guests were

* The Soviet state security organization, the secret police, descendant of the Cheka (Special Commission] of the Revolutionary period, and reorganized subsequently as NKVD, and later KGB [Ed.].

aware that ever since 1929 he had been head of the Secret Operations Executive of the Leningrad OGPU and that at the end of 1931 it was his signature that authorized the sentence passed at the show trial of the so-called 'anti-Soviet group of writers in the childrens' section of *Lengosizdat'.* Subsequently Dombrovsky fell victim to the same repressive machinery that he had helped to set up. He was shot in 1937. Life became very difficult for Henrietta – from 1937 to 1947 and from 1949 to 1955 she had to endure sixteen years of prison and camps. In May 1956, after her release, she was to visit Z in Moscow and they would both remember those days of their youth and the uniquely free atmosphere of the editorial offices of the Leningrad children's magazines at the end of the 1920s.

Towards the end of 1930 Henrietta Davydovna was replaced as secretary by Irakly Andronikov, who had just graduated from university. The repertoire of the editorial 'club' was extended by his superb impersonations of the contributors to the magazines. In moments of inspiration he could do solo imitations of an entire brass band. In his memoirs he later gave an account of his impressions on first meeting Z:

> You would certainly never have thought that this was the man who had written *Columns*. He was fresh-faced, had fair hair, cut slanting across his forehead. He wore glasses and spoke in a soft bass voice. He didn't say much and was very serious. His movements were controlled. Nevertheless, there was a hint of humour in the way he spoke and in his eyes. His contributions to the conversation were thoughtful, and his laughter restrained. He had a precisely articulated sense of his own worth.
>
> A huge editors' desk almost filled the entire room. A seat was found for me on Zabolotsky's right. Looking back on it, he seemed very young. Yet everyone seemed to have developed a deep respect for him. His reliability and punctiliousness made me not only respect him, but also feel slightly envious. He always did everything on time. On the appointed day and at the appointed hour he would be handed the sketches and poems for *Chizh* . . . The room would be crowded with people, and the atmosphere noisy, almost festive . . . Z would be laughing and joking, and at the same time measuring, pasting up and numbering the pages of the mock-up.

It was indeed the case that Z did all his work by the agreed deadline, both the editorial work and his own freelance writing. He always managed to produce *Chizh* on time, and if a gap needed filling he would supply some children's poems of his own, or an article, or an amusing

* Leningrad State Publishing House [Ed.].

caption to a drawing. It was not for nothing that the editorial staff used to say jokingly about him, bearing in mind his pseudonym, 'You can always rely on Yasha Miller.'

In the lunch breaks or after work the staff would cross to the other side of the Griboyedov Canal and settle into the 'Kulturnaya' beer-hall. Here the talk was about everything imaginable, except politics. The fact was that since the beginning of the thirties they had all been aware that everything they did and said was being watched and reported on to the relevant authorities. Sometimes they would hand each other a newspaper or magazine containing one of the by now regular crushing reviews. In April 1930, Oleynikov without a word handed to Z a copy of the youth paper *Smena*. In it the latter found a review of the last performance of the *Oberiu* poets Levin and Vladimirov at the student hostel in Leningrad University. The review said:

> The *Oberiu* writers are far removed from the work of construction. They are full of hatred for the struggle which the proletariat is waging. Their remoteness from real life, their meaningless poetry, their juggling with sheer sound is all a protest against the dictatorship of the proletariat. For that reason their poetry is counter-revolutionary. It is a poetry which is alien to our people, the poetry of the class enemy: that is what the proletarian student body has made clear.

Some time passed, and then not only the press but also the organs of repression began to take an interest in former members of *Oberiu* and their colleagues. In December 1931, a group of writers and artists working in the children's section of *Giz* was arrested. The group included Kharms, Vvedensky, Bakhterev, Tufanov and Andronikov. Using as a pretext the struggle against counter-revolution, an attempt was made not only to suppress any independent tendency in children's literature in Leningrad, but to frighten all those writers who refused to submit to official precepts and stereotypes. During their interrogations many of those arrested were forced to confess to membership of a group which was alleged to be hostile to Soviet power. The statement signed by Vvedensky, for example, read: 'Together with the writers Kharms, Bakhterev, and earlier Zabolotsky and others, I formed part of an anti-Soviet group which composed and distributed objectively counter-revolutionary poems.' Tufanov's statement contained the words: 'Our organization, which had as its aim the establishment and dissemination of *Oberiu* beliefs as a weapon in the struggle against Soviet power, counted amongst its members Kharms, Vvedensky, Zabolotsky, Vigilyansky, myself, Markov, Bogayevsky, and others.'

Attached to the records kept by OGPU on case no. 4246 were some curiously interesting pages written in Andronikov's own hand. Though they tried not to stray too far from the truth all they did essentially was to pour oil onto the flames of the investigation. On 27 January 1932, he wrote:

> The ideological closeness of Shvarts, Zabolotsky, Oleynikov and Lipavsky to the Kharms–Vvedensky group was expressed in their reading their latest poems to each other, normally in private; in conversations that were sometimes of an intimate nature, and in the exchange of impressions and opinions which made me think how much these people had in common from the point of view of ideology and interests. Kharms and Vvedensky were constant visitors to the *Giz* offices, spending almost all their time in the company of Shvarts, Oleynikov and Zabolotsky. They were often joined by Lipavsky, and would stay together for hours on end. Whenever they wished to discuss anything serious they would all go to the pub together, under the pretext that it was the lunch hour.

And further in the same document:

> The occasional visits Shvarts, Kharms and Vvedensky made together to symphony concerts, and the fact that Shvarts and Kharms went together to exhibitions of paintings by the artist Niko Pirosmanishvili and to the opening of an exhibition by Filonov, at which I also met them, and an exchange of opinions on this subject in the editorial offices at which Vvedensky, Zabolotsky, Oleynikov, and Lipavsky were also present, all this finally convinced me that these people were linked together by a common ideological position, expressed in their views and their attitude of mind.

At that juncture the punitive organs were not as virulent as they were to become a few years later, and not all those mentioned in the depositions were punished. Andronikov was released. Kharms and Vvedensky spent some six months in prison, and on release were exiled for a few months to Kursk. Tufanov was sentenced to five years in the camps, followed by exile. Z was not arrested at that time, but in view of the fact that he had been mentioned on more than one occasion during the investigation as a member of a supposedly suspicious or simply anti-Soviet group of writers, it can be safely assumed that his name had been entered in the OGPU (later NKVD) record files.

It has to be admitted that, looked at from their own point of view, the OGPU agents were to a certain extent justified in acting as they did: Z and his colleagues naturally had no sympathy with the current situation, not only in Soviet literature, but in the country generally. Not only that, but they were awkward for the authorities, since they had their own original views, and were prepared to stand by these views in their work. But naturally none of them had made any attempt to fight against the regime in power, unless it were by the original method of writing their poetry or by adherence to the avant-garde views on art represented by Filonov.

It also proved next to impossible to avoid talking about politics in their conversations. On one occasion, at the beginning of 1933, Oleynikov came to see Z and began talking agitatedly about the situation in the country, about the famine in the Ukraine and the south of Russia, and about the desperate situation of the peasantry. As a descendant of Cossacks, a member of the Party and a participant in the Civil War, he knew more about what was happening than any of his friends, and now made no attempt to conceal his rage and scepticism. It was a dangerous subject which it was better not to mention to avoid suspicion. This time, however, there was a pressing reason for the conversation – Oleynikov had been conscripted into a requisition detachment to extort the last remnants of grain from the peasants, and he had come to seek advice on how he could get out of taking part in this plunder. In the end, after starving himself for a week, he was able skilfully to feign the symptoms of an aggravated ulcerous condition, and was classed as unfit by a medical commission. Z guarded his friend's secret religiously, and only much later did he tell his wife about what had happened – he could trust her.

In the company of Oleynikov, Shvarts, Kharms and Lipavsky, Z used to like to visit the hospitable household of Boris Stepanovich Zhitkov. The latter had until recently been a loyal associate of Marshak in their common struggle to make children's literature independent of official and bureaucratic pressure. He would present his guests with a wide selection of home-made liqueurs and regale them with accounts of his sea-voyages round the world. Many of these stories later found a place in his books. There was always a special liveliness about these feasts at the Zhitkovs' table. Shvarts later recalled the meetings: 'We were all happy. Happy to such an extent that we were silly, stupid and inspired.' Part of the ritual at the table consisted of the repetition of a particular set of 'in' jokes, and at the same time new ones would be thought up. Then there would be the solving of all kinds of conundrums thought up by their host, and they would have a good laugh at the more ridiculous aspects of literary life. Zhitkov would show them new tricks which he had taught his cat and dog. The basis of the company's wit was not the humour of the anecdote or the pun – these were less appreciated – but leaps of logic that destroyed common sense and allowed free rein to the imagination. It was just such humour that Z liked best of all.

At times, however, the amusement was laced with a sense of malice which was usually purveyed by Oleynikov. This was the reason why Marshak, who was well aware of how dangerous it was to fall victim to the latter's tongue, composed the following epigram:

Beware of Nikolay Oleynikov,
Whose motto is: let no one off.

Everyone knew that Oleynikov would not spare even those sitting at the table, and sometimes they secretly took offence, but they almost always forgave him because he did it in such a witty and talented way. Although Z knew that Oleynikov valued his poetry, he still found his subjects being parodied and himself being called Foma Opiskin the Scribbler* to his face. Shvarts, who had taken some time to find his way into drama, now faced being tormented with not having written much. Shvarts noted bitterly: 'There was yet another wicked talent that Oleynikov possessed: he could spatter both his friends and those he did not know in their most vulnerable places with sulphuric acid.'

A favourite target at table at the Zhitkovs' was Marshak. Stepanov, who was an occasional visitor, recalls:

For some reason I remember in particular how we talked about Marshak, who was unanimously condemned for his hypocrisy, servility and lack of principles. This was evident already at the time of the split between Zhitkov and his former friend. Oleynikov's attacks on Marshak were especially sharp and spiteful. He made great fun of the gushing way the latter spoke ('my dear'), and of his constant striking of attitudes.

Despite his generally positive attitude to Marshak, Z also spoke of him in ironic terms and laughed at his predilection for posing.

The meetings at the Lipavskys' were of quite a different kind. Z was a very frequent visitor from 1931 to 1933. The hostess was Tamara Aleksandrovna, who at that time had just left Vvedensky and married Leonid Savelyevich Lipavsky, who wrote under the pen-name Savelyev. She knew how to make these gatherings warm and cosy. As he entered the Lipavskys' apartment Z would invariably repeat a special ritual joke of his. With deliberate seriousness he would turn to Tamara and recite:

Oh, beautiful Tamara,
If only you could witness
The fiery flames of passion
In that place where virtue
Has found refuge for itself!
Where? In this place. Here!

* A buffoonish character in Dostoyevsky's *Village of Stepanchikovo* [Ed.].

As he pronounced these last words he would beat his breast with an extravagant gesture, and just the hint of a smile would appear on his crafty face. In addition to Lipavsky, Z, Kharms and Oleynikov, another visitor to the house was a colleague of Lipavsky's from his time at the Philosophy Faculty, the musician and mathematician Yakov Druskin, and on occasions they would be joined by others. They would talk, read poetry and play board games. As he played, Z would sing to himself a simple little song of his own creation: 'One adjutant had an epaulette, the other adjutant hadn't got one yet.'

What was so special about the evenings at the Lipavskys' was the discussions that took place on the most varied philosophical topics – mathematics, the philosophical meaning of time, inspiration, death, academics and philosophers, books which they had all read, the nature of talent, how pleasant it was to give presents, about harmony, and about many other matters. Also current were some special kind of word games, which consisted, in Lipavsky's words, 'in transforming, substituting and juggling words in accordance with a kind of indefinable stylistic system'. On one occasion they all decided to write down on separate pieces of paper what it was that interested them most in life. Z's list of interests ran as follows:

Architecture, the laws governing large structures. Symbolism. The representation of ideas in the form of the conventional disposition of objects and their constituent parts. The practice of religion by the use of such objects. Verse. Sundry common phenomena – fighting, food, dancing. Meat and pastry. Vodka and beer. Popular astronomy. Popular numerology. Sleep. The dispositions and figures of revolution. The peoples of the north. The destruction of all 'frenchies'.* Music, its architecture, fugues. The structuring of pictures of nature. Domestic animals. Wild animals and insects. Birds. Goodness – Beauty – Truth. People and situations in military actions. Death. Books, and how to create them. Letters, signs and numerals. Cymbals. Ships.

What is interesting about this list is that we can guess from it some of the poet's innermost thought-processes that were reflected in his poetry.

Lipavsky kept a record for the years 1933–4 of the conversations that took place in his house. There was one occasion when Oleynikov said: 'I have several times dreamt that I was dying. While death was drawing near it was very frightening, but as soon as the blood began to flow out of my veins, it was not frightening at all, and dying was easy.' At this Z

---

* By 'frenchies' Z means those superficial, empty people who are always striving for outward show (cf. 'The little Frenchman from Bordeaux' in Griboyedov's play *Woe from Wit*). Z particularly disliked such types [Author's note].

remarked: 'I think I have dreamt even more – the moment when I was already dead and I was beginning to disperse into the air. That was simple and pleasant too . . . Generally speaking emotions are remarkably clear and fresh in dreams. The most acute sorrow and the most passionate love are experienced in dreams.'

When he fell asleep Z went on living that special kind of life that enriched his existence. There were instances when he would wake in the middle of the night, jot down a line of verse, and then go back to sleep again. Sometimes his dreams provided material for whole poems, such as 'Figures of Sleep' of 1928 and, from a much later period, 'Dream', 'The Flight into Egypt' and 'Juniper Bush'.

The meetings at the Lipavskys' lasted until Z and Oleynikov moved into the co-operative flats project on the Griboyedov Canal. Already by the beginning of 1934, however, the members of the company had begun to disperse. Z had already started to lose interest in Lipavsky's and Druskin's philosophical views. In the summer of 1932 he had attempted to steer the discussions in a direction which interested him – natural science. The friends decided to meet once a week and talk about questions of natural science, labelling these gatherings a 'school for semi-literate scholars'. But after the second such meeting the idea of a strictly adhered-to theme began to get lost, and nothing came of this undertaking, so Z had to resign himself to what he considered the trivial nature of these occasions. For their part, Lipavsky and Druskin, both of whom were enthusiastic about Z's *Columns*, found themselves out of sympathy with his change of topic, and more especially with the change in his poetic system.

Lipavsky once said to Kharms about Z's writing: 'His poetry is the effort of a blind man opening his eyes. That's where his greatness and his talent lie. But whenever he makes it seem as though his eyes are open already, it all goes to pieces.' Kharms might well have replied with the words he used in a letter to the Youth Theatre actress, K.V. Pugachova:

I have been thinking how splendid everything is that is fresh. How splendid is the first flush of reality. How splendid are the sun and the grass and the stones and water and a bird and a spider and a fly and a man. But a glass and a knife and a key and a comb are just as splendid. Yet if I were to go blind and deaf, and lose all my senses, how could I know all this splendour? Everything would have disappeared, and for me there would be nothing. Then I would get back my sense of touch, and a whole new world would appear. I would start to hear again, and the world would be significantly better. I would get back all the other senses, and the world would be even bigger and better. The world only starts to exist as soon as I let it into myself. Let it be as disordered as you like, all the same it would exist! Yet I have begun to put the world into order. And that is where Art comes in.

Kharms might have objected to Lipavsky that Z's greatness lay not only in looking at the world for the first time, but in his effort to put the world into order, in the fact that he created, as Kharms would have said, 'the purity of order'. It is in this idea that we can perceive the development of Z's method of writing: moving from looking at the world 'with naked eyes', to making meaning out of it, to elaborating a sense of order for it, and then to reflecting this sense of order in his poetry.

In the 1930s many admirers of Z's work were disturbed, and even disappointed, by the appearance in his poetry of what they considered to be too much reasoning, too much rationalism. In 1933 Lidiya Ginzburg said to Oleynikov: 'A sort of coldness has come into Z's work . . .' Oleynikov, who, like Kharms, understood the peculiarities of Z's chosen path and his deeper thought processes, replied, as Lidiya Ginzburg recalls, in a particularly serious tone: 'Never mind, he's got every right to go through this stage. Pushkin was cold when he wrote *Boris Godunov*. Z is now under the influence of *Boris Godunov*.'

This 'coldness' of Z's, Oleynikov's ever-increasing sense of doubt under the pressure of the frightening events of the 1930s, and Lipavsky's and Druskin's apartness, threatened the little group, and finally led to its breakup. Z, who liked everything to be clear-cut, and who was always ready to subject his own interests to those of his work, finally said, on one of those evenings at the beginning of 1934:

We're all living as though we are shut in a box. We can't go on like this. The box is stopping us from writing. We are all different as people, and it's only natural that we shouldn't want to do everything in the same way all the time. It's not our fault – we've no freedom of choice in this. This is more glaringly obvious than ever in questions of art. We just have to write as often as we can, because success doesn't depend on us – so let's have as many chances as we can.

Lipavsky agreed with him: 'You're probably right. And after all we're not factory managers, who can't work as isolated individuals. You may only be a bus-conductor, but it all depends on you whether you go on being a conductor, and whether you're a good one or a bad one.'

Z was happy to see that he had been understood and so he went on:

That's what it's all about. You have to create conditions where you can give the maximum to art. Our box has turned out to be a bad kind of accommodation: that means we have to break out of it. So, then, our little group is breaking up, and that's a cause for sorrow. When I had to leave the friends I had made at secondary school, I thought I'd not be able to live without them. But life creates new friendships all the time. It's not a matter of our group now, it's a matter of each one for himself!

The demise of the friendly gatherings at the Lipavskys' was summed up by Kharms in verse:

> Here is the group of friends, abandoned by fate:
> It pains us to hear each other speak;
> No longer can we leap up, or be ourselves,
> Or get boredom off our back with a bitter joke.
>
> Long abandoned is the argument, the pointless talk
> Has dried up of itself, and silently each glance,
> Full of disdain, files lance-like at our neighbours,
> Knocking the words from their lips; and conversation dies.

When the meetings at the Lipavskys' came to a stop, the close and friendly relations between individual members of the group were not affected. Z went on meeting Oleynikov and Kharms, and, less often, Lipavsky, until they were torn apart by circumstances beyond their control.

In 1933–4 it was quite possible to escape from the 'box' of a gathering that had outlived its usefulness, but where could you go to escape from the oppressive and constricting atmosphere that surrounded literature at the time? Z was becoming more and more aware that a time had arrived when it was difficult to display talent and individuality. But we shall be discussing his creative activities in those years shortly. For the moment we shall describe one particular meeting of friends.

In the summer of 1933, when Z's family were living out at Siverskaya, and such meetings were very frequent, Z, Kharms and Oleynikov got together one day and decided to visit the Kaverins and the Shvartses who were living in a dacha in Sestroretsk. The Kaverins had rented the ground floor of the house, and Shvarts and his wife Yekaterina were living upstairs. Since they had absolutely no money at all, and for a variety of other reasons, the general mood was not bright. Uppermost in Z's mind was the fresh wave of hostile criticism directed at him, and the difficulties he was having in getting his poetry published. He needed something to take his mind off all these unpleasant matters.

When they arrived Kaverin was still completing the time he had set himself for work, sitting at a table on the ground floor of the dacha and writing. So as not to interrupt him the friends went for a walk with Shvarts in the direction of a small clump of oak trees by the slope down to the beach. Oleynikov, who came from the south, was healthily critical of everything he saw around him, the northern landscape, the gnarled oaks, the cold sea, the weather, and especially the peculiar people who rent dachas in such unprepossessing places. In order to change the subject the emotionally sensitive Shvarts asked Kharms: 'Daniil, you've written so wonderfully about God and a grain of sand, please recite it to us.' They all sat down under one of the oaks, and Kharms began to recite, as usual with great expression:

> God awoke and opened his eyes,
> He took a grain of sand – and threw it at us . . .

Z listened and thought of his latest long poem, which, just like Kharms's verse, would probably never be published. Oleynikov suddenly began to talk about Kaverin:

'Veniamin is working like a spring that has been wound up – searching all the time for a new form. In doing so he thinks he's like you – Kharms and Z. But in the first place he's working in the traditional literary manner, and he's not an innovator. In the second place, are you looking for a new form? You're not looking for anything. You just simply don't know how to write any differently from how you write now. And you're sick of everything that has been called literature before you.'

'We should still know about everything called literature, and about the laws that govern it as well', remarked Z. 'All of us, not just me, but Daniil too, are dependent on those who have gone before us. An empty place will always remain empty.'

Oleynikov did not agree:'If you followed the laws of literature that are in force at the moment, then you would write falsely, yet you are still correct in what you say. That's the whole bind of it. You're absolutely right. That's exactly why you can't stand the lie in human relationships. I find it amazing that so few people understand that.' Then they began talking about the Symbolists and the Post-Symbolists, the general outcome being one of all-round condemnation. Oleynikov exclaimed in annoyance: 'They write words that don't mean anything – but, oh how beautiful they are!'

Gradually the conversation fizzled out, until Shvarts heaved a sigh, and remarked: 'Things don't feel quite right. If I had any money I'd suggest we went for a drink.' It turned out that they all felt like a drink, but no one had any money. There was only one answer: they would have to borrow some from Kaverin.

'I think you should ask him, Yevgeny, you're his neighbour,' Z suggested, 'I owe him money already.'

'No, much as I'd like to, I can't,' Shvarts replied dismally; 'I'm up to my ears in debt to him as well. I feel so ashamed. Katya even has to borrow money to buy bread.'

The other two also felt uncomfortable about asking Kaverin for money. Nevertheless the little group set off for the garden surrounding the dacha, in the vague hope of somehow letting Kaverin know that they would like him to treat them to vodka. As they went Oleynikov mournfully recited his own version of Kharms's poem: 'God awoke – the binge began . . .' They sat down at a table set in the ground beneath a worm-eaten apple tree. The figure of Veniamin Kaverin soon appeared on the terrace of the house. He was pleased to see his visitors, because he thought of them as interesting writers and people to talk to. Shvarts recalls that Kharms and Oleynikov regarded their host dispassionately, as though he were a sample of another species that had nothing to do with them. Z's relations with Kaverin were somewhat closer. They had been on good terms ever since he had gone to see Kaverin one day, to express his opinion about the latter's novel *Artist Unknown*, which had just appeared. Kaverin writes: 'He came to see me carrying a copy of the book, highly excited, and full of ideas that I found very interesting and hadn't in the least expected. That cemented our friendship. It was a relationship between two writers following each other's work with love and interest.'

By now the friends were desperate for a drink, and their only hope lay in Kaverin's ability to take a hint. Oleynikov, who was always very observant, brought to everyone's attention the fact that Kaverin kept giving a little cough and holding his hand up to his throat.

'What's the matter, Veniamin?'

'My throat feels a bit funny. I don't know whether I've caught a cold or what.'

'In that case the only answer is to have a drink,' Oleynikov replied, quick as a flash.

From the expressions on the faces of the rest of the company Kaverin immediately guessed their simple ruse. He had a good laugh and sent down to the shop for a bottle. Not long afterwards Lidiya invited them all onto the terrace. And – horror of horrors! – on the table stood a bottle of sweet red wine, which none of the company could stand. Kaverin, who did not drink at all, thought that any old wine was all right, and the sweeter the taste the better. This great disappointment gave rise to some bitter humour on the part of those assembled and this soon turned into a lively and cheerful buzz of conversation.

This episode stuck so firmly in Shvarts's memory that he twice described it, though a little differently, in his diaries, once in 1954 and again in 1955. In summing up the events he remarked: 'This (the sweet wine) annoyed Z so much that to this day, when we are asked round to the Kaverins', he rings up first and finds out what kind of wine it's going to be.'

Shvarts wrote the following about Z and the relationships between the members of the little circle:

As soon as he adopted a methodical and ordered manner of speaking the others would laugh at him and call him 'Yasha Miller'. He would speak of Goethe with great respect, and I think he was the only one of us to be conscious of his own behaviour. He did not behave as he wished, but in a way he considered proper for a poet. He would deride Vvedensky, who was the direct opposite of him, in a half-joking way, or at least it seemed at first half-joking. He wrote to him:

> Why is it, you devil,
> that you live like a hottentot,
> don't you know the rules,
> of what is done, and what is not?

And this particular episode finished with Zabolotsky behaving strictly, rationally and firmly: he broke off his friendship with Vvedensky . . . Zabolotsky was the son of an agronomist . . . he had grown up in a large, poor family, and in the sort of Russian conditions where you cannot imagine anything more unenlightened. That's why in all his methodical life and his love of Goethe you can detect a very Russian rejection of the disorder and slovenliness of his home background. There is also something of the eccentric and not a little sectarian despotism. Yet all those who teased him and called him 'Yasha Miller' did so behind his back. He had developed the ability to surround himself with a protective stockade. People were not afraid of him, but they were afraid of arguing with him. They didn't want to do it. It wasn't for his importance, nor for his 'wooden' philosophical systems, nor for his methodical nature and his strictness that we loved and respected him. It was for his strength. For the strength that found expression in his poetry. Even the harshest of all his critics, Nikolay Oleynikov, was forced to admit: 'You have to grant that when he writes poetry, he's strong. It's like muscles. Some people have them and others don't' . . . For all the exceptional strength of will that was evident through his behaviour, essentially he lived like the rest of us. Whether he liked it or not he took on the colour of his surroundings, without realizing that he was doing so. And yet, for all that, he was methodical, rational, severe and pure.

III

Z's natural-philosophical ideas underwent an exceptionally rich period of development in the years 1929–33. He now had his own distinctive poetic voice, and became deeply immersed in working out the view of the universe which had arisen in his mind in his earlier years. He wanted to make his ideas clearer and more ordered, to enrich them by reading scientific and philosophical literature, and to polish them in discussions with his friends. An idea, taken to the limits of possible clarity, became material for his poetry. On what basis his views were formed is hard to say. Z had absorbed a great deal from being with his father as a child, from his own observations, and from the many books he had read. There was a characteristic peculiarity about the way he worked with literature, about the way he reacted to art, and about his conversations with people who were experts in their fields – from all these sources he took for himself only those pieces of information and ideas which confirmed or could enrich his own concept of the world. It was as though he were filtering the information he was taking in, and rejecting what he could not use as of no interest. Yet even such unnecessary information was not abandoned altogether. He stored it somewhere deep in his memory, and then at the appropriate moment he would demonstrate a quite unexpected breadth of knowledge. Such a process of selection was, in the final analysis, subjected to the interests of his work. Among the literary sources known to us from which the poet drew his ideas, we should mention the works of Plato and of Engels, Goethe and Khlebnikov, Grigory Skovoroda and Timiryazev, Vernadsky and Tsiolkovsky. But of course this list is far from exhaustive.

Z extracted much that was of interest to him from Vladimir Ivanovich Vernadsky's writings on the biosphere. His seminal work *The Biosphere* had appeared in Leningrad in 1926 in a printing of only 2,000 copies, but it had come to Z's notice and he had read it with close attention. He referred to it more than once in his discussions of natural philosophy. It is quite possible that he had also read other works by Vernadsky; he would have found them attractive because of the broad sweep of the subjects covered and the depth and independence of the philosophical thinking. What he found especially to his liking was the bringing together of living creatures and all inanimate matter into one unified, elegant process of formation of the outer surface of our planet. The writer equated living matter with dead, inorganic formations on a planetary scale, and affirmed, moreover, that the transformation of the face of the Earth was to the ultimate degree dependent precisely upon living matter, life. Such a view enabled life to be seen not as a chance phenomenon in the vastness of the cosmos, but as the natural, highest stage of development of matter, a stage at which matter acquired the capacity for self-knowledge and self-regulation.

There was one occasion when the writers and philosophers who had gathered at the Lipavskys' were discussing a book by the famous English astronomer, James Jeans, which, as Vernadsky had remarked in his critique, reduced all the phenomena of life 'to the position of insignificant details in the Cosmos'. The whole of Z's way of thinking revolted against such a point of view. Jeans wrote:

When we observe the Universe we are seized with a sense of terror. The Universe terrifies us with its huge, meaningless distances, its immense chronological perspectives, reducing human history to a matter of a few moments, it terrifies us with a sense of our utter isolation and the material insignificance of our planet, which makes up only a millionth part of the innumerable grains of sand in the galaxy. But more than anything else the Universe terrifies us because it would seem to be indifferent to any form of life such as ours; feeling, striving and achievement, art, philosophy and science – all this would seem to be alien to its plans. Rather it would be more accurate to say that the Universe is actively hostile to life. (J. Jeans, *The Movement of the World*, translated as *Dvizhenie mira*, Moscow, 1933, pp. 124–5).

Z could never agree with such an analysis, and he responded to it firmly:

Jeans's book is far too sombre, and it doesn't provide a single answer to anything. What comes across is the terrible emptiness of the Universe, the exclusive nature of matter, and the even more exclusive nature of the planetary systems and the almost absolute impossibility of life. All astronomical matters are the result of chance – and a highly improbable one at that. What an exceedingly inhospitable Universe!

Leonid Lipavsky tried to defend the book: 'Nevertheless, it shows that the Universe has its own birth, growth and decline. It is a more dramatic and more individual thing than people had previously believed.' Z agreed:

Of course, the Universe has its own destiny. The stars cannot be compared to machines – that is just as absurd as considering a radioactive substance a machine. But just look at one particularly interesting drawing in the book – a depiction of the conglomeration of the spheres in the surface of the Milky Way. Does it not seem to you that these dots form the shape of a human figure? And the sun is not in the centre of it, but where the sexual organ is. The Earth is like the seed of the Universe.

Here Z had discovered an image that corresponded to his views. It corresponded to Vernadsky's teaching, and to the works of Tsiolkovsky which he had already read by then, that the development of matter

117

progresses from its most primitive forms, through various minerals to organic life, and to its highest form – the harmony of matter organized by reason. In that case the appearance of life on Earth is not the result of chance, but the logical outcome of development. The only area of chance could be in the fact that it was on Earth that matter reached the supreme point of its development, but from here life should spread throughout the whole expanse of the Universe. That is why the Earth should be, as it were, the Universe's seed, which, when the time comes, will grow and involve the matter of the Universe in a new form of existence.

In that way even greater responsibility is placed on reason as the decisive factor in turning cosmic matter into some form of single harmonized organism of nature. When he considered the present-day state of nature Z was acutely aware that in a mutually interdependent world there were no limits to the spread of reason, that in its elementary form it was inherent in all of nature, and that was why, in its miserable present-day state, it was reaching out to human reason and, through it, striving for active development. It was as though all the dispersed wisdom of creation was concentrated in mankind.

Z had read and made notes on Engels's *Anti-Dühring*. At the head of his notes he had written out the following sentence:

> But if we then come to ask what are thought and consciousness, where do they come from, then it transpires that they are products of the human mind, and that man is himself a product of nature, developing in and together with the world around him; from which it follows naturally that those things that spring from the human mind are, in the last analysis, also products of nature, and they do not contradict but agree with the whole of the rest of nature.

Z was also excited by reading what Timiryazev had to say in his popular science work *The Life of Plants*, which seemed to develop Engels's ideas further. Timiryazev posed questions which meant a great deal to Z:

> Does a plant have a consciousness? Let's answer this question with another one: do all animals possess such a sense? If we grant this to all animals, then why do we deny it to plants? And if we deny it to the most primitive of animals, then tell me where, on which rung of the ladder of organic development, is this *threshold* of consciousness? Where is the boundary beyond which an object becomes a subject? How can we find a way out of this dilemma? Should we assume that consciousness is spread throughout nature, that it glimmers dully in the lower orders of

creatures, and only burns like a bright flame in the human power of reason?

That is why it is precisely the bearer of reason – mankind – who should recognize his mission, and take on the task of caring for all non-human nature, and of resolving those agonizing contradictions which control this planet's nature at the present stage of its development. But is mankind prepared for the role allotted him by destiny? Z had to recognize sadly how imperfect were the relations between humanity and nature, just as there was a lack of harmony in all of nature in its present form. As early as 1928 he had written about man's dwelling-place:

> . . . there the primus is set up like a rack,
> on it, crackling in terror,
> moans a poor fish,
> covered in oily green pimples;
> there the corpses of washed-out animals
> lie on cold griddles
> and iron pots – the fonts of tears –
> crown this apotheosis of evil.

Then, in 1929, filled with sympathy for nature in its painful process of evolution, he wrote the poem 'A Walk', which begins with the words:

> The animals have no names –
> who ordered them to be called anything?
> equality of suffering –
> that is their unseen lot.*

Further on we find: 'The whole of nature was smiling, like a massive prison', 'and all of nature laughs, dying every minute'. And again in the poem 'Snakes': 'And nature, bored in an instant, stands above him like a prison.' Much as he was aware of the Darwinian concept of competition in nature, Z was trying to find something to counter the egotistical battle for survival. One of these early attempts at an optimistic interpretation can be seen in the poem from 1928, 'The Bakehouse'. In it mankind's urban existence is depicted as something unnatural, suppressing all the vital forces of nature. The evening is dying 'like a light-bulb in a glass jar', and further:

> The sunset fires of evening, like fantastic wounds,
> were smoking, as they subsided downwards;
> on the roofs the house tiles
> met them in the simulacrum of faces,
> drawn in a half grimace of malice.

---

* Full translation on p.350.

And in the midst of this city with its malevolent face there wanders something animal and elemental (in the manner of Filonov), symbolized by rising dough. Nothing, it would seem, can stop its 'triumphant progress'. But no! There emerge as tamers of this hostile element the bakers, who by dint of their reason, will and labour are called upon to give form to its primitive savagery. As a result of the transformation that takes place in the oven the dough becomes the infant bread – symbol of the birth of a new, perfected world ('the infant bread raised its arms and seemed to speak words of harmony'). This was the poet's first expression of the idea of the organizing role of thinking humanity in the taming and shaping of the elemental principles of existence.

This theme was developed further in 'The Triumph of Agriculture'. The image of the 'infant bread' was transformed into the 'infant world', where mankind, having perfected its own society, ceases to exploit the animals and the rest of nature and sets about creating new, harmonious relations between all its elements. In this long poem Z also gave expression to. Vernadsky's important idea that human reason should change the very structure of the organism of mankind itself, directing its development towards acquiring the capacity for autotropy, in other words the ability to absorb directly the energy of the sun and mineral substances, in the same way as chlorophyl plants do. Mankind would thus become physiologically independent of other forms of life, and need no longer consume them, but create relationships based on the highest ethical ideals.

In 1931 Z wrote 'The School for Beetles' and a long poem 'The Crazy Wolf'. Before setting about the writing of 'The School for Beetles', in the room on Bolshaya Pushkarskaya, he got out from under the bed a little wooden chest with his collection of polished pieces of wood from various species of trees, and he looked at the design of the tree fibres and tried to figure out in it the sense of this secret script of growth. In the twisting shapes of the year-rings of a maple he imagined he could see the surf on the shore, in the wood of the plane tree he could see the prototype of weaving, and in that of the ash tree the shapes of the clouds. In the poet's mind there was born the metaphorical image of a single world, the multitude of whose interpenetrating constituent parts were recast from shape to shape and reflected in themslves the multiform nature of the whole. When this world is ordered by consciousness, a thinking cow will take a course in buttermaking, and the camel will dance around a dish which catches the energy from the sun, the body of the potato will develop an organ for thought, and selfless humans will symbolically transfer their brains to asses, 'so that the thinking kingdom of the animals shall blossom'. Reason will become a universal attribute of nature. Such is the fundamental idea of 'The School for Beetles'.

In 'The Crazy Wolf' Z once more developed the idea of the awakening of reason in animals and plants. The poet imagines a world in which there are 'well-behaved wolves, dressed in light clothing, and devoted to lengthy scholarly discussions', while a wolf philosopher, having overcome the power of the Earth's gravity, is floating about in the air, 'so as to teach the burdocks the geometry of the sky'. Here it is difficult to distinguish where the artistic image, the grandiose metaphor, shades into Z's actual perceptions about the development of the world. It could well be, in fact, that the essential meaning of the poem resides in a consideration of the dialectic unity of dream and reality. Well aware of the fantastic and fairy-tale nature of his images, the poet, as it were, answers sceptics and opponents:

> The Madman's dreams are absurd,
> but anyone who is not blind can see, –
> any one of us, baking loaves,
> seems absurd to the old world.

> The ages pass, the years go by,
> yet all that lives is not a dream:
> it lives and supersedes
> the truth of yesterday's laws.

We have to interpret 'baking loaves' to mean, in the context of Z's other writings, building new relationships in the world – relationships based on reason and justice. He himself did not consider his ideas and images either absurd or remote from the world around him. He regarded his natural-philosophical ideas as proper material for poetic revelations, in just the same way as other poets looked upon their feelings for the woman they loved or their delight in the external beauty of nature.

The unexpected image in the poem of the crazy dreamer-wolf represented for Z the perfectly real dreamer-man. At the end of 1931 there came into his hands a slim 32-page pamphlet by Konstantin Eduardovich Tsiolkovsky, published by the great man himself in 1929 in Kaluga. The very title of the booklet, *Plants of the future. Animals of the cosmos. Spontaneous generation*, could not but attract the attention of the author of 'The Triumph of Agriculture' and 'The Crazy Wolf'. In his work Tsiolkovsky dealt with the imperfection of earthly organisms and the direction of their development, with the conscious remodelling of plants, soils and the make-up of the atmosphere, with the possibility

121

for mankind of autotropic nutrition, and with the development of the more perfect organisms of the future and their relations with those less developed. So gripped was Z by the scientist's bold imagination that he immediately wrote him a letter with a request that he send him other works he had written on similar themes. He made the request not only in his own name, but also on behalf of his friends: 'I feel that your books will be of great significance to me and to my friends, and we shall be eternally grateful to you for them.'

Tsiolkovsky responded to the poet's request at once and sent him several of his pamphlets published in the years 1925–30: *The Monism of the Universe, The Reason for the Cosmos, The Perfect State of the Earth, The Past of the Earth, The Future of the Earth and Mankind, The Will of the Universe* and others.

On 18 January 1932, Z wrote another letter to Kaluga, in which he thanked Tsiolkovsky for the books he had sent, and gave him his first impressions on reading them. He wrote:

> I received your books, and I thank you from the bottom of my heart. I have read almost all of them already, but I have done so very much at a rush. Something so new and so huge has come upon me that I haven't the strength to think it right through to the end: my head is too much in a whirl.
>
> I cannot find words to express my appreciation of your life and works. I have always known that the life of outstanding people is a selfless feat of great heroism. Yet each time that I actually come face to face with such a feat, I am amazed over and over again: how strong humanity is capable of being! And now, when I have come into contact with you, my heart is full of joy again – the best of all earthly joys – joy for man and mankind.

The part of the letter quoted was published by Tsiolkovsky in a section headed 'Critical Responses', contained in a pamphlet brought out in 1932 and entitled *The Semi-jet-propelled Stratoplane*. The author sent a signed copy of this to Z, who immediately bound together the eighteen pamphlets he had already received into a single book, placed in it the article with the author's signature which he had just received, and valued the whole collection highly for the rest of his life.

Tsiolkovsky's letters to Z have not been preserved. But they did exist. On 26 January, on the day after the birth of his son, Z told his wife when he visited her in the maternity home: 'I have had a very friendly card from Tsiolkovsky. The old man is a splendid fellow!'

Z made a close study of the works of the dreamer from Kaluga, and in the letter to him dated 18 January 1932, he said: 'I find your ideas

122

about the future of the Earth, mankind, the animals and the plants enormously exciting, and they are very close to my own. I have tried to resolve them, as best I can, in my unpublished poems. Now that I have become familiar with your ideas there is much that I shall have to rethink.' Further on in the letter Z introduced extracts from 'The Triumph of Agriculture' and 'The School for Beetles' to show how close his ideas were to the themes contained in Tsiolkovsky's writings.

Where the nature of Tsiolkovsky's natural-philosophical ideas was concerned Z was attracted primarily by their monism, which affirmed, in essence, the absolute material oneness of the world. All-embracing matter in its various forms of existence, the reflection of the great in the small, and the small in the great, did not allow for the contrasting of such concepts as macrocosm and microcosm, Earth and the Universe, living and dead, humanity and the surrounding world, reason and matter. Proceeding from the monism of the Universe, and the infinity of time and space, Tsiolkovsky rejected the exclusiveness of life on Earth, and maintained that reason was an attribute not only of humanity but of other beings in the Universe. As a result he drew bold and sometimes fantastic pictures of the future of the Earth, nature and mankind. He proclaimed the immortality and eternal happiness of highly organized thinking beings.

He perceived living beings as an accumulation of atoms. In the form of a living being, and especially of the brain, these atoms realize their potential for feeling. Outside living matter they exist in a state of semi-consciousness so that in practical terms time does not exist for them. After the death and decay of the living organism sooner or later the atoms find their way into the make-up of another living body, and begin to live and feel once more. In this way for atoms life is practically unbroken and infinite. But the life of matter in imperfect organisms, such as the animal kingdom on earth, is full of suffering. For this reason animals should be gradually and painlessly excluded from life, so that in the future only super-developed beings will remain.

Despite his respect for Tsiolkovsky's ideas and his desire to make them part of his own thinking, Z could not agree with some of the scientist's conclusions, though he fully accepted the concept of monism. In the same letter to Tsiolkovsky he complained that he could not understand everything in the latter's discussions of immortality. 'It's not clear to me, for example,' he writes, 'why my life will continue after my death.'

If the atoms which make up my body are wandering round the Universe, and they become part of other more developed organisms, then their

previous links will not be renewed, and it follows that I cannot be reborn
. . . It's all a matter, obviously, of how man understands himself and
feels. You obviously feel yourself so firmly and clearly in the kingdom of
the atoms, while we, your correspondents, cannot get away from looking
at ourselves as something whole and indivisible. After all, it's one thing
to know something, and another to feel it. A conservative feeling, bred
into us over the centuries, clings to our power of knowledge, and
prevents it from moving forward.

Neither could Z agree with Tsiolkovsky's view that the lower forms of
life must gradually be liquidated. Z believed that they would be
organically absorbed into the general system of the renewal of
existence, and with the help of human reason they would develop
within this system, making their unique contribution to the total moral
and physical value of the world.

Z believed, in addition, that all objects in nature contained those
laws of its development and perfection without which humankind could
not conduct its activities. Thus every blade of grass was of the utmost
value to the whole of the rest of nature. Such a way of looking at things
was deeply moral.

As a natural consequence, there also developed in Z's poetry the
concept of the wisdom of nature, displayed not only by mankind, but,
in their contact with it, by all branches of existence. As early as 1926 he
was writing about this in the poem 'The Face of the Horse'. Now he
began to maintain that hidden within nature were all the preconditions
for its transformation with the aid of human reason, and that in this
sense nature was the teacher of mankind. The task before us consisted
in uncovering these riddles of nature, solving them, and using the
answers gained for the common good.

This idea is especially clearly expressed in a poem from 1932,
'Autumn' ('In a sheepskin cloak . . .'):

> . . . In nature unconcealed,
> so severe, malevolent and imperfect,
> so luxuriant and so mean, –
> there is a wonderful power. Take it in your hands,
> breathe it, renew its particles –
> and you will be freer than a light bird
> among the perfect rivers and the enlightened cliffs.

In the poem 'Garlanded with Fruits' Z gave his own interpretation of
the biblical legend of the apple from the Tree of Knowledge, and wrote
about the fruits of plants:

I would include you in my library,
I would read you and write out the laws,
that you have preserved . . .

Z's perception of nature rested on a double understanding of its role. He viewed it as being at once both pupil and teacher, a receptacle of chaos and savagery and at the same time the bearer of wise laws, directed at achieving harmony. The lack of equilibrium between these two principles at times caused him emotional confusion. Thus the hero of 'Lodeynikov', a poem of 1932, has conflicting pictures of nature revealed to him. He sees the savage struggle of plants for existence:

And this was the battle of the grasses, the silent struggle of the plants.
Some, stretching forth their sappy stems
and opening their leaves, crush others with their weight,
and the tautness of their joints puts forth
a thick slime. Others have crept into the gap
between the leaves of yet others. There are some too
have lodged themselves on neighbours as on a bed
and pulled them back and worn them out . . .

But Lodeynikov also sees a second picture that would seem to cancel out the first one:

. . . above the village
rose the misty horn of the moon,
and gradually the rustle of the grass and the silence
was turning into singing.
Nature was singing. The forest lifted up its face,
and sang together with the meadow. The pure body of the stream
echoed it all, like a resonant ring.

In 1933 Z wrote three long poems on natural-philosophical subjects – 'The Trees', 'The Birds' and 'The Clouds'. In 'The Trees', written at the beginning of that year, an attempt is made to explain and justify the dual character of nature. The main character, Bombeyev, like Lodeynikov, has discovered in the whirlpool of nature 'the terrible traits of cannibalism' and has tried to bring an end to this mutual destruction. Yet his 'gaze is sorrowful', he does not know how to achieve his goal. He realizes that he simply has to place his trust in the fact that at some time or other every little gnat, 'reading in its gnat language, will be filled with noble doctrine'.

As a contrast to Bombeyev we meet Lesnichy (meaning Forester), the man of science. Just like the Soldier in 'The Triumph of Agriculture', he regards the world from an optimistic point of view, and sees it as

125

foreshadowing the future ideal world, while he sees mankind as the builder of this world. By a process of painful evolution nature has given birth to man, at the price of ghastly sacrifice it has developed in him the power of reason, and the sacrifice has not been in vain: man's reason is the guarantee of the liberation of nature. Forester instructs Bombeyev:

> Through the mouths, the stomachs, the gullets,
> Through the intestinal prison
> Lies the central path of nature
> To the blessed mind.
> So, long live the battle,
> And the roar of the beasts, and the thunder of the guns,
> And the transfiguration of all living things
> In one world consciousness!

As we can see, Bombeyev and Forester have a common aim – to liberate nature from suffering and self-destruction, but only Forester knows the effective means to achieve this aim. There is no point bemoaning the ox you have just eaten; you should trust in the laws of nature, which, though they may be savage at times, are nevertheless wise.

The poet placed great value on the idea that nature contained within it a skilful blueprint for its own perfection, and if we did not always recognize this blueprint, and did not always like it when we did, then this was not nature's fault, but the result of our own limited powers of understanding. According to Z the education of nature by man, its thinking transformer, was not the whole purpose of its wisdom. In the concluding section of the long poem 'The Trees' there is a symbolic description of the complex life of the forest, of the music of its work, which brings together the complementary views of Forester and Bombeyev. The universal wisdom of nature exists outside mankind, and is directed through its laws at developing the world towards Goodness-Beauty-Truth. Though they are still not attainable by reason these laws are spread throughout the world as some kind of 'pure concept'. 'Mind, do not seek among the trees: it is among them, and to the side, and here, and everywhere' – these are the words with which 'The Trees' concludes.

In March 1933, Z wrote the long poem 'The Birds',* in which he also affirmed the dialectical oneness of nature as mankind's pupil and as his teacher. The poem's content is briefly as follows.

An old teacher and his pupil are engaged in the study of the

* See full translation on pp.358–63.

anatomical structure of birds, using a dove as a sacrifice to scientific knowledge. Birds fly in from all the surrounding areas to take part in the lesson. Man is anxious to probe the mystery of flight which the birds understand, while magpies, herons, crows, jays, robins and warblers can become familiar with the way they are built, and can share in man's ideas. Sensing the approach of death, yet aware of a growing feeling of oneness with nature, the old teacher is ready to meet his end in peace and wisdom. Just before his death the old man exclaims (and these words contain the quintessence of the author's ideas):

> Could I assimilate this will of mine to the will
> of Nature, my word to the visionary word,
> could I envisage how all that I see – birds, animals, trees,
> stones, rivers and lakes – were homogeneous limbs
> of a single marvellous body, then, without doubt,
> should I be the better creator, my reason not blunder,
> striding the highroad of truth. Benighted my science;
> yet even now something speaks of the mighty chain
> of creation, where all metamorphoses are directed
> to a single wise end: that old, worn-out forms
> should be recast into vessels of more perfect aspect.

This is what Z was striving for – to recognize all that exists as being part of the construction of the one miraculous body of nature. And at that point death disappears, and human reason becomes the common property of the animals, the birds, the trees, and even the rocks, the rivers, and the lakes. Also built in to this miraculous body is a law maintaining its movement in the direction of perfection, of moral purity and harmony.

Z gave the typed-out text of this poem to Stepanov so that the latter could read it through and then find a place for it in a journal. Beneath the title he had placed the dedication 'To the memory of my father'. In doing so Z confirmed that the model for the hero of the poem, the elderly natural scientist, had been his father – the agronomist Aleksey Agafonovich. Some time afterwards Z and his wife visited the Stepanovs, and on that occasion alterations were made to the text: some small corrections were made, the dedication was removed and the lyrical ending to the poem was replaced. The new concluding lines gave firm expression to the author's views on the role of humanity in the transformation of nature:

> Past the houses walks Sleep . . . Earth, mother mine, I know
> your immutable law. Not as plunderer, but as wise husbandman
> man has now come, and acting for everyone's good,

will manage your life. That I know. With what love
grasses nestle to grasses! With what chirping and whistling
birds circle birds! How incorruptibly splendid
Nature will be! And thought, coming home to the heart,
thought of mankind – how triumphantly will it be kindled!
Feastday of Nature! I place my trust in your coming.

[version of 1936]

The poem remained in the editorial offices of the journal *Zvezda* for a long time, yet it was never published.

In a letter to his wife at Siverskaya, dated 26 May 1933, Z told her that the composition of a new long poem 'The Clouds' was progressing and that he had already written the second section, consisting of a hundred lines. He was not going to read the poem to anyone until he had finished it. Further on in the letter he wrote: 'Kaverin has suggested that I write a filmscript for a young audience – I turned it down because I am very much afraid that the same thing will happen as happened with the book for Lyadova and Zhitkov. At the moment, while something adult is getting written, I shouldn't waste time on anything else . . .'

'The Clouds' has not survived, and would seem to be the greatest loss from Z's poetic legacy, since, by all accounts, it contained a broad, generalized presentation of the poet's view of the world. Z began to read sections of the poem to his friends in the autumn of the same year. On 16 October he visited Kharms, and read the whole poem to him. On the same day we find Kharms writing to K. V. Pugachova:

Zabolotsky was here today. He's been interested in architecture for some time, and now he's written a long poem full of remarkable ideas about architecture and human life. Lots of people will be very excited by this, I know. But I also know that it's a bad poem. It's only good in a few places, and then almost by accident. There are two categories involved.

The first category is understandable and simple. It's quite clear what has to be done. You can see what you've got to aim for, what to achieve and how to do it. You can see a pathway. You can discuss this, and there'll be a time when some literary critic will write a whole book about it, and some commentator six volumes about what it means. In this category everything is fine.

But about the second category nobody will say a word, even though it's what makes all the architecture and the idea about human life worthwhile. It's unintelligible, unfathomable, and at the same time beautiful – the second category! But you cannot reach it, it's even absurd to try to do so, there are no paths leading to it. It's just something like this second category that would make a man give up everything and immerse himself in mathematics, and then suddenly give up mathematics and become interested in Arab music, then get married, then murder his wife and child and lie on his stomach and look at a flower.

This is that very unsuccessful category from which genius emerges. (Incidentally, I'm not talking here about Z, he hasn't murdered his wife yet, and he hasn't even been enthused by mathematics).

Kharms inwardly could not come to terms with the fact that, as the *Oberiu* writers put on their placard, 'Kolya's gone to sea', in other words Z's poetry had diverged from the 'classical' *Oberiu* line and gone off into uncharted waters. It was the aspect of the poem that had a paraphraseable content and reflected this new direction to which Kharms was objecting; the parts that came from the *Oberiu* background – the indefinable and irrational impulse – were the ones that he liked. It is also clear, however, that the poem as a whole produced a great impression on him. Not without justification did he maintain that a lot of people would get very excited about it. From surviving remarks jotted down in his notebook we can get some inkling about the characters in the poem, and some approximate idea of its contents.

As far as the philosophy in 'The Clouds' is concerned it would seem that it owes much to 'The Triumph of Agriculture', 'The Trees', 'The Birds', 'Autumn' ('The Signs of Autumn') and to other works by Z from this period. The poet reproduced the architectural ensemble of creation, the 'structure of pictures of nature', in which the complex picturesque whole is formed from the mutual interaction of the parts. To judge from Kharms's notes, the main characters were the clouds ('misshapen, puffy and depressed'), a stream, peasants, a shepherd and an old man, animals, ancestors, the Philosopher and the Builder, and messengers. Bathing took place in the stream, the shepherd died, the messengers conducted conversations, a 'window of second sight' was revealed, and the Philosopher sat talking with someone until the early hours . . .

Regardless of the complexity of the poem's construction, Z was happy with it, just as he was generally happy with the results of his work in the first six months of 1933; his friends noticed this. Kharms wrote at the time: 'Man finds salvation in his work, and so he should always be at his work, so as to be happy. Only belief in the success of your work will bring happiness. Zabolotsky must be happy now.'

But that same year 1933 was also to bring severe trials for the poet who was tasting creative happiness.

IV

As early as 1932, before he left for Belorussia on military service, Z had decided that the time had come to publish a new collection of his poems. The wave of articles roundly condemning his first book *Columns* had already receded. A decree on the reconstruction of literary and artistic organizations had been issued by the Central Committee of the Party, and as a result RAPP, the Association of Proletarian Writers, had been closed down, and a more gentle policy towards all writers had been introduced. True, this was only if they were genuinely attempting to understand and depict socialist construction. In such circumstances it was to be hoped that Z's book might get through the official filters.

Z assembled the collection with great care. He divided the poems into two sections, headed 'Columns' and 'The Trees'. A third section was devoted to the long poem 'The Triumph of Agriculture'. The section 'Columns' contained thirty poems, among them all those, with one exception, that had been included in the eponymous collection of 1929. This was a brazen attempt at a second publication of *Columns*, and of the full text of 'The Triumph of Agriculture', sections of which had also been sharply criticized when they were published separately. From this we can see that the poet had not obediently fallen into line, had not accepted the 'lessons' of his critics, but had remained true to his creative intention. The section entitled 'The Trees' included poems which represented the latest direction of Z's poetic thought, although in thematic and chronological terms they were closely related to the preceding section. 'The Crazy Wolf' had at that time not yet been classified as a separate long poem*, and was placed in the section 'The Trees'. The long poems of 1933 were still unwritten and therefore could obviously not be included in the book. The resulting collection was reasonably extensive, and was put together exclusively in accordance with the taste and wishes of the author, without any deference to the party line or to official requirements. It was naturally a matter of pressing concern to Z to have it published exactly as it stood. The publication of this new book would demonstrate to everybody that the poet Z was alive and kicking, was maturing, and was conquering new poetic territory.

It was not without humour that Lidiya Ginzburg recalled how the

---

* Russians make a generic distinction between the short or lyric poem, *stikhotvoreniye*, and the long or epic poem, *poema* [Ed.].

text, with the simple title 'Poems 1926–1932', was handed in at the Leningrad publishing house:

Zabolotsky brought his material for the new collection to the Writers' Publishing House. In the end they said that they would have a go at it. But they kept finding things they did not like. They did not like 'The ass was singing of freedom in the cattle-shed'. He sat down there and then and corrected it to: 'The ass was singing of nature in the cattle-shed' (actually he wrote: 'In the cattle-shed the ass was singing of nature' – N.Z). They did not like: 'in Red Army bonnets'. He corrected it to: 'in Red Army spiked helmets'. They did not like: 'the sentry stands like a doll'. He at once wrote out: 'the sentry stands like a turnip'. But they liked that even less.

Z became a regular visitor at the publishing house, settling every conceivable kind of question that arose as the collection made its way through the publishing process. On 2 August he wrote to his wife at Siverskaya:

Yesterday the Writers' Publishing House accepted my book of poems for printing – with some small alterations and a preface which they want Matveyev to write. We can't start leaping up and down yet, though. The book has still got to pass the censor. All the same, I shall be signing a contract on the 5th, and they have promised some money. I shall ask for more money – they have got to help us get through.

On his return from Belorussia Z was full of bright hopes and was already savouring his pleasure at the new edition. In a letter to his old Urzhum friend Kasyanov he wrote:

Dear Misha, I'm so glad that I have managed to track you down. *Columns* is my only book of poems. It came out in 1929, and was sold out within a few days, both in Leningrad and in Moscow. So far it has not been republished because it caused a rare old scandal and I was excommunicated . . . As to the book itself, my last copy was pinched two years ago, and even in my work now I'm using someone else's. But this winter I hope to bring out the first volume to contain the whole of *Columns*. The book has already been accepted for printing, and if there are no further complications, everything will be all right. As soon as the book comes out I shall send you your own copy. (10 September 1932)

It was, of course, Z who had proposed that the preface be written by V. P. Matveyev, under whom he had worked at *Soyuzfoto*. He came from a long line of revolutionaries, and was a renowned Civil War hero. He was an associate of Kirov and was one of his supporters in the Leningrad party. As a brave and honest man, he wholeheartedly opposed the way people were currently being watched and informed upon. His opinions were sharp and outspoken, and he opened the eyes of Z and his colleagues to much that was going on. Stepanov records in his memoirs:

> On one occasion Zabolotsky and I were invited to visit Matveyev. There were six in his family, and so it was rather crowded at table. I was surprised to find how sharp he was in his sarcastic denunciations of bureaucratic procedures and the philistine stupidity of officials. He was outspoken and witty about matters which we had decided to discuss in only the closest of circles . . . After Kirov's murder he was one of the first to be arrested, and was evidently shot almost at once.

It soon became clear that the hopes of Z's book coming out quickly had been premature. To begin with there was difficulty with the introductory preface. In the end it was written by the editor-in-chief himself, I. A. Vinogradov. It was not badly written, and showed some understanding of Z's work, but there were all kinds of reservations, corrections and mistakes, and these grew in number the longer the book remained in the publishing house. After someone had been through the article with a red pencil, the following kind of marginal note appeared: 'There is a significant ideological flaw in the very understanding of nature itself. Moreover, nature pushes the life of society into the background.' In the place in the article where Vinogradov had written: 'The kulak is depicted primarily as an enemy of nature, as someone who destroys the harvest', the following instruction had appeared in the margin: 'Remove these sections from the poem' (not from the article, but from the poem 'The Triumph of Agriculture'). It was considered a great sin to write about nature outside the context of the class struggle, or not according to the established stereotype.

In this connection it is interesting to look at the review of Dovzhenko's film *Earth*, which Z admired very much. In issues 11–12 of the newspaper *Smena* for 1930 the reviewer wrote: 'In his attempt to show the class struggle in the Ukrainian countryside, Dovzhenko in places loses his control over the subject and starts to let nature take the upper hand. The biological episodes (the death of the old man, the woman's pregnancy, the girl's love, the flowering of the apple tree) at times begin to take precedence over the social ones.' Even such subjects as old age and death, a girl's love, and the blossoming of the trees were considered by this critic as something reprehensible and impermissible.

Another heinous sin at this time was formalism, by which was meant the alienation of objects from their 'new relationships with the surrounding reality' (Vinogradov), in other words, once again, from the struggle with the class enemy. Through no fault of Z's, the revised introductory preface was far from lucid.

Despite his worries about the difficulties the book was having at the publisher's, at the beginning of 1933 Z was in a hopeful mood, and wrote the long poems 'The Trees', 'The Birds' and 'The Clouds' in quick succession. Every time he arrived at Siverskaya to visit his family and bring them the food he had collected on their ration cards, Yekaterina naturally wanted to know straight away how things were at the publishing house, but, by a well-established ritual, she could not ask her husband about it as soon as he got through the door. First he would get his breath back after the journey, have something to eat, and only then would he tell her about the book and what was going on in literary circles. Either in the winter of 1932 or at the beginning of 1933 he told his wife that he had taken the long poem 'The Triumph of Agriculture' and two shorter poems – 'The Signs of the Zodiac are Growing Dim' and 'Lodeynikov' – to the offices of the journal *Zvezda*. Nikolay Tikhonov, who was in charge of the poetry section there, promised to get them published. Now this publication, as well as that of the book, was awaited with impatience.

One early spring day Z was held up at the editorial office, and it was already getting dark when he arrived at the dacha. He had to walk some two and a half kilometres carrying a heavy bag of shopping. In the growing darkness he blundered into a ditch full of half-melted snow, and got wet up to the waist. When he finally reached the dacha, he had to change his damp clothing, and in his fluster he momentarily forgot what it was he had been so anxious to tell his wife. There had been a row about the publication of *Zvezda*. After the run of Nos. 2–3 of the journal, containing the selection of his poems, had already been printed, someone up above had demanded that the title of chapter three of 'The Triumph of Agriculture' should be changed. The chapter dealt with a kulak, and the demand was that it be called 'The Enemy' instead of 'The Exile', and that corresponding abbreviations and corrections be made to the text. It was not permissible to show sympathy towards a kulak by referring to him as an exile: he had to be given the generally acceptable label – enemy. Making these special alterations had delayed Z in the city on that particular day.

From the already printed copies of the journal two pages were cut out and replaced by others, containing the newly set-up text. Only a few copies of *Zvezda* in the original format managed to get distributed and have survived.

Z's poems in *Zvezda* appeared at exactly the wrong moment. Neither the dissolution of RAPP, nor the new chapter heading – 'The Enemy' –

could save them. Somehow Z's works always contrived to be out of step with the outside world. A terrible famine was stalking the countryside and the villages, the newly established collective farms were on the point of collapse – and at that very moment a poem appeared with (from the authorities' point of view) the sarcastic title 'The Triumph of Agriculture': a poem, moreover, which advocated entirely new aims for the transformation of agriculture, aims that were unintelligible to the proletariat. The publication in *Zvezda* proved to be a gift of a target for the critics.

One of the first to attack the renewed publication of his poems was the critic Ye. Usievich. In her article 'Behind the Mask of Buffoonery' (*Literaturny kritik*, 1933, No.4) political accusations were to the fore, as was to be expected. Once more such expressions were used as 'a malicious caricature of socialism', 'a lampoon on the collectivization of agriculture', 'we must fight him, and unmask him as an enemy'. Usievich was particularly disturbed by what she saw as the growing 'pernicious' influence of Z on younger writers. Usievich's article acted as a signal for a new wave of persecution of the writer, conducted in the 'best' traditions of RAPP criticism. In *Literaturnaya gazeta* of 11 July 1933, for instance, O. Beskin wrote the following about 'The Triumph of Agriculture':

> This nonsensical idyll is objectively opposed (whether Zabolotsky intends it or not) to the building of socialism and the classless society, which is being conducted in conditions of the most intense and widespread class conflict. A socialist triumph of agriculture, attainable by the coming together of animals (and at the same time fruits) with people, the tractor in the role of liberator of domestic animals from slavery – this is not only simply *Oberiu* nonsense, but some sort of politically reactionary religious mumbo-jumbo, which finds common cause with the kulaks in the villages, and in literature with the Klyuyevs and the Klychkovs.

The main critical assault on Z followed on 21 July 1933; the national newspaper *Pravda* published an article by V. Yermilov entitled 'Poetry that fools about and poetry for the millions'. This savage attack led off with an extensive quotation of Stalin's words about tearing the mask from the face of the disguised enemy. The quotation included the following: 'Today's kulaks and petty kulaks, today's anti-Soviet elements in the countryside are for the most part "gentle" people, "nice" people, almost "holy". . . . In order to see through such a cunning enemy, and not to succumb to demagogy, we have to maintain revolutionary vigilance, we have to be capable of tearing the mask from our enemy. . .'

The main aim of the rest of the article was to show that in poetry Z had become just such an enemy. His 'Triumph of Agriculture' was 'the basest of lampoons on collectivization'. The article finished with a call to sweep out of poetry all vestiges of buffoonery and stupidity, which included, in Yermilov's opinion, Z's works.

Soon afterwards, on 30 August, *Pravda*, in an article signed by S. Rosental, once more maintained that Z's 'crazy poetry is definitely kulak in character'. Alongside Shklovsky, Mandelshtam and Vaginov, Z was categorized as a remnant of the old classes and literary movements, going back to such 'enemies of the revolution' as Merezhkovsky, Berdyayev and Filosofov. The absurdity of making a connection between 'kulak' poetry and 'the shadow of Petersburg' (that is what the article was called) evidently did not seem to have occurred to anyone. Usievich, Yermilov and Rosental were joined in their attacks and denunciations of Z by such influential critics at the time as K. Zelinsky, A. Tarasenkov, D. Mirsky and V. Druzin. Nothing that they wrote had much to do with the real essence of Z's poetry. They were simply following the official requirements of the time. In Tarasenkov's article, for example, that bore the ironic title 'In Praise of Zabolotsky' (on the model of Erasmus's *In Praise of Folly*), a typical passage was:

He has depicted mankind's greatest struggle in the world as a stupid and pointless pastime. He has pranced about playing the fool, sticking his tongue out, telling dirty jokes in places where he was talking about the cause led by the Leninist Party, guided by its leader, the steel Bolshevik with the name of steel [Stalin]. . .

In a letter to Tikhonov dated 14 November 1933, written after he had read this article, Pavel Antokolsky complained:

Have you had a chance to see Tarasenkov's article on Zabolotsky in *Krasnaya Nov*? Although the author is a friend of mine, I must admit that his article is an example of impotent rage. How offensive it is that things are going so badly for Zabolotsky, and that he's being so wilfully and savagely misunderstood! And yet there's an outward appearance of truth in what Tarasenkov says, he's got every right to solve such indeterminate equations in this way. . . But that makes it worse!

Such a tense atmosphere had grown up around Z that even his book at the Leningrad Writers' Publishing House was coming under threat. Despite the fact that it had already been typeset, a round of fresh rearrangements and excisions began, as the publishing house was still unhappy with what the author had submitted. In the middle of July, fourteen poems and 'The Triumph of Agriculture' were removed as unsatisfactory. To replace them Z supplied four new poems. But even these changes to the contents could not save things. Following the *Pravda* article the type was broken up, and the book never came into existence.

After this failure Z never in his life had the chance to put together a collection of his poetry for publication in the way that he wanted to – without taking any of the publishers' demands into account. The proof copies of the book were, however, preserved. Z rebound one himself in a dark red binding, and treasured it as part of his own archive.

The violent critical attacks, the threatening political accusations, the crushing of his hopes for a new collection of poems – all this had a disastrous effect on Z. To make things worse it had become clear that Party policy towards literature had not only not changed for the better, but, if anything, had become more severe and more tendentious. And while Z had managed to bear the blows of the critics reasonably stoically so far, he now realized that in the conditions that had arisen it was impossible for him to go on following his own, original line in literature. The year 1933, which had begun so well and so fruitfully for him, saw the start of deep depression and disillusionment, and a falling off in creativity. Nor could he derive much pleasure even from his publications in childrens' magazines, which included some of his best poems for children, 'The Tale of the One-eyed Man' and 'How the Mice fought the Cat'. When all was said and done, writing for children was a sideline, and could never provide complete satisfaction.

Z did not want to believe that his philosophy and his poetry were not suitable for Soviet literature, but he had to stop and take thought. For a long while he stopped writing original verse. After finishing work on 'The Clouds' in the summer of 1933, he did not write a single poem until December 1934. At that time he wrote two, in 1935 another two, and only in 1936 was there a period of greater activity. During the period of silence he directed all his creative efforts to the reworking of foreign classics for children and young people, and to the translation of poetry from other languages.

Some time before, when Z had been living on Konnaya Street, there lay on his desk a large format edition in French of Rabelais's *Gargantua et Pantagruel*, with illustrations by Gustave Doré. It was possibly then that he conceived the idea of using motifs from Rabelais as the basis of a new work for children. Now the time had come for such an undertaking. He decided to rework the book for younger readers. In the third issue of *Yozh* for 1934 there appeared the first part of 'The Tale of the Amazing Life of the Great Gargantua', with a foreword by Z. At the end of that year, after the whole work had appeared in *Yozh*, he set about preparing a separate edition of the book, checking the text once more, and consulting with experts in the French of the period.

The work was unusual and difficult. In the course of it Z elaborated the method of reworking and translating that he was to use in all his later projects of this kind. In the article 'Rabelais for children' (1935) he described it in the following way:

> It enabled me to escape completely from translator's language, with its inevitable artificiality. In its place I worked out a sort of linguistic system of my own, which, although it was further from the original in the literal sense, was nevertheless in essence near to it. It was not formal accuracy that interested me here, but an inner closeness to Rabelais.

Over the years 1934–5, at the suggestion of Yury Tynyanov, Z transposed into blank verse the longish poem by Grigol Orbeliani, 'The Toast of Honour'. This first attempt at translating Georgian classical poetry proved to be successful. Next he wrote the scenario for a film for children, 'The Adventures of Baron Münchhausen', based on the well-known work by Raspé. Encouraged by his success in reworking Rabelais, in 1935 he began work on a similar project, using the book by Charles de Costière, *Til Eulenspiegel*. Z's *Eulenspiegel* appeared in the magazine *Kostyor* (*Bonfire*), and came out in book form in 1936 and 1937. He also rewrote for children part of Swift's *Gulliver's Travels* – in *Chizh* this work was published under the title 'Gulliver in the Land of the Giants'.

The work on translation and rewriting interested Z, and brought him financial and literary success, but it could not take the place of the hard-won joy of producing his own original work, nor could it suppress the anguish at all the ideas he had been forced to abandon about the building of nature, about the direction of its development, and about the future harmony of the world.

V

In the spring of 1934 the Zabolotskys moved to their own self-contained apartment in a co-operative extension to No. 9 on the Griboyedov Canal. It was an attractive and comfortable place. A little way up, the Griboyedov Canal was crossed by Nevsky Prospect. At this intersection was Dom Knigi (The House of the Book), containing the publishing house and the editorial offices of the childrens' magazines where Z frequently had to go on literary business. Beyond the Nevsky was the Kazan Cathedral, with its colonnade surrounding a little square with a fountain and memorials to the Russian military leaders of 1812. If you looked from No. 9 in the opposite direction from the Nevsky, you could see close at hand, on the bank of the canal, the Church of Christ 'on the Blood' [where Alexander II was assassinated – Ed.] with its multi-coloured domes, and the ornamental iron railings of Mikhaylovsky Gardens. Beyond that it was not far to the Field of Mars, the Neva, and the Summer Gardens. Opposite the house, beyond the canal, Rakov Street led to Mikhaylovsky Square, with its theatre and the ensemble formed by the Russian Museum, the Philharmonia and the Yevropeyskaya Hotel.

The apartments in the two-storey extension were all occupied by writers who knew each other either closely or reasonably well: Kaverin, Shvarts, Oleynikov, Gitovich, Zoshchenko, Eykhenbaum, Tomashevsky, Spassky, Kozakov, Gruzdev, Tager and many others. In order to get to the Zabolotskys you had to go in at the main door from the side street, opposite the Perovskaya Hospital, go up to the third floor, along the corridor, and ring at apartment No. 45. The windows of the two rooms of the apartment looked out over the canal. The little kitchen was dark, with a wood-fired stove. This was the first self-contained accommodation of his own Z had ever had. One of the rooms, the one on the left, became a study-cum-dining-room, and the other was occupied by Yekaterina and their son. Gradually they began to acquire some furniture. At the end of the study, under the window, was a writing table, and to the left of that was a green ottoman with bolsters and cushions made of carpet material. When he grew tired of working at the table, Z would lie on this couch and write there. If, while he was doing this, his little son came running into the room, he could either ride on his father's knee or listen to him reading poetry.

Now that they had their own apartment it was possible for Z to begin making a collection of some of the books that interested him. Shelving was put on the right-hand wall of the study and this began quite quickly to fill up with the volumes of their own domestic library. Z set about selecting the books methodically and carefully – a sample list of editions was drawn up and passed to Rakhlin, the well-known Leningrad book dealer and manager of the Writers' Bookshop. Preference was given to solid editions, in good bindings, with illustrations. But there were some with worn paper covers. When there were books in this condition that were of special interest, Z would send them off to the binders. Over the course of two years the shelves filled up completely, and books began to be kept in a cupboard in the hall, or in the passageway. In this way all his favourite writers were collected. The collection also included books that were vital to his work like encyclopaedias, dictionaries and reference books. Among the collected works were those of Pushkin, Tyutchev, Boratynsky, Lermontov, Goethe, Gogol, Dostoyevsky, Bunin, Byron, Shakespeare, Schiller, Molière, the Bible, a world history and many others.

Sometimes Z would take from the shelves a small volume of A. K. Tolstoy, and read poems to his wife and son. He would pronounce the first words of each line in a sing-song voice and the last very jerkily:

> Conceit walks all puffed up,
> Swaying from side to side . . .

And to amuse his son he would even imitate how Conceit walks. He loved to read out Boratynsky, Tyutchev, Pushkin, Batyushkov and, less often, Khlebnikov.

When he had done the necessary amount of work he would go into the nursery and play with his son, building towers and the walls of make-believe castles out of bricks. Or he would sing to a guitar 'In the steep valley of the Daryal. . .', 'Oh, out in the porch, my porch. . .', 'There is one beautiful song of the nightingale. . .' At times like this he would forget all his professional worries and find peace and quiet contentment.

The family's life began to improve in their new accommodation. The translation work paid reasonably well – and for once in the household they had everything they needed. Their friends would frequently meet around the dining-table in the study, thanks to the fact that several of them lived in the same house. To look after their little boy, who was often ill, they engaged a nurse called Sasha – a kindly, quiet woman, who was a great help to Yekaterina. At that time many young country women, escaping from the harsh, hungry life in the countryside, came to the city in search of work, and it was easy to find a maid: even not very well-to-do people had one.

We get some idea of how the family lived from a surviving note of Z's which he wrote to his wife while she was in hospital at the end of 1934:

> Everything's fine here. Last night I played (quietly) with Nikita, then he went out for a walk with Sasha for an hour, then we put him to bed . . . This morning he went for a walk for half an hour, had something to eat, then looked at a German book with me, which he liked a lot. We're having some lunch at the moment, and then I shall send him out for a walk with Sasha . . . The milk woman called, and I gave her one rouble. I'm still expecting some money from Moscow, but I can't wait for it. Yesterday Oleynikov got the food and consumer-goods pass which I had asked him to collect for me. The pass is for the writers' ZRK [restricted access retail co-operative]; I've registered one of the cards there . . .

139

Nikita has just come running in and asked me if you are taking your medicine.

Z would often go out in the evenings to visit artist friends or to the Shvartses' or the Oleynikovs', and from 1936 onwards to the Gitoviches'. On one occasion the artist Eduard Budogosky took Z with him to the house of a friend, also an artist – G. Shevyakov, who lived on the Eighth Line* on Vasilevsky Island. Here the poet found a gathering of the pupils and colleagues of V. Lebedev, generally recognized as the leading figure among the illustrators working in children's literature. Z was pleased with the general attention paid by the happy, noisy company to him and to his poetry, and he paid several more visits there. Yet he would get even more pleasure from a quiet chat with the artist Pyotr Sokolov over a glass of beer in one of the bars he liked so much. Whenever Z visited the Gitoviches he always admired two paintings of Sokolov's that hung there. He was specially fond of one called 'The Cyclist' – a little man with a beard riding a bicycle across a field.

Z waited with excitement and some trepidation to be admitted to the newly formed Writers' Union. After what had been written about him in the press and in the journals, he was quite likely to be refused admission. Nevertheless he was accepted, and got his brand new member's card, signed by Maksim Gorky. Z was specially amused to find himself in the same organization as the former RAPP members, and he read his friends a humorous couplet which he had written about it:

> From now on I'm Unionized,
> I'm not lost to the world.
> My instructor is Valka Druzin,
> My corporal – Libedinsky.

Back in 1928, when Druzin had been editor of the literary supplement of *Leningrad Pravda*, he had published some of Z's verse, and had then been one of the first to write a review, admittedly in restrained but businesslike tones, of *Columns*. Subsequently he had changed his tack and adopted a sharply negative approach. Z had not forgotten how, on one of the literary evenings after this, when he had been reading his poetry, Druzin had stood up and started lecturing him on how and what to write. He had found Druzin's words offensive, collected his coat, and made for the exit. Meanwhile Druzin, pointing at the poet as he made

* Houses in the old quarter of Vasilevsky Island are identified by their 'line' – each representing one side of a north–south street [Ed.].

140

his way to the door, shouted out gloatingly: 'Look, look, Zabolotsky's leaving, he's leaving Soviet literature!' That was why Z described Druzin ironically as 'my instructor'. As for Libedinsky, he was one of those people in literary life who enjoyed Z's poetry, but either could not or did not want to write about it for fear of jeopardizing their position. In fact at one of the Moscow literary evenings Libedinsky had spoken about Z's verse in very appreciative terms.

In August 1934, the First All-Union Congress of Soviet Writers took place. Speeches on poetry were given by Bukharin and Tikhonov. Z's name was not mentioned, but this is easily explained since he could not be talked about without some evaluation of his works. The speakers had evidently decided diplomatically not to become embroiled in this affair, even though they both rated Z's works quite highly. Instead it was A. Bezymensky who brought up the subject. He made a polemical speech commenting on what Bukharin had said. He proposed to talk about 'those poets who are the mouthpiece of the class enemy', and, in particular, about the 'hostile activities' of Z. He said: 'The mask of buffoonery, which the enemy is adopting, is much more dangerous. This sort of poetry is represented by Zabolotsky, who was not mentioned as an enemy in Comrade Tikhonov's speech either.' Having so roundly condemned Z's work, and also that of Pavel Vasilyev, Bezymensky then maliciously offered them a chance of surviving in literature: 'Neither Zabolotsky nor Vasilyev is completely beyond hope. The re-educative power of socialism knows no bounds.'

The poet Dmitry Kedrin wrote an epigram on the subject of this particular speech:

> A poet's lot is strange,
> The weak oppress the strong:
> Zabolotsky is nameless,
> While Bezymensky is famous!*

In the midst of these sombre and troubling times Z received an unexpected telephone call from *Izvestia*, at that period edited by Bukharin. He was asked to provide some of his latest poems for publication. Thus on 18 November 1934, *Izvestia* printed 'Signs of Autumn' ('Autumn') which had been written two years previously. This publication did a little to cheer Z up.

On 1 December a fateful shot rang out at Smolny: Sergey Kirov had been murdered. The whole of Leningrad was shocked by this event. Even at that time there were many who realized that any political

---

* 'Bezymensky' derives from 'nameless' in Russian [Ed.].

assassination would only serve the purpose of those people who were exaggerating the danger of the so-called 'intensifying class struggle' in order to shackle the country with emergency measures and Stalin's absolute power. There was a suspicion that OGPU, which had just been reorganized as the NKVD, was implicated in the killing, and everyone fearfully awaited reprisals. Hardly anyone at the time could even guess that Kirov might have been killed on Stalin's personal orders.

Z was afraid that he too might be affected by the anticipated repressive measures: there had been too many public references to him as an 'enemy'. And then, on 2 December, there was another telephone call from *Izvestia* asking him to write a poem dedicated to Kirov as soon as possible. Z interpreted this request as an attempt to protect him on the part of the editor-in-chief Bukharin, since an immediate response to the murder in one of the central papers would, to a certain extent, act as an insurance against any possible trouble. He had never had to write a poem of this kind before, and now the time at his disposal was limited – the copy had to be handed in at the paper's Leningrad office before noon on 3 December.

Like many Leningraders, Z was generally sympathetic towards Kirov, the more so since they came from the same part of the country – both had spent their childhood in Urzhum. V. P. Matveyev had hinted at Kirov's situation, and what Z had heard had encouraged him to feel more sympathetic. All the same, he just could not get any of the poem down on paper. Yet it definitely had to be written. Next morning he had got the bulk of it done, but simply could not work out an ending. Time was already running out, he would soon have to go to *Izvestia*, and the closing lines had still not been written. In the end, when he had already put his coat on, Z perched on the edge of a chair, and, almost without thinking, wrote the last lines and turned to his wife and said:

'I think it sounds like nonsense. Just listen to this ending:

> And the world, gigantically splendid,
> Shone over the wordless tomb,
> And it was firm and strong,
> Like the form of the heart that had perished.'

Yekaterina liked this, and said encouragingly to her husband: 'But those are the best lines in the poem! There's no need to worry at all.' Z's poem, bearing the title 'Farewell', was printed in *Izvestia* on 4 December. In the same month *Chizh* published his poem for children 'Night in the Steppes', also dedicated to Kirov.

Encouraged by the attention paid him by *Izvestia*, after a break of eighteen months Z tried to return to poetry about natural philosophy, and wrote a variant of his earlier poem 'Lodeynikov' – 'Lodeynikov in the Garden'. This latter work contained an even more closely defined depiction of the dual role of nature, and its imperfection appeared in an even starker and more concrete form. In the depiction of the 'eternal winepress' of nature there was an indirect reflection of the way the poet perceived the social situation in the country. He wrote:

> Nature, turning into hell,
> went about its business without fuss.
> the beetle ate the grass, the bird pecked the beetle,
> the polecat sucked the brain from the bird's head,
> and the fearsomely distorted faces
> of night creatures stared from the grass.
> Nature's eternal winepress
> united death and existence
> in one club. But thought was powerless
> to join together its two mysteries.

But the time was still not ripe for an integrated, fully considered poem about Lodeynikov. After Kirov's murder a wave of arrests swept Leningrad. Among the poet's close acquaintances who were picked up was Matveyev. In such circumstances Z thought it wise to switch all his efforts to preparing a separate edition of *Gargantua and Pantagruel*, and to a re-working for children of *Til Eulenspiegel*. Over the whole of 1935 he wrote only two poems – 'The Beginning of Winter' and 'Spring in the Forest', in which lyrical depictions are firmly based on his natural-philosophical view of the world. He himself considered 'The Beginning of Winter' to be one of his most successful poems.

By the beginning of 1936 the atmosphere had eased somewhat. On 11 February *Izvestia* published a new poem by him entitled 'The North', about man's conquest of the harsh environment of the Arctic, and about the heroic feats of the men of the ship *Chelyuskin* and their rescuers, which were still fresh in everyone's memory. Here the poet's talent had switched to a new field of epic activity and, as in 'Farewell', it was treating a contemporary theme. Also in February he participated in the plenary session of the directorate of the Union of Writers, which took place in Minsk, and had poetry as its main business. In March he was to speak at a discussion of Formalism at the Leningrad House of Writers.

He had to prepare a text for this speech. Z gave a businesslike account of his development as a writer, and explained his views on nature and his position with regard to the form of poetic works. Aware that the speech could have serious consequences for him, he decided to seek the advice of Nikolay Stepanov. When he read the text Stepanov was horrified.

'Kolya, whatever are you doing?' he cried. 'They expect you to recognize your mistakes and renounce your previous errors. There's nothing you can do about it, you have to recant! That's the way things are. And here you are casting pearls before swine.'

'But my dear Nikolay, a poet has some dignity. It's not worth becoming a swine oneself.'

Seeing the stubborn expression on his friend's face, Stepanov began to get extremely concerned. He considered it his duty to save a great poet for Russian literature, and could see no other way out but recantation. Almost in tears, he began to try and persuade Z to rewrite the speech:

'You've written very well about Kirov and about the North. Now you should build on your success and throw them another bone. When they are satisfied, you can write your own thing. You can't afford to take the risk. What's more, your latest poems are splendid. Maybe that's the way you should be developing? Let's hope nobody brings up our good relations with Matveyev. You know what I mean. . .?'

In the end they both sat down and began to correct the text of the speech together. Stepanov dictated the opening sentences to Z:

> In the articles in *Pravda* criticizing Formalism I can see an answer to the doubts and questions which have come up in my own mind over the course of the last few years. For me these articles are evidence of the care and attention which the Party is giving to literature.

After that he added some words about rejecting any new form which was separated from content, and breaking with his ideas about the building of nature and the future union of man and nature. When Stepanov attempted to persuade him to delete the passages where he discussed the disgraceful tone of the criticism of him, Z dug his heels in: 'No, I'm going to leave that. I've got the right to defend myself!' So, when he got to the House of Writers, he said, without a trace of slyness:

> And what of criticism? Has it helped me as a writer? Has it explained to me in detail and in plain words how I have sinned against the reader? . . . No Soviet poet, it would seem, has been mocked by the critics as much as I have. Whatever my literary sins are supposed to have been, articles and speeches like those do not bring any honour to modern criticism. They only serve to disorientate the writer even further, and to alienate him from art. That is all they do.'

Z said in conclusion, quoting *Faust*, that the basic thing in art was the idea, and it had to be expressed in such a way that it was accessible to the mass of the people.

A shortened version of the speech was published in *Literaturny Leningrad*, beneath a title supplied by the editors, 'The Articles in *Pravda* Open Our Eyes'. There was pleasure in official circles. A leader in the same issue of the paper said:

> Zabolotsky's speech was full of the self-assurance of an artist who has freed himself from the dead hand of Formalism, of an artist organically accepting the new principles of poetry, and aware of the broad creative horizons opening up to him.

When his friends came to see Z in his apartment they tried to persuade him that by making the speech he had not demeaned himself, and that he had come out of a difficult situation with honour. But Z was sickened by any two-faced behaviour. Even in the forced rejection of the 'Formalism' of his earlier works, he was basing himself on the actual development of his poetic manner, which had begun organically even before the critics rained down their blows on him.

The poems 'Farewell' and 'The North', the speech at the discussion of Formalism, the absence of any other poems which the critics might consider harmful – all this contributed to bringing to an end the unconditional abuse directed at the poet. Even if he continued to be reviled, out of inertia, for his earlier 'sins', at least he was not considered an enemy, and it was recognized that he did have one or two good poems.

In the middle of the thirties Z began to make a closer study of Georgian poetry, and to realize what enormous possibilities there were for translating it into Russian verse. His interest in Georgian literature was further fostered by his growing friendship with Simon Chikovani and Titsian Tabidze. Z had met both these poets at the end of 1935. Chikovani recalls their first meeting:

> I first met Zabolotsky . . . in the Leningrad Writers' Club, at an evening of Georgian poetry . . . I had imagined that the author of *Columns* would have a decidedly poetic look about him, and would be brilliant and authoritative by nature. Imagine our surprise, myself and Titsian Tabidze, when one of our old friends introduced us to a young fair-haired fellow, rather stout and of medium height. He wore glasses, and had a calm and serious expression on his face. Our friend said: 'I'd like you to meet Nikolay Zabolotsky, the poet.' I stared at him in amazement; he certainly didn't look very convincing as a poet. He looked more like a respectable scholar. But it was Zabolotsky himself who made us revise our opinions about him. He shook us warmly by the hand and

said in a friendly way: 'I'm a great admirer of Georgian poetry. I know I haven't been studying it for long, but I've already come to love some of the Georgian poets' . . . He spoke in a calm voice, not at all effusive, and it seemed as though every word he used had been carefully chosen, thought over, and weighed in advance. This disparity between his outside appearance and his creative self fascinated me and I attempted there and then to strip away the armour of apparent impenetrability that surrounded my new acquaintance. This turned out to be not a very difficult task. At the time he was engaged in translating Orbeliani's 'The Toast of Honour', and I only had to mention this subject when the ice began to thaw, and soon to melt altogether. I at once realized his sensitivity and nobility of spirit, and we began to talk in a frank and friendly fashion . . .

That evening in Leningrad tied the knot of our friendship which strengthened when we met a year later in Minsk at the Writers' Union plenum. My new friend invited Mikola Bazhan, some colleagues from Moscow, and myself back to his hotel. There he read to us his latest poems – 'The North', 'Lodeynikov', 'Autumn', and 'The Beginning of Winter'. Our reaction was one of great excitement and appreciation.

We should add the fact that Z in his turn was full of praise for the poems by Tabidze and Chikovani which were read to him in Georgian and then paraphrased in Russian. He discussed with them the possibility of translating modern and classical Georgian poetry, and in particular their own poems. They talked a great deal about Rustaveli's long, narrative poem *The Knight in the Panther Skin*, and the unsatisfactory nature of the existing translations of it into Russian.

On 1 July Z wrote to Tabidze about his idea of re-working Rustaveli's poem in translation for young readers, and about what he needed to do to prepare for this project:

> Leningrad *Detgiz* has commissioned me to do an abridged translation and re-working of Rustaveli for children. The initiative came from me. I think it's something that needs to be done . . . I plan to come to Tiflis* in September, at the very beginning of the month. I shall have to get into contact with the Rustaveli Institute and with the people who are preparing his centenary. I just have to breathe the air of Georgia, and appreciate Rustaveli in his own country. This is all the more necessary because what has been written in Russian does not contain even the most elementary information about this great poet . . . Titsian Iustinovich, if you are going to be in Tiflis in September, I shall ask you to give me some help, and put me in touch with the right people.
>
> Until quite recently I have been snowed under with prose re-workings,

---

* Nowadays generally known in its Georgian form, Tbilisi [Ed.].

and I am only just finishing them off now. I had hoped to be getting down to Vazha Pshavela, but now this other urgent business has somewhat delayed the translation of 'Aluda Ketelauri' . . .

On 8 or 10 July I'm leaving for the Ukraine, where my family is living. I have fixed up a little dacha on the banks of the Dnieper, outside Kanev. It's the beautiful, rich countryside described by Gogol in *Viy*.

Earlier in the spring of 1936, Z had travelled to Kiev at the invitation of the Ukrainian poet M. P. Bazhan on some kind of literary business, and had arranged for his family to rent accommodation for the summer in the village of Prokhorovka on one of the tributaries of the Dnieper. At the beginning of the summer he took his wife and son there, and he joined them himself in July. The Zabolotskys' rented rooms were in the house of the local lawyer, with windows looking out over the orchard with its beehives, and a verandah thickly overgrown with hops. The summer that year was very hot and dry. Together with Kaverin's brother, David Aleksandrovich Zilber, and his family, who were living in the house next door, the Zabolotskys went swimming every day. The path leading down to the river described a wide curve round an old oak tree, occupied by a nest of fearsome hornets and numerous horned stag-beetles. Z observed these huge beetles with great interest, and watched dung beetles rolling little round balls along the dusty path. In the sandy inlets of the river there were horned snails, and as he listened he could hear larks singing in the sky, and grasshoppers in the grass, yellow from the heat.

For lunch they would have exceptionally tasty Ukrainian borshch, served by the household maid, the countrywoman Marfa. When she had put down the dish with the borshch and the plates, Marfa would perch on the rail of the verandah and tell them about the recent terrible events that had emptied the Ukrainian countryside. It was from her stories that Z first learnt in full detail how violently collectivization and de-kulakization had been carried out, and what merciless famine had visited the Ukrainian peasants in 1932–3. The farms in the Ukraine were rich, and many peasants were classed as kulaks: men able to work were herded together and taken away somewhere, every speck of grain was requisitioned, so that there was none left, even for the spring sowing of 1933. Marfa told them how officials had come from the city to search out grain, and how in the winter the peasants had eaten up all the potatoes, slaughtered the cattle and even dug up acorns from under the snow. In the spring they had eaten tree roots, skins, mice, and even worms. They had waited impatiently for the first green shoots, and then the first spikes of wheat, but there were already signs of the most terrible thing starting – cannibalism. Marfa said that there was a woman still living, who came from her home village, and whose daughter had been stolen and eaten. Countryfolk had been prevented from getting into the city. There were detachments of soldiers along the roads and at the railway stations, and the people had not the strength left to offer any resistance. Nevertheless, Marfa had managed to escape from the dying village where she had been born, and she had survived.

Z listened to this tragic story, and thought how nature's eternal winepress, its bestial, chaotic features, had affected mankind as well and how mankind too was in need of that ennobling moral principle which, like reason, replenished nature itself.

After lunch the whole family would rest on a rug spread out on the grass. Once, when their son was being naughty, walking round the rug and spitting into the grass, Z said to him very seriously: 'Don't spit, Nikita, or you'll spit everything out from inside yourself and nothing will be left. It happens to some people.'

Meanwhile lines of verse were already forming in the poet's mind:

> Everything that was in my soul, everything seemed lost again,
> I lay in the grass, exhausted by anguish and sorrow.
> and the splendid stem of a flower rose up over me,
> and a grasshopper, like a little sentry, stood before it.

The sense of sorrow, anxiety and confusion which we find in Z's poems that are linked with his stay in the Ukraine has its origins naturally in his emotional state during these years. When he returned to the ideas about the psychological affinity of man and nature, he was again convinced that there was something to learn from nature. In the poem 'Drought' he writes openly about his emotional state, without a trace of irony:

> But my life is a hundred times more sad,
> when my lonely reason is sick,
> and my thoughts sit like monsters,
> raising their snouts above the rotting sedge.
> My poor soul is in a faint,
> and my doubts creep like snails,
> and on the sands, swaying and quaking,
> plants stand black like coals.

Watching the revivifying effect of the squalls and downpours of a summer storm on the drought-stricken countryside, the poet was seeking the wellspring of life in his own soul, and exclaimed: 'Let the rain and the wind strike together, so that my reason should be cured!' 'Do not fear the storm! Let the cleansing force strike nature in the breast!' At the end of the poem he turns to nature with gratitude for showing him the path to recovery:

> Teacher, maiden, mother,
> you are no goddess, neither are we gods,
> yet how sweet it is to understand
> your inchoate and jumbled lessons!

While still in the Ukraine Z received a letter from Titsian Tabidze. The latter thoroughly approved of his plan to translate and re-work Rustaveli, and sent him literal translations of his own poems 'In the Gorge of the Aragvi' and 'The Birth of the Word'. They clinched the matter straight away, and on 2 August Z was writing back to say that he had made a verse translation of them. What excited him about Tabidze's work was something he valued more than anything else in poetry:

> What captivates me about your poetry is the amazing affinity between the spiritual world and the world of nature. In your writings these two worlds blend together into one inseparable whole – and in our times that is a most rare quality. Very few modern Russian poets love and feel for nature.

Z wanted his wife to accompany him from Prokhorovka to Georgia, while their son was to stay with old Pelageya Semyonovna, who had just arrived in the village. They planned to go down the Dnieper by boat and then to take the train to Tbilisi. But all this came to nothing. Little Nikita made it very obvious that he did not want to stay with this 'grandmother' who was not really a relative. There was nothing for it but to change their plans: Z arranged accommodation for his family in the Ukrainian Writers' House in Svyatoshino outside Kiev, and at the beginning of September he set out alone to see his new friends.

This was Z's first acquaintance with Georgia, its luxuriant countryside, ancient culture and hospitable people. The Georgians, and in particular Chikovani and Tabidze, at once recognized in Z a powerful poetic talent and an unusual personality, and they developed a warm affection for him. An evening was organized for him at the Georgian Union of Writers. Z reached an agreement on re-working Rustaveli's poem and on other translations, visited Mtskheta, Tsinandali and Gori. On 18 September he wrote from Tbilisi to his wife in the Ukraine:

> I've had tremendous success here. Every day I am invited to banquets by well-known writers and distinguished people. They make me read my poems, and they cry out with delight. If Russian writers treated me like Georgian ones do, I'd be a famous man. They are going to interview me

and put my picture in the paper. They are going to take me all round Georgia. I'm making an agreement with Iordanishvili for a word-for-word translation. We're going to various theatres.

Every time I go to a banquet there are several toasts to your health and Nikita's, and they all want to meet you. We must visit Tiflis together.

Despite the banquets, and they are huge ones (the day before yesterday there were twenty people at Titsian's, and we drank 2½ buckets of Kakhetia wine), I am getting on with my business, and even doing some writing. I have translated a poem for children by Kvitko and it seems to have gone down well. I am also sending a collection of Kvitko to *Chizh*.

I haven't had any letters or telegrams from you yet. I console myself by thinking that if anything had happened you would have sent a telegram. Letters take a long time to get here anyhow. [In point of fact something had happened. In Svyatoshino first his wife and then his son had fallen seriously ill – N.Z.]

I'm finding my trip here very good and useful. I've met a great many interesting people. The women here are stunningly beautiful, but I am too old and fat for them, and besides, I don't want to cause my nice little wife any unpleasantness. The Georgian men are quite good at giving you a clout round the ear too!

The countryside is beautiful. I shall write about Georgia. I've been asked to do a lot of translating. Goodbye. A kiss to you and our little boy . . . Your Papa.

Z spent thirty days in Georgia, and these days played a vital part in his development as a writer. In the early days of October he went with Simon Chikovani to Gori – the town where Stalin was born and grew up. In accordance with the normal ritual both poets visited the Museum of the Leader, and then they immediately went off to a wine-bar that Chikovani knew of where they had some of the famous Ateni wine. This wine is so delicate that it will only stand being moved from Ateni to Gori. When they emerged from the cellar, they made their way up the hill to the old fortress, and from there looked out over the city, the surrounding fields, gardens, and vineyards, framed by the distant craggy peaks, and bathed in the evening sunshine. After their friendly talk, and the Ateni wine, everything in the world seemed splendid. They both experienced that sharp joy at simply being alive, and they swore to each other there and then, at the foot of the Gori fortress, that they would each without fail write a poem about that evening.

The letter that Z wrote to Chikovani immediately on his return from Georgia is full of emotional uplift and gratitude for all that he had experienced in the past month:

When I got back to Leningrad, I called my friends together straight away, and your nine bottles were consumed to the sound of jubilant toasts to you, to Marya and to the health of all our Georgian friends . . . At the moment I am still under the spell of the charm of your hospitality, and I keep thinking that I shall see you, fat Titsian, and handsome Ilo Mosashvili, and that we'll go to the bar together and I shall once more hear the songs 'Svetlyachka' and 'Suliko'.

I shall naturally never forget my first acquaintance with Georgia, and the memory of the month in Tiflis will be one of the most cherished memories of my life. I just can't tell you how grateful I am to you all, principally to you and to Marya, for the wonderful time I had, for the trips we made, for the feasts we enjoyed, and for the conversations we had.

Here in Leningrad it is deepest autumn. In front of me at the moment, outside the window, damp snow is falling fast, covering the roofs, and melting on the dirty pavements below. I find that my affairs here are generally proceeding as normal. *Til Eulenspiegl* has gone off to the printers. *Literaturny Sovremennik* is asking for translations of Galaktion Tabidze. Today I'm going to present a report about my trip and about Rustaveli. My wife and son are better, which is a source of great pleasure. Nikita is delighted with the strap and the dagger. (15 October 1936)

On 14 November 1936, Z informed Chikovani that he had kept his part of the promise, and written the poem 'Gori Symphony':

You insisted that I write something about Gori. Well, here you are, I'm sending you a manuscript copy. The verses came into being thanks to you, so read them and enjoy them. Joking aside – they don't seem bad at all . . . Now, my dear colleague, it's your turn! I await your poem about Gori – you remember what we agreed! Because I've been busy doing this I haven't had time to translate your things. But I'll do them in a couple of days, and I'll send them to you straight away.

The poem 'Gori Symphony' was essentially dedicated to all of Georgia, its people and its countryside. Written on the crest of the wave of emotion which the two poets had experienced as they stood beneath the ancient fortress that autumn evening, it also touched on the subject of Stalin, although his name is never mentioned. The 'leader of the peoples of the world' interested Z more as a political figure: there was, naturally, no question of a worshipful attitude. However it should be said, to be just, that the words of the poem devoted to Stalin were put there with a certain *arrière-pensée*: Z was hoping to strengthen his still shaky position in the face of official opinion. In 'Gori Symphony' he wrote:

> The city has gone quiet, peaceful and still,
> and this shack – the poorest of shacks –
> seemed to us smaller and darker.
> But how my thoughts were attracted to it!
> I recalled the years of adolescence,
> I wanted to know, how in such remoteness
> was formed by the action of nature
> the first shape of his soul –
> how he looked at the great dome of the sky,
> how he stroked the cattle, how he learnt his lessons,
> how, in the recesses of his soul, he nurtured
> what he could not even express.

The general context of the poem, its jubilant and elated tone, yet another reference to the 'leader of the peoples of the world', lent these lines the accepted air of adulation. Yet it was also possible to understand them differently, even to see in the last two lines of the passage quoted a veiled sense of menace.*

Z reckoned right. After the publication of the poem in *Izvestia* on 4 December, Z told his friends in Georgia:

> I'm glad that my poems were to your taste. They've got things moving for me again, and now the book of my poetry is going ahead. It has already been included in the plan of the Leningrad GIKhL (State Publishing House for Literature) – it has been confirmed by Moscow, and if all goes well it may be out by the spring. Two of the Leningrad journals (*Literaturny Sovremennik* No.3 and *Zvezda* No.2) are proposing some articles about me (Zoshchenko among the authors) and around 600 lines of poetry. There was a big evening here in my honour, and it went off well.

VI

Of course, the main thing for Z was to get a book of his poems published. He was by now an established poet whose name was widely known, and yet, apart from one slim volume published some seven years earlier, there was no separate edition of his works. He could not forget the failure with the collected poems in 1933, when the type had been broken up. Now he was stubbornly aiming at getting another edition off the ground – one that would cover all his writing – from *Columns* to his

---

* After Khrushchov's denunciation of Stalin in 1956 this fine poem was in turn censored from Z's collections for promoting the 'cult of personality' [Ed.].

latest poem. Even before the trip to Georgia, when he had felt a little less under pressure from the critics, he had collected his works together once more, edited them thoroughly, retyped them into three copies, and bound the collections in dark red covers. What Z had achieved was the kind of selection he would have liked to publish if external circumstances had been favourable enough. For some reason or other the long poems 'The Birds' and 'The Clouds' did not find their way into this collection. In anticipation of all eventualities Z gave a copy each for safekeeping to his closest and most reliable friends – Stepanov and Shvarts. Finally overcoming his doubts and hesitation, he sent the third copy to the editor-in-chief of *Izvestia*, Bukharin, with a request for his opinion of the collection – and if it was favourable, that he should recommend the book for publication. Z knew that Bukharin was favourably disposed towards his work, and he was relying on his help. The fact that Bukharin's own position was unsafe was probably not widely known at the time, and Z had no idea of the dangers associated with such patronage. Bukharin, however, did not consider it possible to play any part in the fate of the book, and after a while he returned it together with a polite note saying that he could not be of any help to Z. Shortly afterwards he was removed from his post at *Izvestia*, and later arrested – the infamous trial of the 'Rightist-Trotskyite bloc' was already imminent.

Z realized that without influential support he would not succeed in publishing the book in the form he wanted. Since he had got no help from Bukharin, and so as not to tempt fate, he gathered together only those poems which he personally considered would arouse no objections at the publishing house. The collection, called simply *Second Book*, included 'Gori Symphony' which, as Z said, had got things moving again for him.

Second Book also included two poems which directly continued the natural-philosophical line of development in Z's work – 'Yesterday, Contemplating Death' (1936) and 'Immortality' (early 1937, later retitled 'Metamorphoses'). Both these works contained ideas derived from the writings of Tsiolkovsky and Vernadsky. Throughout the preceding years, whenever the poet felt that evil forces were dragging him away from his work, he would seek solace in reading his favourite books, among them his little volume of Tsiolkovsky. He would go to the passages that interested him most, and when he had read them, he would think with bitterness of the trivial nature of all the literary in-fighting and fuss into which he had willy-nilly been drawn.

As he got to know Tsiolkovsky's works, Z came to consider more and more the great mystery of the interconnection between life and death.

He had derived the idea of material immortality from the concept of the oneness of all of nature's organisms, and the constant metamorphoses to which all the parts of this organism are subjected. The human being is nature's thinking organ, and as such is an inseparable part of it. As long as nature continues to exist he cannot die. If the matter making up his body becomes mixed into other parts of nature this does not alter things, the more so because, so Z believed, even thought has a certain material essence, and cannot disappear without trace. Once dispersed in nature the human being might rise again in any one of its parts – in a leaf, a bird or a stone, and these would then acquire, although admittedly perhaps only to a small extent, its human qualities, just as they had already absorbed the qualities of others who had lived before. If these transformations are looked at from the point of view of the individual then it transpires that human beings as it were pass through a series of forms of matter yet remain themselves. But even the forms of matter which they abandon are not outer shells, not sloughed-off snake skins, but themselves, re-created in other natural objects.

In his considerations of immortality Tsiolkovsky proceeded on the basis of matter, of the atom, which achieves immortality by passing as a unit through an endless series of completed life forms. Z proceeded on the basis of complex natural formations, in which the part possesses, to a greater or lesser degree, the qualities of the whole. Life, flowing from form to form through transformations of matter, does not lose its qualities, but exhibits them in each of these forms. The world is like a complex organism in which each cell carries information about the structure of the whole. That is why, for example, features of humanity can be discerned in a bird:

> Turning its round eye beneath its lids,
> a big bird flies down.
> Man can be sensed in its movements.
> At least he is hiding,
> in embryo, between the two broad wings.

Z's philosophical-poetic idea maintains that man has always existed in nature 'in embryo'. He exists in it in our age, and will not disappear, because his thought and essence are inseparable from any other speck of existence. That is why, in the poem 'Yesterday, Contemplating Death', we read:

> The voice of Pushkin could be heard above the leaves,
> and birds of Khlebnikov sang near the water.
> And I met a stone. The stone was motionless.
> And the face of Skovoroda appeared in it.

> And all creatures, all the peoples
> kept incorruptible existence,
> and I myself was not a child of nature,
> but Nature's thought! Nature's unstable mind!

As we can see, by comparison with the poems of the early thirties, the philosophical idea in these verses has become more bare, more aphoristic and closer to the personality of the author. The writing is to a significant extent devoid of the flowery imagery that formed its outer wrapping; instead it has become highly charged with thought. For that matter the collection *Second Book* is as a whole strikingly different from Z's first book. And to those who did not know the largely unpublished works from the intervening period it might seem that somewhere between the publication of his two books the poet had sharply changed his aesthetic direction.

One day, soon after the move to the house on the Griboyedov Canal, Z was visited by one of his long-time admirers, the poet A. I. Gitovich. Gitovich began to read to him from *Columns*, skilfully imitating Z's voice and intonation. Then he talked convincingly about the qualities of genius in these poems. This amused and even touched Z to such a degree that he began to regard his admirer with renewed interest. Gitovich, noisy, energetic, a great one for drinking and arguing, was not inclined to probe too deeply into the essence of things. On the surface he would not seem to have much in common with the kind of people Z regarded as his friends. Nor did he have much liking for Gitovich's poems. Yet Gitovich had a quite selfless admiration for Z's works, and defended them passionately wherever and whenever he could. At meetings of the Writers' Union he spoke in defence of Z, and at private gatherings, whether the company was friendly or hostile, he would scatter Z's enemies, and call on young people to learn how to write poetry from his idol. Meetings between the two poets became increasingly frequent.

Up until 1936 they occasionally met at the Shvartses', either alone or in the company of their wives. Also present would be Oleynikov with his wife Larisa, Boris Eykhenbaum, and Shvarts's theatrical friends – the actress Yelizaveta Uvarova, the actor Boris Chirkov and others. Oleynikov would raise his glass to their witty and attractive hostess and say, with a look of inscrutable seriousness on his face: 'You charmer, Yekaterina Ivanovna, allow us to drink to you, and through you to all the lady-builders of socialism.' At these gatherings the discussions were always interesting, light-hearted and exuberant. In the breaks in the talk Boris Chirkov would play his guitar and sing all kinds of songs –

pre-revolutionary, black-market, bourgeois . . . Sometimes Z would pick up the instrument and sing little couplets he had made up about some of the writers they all knew. Like this one, for example:

> Oh, fir trees, little fir trees,
> With your crowns like needles.
> If I was Kolya Tikhonov,
> I would have cured my blisters,
> I would still be on a good footing,
> Both in the Gorkom and the Sovnarkom.*

Z respected Tikhonov as a poet, and valued his warm and kindly attitude towards him, but he could not help making a joke out of his constant attempts to follow the official line, hence the reference to Tikhonov's having easy access to important institutions.

From 1936 onwards Z became a frequent visitor at the Gitoviches'. It was there that he met the writer I. S. Sokolov-Mikitov and the painter N. V. Pinegin. He was interested in the stories they told about their travels, and when he got home he would tell his wife what remarkable people they were and how much of the world they had managed to see.

He was most impressed by Pinegin's account of a journey he had made with a brigade of political agitators to an encampment of one of the native peoples of the north. To make their struggle against religious superstitions more effective the brigade had taken with them a radio receiver which they intended to demonstrate as a wonder of modern technology. The head shaman was immediately fascinated by the new gadget, but asked them to delay listening to the radio broadcast until he had summoned the neighbouring shamans and their people. He said that it would not take long to do this, then he went out of the tent, intoned some kind of spell, and returned to his guests. The following morning the agitators were amazed to see approaching the tent the very people the shaman had summoned the night before. They were all impressed by the radio receiver and listened with great interest to music direct from Moscow. Then they politely invited their guests to watch one of the wonders of their world – the dance and music of the ancient forest. The head shaman led them all to a clearing in the trees and then, at his invitation, the forest began to make a noise, the trees began to wave their tops in time to the rhythm he beat out and to make mysterious sounds. The whole created the effect of a forest melody and a dance of the trees. The guests from the city were baffled by the shaman's inexplicable powers.

* i.e. the City Party Committee and the Council of Ministers [Ed.].

Pinegin's story touched something very deep within Z. For the idea of the interpenetration of man and nature, the brotherhood of people and trees, their mutual understanding, was something near and dear to him. Under the influence of this story about the shaman Z wrote a poem of that name, copied it into a school exercise book, and kept it amongst his papers. The contents of the poem, overlaid with Pinegin's story, have remained in Yekaterina's memory, but the poem itself has not survived.

The poem 'Sedov' was written in similar circumstances. Pinegin had himself taken part in an expedition led by the polar explorer Sedov, and gave a very colourful account of it and of the Arctic. Z became interested in the expedition, read material associated with it, and even went to see Sedov's widow, but there was something about the meeting with her that he found unpleasant. Unlike 'Shaman', 'Sedov' was perfectly acceptable for publication, and soon appeared in the favourably disposed paper *Izvestia* (24 June 1937).

Gitovich attempted to bring Z closer to 'official' literature. But whereas similar attempts by Stepanov were guided by a desire to protect the poet, Gitovich was motivated more by a feeling of ambition, a feeling which he tried to engender in Z as well. He believed that a poet like Z ought to be well-known, widely published, and have his own 'school' of followers. A group of young, talented poets had gathered round Gitovich. It included V. Shefner, V. Lifshits, A. Chivilikhin, A. Lebedev, G. Chaikin and Travin. They called themselves the 'Young Association'. At their meetings they read poetry, had heated literary arguments, and criticized each other's work mercilessly. Sometimes they would be joined by Z whom Gitovich was trying to promote as something like the spiritual leader of the group.

After work in the Writers' House they would all go off to the Gitoviches'. There they would have supper and sit till the small hours discussing literature. On occasions, if there was any spare cash around, they would spend the evening in the restaurant of the Hotel Yevropeyskaya where, as Silva Gitovich recalls,

> they always sat at the same corner table which was served by a pleasant waitress – a brunette with her hair pulled back tightly. Zabolotsky almost certainly found her attractive, and when they ordered the meal he would joke with her, laughing heartily, and he was always generous with his tips.

The artist Boris Semyonov recounts a typical episode concerning the discussion of one of Vladimir Lifshits's poems:

> I used to meet Zabolotsky either in the editorial office of *Literaturny Sovremennik* or at parties at G. R. Shevyakov's, where he was much

liked and treated with great respect. I well remember one meeting of the 'Young Association' here, in the Writers' House. It was in the autumn of 1936. Gitovich, the leader of the Association, had invited Zabolotsky to this meeting, which was devoted to the analysis and discussion of *Valley*, the first book of poems by Lifshits. After most people had spoken appreciatively about the book Zabolotsky stood up and welcomed it in general terms, but once he came to a closer analysis he got quite animated and rubbished the work to such an extent that when he had finished there was a painful silence. He had a good word to say about only one piece, a short poem called 'The Last Showing', about the film *Chapayev*. He spoke with much feeling and very conclusively – there was no escaping his message. I recall taking offence on my friend's behalf, and objecting, and for some reason quoting as an example some of Serov's portraits, with their language of gesture. All of these objections were naturally rather naïve: Z simply smiled calmly in reply.

After the meeting was over we all spilled out onto the embankment, and the whole company (six or eight of us) went not to the comfortable restaurant of the Writers' House, but to drink cold beer in one of the floating cafés right opposite the Summer Garden. The wind, the seagulls, the water lapping against the sides – I remember it all vividly. And there was Zabolotsky, laughing, and trying to cheer up the young poet to whom he had given such a pasting, and talking about the value of doubt in an artist, about how necessary it was to nurture and care for these young shoots of doubt.

At this period Z made a number of speeches containing fundamental criticisms of other poets, and he was never afraid to speak the truth, however unpalatable. His assessment of the poetry of Selvinsky and A. Prokofyev are among the best known. In May 1937 he and Gitovich even travelled specially to Moscow together to a discussion of Prokofyev's poetry.

On his return from Georgia, in the autumn of 1936, Z and his family lived for three weeks from the 22 November in the New Peterhof Hotel, which was used by the Leningrad writers as a kind of study centre. The house on the Griboyedov Canal was being repaired, and Z wanted to finish his translation of Vazha Pshavela as quickly as possible. He wrote about his work at this time:

Then I was deluged in work: I wrote several of my own poems ['Gori Symphony', possibly 'Yesterday, Contemplating Death. . .' – N.Z.], translated two poems by Tabidze, three poems by Simon for *Dve Piatiletki*, and finally, in Peterhof, 600 or more lines of Pshavela's 'Aluda Ketelauri'. This is a splendid work. I don't know what the translation's like, but I'm told it's good.

The hotel where the Zabolotskys were living, and where Gitovich soon came to join them, was next to the famous Peterhof Gardens, and they could still go walking there along the snowy pathways between the bare trees and heaps of fallen leaves. In front of them would run a large stray sheepdog that Gitovich had trained, carrying a heavy stone in its mouth. Z and Gitovich would follow on behind, immersed in conversation, and then, bringing up the rear, their wives and little Nikita. 'Gori Symphony' had only just (20 November) been accepted and subsequently published, and Gitovich was busily engaged in working out how best to take advantage of this fact. He said that an evening meeting at the Writers' Union was now a matter of course, and they had to make sure that it was organized in such a way that it became an outright triumph for Z. They made a list of the poems that would be read, and whom they should ask to speak. Gitovich promised to organize it all in the best possible fashion. Among those he approached was Mikhail Zoshchenko. On the very day when the meeting was due to take place Zoshchenko sent Gitovich a note:

> Dear Comrade Gitovich, Zabolotsky is a remarkable poet, and I would be very glad to say a few good words about him, but I'm feeling so ill that I'm afraid I may not be able to make it to the meeting.
>
> I was going to write a short article on him and send it to you so that it could be read out at the evening, but it still needs a bit of work done to it. So I'll save it for the future, and probably get it printed in the newspaper . . . I really do love his poems, and I rate them extremely highly. He is a poet of great power, and his influence on our poetry will be very strong. I'm overjoyed to learn that he has reconsidered the course of his ship, and is now no longer out of step with modernity. Real art, I think, must not be reactionary.
>
> So, if I don't make it, please give my apologies. If he thinks that my article is of interest, I'll willingly get it published . . .
>
> Warmest wishes. M. Zoshchenko.
>
> I'm very annoyed that I don't feel well – I'll do my best to come, if only for an hour. 16/12/36.

Zoshchenko followed Z's work with great interest, but he was unable to do what he had promised and get his article published in the paper. It was 1937 before it appeared, in his book *Stories, Tales, Feuilletons, Plays and Criticism*.

As we learn from a report by Olga Berggolts published in *Literaturny Leningrad* for 23 December 1936:

> On 16 December in the Writers' House there was an evening in honour of the poet N. Zabolotsky. The proceedings took place in a big hall, and there were lots of people present, but the majority of writers and poets,

in particular the so-called venerable ones, once again demonstrated by their absence their indifference to art and to the fate of one of the most interesting and talented Soviet poets.

A speech on Z's development as a writer was given by A. Gorelov – the author of the memorable 1930 article 'The Collapse of Consciousness'. He opened by repeating some of the earlier attacks on *Columns* and 'The Triumph of Agriculture', and went on to recognize in Z 'a great and genuine Soviet poet, whose path to his present poetic output has been a difficult one, has brought real joy to all who love Soviet poetry, and especially to those who were previously sharply critical of him'.

Z then read some of his more recent poems. Kaverin then spoke about Z's courage, and about how he had always found support in his 'awareness of his own uniqueness' and in his closeness to reality, whereas criticism had not helped him at all. Gitovich spoke in the same vein, making sharp attacks on the vulgarizing activities of the critics. The speeches by Kaverin and Gitovich contradicted the official scenario, according to which Z had been bad, but after some of the fundamental criticisms levelled at him had become much better. For that reason both Kaverin and Gitovich were attacked by Berggolts in her report in the paper.

Despite the fact that the evening could be counted an obvious success for Z, the passions surrounding his name had still not died down. The third issue for 1937 of *Literaturny Sovremennik* contained an extensive selection of Z's poetry. As a result a lengthy polemic ensued between *Leningrad Pravda* and *Izvestia*. In *Leningrad Pravda* a certain P. Spidorchuk complained that along with his new poems Z had published some from earlier years. This critic was especially incensed by 'Lodeynikov in the Garden' and 'A Walk'. He wrote:

> But through all this ridiculous rubbish you can see the cap and bells of his 'clowning philosophy' poking.
>
> > In the depths of suffering shine our waters,
> > In the depths of grief rise up our forests!
>
> It is difficult to work out here just what forests are meant that rise up 'in the depths of grief'. Perhaps the 'hidden meaning' of these lines is contained precisely in their ambiguity.

Without even wanting to understand the poem's natural-philosophical content, the author of the article was hinting at its anti-Soviet character. In the happy Soviet land even forests and rivers were forbidden to suffer! *Izvestia* defended Z, but *Leningrad Pravda* had the last word by producing an authoritative argument: 'All the same . . . the poet is not simply a natural scientist, or a child, but an engineer of human souls.'*

Thus, even after the publication of the 'Gori Symphony', Z's position remained delicate. He was well aware of this himself, and at the beginning of 1937 he wrote:

> My position in Leningrad is ambiguous: I have the approval of a large number of respected and authoritative people, but among other poets I can feel a kind of vague opposition. This will no doubt soon become more obvious, and probably on the part of the people in Moscow. This naturally does not frighten me very much, because it is not just a matter of me as an individual, it is true of the situation generally in Soviet poetry.

In fact the best that any real poet could hope for at the time was to be in an ambiguous position. One had to be made of really heroic stuff to be able to look oneself in the face in the prevailing atmosphere of intimidation and repression. 'Faith and Stubbornness, Labour and Honour' – this motto of Z's was tossed about on the stormy sea like a ship battered by a hurricane. But he remained steadfast.

On 5 April 1937, the Zabolotskys had a daughter, Natalya. That evening Z called at the Gitoviches' and announced with pride: 'This afternoon my youngest daughter was born.' Despite the fact that he only had one son and one daughter, from that moment on he would often refer to them as 'my eldest son' and 'my youngest daughter'. Naturally, they had a drink at the Gitoviches' to celebrate the event, and then they all went together to the Shvartses', who lived in the apartment directly below. Silva Gitovich recalls how 'Nikolay sat there at the Shvartses' table, very calm, restrained, and pleased with himself, raising glass after glass with a sense of proud self-importance'.

The Zabolotskys spent the summer of 1937 together with their children and their nurse in a dacha outside Luga. They had rented some rooms with a verandah in a wooden house in the middle of the pine woods, on the edge of a lake. Z sat for days on end over the abridged re-working of Rustaveli's epic poem *The Knight in the Panther Skin*, emerging only at evening to go for a walk in the direction of the lake. Here he would look at a pine that had been struck by lightning, at the crayfish which the summer residents and the local boys caught under the overhanging tree roots, and at the opposite shore in the distance. Stepanov, who was living nearby, would sometimes row over to discuss

---

* A much-used expression attributed to Stalin [Ed.].

the latest news from the city and to read some lines of the new translation.

The news, in fact, was not good. One day, arriving home late from Leningrad, Z quietly told his wife that Oleynikov had been arrested.

Shvarts told Z about his last meeting with their mutual friend. Not long before his arrest, and after he had only just returned from the south, Oleynikov met Shvarts and complained glumly of the difficulty of existing in the general atmosphere of suspicion. He recounted how Kotov, the superintendent of the house on the Griboyedov Canal, had secretly called together the women who cleaned and looked after the writers' apartments and told them that their employers represented a serious threat to Soviet power. The superintendent promised that anyone who unmasked these enemies of the people would be granted the right of permanent residence in the city, and one of the apartments that fell free. The unhappy country women, who had found temporary refuge in the city, were already whispering to each other about the lucky ones who would be getting accommodation as a reward for informing.

Nikolay Oleynikov was shot on 24 November 1937. In the same year, 1937, Titsian Tabidze was arrested and subsequently died. That autumn the Leningrad children's publishing team, led by Marshak, was accused of sabotage and broken up. Many of its members and authors who wrote for it were arrested, among them Z's one-time fellow student Bogolyubov. He also died in the camps. At that time the same fate overtook very many writers, artists, and other completely innocent people.

All the while Z went on doggedly working at the Rustaveli translation. As he produced sections of it they were published in the journal *Pioneer* (Nos. 4–12 for 1937). Finally, Z's little book of his own poems appeared. Naturally, it was not exactly what he had envisaged – a mere seventeen poems were in no way fully representative of his work. The book did not include many items that the author had wanted published. Even as late on as the proof copy he had had to replace 'Lodeynikov in the Garden' with 'Sedov' which he had only just written. But all the same, the slim little volume in its hard binding did bring the poet some pleasure.

At the beginning of November 1937, as part of an ongoing cure for a vascular problem in his legs, Z went to Sochi to bathe in the Matsesta mud-baths. While he was there he wrote to the Georgian literature specialist V. V. Goltsev about his plans for the coming year:

I am very glad that you seem to have found my book enjoyable. It's not a finished piece of work: the ends of the old are sticking out, and you can just see the young shoots of the new. I'm hoping to re-publish the book in a more complete form towards the end of next year. I've got a big task in front of me next year. I have to put the *Igor Tale* into modern Russian verse – it's an interesting project and a responsible one. I also have plans to do a translation of Vazha Pshavela and write some of my own poetry.

Z told Simon Chikovani about the publication of his version of the Rustaveli poem, and he also told him that he wanted to take part in the Rustaveli anniversary celebrations in Tbilisi:

Just lately I've been completely snowed under with masses of work, speeches, and going to various meetings. Now my Rustaveli translation has finally been accepted and should come out in time for the anniversary. The work on the first edition is finished. We've been waiting for you in Leningrad so that we could ask your advice, but we could not wait any longer, time was running out and after checking through the translation in the Rustaveli committee in Moscow it was finally accepted for publication . . . Dear Simon, I still don't know whether I shall be able to join you for the Rustaveli anniversary . . . If my participation is confirmed then I shall come straight to Tbilisi from here on 8 December. . . . I shall bring you and your friends a book of my poems which has just appeared and has sold out long ago.

At the same time he sent a joking letter home to his son:

Respected Nikita Nikolayevich, this is Professor Pichuzhkin writing to you from the city of Sochi. Today I have sent you a book called *The Adventures of Travka*. From this book you will learn much that is new. Goodbye. Soon I shall be writing to you again. Professor Pichuzhkin.

Jokes of this kind were standard practice in the family.

In Sochi Z began to give some thought as to how best to organize his work in the future. It was becoming increasingly clear to him that it would be dangerous to go on writing about his vision of nature and about the real problems of the modern world. An independent-minded treatment of themes like those was impossible, and he could not bring himself to write to the official line, which would have meant compromising his principles and his views. In the situation that was unfolding it was better to concentrate on translations, preferably of classical works. In that respect the translation of *The Knight in the Panther Skin* was an excellent idea – it gave him spiritual fulfilment, provided an income, and even promised some success in official circles. Z decided to continue along the same lines and translate other medieval epics. While he was still in Leningrad he had already begun to collate material about the Old Russian *Igor Tale* and about the German

Nibelungenlied. Next in line after that would be Firdawzi's epic *Shah-nama.*

The Rustaveli celebrations in Georgia were due to take place at the end of December, so that Z had to alter his plans somewhat. At the end of November he went straight from Sochi to Makhachkala, to be present at the funeral of Suleyman Stalsky. He spent several days in Grozny, and then returned home to Leningrad. Once there he immersed himself immediately in organizing his forthcoming work on the *Igor Tale.* On 9 December 1937 he made the following application to the publishing house:

> I am proposing to *Detizdat* that they conclude an agreement with me for a poetic re-working of the *Igor Tale* for older children and for reading in schools . . . I should like to put the *Igor Tale* into rhyming modern Russian. It will be a free re-working, but retaining all the basic stylistic characteristics of the original, and with the intention of making it a clear, accurate and expressive rendering, easy to assimilate and to remember. No Russian poet has yet done this kind of job on it. The work involved will be unusually complex and painstaking, and will demand solid scholarly preparation and good poetic capabilities.
>
> According to my information the anniversary celebration of the *Igor Tale* occurs at the end of 1938,* so that my work could coincide with it nicely.
>
> The artist S. S. Kobuladze has agreed to work on the illustrations to the book. He has already done some excellent illustrations for the Rustaveli poem.

In his application Z stipulated specifically that he be granted consultations with specialists in linguistics and in Old Russian literature, and he also asked to be allowed to travel to the places where the events described in the poem took place – Kiev, Putivl and other towns.

It eventually transpired that he had been included in the group of delegates to the Rustaveli commemorative plenum of the Writers' Union, and at the end of December he travelled to Tbilisi, or as it was then still called, Tiflis. There part of the print run of the high-quality Russian edition of *The Knight in the Panther Skin* was acquired and distributed to the delegates of the Plenum. Z made a speech which was greeted with warm applause from everyone present. For his masterly

---

* The *Igor Tale* was composed not earlier than 1187, so 1938 was taken as its 750th anniversary. Its full title is *The Tale of the Armament of Igor;* it is an anonymous historical tale in highly poeticized prose, rediscovered in a later medieval manuscript at the end of the eighteenth century [Ed.].

translation and re-working of the poem he was awarded a certificate of honour from the Georgian Central Committee.

Z saw in the new year, 1938, on a train somewhere between Tbilisi and Moscow. In the capital he met Gitovich who had just arrived there, and over the course of the next few days he sorted out his publishing affairs, had some meetings with writers, and, apparently took part in a literary evening at the Moscow University Club.

When he returned to Leningrad Z concluded a number of agreements with publishing houses. He was particularly pleased when the Leningrad State Publishing House for Literature accepted a personal volume of his verse translations, and the Leningrad section of the Children's Publishing House agreed to all his conditions and concluded an agreement for the publication of the *Igor Tale*. Now he got down to a really thorough study of Old Russian history and literature.

At the beginning of the year Z had to spend a further period of time on military service. On certain days of the week he had to take training sessions with a detachment of new recruits. One day after work he brought home a long box wrapped in paper. His son decided that the package was intended for him and began to ask his father all kinds of questions. But Z simply smiled and said: 'In the box is a gun I have brought home from military training. You have a look, but be careful how you touch it, in case it goes off.'

In the end it turned out that the package actually did contain a toy for the little boy. They placed the lid of the box upright, and on it were some acrobatic clowns with cups. When a ball was placed in the cup nearest the top, its weight would make the clowns bend forward, passing the ball from one to another, and then it would roll and fall into one of the apertures below. The luck of the player depended on which hole the ball fell into. The parents and son amused themselves by finding out how to play this new game. Their daughter was still very young, and she needed simpler toys. Then they wound up the gramophone and listened to their latest record – the solemn voice of Anton Shvarts reading 'Gori Symphony'. Evenings like this when Z was at home were rare now. More often he would go off with Gitovich to the Writers' House, or to see his artist friends, or to the beer-hall.

On one such evening, when Yekaterina was sitting sadly on her own at home, there was a ring at the door, and standing on the threshold was G. O. Kuklin, a children's writer who lived next door to them. He was a regular drinker, and was in the habit of calling on the Zabolotskys and asking to borrow small sums of money. Z did his best to avoid drunken conversations that distracted him from his work and started to refuse the money. On this occasion Kuklin glanced round apprehensively, stepped inside, and said in a low voice to Yekaterina as she opened the door:

> Don't worry, I'm not after money. I just wanted to warn you: they called me to the Big House and asked me all sorts of questions about Nikolay. I didn't say anything bad, and I didn't sign anything. Goodbye.

Kuklin was arrested soon afterwards. In the apartments on the corridor where the Zabolotskys lived, Berzin, Oleynikov, and Kuklin had already been arrested – who would be next? Even though he knew that the NKVD was interested in him Z had no inkling that he might be the next one. After all, they were interested in lots of people at the time. His situation had become quite safe, he was careful what he did, and did not say too much in public.

Even so, he had a strong desire to express his inner protest. It was probably on one of those days early in the new year, 1938, that Z called his wife into his study, closed the door firmly, and gave her a poem to read about the terrible, oppressive time in which they lived, about the evil Big House with its tower (the NKVD building in Leningrad), about its windows that remained alight all night, and about the dark cells there in which innocent people were tortured. All this was widely known, yet few dared speak, let alone write, about it. 'Now listen,' said Z, when his wife had finished reading, 'now I'm going to read you another poem in which the first words of every line and the rhyme are the same as this one.' And he read out an innocent poem about nature. 'By using the line pattern of this one I shall always be able to re-create the seditious one. After all, things must change sometime!' So saying, he took the dangerous poem from his wife's hands, took it into the kitchen, and thrust it into the stove. 'And now let's forget what was written on it'.*

Literaturnaya Gazeta for 26 February 1938 carried a long-awaited review of *Second Book*. Its author, A. Tarasenkov, who had for some time 'specialized' in Z, dealt first of all with those who had published positive articles on Z's latest works – Stepanov and Dymshits. After that he came to the following conclusion:

> Z has indeed broken with his earlier decadent excesses and his enthusiasm for formalism. This in itself, of course, is a good thing. But unfortunately the enthusiasm for formalism has been replaced merely by the dead hand of academicism, the cold imitation of classical models.

As though trying to knock away the poet's last remaining support,

* Neither version seems to have survived [Ed.].

Tarasenkov had not even anything good to say about 'Gori Symphony', noting tartly that the Leader occupied a far from central position in it:

> ... the formative period of Stalin's genius is viewed solely on one level – as a result of the influence of the primitive nature of the Caucasus. Unfortunately Z completely ignores the social conditions in which the development of the personality of the Leader of the Peoples took place. He does not say a single word about it.

This was a particularly nasty blow, because any accusation, even if made indirectly, of insufficient attention to the Leader's 'genius' was at that time extremely dangerous. The article exhibited that same 'vague opposition' to Z's poetry that he always felt on the part of certain poets, and – more specially – certain critics.

Z got a study permit to the House of Creativity which had recently opened in Yelizavetino, not far from Leningrad, and in the first days of March he travelled there to get away from all the literary fuss and unpleasantness. There he began to translate the *Igor Tale* and to write his own poem 'The Siege of Kozelsk', based on an idea taken from his studies of Old Russian literature and history. All the preparatory work had already been done, and now he found the writing came fluently and easily.

Imprisonment

I

IN THE Writers' House Z unexpectedly received an official telegram from the Party organizational secretary of the Leningrad branch of the Writers' Union, G. I. Miroshnichenko, who asked him to come and see him on urgent business at 11 a.m. on 19 March. His work on the translation of the *Igor Tale* and the long poem 'The Siege of Kozelsk' was in full swing, but, annoying as it was to interrupt it even for a day, he had to go into town. Z decided that there was a bright side to it: he could see the family and read out the parts of the translation he had already written to his wife and to Gitovich. He wanted to test out on his listeners how acceptable an Old Russian poem would be when translated into modern verse.

Arriving in the morning from Yelizavetino, Z briefly went home – his wife was lying down in her room suffering from angina, the children were fine. On the way to the Writers' Union he looked in at Gitovich's flat and promised to come back for dinner and read the beginning of the translation.

In Miroshnichenko's study two NKVD men were waiting for him, and they said they had to have a talk with him in his flat. He was driven back to the Griboyedov Canal and there they showed him an arrest warrant. Normal free human existence came to a sudden end; there now came a fearful time of physical and mental suffering, separation from his beloved work, from family and friends. Although Z knew of the mass arrests in Leningrad, the arrest warrant was a completely unexpected shock. Not yet fully aware of the magnitude and irreversibility of the misfortune that had come upon him, he went up to his wife, cautiously embraced her and showed her the warrant. 'So this is what we've come to!' he said quietly, trying to hide his emotion.

In the presence of a witness – the concierge Yepishkin, drowsing in his chair – they carried out a search. Z and Yekaterina sat motionless on the couch, close together, and watched as the investigator, N. N.

168

Lupandin, searched the writing-table, looked through the papers lying on it and put all the manuscripts he found in a suitcase – where they disappeared for ever as far as the poet himself and Russian literature were concerned. Into the suitcase there also went various suspicious objects such as a blunt Georgian dagger given to him on his last visit, and certain books – such as the Bible. Merkuryev, the investigator's assistant, examined about 2,000 volumes in Z's collection, expertly flicking through them and gathering up the occasional bits of paper that fluttered out. During the search Z's sister-in-law, Yevgeniya Provorova, turned up. Once her identity had been established she was allowed to stay in the kitchen with the young Nikita. Afterwards he was allowed into the living-room, where he clambered behind his parents' backs and had a quiet cry. He already understood that his Daddy was being 'taken away'. After searching the writing-table Lupandin ordered Yekaterina to accompany him round the flat. He searched the shoe-cupboard, the washing in the bathroom, the clothes cupboard. On the landing he found a file containing her old dissertation on Chekhov, but did not look through it – there remained in it, undiscovered, some of Z's old letters and manuscripts. Then the couple sat on the couch and Z stroked his wife's hands and spoke words of comfort, while she kept thinking of the fearful 'evidence' that lay beneath them in the drawer of the couch and prayed that the investigators should not find it. The search was not very meticulous – the investigators omitted to look into the couch. And inside it, together with other books and papers for which there was no other place in a small flat, lay a bound typescript book of Z's poems with a note from Nikolay Bukharin inside it. The content of the note was completely innocuous, but after all the trial of the 'Trotskyite-rightist bloc' had just finished in Moscow, and the chief accused – Bukharin, Rykov and their allies – had been shot four days earlier. The name of Bukharin was associated with the most unbelievable crimes: the wave of repressions struck down his genuine and his supposed supporters alike. In such conditions even a hint of a personal link with Bukharin could cost not just one's freedom, but one's life. Who can tell how the investigators might have directed Z's case, had a note from the leader of the 'Trotskyite-rightist bloc' been in their hands? Realizing the danger of this document, Yekaterina subsequently destroyed it, and for long afterwards hardly anyone knew about it.

At the end of the search, Z said farewells to his family, kissed his little daughter, who then whispered 'Daddy' for the first time, and went along the corridor with the investigators towards the staircase. Then Yekaterina, sensing that she might never see her husband again, rushed after him with a cry of horror. But she was not permitted further than the top of the stairs.

That evening, mastering her despair, Yekaterina put the children to bed, left them in the care of the maid Zina and went to tell the Shvartses what had happened and to discuss what she should do and how her husband could be helped. Yevgeny Shvarts wrote of that evening in his diary:

> We looked into what could be done for Katerina, who's all on her own. She took things calmly, with a real woman's way of comprehending how to stand the pain and shoulder all the burdens life could send her. Sudden bereavement – not quite that, but something close to it. That's how separation was felt in those days.

Straight after the arrest Yekaterina began collecting all her husband's manuscripts that had not been taken in the search. There were not many in the flat – basically the ones that had been in the couch and on the landing. But manuscripts of unfinished long poems and, perhaps, of short poems too still remained in Yelizavetino. Nobody knew if they had been taken away by NKVD men. Gitovich – who well understood the value of all Z's papers – undertook to save them. At crack of dawn, so as to get there ahead of the investigators, he set off to the Writers' House and collected up all the manuscripts that remained there. Among them were fair copies of the introduction and first part of the *Igor Tale*, and two parts of 'The Siege of Kozelsk'.

When Z arrived at the remand prison attached to the well-known NKVD building on Liteyny Prospekt, he immediately encountered a reality that turned out to be more terrible than the most incredible rumours about that institution.

The interrogation went on for about four days and nights without a break; it was accompanied by abuse, insults and threats. He was not given food, nor allowed to sleep. They were trying to get an admission from him that he belonged to a counter-revolutionary writers' organization, supposedly headed by Nikolay Tikhonov. They demanded that he should name the members of this organization, suggesting the names of Benedikt Livshits, Yelena Tager, Georgy Kuklin and Boris Kornilov. They also insisted that Z should confess to the deliberate anti-Soviet character of his work.

Z was overwhelmed by the savage absurdity and cruelty of all that was taking place, but mobilized all his will-power so as to preserve his human dignity and avoid implicating himself or others. He protested against his unlawful arrest and against his rough treatment, referring to his rights under the Soviet Constitution. 'The Constitution stops operating at our front door', the investigator replied mockingly.

The NKVD men worked in shifts, and Z sat motionless on a chair day after day beneath a blinding light that was directed into his face. Eighteen years later he recollected in *The Story of my Imprisonment*:

> My legs began to swell, and on the third day I had to pull off my shoes, since I could no longer stand the pain in my feet. Consciousness started to dim, and I concentrated all my powers on answering rationally and not letting slip any wrong word relating to the people I was being questioned about . . . On the fourth day, as a result of nervous tension, hunger and lack of sleep, I gradually began to lose my reason. As I recall, I myself was by now threatening and shouting at the investigators. Signs of hallucination appeared: on the wall and the parquet floor of the investigators' office I saw some sort of figures in continual motion. I remember that once I was sitting before a whole conclave of investigators. I was no longer the least afraid of them and held them in contempt. Before my eyes the pages of some huge imaginary book were being turned, and I saw different illustrations on every page. Paying no heed to anything else, I was expounding the content of these illustrations to my investigators. It is hard now to define the condition I was in, but I recollect experiencing a sense of inner relief and exaltation that these people had not succeeded in making a dishonourable man of me.

Such behaviour on the part of a poet who was in the process of losing his reason began to annoy the investigators. They pushed him into another room and started to beat him up. In his disturbed state he attempted to defend himself and to attack his tormentors, but eventually they overcame him by means of a powerful water-jet from a fire hose and forced him into a corner. Thereupon he was thoroughly beaten up with truncheons and boots – to such an extent that the doctors who saw him after his ordeal were amazed that his internal organs were still intact. He was dragged unconscious to the prison hospital of the Institute of Forensic Psychiatry, not far from the remand prison. Here he spent about two weeks – first in a violent patients' ward, then in a quiet one.

Z's case was indirectly linked with the destruction of the 'rightist' Bukharinite opposition and with the general task of finding concrete testimony to the connection between this opposition and the supposed activity in the USSR of 'Trotskyite wreckers'. A decision was taken to initiate the unmasking of this Trotskyite-Bukharinite group among the writers of Leningrad as well. The intention of the NKVD was to prove that these writers of counter-revolutionary inclinations headed by Tikhonov should supposedly have received their orders from the Trotskyite centre in Paris, with the wife of Ilya Ehrenburg (who often

171

travelled abroad) as intermediary. The secret policemen reckoned that this could be the basis for the scenario of a large-scale and very promising trial. To realize this plan, supporting evidence from the group's 'members' had to be obtained by whatever means possible. With this in mind they went to work on the writer Benedikt Livshits, who had been arrested at the end of 1937, using torture. At that time 'physical methods' of interrogation were officially permitted and widely used in inquisitorial practice. After many days of so-called 'conveyor' interrogation and beatings Livshits, evidently no longer fully understanding what was going on, signed the statement demanded of him.

The record of Livshits's interrogation reads more specifically as follows:

> In concrete terms Mrs Ehrenburg indicated the necessity of forming a bloc consisting of the already existing rightist group of Leningrad writers headed by the president of the Leningrad branch of the Writers' Union, Nikolay Tikhonov . . . Sheltered by Tikhonov, Akhmatova long continued the publication of her reactionary verse. Mandelshtam republished a volume of his anti-Soviet writings with *Goslitizdat* (State Literary Publishing House). With Tikhonov's connivance the depraved novels of Vaginov, slandering Soviet reality, came out one after another from the Leningrad writers' publishing house; Tikhonov pronounced over Vaginov's grave that the latter's poetic heritage was immortal.
>
> In the poetry section of *Zvezda* (*Star*), edited personally by Tikhonov, there was published Zabolotsky's contemptuous poem 'The Triumph of Agriculture' – praised to the skies by Eykhenbaum and Stepanov despite its clear counter-revolutionary nature. In general the entire odious, counter-revolutionary personality of Zabolotsky was for a long time supported by Tikhonov's recognition of him.
>
> These facts – and many more could be adduced – point clearly enough to the counter-revolutionary essence of Tikhonov . . .
>
> Tikhonov for his part has informed me that he has set up a group among whose participants are the poets Zabolotsky, Kornilov, Dagayev and Akhmatova, and he has indicated his close links with the formalists Eykhenbaum and Stepanov. Furthermore he indicated to me that he is linked with counter-revolutionary nationalist organizations existing among the Georgian writers.

There is evidence that the unfortunate Benedikt Livshits completely lost his reason during interrogation, signed a 'confession' at the end of the interrogators' record that he had incited terrorism, and was soon afterwards shot.

Z was arrested two months after Livshits's interrogation and his inquisition began immediately, lasting from 19 to 23 March without

Zabolotsky in Leningrad 1929.

Daniil Kharms with Alisa Poret, an artist
belonging to the Filonov circle,
Leningrad 1931.

Aleksandr Vvedensky in Leningrad
in the 1930s.

Yevgeny Shvarts. Leningrad,
17 September 1934.

The third block from the left is the house on the Griboyedov canal in Leningrad where the Zabolotskys lived on the fourth floor and where the poet was arrested on 19 March 1938.

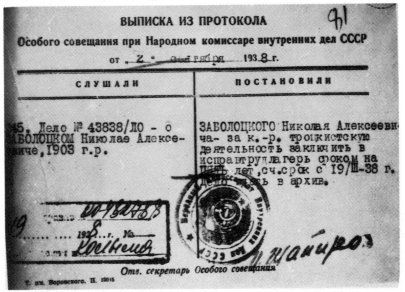

ВЫПИСКА ИЗ ПРОТОКОЛА

Особого совещания при Народном комиссаре внутренних дел СССР

от „ 2 " октября 1938 г.

СЛУШАЛИ	ПОСТАНОВИЛИ
45. Дело № 43838/ЛО - о ЗАБОЛОЦКОМ Николае Алексеевиче, 1903 г.р.	ЗАБОЛОЦКОГО Николая Алексеевича- за к.-р. троцкистскую деятельность заключить в исправтрудлагерь сроком на пять лет, сч.срок с 19/III-38 г. Дело сдать в архив.

Отв. секретарь Особого совещания

Т. им. Воровского. П. 18015

The official decree sentencing Zabolotsky to five years' imprisonment in a corrective labour camp following a special NKVD meeting. The stamp in the bottom left-hand corner notes the place of imprisonment as the notorious Kolyma, but in fact he was sent elsewhere.

Yekaterina, Zabolotsky's wife, with their children Nikita and Natasha, in 1939 when they were exiled to Urzhum. This photograph was sent to Zabolotsky and kept throughout his years in the camps.

Four poets, from left to right: Zabolotsky, Mezhirov, Tikhonov and Antokolsky in Tbilisi in May 1947.

Aleksandr Gitovich, poet and
staunch defender of Zabolotsky.

Vasily Grossman (left) with Zabolotsky,
Z's wife Yekaterina and daughter
Natasha in Moscow, June 1951.

Zabolotsky in the birch woods at Tarusa, 1957.

interruption. However only one page of notes in his file reflects those days of interrogation. The prisoner determinedly and repeatedly rebuffed all accusations of criminal anti-Soviet activity. From Z's own later testimony it is known that he was questioned about writers whom he had known or with whom he had literary dealings, but his answers were so brief and uninteresting that they did not even enter them in the record, hoping that he could be broken anyhow. But beatings and tortures, hunger and sleeplessness had the sole result that Z needed to be sent to the mental hospital.

The writer Yelena Tager, who had been arrested almost at the same time as Z, was interrogated about the same matter and by the same methods. To the file of documents pertaining to Z's interrogation is attached the record of her 'supplementary interrogation' of 11 June 1938. Her interrogator was the same Lupandin, who had particularly interested himself in the 'Trotskyite' Livshits, Tikhonov and N. Chukovsky. In particular her record contains evidence intended to confirm Z's participation in the counter-revolutionary group headed by Tikhonov:

> From approximately 1931 there was a group of writers with anti-Soviet tendencies around N. S. Tikhonov: N. A. Zabolotsky, B. P. Kornilov, L. I. Dobychin, O. Mandelshtam, Tsirelson, S. A. Kolbasyev, V. I. Erlikh, I. T. Dmitrochenko and P. Kalitin. Tikhonov and his group enjoyed great attention and support on the part of Bukharin, who was invariably ready to print their works on the pages of *Izvestia*. In its counter-revolutionary activity the group had a distinctly rightist tendency. Its members' works had a counter-revolutionary kulak character . . .
>
> Links between our anti-Soviet organization and the nationalistically-inclined Georgian writers were set up in 1933, and from then till my arrest they were regularly encouraged by members of the organization: Livshits, Tikhonov, Zabolotsky, Spassky . . .
>
> Tikhonov in every possible way promoted the writing careers of N. A. Zabolotsky, author of a series of anti-Soviet works (*Columns*; 'The Triumph of Agriculture'), Boris Kornilov (whose kulak works are also well known), Volf Erlikh, P. Kalitin, S. A. Kolbasyev, Tsirelson, Mariya Shapskaya. These people's works were raised up aloft by us without deserving it in any way. As I indicated before, this group had Bukharin's support.
>
> After the fiasco of Zabolotsky's 'The Triumph of Agriculture' Tikhonov and other members of our anti-Soviet organization immediately set about his rehabilitation, declaring Zabolotsky had been 'unlucky'. Speeches of 'repentance' by Zabolotsky were quickly organized. A laudatory article about him was published by Zoshchenko.

173

Meanwhile, on 2 April, after ten days in the prison mental hospital Z was again put in the cells. The forensic psychiatric verdict declared, 'N. A. Zabolotsky had undergone an acute reactive psychotic condition with intermittent obscuring of consciousness. At present Z is neurally healthy and sane. He shows signs of a neuropathological condition.'

Not yet fully recovered from his injuries and psychological shock, Z was returned to prison confinement and put into one of the common cells, filled to bursting with other prisoners. 'Clouds of steam and the special prison stench reached me while still in the corridor, and I remember being astonished by it', he recalled. 'They could hardly shut the door after me, and I found myself in a crowd of people wedged tight against each other or sitting in disorderly heaps, all over the cell. Learning that the newcomer was a writer, my neighbours informed me that the cell contained other writers too, and soon they brought along P. N. Medvedev and D. Vygodsky, who had been arrested before me. Seeing the sad state I was in, my comrades fixed me up a place in a corner. Thus began my prison life in the proper sense'.

Every night Z waited to be summoned to interrogation with accompanying torture and beatings; each night he listened, horrified, to the groans and soul-lacerating shrieks from the investigators' offices. To drown out these noises heavy lorries were stationed in the courtyard with engines running, and from the noise of these and from the imagined pictures of torment the prisoners reached an extreme pitch of nervousness.

In his memoirs Z wrote: 'After my return from hospital I was left in peace and not called before the investigator for some time. When interrogations did begin again – and there were still a few to come – no one hit me any more, and things were limited to the ordinary threats and abuse. I didn't budge, and the investigation marked time.'

All in all the investigator was well-informed about Z's circle of acquaintances, and also about the multitude of critical articles attacking his work politically. The junior lieutenant Lupandin, not very well up in literary matters, took instuctions from the former RAPP writer N. V. Lesyuchevsky. It is quite possible that the latter helped in putting together the record of the arrestees' interrogations.

While Z had been in the prison hospital, for some unknown reason the NKVD lost its active interest in the further disentangling of this wide-ranging case. Its central protagonist – Tikhonov – was not arrested. Perhaps there were insufficient 'testamentary depositions', perhaps the authorities would not sanction the arrest of such a major figure as Tikhonov at the time: and without him the whole story of a group of anti-Soviet writers around him fell to pieces. In *Epilogue*, his book of memoirs, V. A. Kaverin voiced the supposition that what protected Tikhonov was the favourable impression made on Stalin by Tikhonov's speech in the Bolshoy Theatre on 10 February 1937, at the formal session devoted to the centenary of Pushkin's death. Stalin was present and, according to Kaverin,

> not only approved the speech, but let the fact be known. He fell for Tikhonov, and Tikhonov fell for Stalin – sincerely, unselfconsciously: it is significant that even now, when he is over 80, he still has Stalin's portrait hanging above his desk. As I see it that is what prevented realization of the grandiose plans of the Leningrad police. To put Stalin's favourite behind bars, to make him head of a counter-revolutionary plot – that would have taken a very bold initiative, resting on firm evidence.

In Z's case-file there is only one record of an interrogation after his return from hospital – on 22 June 1938. In an attempt to unmask the prisoner, Lupandin referred to 'depositions of evidence' by Yelena Tager (11 June) and Benedikt Livshits. He read out extracts from their interrogations to Z, but the latter refused to believe in their authenticity. He was not allowed to see the depositions with his own eyes, and could not obtain a personal confrontation with Livshits and Tager. Up to this last interrogation Z continued his categorical denial of all charges brought against him. On the same day he was informed the investigation had ended. However, so as to close Z's case they still required an 'authoritative' conclusion about the 'counter-revolutionary' nature of his work. As usual the NKVD turned to its consultant N. V. Lesyuchevsky: without any need for 'physical methods' he found no difficulty in coping with the tasks his bosses set him. Thus in May 1937 he had written a long denunciatory article 'On the Poetry of Boris Kornilov', in which, defying all logic and common sense he furnished the investigators with the conclusion they needed about the anti-Soviet, counter-revolutionary and kulak nature of his work. That caused Kornilov's tragic death. Now a similar denunciation was required for Z.

Lesyuchevsky did not need to rack his brains for long. He was no novice; anyhow rich material for denunciation could be extracted from the earlier critical articles about Z's works. Under his standard title 'On the Poetry of Nikolay Zabolotsky' he produced a document of stunning mendacity and cynicism, entirely characteristic of that dark epoch.* Now that the denunciation has been made public, its lines read like some crude farce, nasty parody or simple idiocy, but at that time they

---

* Translated in full in Appendix I.

175

were not so stupid and indeed provided an entirely adequate basis for an accusation. Its date deserves to be noted: 3 July 1938. That means it was written three and a half months after Z's arrest, after the 'case of the counter-revolutionary writers' organization' had already foundered.

On 31 July 1938 the deputy head of Leningrad NKVD, Khatenever, signed the prosecutor's statement on Z's case. It contained the phrases 'belonged to an anti-Soviet rightist organization', 'was the author of anti-Soviet works', 'did not admit his guilt, but was fully unmasked by Livshits's and Tager's depositions'. That was enough: on 2 September 1938, by decree of a Special Commission (that is, without trial) Z was sentenced to five years' detention in the corrective labour camps 'for counter-revolutionary Trotskyite activity', and after two more months was dispatched to the Far East of the Soviet Union.

In early November Z had a meeting with his wife in a special room at the 'Kresty' transfer prison (see p.216). She gave him the things he needed and told him that she and the children were being exiled from the city. Within permitted limits one could choose one's place of exile, and Yekaterina decided on Urzhum, of which she had heard much from her husband and which was therefore not a totally unfamiliar place. Through a double grille the Zabolotskys again made their farewells, not knowing if they would ever meet again.

The day after his family left Leningrad, on 8 November, Z too was sent on his way. The first stage, to Sverdlovsk, was covered quite quickly in two days. Here they off-loaded the prisoners and put them in the Sverdlovsk transit prison to be sorted and prepared for the next stage. When, a month later, it was Z's turn to be sent on, he was transferred to a vast room, where hundreds of prisoners selected for dispatch were crowded together with their possessions. A grey-haired man, thirty-six years old, came up to him in this room and introduced himself as Gurgen Georgievich Tatosov, a lawyer from the town of Grozny. He said he already had experience of prison life, and a month ago, communicating in sign language through a window-grille with people in other cells, he had learnt that the poet Z, whose work he knew and loved, had arrived at the prison. The two of them talked for a couple of hours about poetry, about the misfortune that had come upon them and about their families, still at liberty. Z sensed in his new acquaintance a strong, honest, benevolently inclined person and felt trust and sympathy for him. They agreed not to be separated, but in the loading-up operation they were put into different wagons. Everyone knew that the destination was supposed to be Kolyma; but for some reason or other, while already under way, the convoy was redirected to Komsomolsk-on-the-Amur.

Let us quote again from Z's memoir:

Sixty and more days we toiled along the main Siberian line, lingering in sidings for days at a time. There were some forty men in the wagon, as I recollect. A fierce winter had started and the frosts became more severe every day. A little iron stove was lit in the centre of the wagon; the orderly sat near by and looked after it. At first we lived on two levels – one half underneath, the other half above on high wooden planks ranged along the sides of the wagon, a little lower than a man's height. But soon the cold drove all those below on to the plank bunks; even here, however, packed into a heap for bodily warmth, we suffered cruelly from the cold. Bit by bit life turned into a purely bodily existence without higher interests, where a person's entire concerns were reduced to not dying of hunger or thirst, not freezing through and not being shot like a rabid dog.

Each man received 300 grams of bread a day, hot water twice a day and a dinner of thin *balanda* (soup) with a ladle of gruel. For starving and frozen men this food was of course not enough. But even this pitiful ration was given out irregularly – and evidently not always through the fault of the privileged criminal prisoners who served it to us. The fact was that the provisioning of this whole vast mass of prisoners moving at that period through Siberia in endless waves presented a complex economic problem. At many stations severe cold and poor administration made it impossible to supply men even with water. Once we received no water for about three days, and as we greeted the new year of 1939 somewhere around Lake Baykal we had to lick black sooty icicles that had formed on the walls of the wagon from our own exhalations. I shall never succeed in forgetting this New Year's Day feast to the end of my life.

In that wagon I first came up against the world of criminals, who became a constant torment to us who had to drag out our lives alongside them, and often under their command . . .

Somehow of its own accord, our wagon divided into two groups: those sentenced under Article 58* settled on one side, the criminals on the other. Condemned to coexist, we stared at each other with concealed hostility, and only occasionally did this hostility break through to the surface. I remember how once, without any provocation from my side, one of our criminals who was liable to fits and some sort of instantaneous hysteria attacked me with a log of wood. His comrades restrained him and I was unharmed. But an atmosphere of peculiar psychological tension never left us for a moment, and put its stamp upon our life in the train.

From time to time the authorities appeared in the wagon to carry out a check. In order to verify the numbers they made us all go on to one ledge

* Political prisoners [Ed.].

of planks. At a special command we had to crawl across a plank to the other ledge, and they counted us as we did so. The picture is as vivid before me as if it were happening now: black with soot, beards sprouting, we crawl one after the other on all fours like monkeys across the plank, lit by the dim glow of lanterns, while a semi-educated guard holds us at rifle-point and counts and counts away, getting muddled in his tricky calculations.

Insects devoured us, and the two baths arranged for us at Irkutsk and Chita did not deliver us from this affliction. Both these baths were sheer torment. Each was like an inferno filled with a wildly cackling throng of devils large and small. There was not the remotest possibility of washing. One felt lucky if one managed to save one's personal possessions from the professional criminals. Loss of possessions indicated almost certain death on the journey. This indeed happened to certain unfortunates: they died without reaching camp. In our wagon there were no fatal incidents.

For more than two months our sad train dragged its way along the main Trans-Siberian line. Two small iced-up windows under the ceiling allowed faint light into our wagon during the short hours of daylight. At other times a candle-end glowed in a lantern, and when candles were not given out the whole wagon was plunged into impenetrable darkness. Pressed tightly together we lay in this primordial gloom, listening to the thudding of the wheels and sunk in disconsolate thoughts about our fate. In the mornings we could only just manage to peer out of the window at the limitless expanse of the Siberian fields, the endless snow-covered forest, the shadowy villages and towns dominated by columns of vertical smoke, and the fantastic sheer cliffs of the shores of Lake Baykal. We were being taken further and further, towards the Far East, towards the end of the world . . .

In the first days of February we arrived at Khabarovsk. Here we stopped a long time. Then we were suddenly moved backwards, reached Volochayevka and turned northwards off the main line along a newly built branch line. Along both sides of the railway there were glimpses of camps with their watch-towers and settlements of modern 'gingerbread houses' all built to the same pattern. The kingdom of the BAM (Baykal-Amur Railway) was awaiting us, its new settlers. The train stopped, there was a rattling of bolts, and we stepped out from our hiding-places into this new world, flooded in sunlight, shackled in a frost of minus fifty, encircled with the apparitions of slim Far Eastern birch-trees rising to the very heavens.

Thus we came to the town of Komsomolsk-on-the-Amur.

II

The grey mass of exhausted prisoners, weak from their journey, was brought to the transit point. Here Z again saw his Sverdlov prison friend G. G. Tatosov, with whom he was to live side by side almost uninterruptedly till 1943, when they were fated to go to different camps. As Tatosov describes it this is how the dispatch camp at Komsomolsk looked:

> The vast barrack-hut, 35–40 metres long, in which oil-lamps burned day and night, was cold and damp. Wooden planking stretched along the walls, two tiers high, with sticks instead of boards laid across: you can imagine what it was like to lie on them. Criminals and political prisoners were in there together, and that led to an appalling existence for us. Once a man was forcibly stripped, since without his knowing it some card-players were gambling for his clothes. Somewhere else there would be torrents of blood flowing after a senseless fight which would flare up for some trivial reason. The air would be thick with cynical, indecent and blasphemous oaths – and there would be far too much else going on to try and describe in a short letter – things that anyhow you might prefer not to commit to paper.
>
> That's where we lived for about three weeks. We were sorted, checked and prepared for the next stage. On one ill-omened day Zabolotsky had all his possessions stolen. Distressed and confused, he wandered around the barrack-hut and naïvely enquired who had taken his things. He got some nasty answers; someone said Yashka had them, and when Z asked which Yashka he just got a scabrous rhyme back.
>
> I was well acquainted with all the filth around us since I'd worked as a lawyer, had met a great deal of it, knew the language, and I was not considered a total sucker like most of the intelligentsia. I told Z that he should not even give another thought to his possessions – they had long ago been spirited away from the hut and sold – that all we could do was to hang on to each other so as to suffer a bit less from the lawlessness around us. We settled ourselves on the sticks, and so began our prison-camp lives.

Z and Tatosov got into a group of political prisoners sent from the transfer prison to a settlement called Start, situated in deep forest about forty kilometres from Komsomolsk. Before he left Z was handed out some kind of prison-camp clothing, or else he could never have stood the bitter Far-Eastern February frost. Even in this he was frozen through when he had to stand for about an hour and wait in front of the barbed wire, looking at slogans hanging on the gate saying: 'Labour is a matter of honour, glory and heroism', and another, directly related to it: 'Death to the enemies of the people!' Finally the gate opened and the icy prisoners were let in to the empty, cold barrack-hut intended for them. They lit the iron stove in the middle and distributed themselves randomly on the two-tiered plank beds. It was warmer on top (to the point where they shouted 'stop feeding the stove'!) but in compensation there were so many bed bugs that they had to be scooped out by the handful and hurled down. On the tier below there were fewer bugs, since the cold put them off just as it did the humans.

The trivialities of their endless days were nearly unendurable. Before dawn the prisoners would be led out to their labours. As he emerged from the hut Z would manage to take a look about him and drink in what he later described in his brief sketch 'Pictures from the Far East':

At night an utterly black sky studded with a glittering multitude of brilliant stars would arch over the snow-white earth. Above the settlement, where stoves kept going day and night, there would tower a many-pillared colonnade of smoke. Each white pillar was virtually immobile and colossally tall, and only high up aloft would they all spread out into a single layer propping up the black heavens. Low down, resting its tail against the horizon, glittered the Great Bear. And on a pole above the huts, fixing its eye on a snowdrift, sat a polar owl, watching out for the rats that bred multitudinously where people lived.

At first Z and Tatosov worked as a team cutting timber. They had to fell a tree not more than ten centimetres above ground level, trim off the branches, saw the trunk into planks of a certain length and stack them up. People worked in a close bunch, since it was easier for the marksmen to guard a smaller area. From time to time a shout of 'Timber!' would ring out, and a huge tree crashed down, hitting the neighbouring tree-tops and endangering those people working nearby. Then they would have to run for it blindly and were in danger of being hit in the face by branches.

On one occasion Z and Tatosov selected a massive, as they used to say 'rock-solid', birch, thinking that if they got that one down they would have done half their day's work. Somehow they felled it, and then found they could not cut it up – it jammed the saw. They started observing how the Finnish prisoners, great forestry experts, went about their work. They learnt how to fell a tree, when and where to knock in wedges, how to make a wood-stack look as big as possible. They tried to work flat out, but none of the new arrivals could complete the daily norm – and failing to reach it could mean dying of hunger. Those who could not cope with the task used to receive a mere 300 grams of bread and a ladle of thin soup for supper. For men working in sub-zero temperatures that sort of ration meant speedy emaciation and dystrophy.

There were tables in the food-hut set aside for those who fulfilled the norm: here there was better food and more of it – several helpings of kasha, a sufficiency of bread.

But without being used to physical work, or knowing how to use axe and saw properly, it was impossible to fulfil the norm, try as you might. At the end of the working day the foreman noted work done on a special board. Suddenly on one such day, when strength had almost gone (there were not yet any food-parcels from home), a miracle occurred: the guard watching over the workmen went up to the tally-keeper and, pointing to Z and Tatosov, ordered: 'Put down 120 per cent for these two. They want to work well even if they can't.' Thus thanks to the guard's humanity it was occasionally possible to get a better level of nourishment. Gradually the work grew more familiar to them and the norm not so unattainable.

On 27 February 1939 Z wrote to his wife:

My dear Katya and children! I am well, and sent my first letter to you two weeks ago. Too early to expect an answer, but I'm waiting impatiently. My address: Komsomolsk-on-the Amur, NKVD camp, 15th section, 2nd column, then my name.

I'm working on general duties. It's hard because I'm not used to it, but I've begun to reach the norm. I've asked you to send fifty roubles, if you can manage it, and a food parcel – lard, sugar, soap, underwear, a couple of pairs of socks and leg-wrappers. I need Vitamin C too. I've heard tell you can get it in wafer form for 1½ roubles a box. If it's true do please send me some, dearest. It'd also be good to have some onions and garlic. Don't send anything expensive.

There's not a single hour when I don't think about you, my family! I pine for the children and I'm grief-stricken for you, Katya. How are things going? Write as soon as you get this letter, and keep on writing. I'm able to send letters twice a month. Tell me about yourself and the family. I don't yet know your new address. Send some paper and stamps.

I've got one hope in life: that my case will be reviewed. I'm waiting in the belief that'll happen. However hard it is I'll be patient and wait for the Ministry to reply. Lots of kisses to you and to my Nikita and Natasha . . . If I only knew how you all were and what's become of you.

Keep well, keep patient and sensible. Your loving Dad N.Z.
P.S. I need glasses for shortsightedness: 1.75. If you can order them send them in a case.

Letters had to be given in unsealed, so that the camp censors could check them. It is possible that Z wrote about fulfilling his norm specially with the censor in view, so as not to give away those camp guards who were well-disposed, though it is also possible he had already got into the swing of his work and really was managing it.

By no means all the armed guards behaved humanely to the prisoners: more often they would shout, swear and mock at them. Once when spring had come Z and Tatosov were sent to dig post-holes somewhere outside the camp precinct. The earth was hard, the spring water quickly filled the excavated holes and they had to work standing in icy water. Suddenly a guard with a dog appeared out of nearby woodland. Maybe the workers had sat down for a breather, maybe there was no specific reason, but he gave a command, pointed at the two prisoners and let the guard-dog off its lead. Z stepped back as it hurled itself at him and he fell into the water-filled pit, so that only his head and feet stuck out of the water. Tatosov hit the dog with the crowbar he had in his hands so that it dropped down with a howl. Cocking his rifle the guard ran up and yelled at Tatosov (who had gone grey in the committal prison), 'What have you done with the dog, you louse?', and took a routine hefty swing at his mouth.

A decade afterwards one of his friends asked Z whether it was a hard life in prison.

'It was hard often enough,' he answered laconically.

'How was it hard, then? Tell me.'

'It's pretty hard, isn't it, when you work till you're dropping, take a quick breather, and they set the dogs on you?' answered Z, frowning and changing the conversation to another topic.

Yet even so, after the experience of the investigation, seven months of prison torments, the month spent at Sverdlovsk in transit, the two-month journey through Siberia and the time in Komsomolsk – after all this, hard convict labour actually seemed attractive at first. After the confined, stinking air of the cells and the railway-wagons the forest air smelt sweet. The possibility of looking out at mountains, touching the trunk of an Eastern cedar or a larch, spotting a woodpecker or a chipmunk gave at least a moment of inner joy. Even the most intolerable work drowned out mental pain and suffering, spared one for a time from the oppression of overseers or of real criminals, brought oblivion from the horrors of reality. Occasionally Z was even able to find a certain satisfaction in it. Thus eight years later he was to write in the poem 'Starting Construction':

> When in the forest thickets age-old cedars,
> cracking under the axe one by one,
> suddenly start inclining their grey necks,
> I am no longer master of myself!

For a certain brief moment
I am replete with that abundance of energy,
that blessed thirst of creativity,
such as would raise the dead out of their graves.

With a twelve-hour working day there was little free time. After eating and before going to sleep they just about managed to mend clothes, do other small but important tasks and twice a month write home. But after exhausting work in sub-zero temperatures sleep was demanded. Only the cold and the vicious bedbugs would wake anyone up.

After a time the work changed – the prisoners started having to quarry stone. The technology of preparing stone rubble was not complicated, but did require a certain degree of knowledge and joint effort. Explosives made it easier. To get them ready someone had to clamber up the sheer face of the quarry so as to fix stakes and attach ropes. Z was among those who had to undertake this dangerous work. Once he was inching his way up the cliff, spread-eagled against it and carefully seeking out the scarcely noticeable footholds. All of a sudden a tree root sticking out of the rock-face hooked on to his spectacle-frame, and his glasses hung from one ear. For a short-sighted person their loss would probably mean a fall, and there were sharp rocks beneath. Both hands were busy hanging on, and only by contorting his whole body with immense efforts could he push the glasses back into place.

The task was successfully completed. Men were able to climb up the ropes attached to the top of the cliff and place fuses for explosive charges at the proper height. After the explosion the shattered seams of rock had to be collected up. Here Z as he worked could examine the revealed strata of rocks and minerals, and ponder the geological cataclysms that had given rise to them. In his 'Pictures from the Far East' he wrote: 'At the quarries we lay bare and break up the age-old bands of rock: it is strange to look at their dusty surfaces, newly revealed and witnessing the sunlight for the first time since creation.'

Z lived through much during those first months of hard labour. Once in heavy frost he fell into a fast-flowing stream. His clothing instantly became an icy suit of armour: he could scarcely move and cold went through him in a great wave. In his iced-up clothes he had to go to the quarry with a party of prisoners and only there could he dry out at the big bonfire. Strange to say this icy bath did not even give him a cold: the continuous tension and sense of danger mobilized the organism's resistance.

Among the political prisoners Z was able to stand up to life

183

comparatively well, thanks no doubt to his peasant blood and to the toughening experience of hunger and physical labour in his first years of independence. He was also at the best age: the very young and old had a harder time. But after two months of hard labour and prison-camp food he realized with alarm that his strength was on the wane and that he was doomed to share the fate of the camp's 'no-hopers'. He still believed that his case would be reviewed and he would soon be freed. How ridiculous it would be if he could not last out till liberation and would have to perish in some prison-camp complex.

He was saved by a fortunate accident.

At that time the Lower Amur camps were providing a workforce for several massive construction projects, chief among them the laying of a new section of main railway line, the pre-war BAM (Baykal-Amur Railway), between Komsomolsk and Sovetskaya Gavan, together with an oil pipeline connecting the wells on Sakhalin with the Komsomolsk oil refineries. The scale of the task was enormous: many approach-roads had to be built through virgin forest, and settlements and factories producing building materials had to be constructed, together with numerous subsidiary works. To achieve all this the camp had to appoint manual workers, foremen, planners, economists, lawyers, service personnel etc. No doubt the great increase in demand for labour in that area was the reason why Z was sent to Komsomolsk instead of Kolyma. From time to time a necessary specialist would be sought from among the prisoners. In the spring of 1939 technical and mechanical workers – among them draughtsmen – were needed for the newly-established planning office of the building directorate.

When it was announced to the row of prisoners that a draughtsman was needed, Z instantly understood that he had a miraculous opportunity to get away from the crippling labour in the quarry. A long time before, at school in Urzhum, he had been good at drawing; he had always been attracted to graphic art and now decided to chance his arm. He took a pace forward and boldly announced, 'I'm a draughtsman'. His abilities could not be tested on the spot, since his hands were cut up and swollen. By the time they were better he had mastered the job. Well-disposed people helped him. The planning office staff understood that their new colleague was not too well-informed about technical drawing, but they did not give him away and helped him to learn in all sorts of ways. At the outset, when his hands could not yet obey him and lice would fall out of his clothes on to the tracing-paper, one of the draughtspeople, a woman (not a prisoner), showed him the various methods of making copies.

In his letter of 14 April 1939 Z wrote home:

Today I've had your first letter, dated 23 March . . . I'm working as a draughtsman and get a bonus payment of thirty roubles a month. That's quite enough money for people in our situation – enough for sugar and coarse tobacco. I get better food and now feel a good deal healthier than at first . . . It's amazing: in Leningrad I often used to go down with flu or angina – so far I haven't been ill here once . . . Don't send any good-quality things – there's no point.

Clearly with a view to the camp censor he added: 'I've even remembered my old draughtsman's skills and after a few days it was all going fine.' By autumn he was writing: 'I've begun drawing much better – I love doing it.' In the summer of 1940 he was telling his family: 'In a year I could become a technician and do simple independent blueprints. I only need to get back my maths and read up something about building methods. However I haven't a moment to spare – it's all taken up with work.'

Within the area of the second column of the camp a special hut was set aside equipped with desks and drawing-boards. Those seconded to the planning office lived as before with the criminals and slept on planks, but worked apart in a clean, heated hut. After general duties in the forest this was happiness. The working day began at 8 a.m., from 4 to 7 p.m. there was a break and then work continued till 11 p.m. Those working on the project for the oil pipeline and its associated works were made to sign a promise not to give away state secrets, and when a senior guard came into the hut Z would hide his drawings under a sheet of paper.

'What have you got there?' the guard would ask suspiciously.

'I have no right to show you,' the draughtsman would answer.

Then the guard would grumble: 'I'm meant to guard these enemies of the people who get trusted more than I do. They ought to be lined up and shot after all this.' The prisoners were much amused by the situation.

The head of the planning office at the time was the prisoner Kormilitsyn, former operational manager at the Ministry of Communications. Also working in the office were the former chief engineer of the Tula weapons factory, Mamayev, and other specialists – a dozen or so people. Two of these, A. L. Sokolovsky and L. B. Zalkind (former editor of a chess journal), who had experienced the Menshevik trial of 1931, were men of great culture and erudition. Both were splendid conversationalists and companions. After a time Tatosov too was seconded to auxiliary work in the office and thus joined Z in his work again. 'Soon I too got into the planning office,' Tatosov recalled.

How I managed is a long and not very interesting story: the chief thing is that I found a haven at a time when I hardly dared hope to survive. I was being devoured by scurvy and all my strength was drained. After all I had been under investigation from January 1937 to October 1939. I had exhausted all my energy on that horrific period. Our life was relatively quiet. I say relatively since it was not uncommon for us to be woken up in the night and sent off to load stone into railway-wagons.

Such emergencies sometimes lasted several days, but in general Z's situation improved considerably. The high work norms demanded in the drawing office were nevertheless easier to fulfil than in wood-cutting or at the quarry. In the eating-hut Z now sat among those who overfulfilled their norms, where there was quite enough coarse food, though as before there was virtually no source of vitamins, no fats and no sugar. The starving prisoners looked on from other tables, waiting for the moment they could get their hands on the left-overs. Z knew from his own experience how desperately one wants to eat after hard labour in the forest or the quarry, and when he could he shared his bread and kasha with the hungry men. From May 1939 he was receiving food parcels from his wife, and these noticeably improved and varied his diet.

In spare moments Z agonized about his family, about his wasted talent, about the need to get a review of his case. Almost every night he dreamed of Leningrad, of his wife and his children. He understood that his place in the planning office depended on many chance factors and that at any moment he could be sent back to general duties at the bosses' whim. What saved him was the respect of his comrades working in the office and the enthusiasm he put into his drawings.

Life in the huts was darkened by ceaseless swearing, robbery, mockery, dirt and insects. The presence of the convicts meant always being on one's guard. Z's glasses were stolen more than once when he took them off to wash or go to sleep. A fee had to be paid for their return – a hunk of bread or pinch of tobacco. With Tatosov's help Z slowly established tolerable relations with his hut-neighbours. The criminals came to respect his firm principles and particularly his ability to tell interesting stories. Tatosov sometimes retold them bits of The *Count of Monte Cristo* and Z, Hugo's novel *1793*. They also summoned up the memory of other entertaining stories they had once read. But there was not much time for this anyhow.

With the coming of spring Z began particularly strongly to miss both his family and his work as a writer. Now when he was sent out on temporary work in the forest he could sadly observe the signs of spring: birds and animals, running streams, opening buds. In the bushes close to the stream a nightingale would sing: unexpectedly the lines of a poem that he was later to call 'Nightingale' began to form in his consciousness. He did not write it down, recited it to nobody, but polished up its stanzas privately and repeated them over and over again so as to memorize them and one day commit them to paper.

Renewed contact with poetry was both delightful and tormenting. Z knew that now was not the time for him to write poems, that he had to forget about art – but he was unable to fight against this sudden inspiration. 'Nailed to art' is how he described the nightingale in this poem, but simultaneously he thought of the heavy cross he himself had to bear for being a poet. With his own calling in mind, he sadly addressed the nightingale:

> Why, leaving the evening groves,
> Do you rip my heart into pieces?
> I am sick with you, whereas it would be simpler
> To part with you and step back from the abyss.

But it was impossible for him to part completely with art.

While deprived of freedom Z composed two poems: 'Nightingale' and another, dated 1938, 'Forest Lake'. When, though, was the latter (which was very highly regarded by the poet himself) composed? Its first idea had come to him in the summer of 1937 at Luga during a walk to Lake Glukhoye. Z began to write it down at the Writers' House at Yelizavetino: after his arrest a variant of its first two lines was found among his notes there. It was fully written out for the first time, like 'Nightingale', in 1944. One is left with the almost incredible conclusion that it was composed either in the Leningrad prison or during the journey to the Far East: after all the author noted '1938' as its date.

At the end of 1939 the living conditions of the nineteen people who by now worked in the Planning Office noticeably improved. They were given their own hut to live in: together with the work-hut and toilet block it was separated off with barbed wire. At the edge two guard-towers were put up, thus creating a small special zone within the general territory of the camp. Maybe this isolation was imposed because of worries about the secrecy of the planning work in the office.

One contact with the outside world was set up. One of the engineers, I. I. Prokhorov, was an excellent radio mechanic: he built a receiver in the hut and they began listening to broadcasts. They were allowed to read local newspapers. Two more free workers came to work in the Planning Office. They were well-disposed towards the prisoners and sometimes brought them books to read, and even a gramophone with records. Z. A. Sergeyeva, a free engineer, was head of the office for a time; she had known Z's poems before she met him. She brought him books, talked about literature and helped in his work. In case of need letters could be sent to the outside world through the free workers – without going through camp censorship. It can be guessed that this was how Z sent off petitions to the USSR Procurator and the directorate of the Union of Writers.

In between the huts they made an area where they could play *gorodki.** Z much enjoyed this popular game after many hours over the drawing-board in the airless hut. The armed guards in the machine-gun towers followed the game and gave their advice. But they also paid strict attention to the daily timetable. On summer evenings in the few free minutes before sleep the workers would sit outside the hut and sing songs.

This curious prison-camp idyll was interrupted by alarms, searches and orders to report to the camp commanders who gave educational talks and tried to drum up informers. Z when summoned refused to report on his comrades, as (according to Tatosov) did all the others who worked at the office.

The summer of 1939 came to an end. The prisoners began heating their huts; they filled in the space between the double plank walls with earth and put clay in any cracks. The days dragged out wearily in perpetual hope of news from home and some kind of response to petitions requesting just treatment and a review of their cases. Sometimes before sleep overcame them Z would tell Tatosov about his family, about poetry and about poets he had met, about his work translating Rustaveli, about visiting Georgia.

On 29 December 1939 Z wrote:

Dearest Katya and children! We're two days off New Year – I'm sending my kisses and once again all best wishes for health and happiness. Today I got your New Year's telegram: thank you for your wishes and for the good news about the review of the case. Before that there was a telegram about the transfer of the case to the Leningrad regional prosecutor's office. I'm happy to know my case has begun to move: I firmly hope and expect it'll take a turn for the better . . . Time passes quickly. Now December is almost over – one of the two coldest months. The weather is changeable – one day it's below minus 40°, on another it's quite mild. It's worth mentioning that the frosts here are easier to stand than those in Leningrad. A little chipmunk has been living all winter with us – a bit like a squirrel with stripes. It's got used to humans and runs around under our feet. Someone caught a woodpecker, and it lived here for a few

* A Russian game somewhat resembling rounders or baseball [Ed.].

days in a cage, wrathfully drummed on the bars and devoured the grubs we found in the firewood – in the end we let it go. All these small diversions go some way to enliven our admittedly brief leisure hours.

They had a good New Year's celebration. The guards and overseers decided to let them hold a special supper in the hut. All the workers in the Planning Office made contributions to the kitty – sausage and biscuits they had been awarded for especially good work, and a few delicacies saved up from food-parcels, bacon fat, onions, sweets. Tatosov had oriental sweetmeats sent from home, while Raychenko, the former military engineer of the Kiev military district, had a three-litre tin of apple preserve. Z too brought something from a food parcel. The women engineers made themselves up and set out the treats on the festive table, pouring water into bottles in place of wine. The guards came in, checked the foodstuffs, sniffed the bottles – all was in order, so off they went.

They sat down at table, opened the tin of preserve and unexpectedly discovered that instead of apple jam it contained pure spirit. The Kiev engineer's thoughtful relatives had sent him a New Year surprise. They cut the spirit with water and handed it round in mugs. Tatosov stood up to pronounce a festive toast but could not say a word for tears. It was all so unexpected for the hut: so many heart-warming distant memories from the past enveloped this carefully organized New Year's table, so powerful was the deceptive sense of their long-lost freedom! All of them wept. But they drank and were all soon drunk. They began to react against their recently felt inner pain and against everything around them. There began merry-making, loud conversations, songs and dances. The hut was in an uproar. In burst the guards and discovered everybody drunk. They had no option but to tell of the surprise in the tin. Thereafter whenever there were inspections all tins in food-parcels were prodded and sniffed. So began the year 1940.

The endlessly monotonous days dragged by: in place of stern winter came a chilly spring, then a rain-soaked summer. Neither the work nor the daily life of the prisoners attached to the planning office changed at all till November 1940. One hut to live in, one hut as office, barbed wire, sentry-towers; around them the other huts of the camp, to one side a small settlement for the guards and the free workers, beyond them deep, endless forest. Ten to twelve hours a day – often more – were spent at the drawing-board; in the few hours remaining from work, sleep and food, there were small daily tasks, bitter thoughts of family and freedom, chats with neighbours, sometimes permitted relaxations such as games of *gorodki*. Letters from home brought joy; occasionally it was possible to read the odd book. And still the hope lingered of a legal review, of rehabilitation, of early liberation – of a return to writing and to the family. These were deadening months of monotony and fading hopes; but expeditions into the forest for emergency jobs revived the memory of another, harsher life. And then Z would be continually grateful to the fate that brought him his draughtsman's work.

He wrote to Yekaterina:

13 March 1940. My dear Katya – I have had two telegrams (3 and 8 March) and a letter (dated 9 January) from you in the last two weeks.

On the 19 March – six days from now – I'll have been inside for two years. Two years out of the best time of one's life. Strange how my destiny has turned out.

Something amazing happened yesterday. As always I was working, hunched over the desk. The radio was chattering away at the other end of the hut. It was relaying Moscow. Suddenly I was aware that an actor was reading something familiar. At the second line I recognized it – my translation of Rustaveli! – the battle of Artandila and the pirates. The actor didn't read very well – but my heart was fluttering from those half-forgotten but familiar lines, and the Moscow reader was like a voice from the other world. Then they put on some music – Berlioz's 'Symphonie Fantastique'. What a shattering piece – specially the fourth movement. What a joy to have the radio, far away in the forest as we are . . .

30 April 1940. Dear Katya, my beloved children! The time to write to you has come round again, but truth to tell, there's nothing really to write about . . . I live, or rather exist, in the same old way. All my time is taken up with work and the habitual melancholy thoughts about my family. I daydream about you now as once I did about my fine future plans for poems . . .

3 August 1940 . . . Summer is on the way out, yet we've hardly seen it, since there were only a few sunny days . . . My inner poetic instrument is coarsening without use, my perception of things is dimming, but despite the exhaustion, the inner tiredness, the whole endless burden of continuous waiting – despite all these I feel myself still an integrated person, with life and work in me yet . . .

28 September 1940 . . . Since I'm busy absolutely the whole time there's no opportunity to get bored and homesick. When you finish work here you drop down into a dead sleep and the only thing that could wake you up is the cold. That's how the days go by one after another – just the same, without events, without thoughts. I'm very glad that I've taken up technical work lately, to fill the emptiness inside my head that I've never had to live with before.

What do I need? Trousers. Old ones would do so long as they're warm and tough. It doesn't matter what they look like or who wore them before. If you get a chance send me a pair. These blue ones I've got have been worn two years uninterruptedly and are already falling to bits, not to mention their incredible appearance. And if you do send them don't forget some tobacco as well – even the coarsest or cheapest so long as there's plenty of it. I'm lost without it and there's nowhere to get any here. Actually though the trousers and the tobacco don't matter – I can get along without them.

6 December 1940. I've had your postcard of 17 November. Sadness itself must have written that little note. I'm rather tired, you write, and I'm ready to weep at that 'rather', my poor, tired thing. And I see the picture of that sickly, lonely little boy, sad beyond his years – your 'little turkey' as you call him. Maybe we really will be together, be able to relax, bring up the children – but my soul has been so undeservedly and fearfully wounded for all time. Surely, there must be some kind of meaning that we can't comprehend in all this?

At the end of October 1940 the nineteen inhabitants of the separate hut were ordered to get ready for a move. The planning section, now directly attached to the camp directorate, was transferred to Komsomolsk-on-the-Amur.

Their way of life changed noticeably. After the settlement of Start, deep in the forests, it seemed to the prisoners that they had once again arrived in the civilized world, with brick and plaster houses, with central heating at the directorate, with free inhabitants who could be seen on the road from the prison-camp to the office, with fresh newspapers and even cinema-films that were occasionally shown at the camp. The free workers at the directorate behaved pleasantly towards the prisoner-experts in the new section. Z, who always called forth the respect of people with whom he had dealings, was even noticed by the boss of the whole camp, Barabanov – someone who was on an immeasurably lofty and unattainable level. He reckoned himself an enlightened figure, well disposed to intellectuals and particularly writers. It was said that one prisoner summed up the nerve to say to Barabanov: 'All the others are simply killers, whereas you're a cultured killer.' It should not be forgotten that the directorate workers were in a privileged situation, while around Komsomolsk, in the construction of roads, the pipeline and other sites, thousands of prisoners were perishing from the intolerable work and inhuman conditions: so 'killer' was a precise definition.

Might it not have been then that an incident took place that Z often recalled and that haunted him like a nightmare, despite its apparent harmlessness? A section boss or overseer paraded the prisoners for an inspection by the head of the camp. The latter made his appearance – decisive, hard but 'cultured'. He already knew that Z was serving his

191

sentence in his camp, remembered him by sight and wished him no harm. He went up to the parade, recognized Z and being in a good mood enquired of his immediate boss: 'Well, how's Zabolotsky getting on here? Not writing poetry?'

'No bad marks against prisoner Zabolotsky for his work or his conduct' reported the section head. And with a guffaw he added, 'I gather he won't be writing any more poems ever again.'

'Well, that's that then.' The inspection went on. What a painful blow this little conversation struck at the poet's deepest feelings!

The workers at the planning department now lived in a quite warm hut at the edge of town, three kilometres from the camp directorate. This distance had to be covered four times a day – in the morning and evening, and also for the daytime break, since they ate in the prison zone. Almost all their free time was spent on foot; in winter, when the frost could reach minus 40° and the wind could be strong there was additionally the threat of getting frozen. Thus these journeys seemed naturally unpleasant and the prisoners remembered with some nostalgia the camp in the forest where they had to go only 20–30 metres from living to working quarters. But Z found a positive side too in these walks. 'It's good to an extent', he wrote to his wife, 'since we spend this time out in the air and in movement, a good contrast with my desk-work.' In any case the conditions of life in Komsomolsk gradually improved. The workers at the directorate were allowed to walk apart from the general column, and even unguarded: the most privileged even received a pass to leave the camp zone.

Soon after the transfer to Komsomolsk, at the end of November 1940, Z was temporarily put under the command of V. N. Azhayev, formerly a prisoner, at that time a free worker, later a well-known writer and author of the novel *Far from Moscow*. A group of prisoners under Azhayev was busy establishing a social centre for the whole camp. About this job Z wrote: 'I'm working round the clock, only snatching 5–6 hours' sleep. I'm having to be an artist, a draughtsman and much else too. Though it's very tiring at least it means much better food.' This job went on for a couple of months and during that time he was fed in the dining-room for free workers. 'If only you knew how delicious it is after two years of camp food!', he wrote home.

On 1 January 1941 he got back from work at 7 a.m. – the time when in Moscow the New Year was just being celebrated: the radio was broadcasting toasts and the chink of glasses. Just then the post arrived at the hut, including a parcel sent by Nikolay Stepanov containing a two-volume edition of Pushkin. Z exclaimed gratefully in a letter: 'What a breath of warm friendship and sympathy! Thank you. That way I was able to meet my New Year in Pushkin's company . . .' In the same letter he wrote:

> When I get back at night from work I want to think, think and think. But there isn't time: tiredness takes its toll. I do battle with the bedbugs and slip into a dead sleep. Now sometimes I manage to read Pushkin. And at times he seems to be a young man of genius. Young, because I'm now significantly past the age that Pushkin had reached when he died.*

Z took every opportunity to take part in life outside the camp. When a film was shown in the clubroom attached to the commandant's section he made efforts to see it. If a book turned up, he read it at the expense of his sleep. Once a copy of the journal *Literary Contemporary* fell into his hands. He was excited to read in it the transcript of a speech by his Leningrad friend Aleksandr Gitovich and a poem by him. He was heavy-hearted when he recognized echoes of their own conversations about poetry, and when he guessed the poem was addressed to himself: 'Long long ago, I don't know why, I lost my comrade . . .' At the time Gitovich said that he would give much for Z to be able to read that poem. Fate decreed that his wish should come true.

At the beginning of April 1941 he got a parcel containing five volumes of nineteenth-century poetry selected by Irina Tomashevskaya and Nikolay Stepanov. At a routine search he had four of the volumes confiscated: he was told that for educational purposes he was allowed to have only Soviet writers. Z particularly wanted to keep the poems of Boratynsky (1800–1844), whom he adored. He pointed out to the guard the name of the publishing house *Soviet Writer*, and Boratynsky was able to pass as a Soviet poet: Z was allowed to keep the book.

He wrote to his wife:

> Thank you for your nice letter and the books. The little volume of Boratynsky gives me a great deal of joy. Before going to sleep and in breaks I manage to read a few poems, and I carry the book around everywhere. Of course his view of the world isn't identical with mine, but his subject-matter and the fact that he is a thinking, pondering poet bring him close to me: I often get the idea that Boratynsky and Tyutchev among nineteenth-century Russian poets achieved what was so evidently missing in Pushkin and what was so splendidly and powerfully apparent in Goethe. But I like Boratynsky not only as a thinker but as a poet: in his late work (which he wrote at about my own age and later) there's so much poetic daring – far more than in his young poems which are Frenchified, in the spirit of the times. And I have to tell you it is

---

* i.e. 37 years 8 months; Z was at that time only one month older [Ed.].

sometimes bitter for me not to have the opportunity to write myself. And the question comes into my mind: can I really be the only person to lose from this? I feel I could still do a lot and could write better than I did before.

You write about meeting. Even if it was allowed there'd be no point in trying to arrange it – not to speak of the money, which we don't have: just imagine all the effort and deprivations that a journey here, to the edge of the world, would cost you. You'd come worn out, tired, strained, all just to spend a few hours with me. It wouldn't make things easier for either of us: on the contrary we'd just open our wounds all the deeper. Don't imagine I don't want to see you. For a single sight of you I'd give God knows what, but after thinking things over soberly I reckon it's not right to come . . .

In spring the sharp yearning to get back to writing and hopeless regret for the lost years of his life were particularly keenly felt. Z wrote home:

My head wants to get back to thinking – it hasn't lost the capacity, and this single fact cheers me up. I'm not the only person to suffer in prison, but I find it harder to endure than many others do because I've been given a mind and a talent. If I were now able to write I'd start writing about Nature. The older I get the closer it becomes to me. And now it is standing in front of me as a vast theme, and all that I've written about Nature up to now seems like slight and timid attempts to approach this theme [19 April 1941].

And in a letter to his wife of 8 May 1941 she read:

I often remember Nikita's childhood – how at Siverskaya he first stood up, how he clambered under the table to get a ball and straightened up and hit his head there, which taught him a lesson, how he played hide-and-seek, how he watched me shaving while I made amazing faces at him which he was so happy with; how he rocked his little sister; how she murmured 'Daddy' when she parted from me. Or did I just imagine it? Do write about the children, Katya. Fate has parted me from my daughter – her childhood is going by without me.

Thus with his monotonous draughtsman's work and with comfortless reflections on his lot passed eight months of life in the town of Komsomolsk. And he had already spent more than three years of imprisonment.

III

Immediately after Z's arrest his wife and friends started thinking about how to help him. It would be possible to do something to ease his lot only after the investigation was completed and sentence pronounced, but as to what and how, nobody had a clue. It was not known what he was accused of; there was no court before which he could be defended.

The first to take a decisive step was Professor V. A. Desnitsky, who had followed Z's progress as a poet attentively and thought him one of his best students. Before the Revolution Desnitsky had worked for the Bolsheviks, knew Stalin personally and now decided to make use of this acquaintance to try and defend the poet. Soon after Z was sentenced Desnitsky wrote a letter begging the Leader to intervene in his pupil's case. He wrote that he had known Z from his very first day as a student, rated his poetry highly and could guarantee that the author of 'Gori Symphony' could not be an 'enemy of the people'. The letter addressed him as 'Koba' (Stalin's Party code-name) and was signed with his own code-name 'Desnitsky-Lopata'. It had no discernible consequences.

While still in Kresty Prison, immediately after learning the decision of the Special Commission, Z wrote requesting an appeal hearing. Soon after getting to the camp in the Far East, while still engaged in exhausting manual labour, he chanced to come across a torn bit of *Pravda* of 1 February 1939, which had been part of the wrapping around a fellow prisoner's parcel. It was already being used for rolling cigarettes when Z asked if he could read what was left. As he looked at it he could hardly believe his eyes: there was a decree announcing awards to a large group of writers. The poet Nikolay Tikhonov was among those to receive the Order of Lenin: whereas Z had imagined that Tikhonov had long before been arrested and would be in prison. If Tikhonov was at liberty, and furthermore the recipient of high honours, it meant that the accusation of belonging to a counter-revolutionary organization supposedly headed by him was simply ridiculous. So Z got down to writing appeals to the Interior Ministry, the Director of Prosecutions, then to Stalin. He protested against his unjust imprisonment and demanded a review of his case and abrogation of his sentence. Such appeals had to be handed in to the camp directorate to be forwarded to their destinations, and the prisoner would be informed when this had happened. The process was protracted and unreliable.

Yekaterina also tried to help her husband. In her Urzhum exile, after putting the children to bed, she would light a candle so as not to disturb her neighbours with the electric light (the partitions did not reach up to the ceiling) and would get down to the job of writing the next letter to Moscow. But all these letters of both husband and wife got lost somewhere in the bowels of bureaucracy and did nothing to assist their case.

At the end of April 1939 Yekaterina, in Urzhum, received a letter (his second) from Mikhail Zoshchenko, in which he wrote:

> Dear Yekaterina Vasilyevna! Please don't get the idea that we've forgotten what has happened to Nikolay. Many of our colleagues have promised to help. I've personally written a letter to Moscow asking if there's any possibility of reviewing his case or at least lightening your burden and his. Now I'm waiting for an answer. I think there'll be a good outcome. My heartfelt wishes to you and Nikolay. Mikhail Zoshchenko. 23.IV.39.

As it happened the times were relatively favourable for complaints about illegal convictions and appeals for the setting aside of sentences. Late in 1938, after the unprecedented fury of the repressions, Stalin decided to indulge in a characteristically hypocritical manœuvre. In the Central Committee and Councils of the Republics a resolution was passed proposing the softening of harsh methods of investigation and changes of cadre in the NKVD organs. After the appointment of a new Interior Minister (Beria) and the disappearance of Yezhov in December 1938 the character of the repressions temporarily changed. Mass arrests began among the members of the NKVD. And although Beria was in no way better than Yezhov, while Stalin's political line on the repressions remained essentially the same, confusion reigned among those who actually worked in the instruments of repression – arrests of 'enemies of the people' were reduced to a trickle, prisoners' cases began to be reviewed, a few were rehabilitated. The prisoners began to hope for justice.

In the summer of 1939 Z wrote to his wife: 'It's said they're reviewing a lot of cases', 'it's said that complaints are being dealt with more quickly', 'a lot of long sentences are being reviewed and altered. All quiet on our front. I guess we have to wait our turn'. On the 23 July 1939 Z wrote a long statement addressed to the Chief Prosecutor of the USSR, and to get round the ordinary complaints procedure sent it to his wife. Yekaterina received it in Urzhum and realized she had to do everything possible to get it to the Prosecutor's office. She made use of the changed situation, sent a telegram addressed to Beria and received permission to make a journey from her place of exile to Leningrad for the children to get medical treatment. From Leningrad she went with Nikolay Stepanov to Moscow in order to organize high-level support for the petition. In his uncompleted memoirs Stepanov wrote:

> We went and saw Shklovsky, who then lived on Lavrushensky Lane. He
> told us we had to go and see Fadeyev at Peredelkino. We all three went
> together. At that time Fadeyev's dacha didn't have the high fence that
> was built round it soon after the war, and anyone could easily get to see
> him. He received us in a friendly and straightforward way. He heard
> what we had to say and promised to find out about the case. In those
> years that was amazingly good news – after all, everybody would
> normally keep as far away as they could from such matters.

On 9 September Fadeyev met M. I. Panfilov, the Prosecutor, and
handed him Z's statement. The Prosecutor promised to review the case
speedily and turned it over to his Special Section. The family, temporarily back from exile, was given permission to live in Leningrad, which
allowed Yekaterina to be fully active on her husband's behalf. She sent
an immediate telegram to the Far East reporting the Prosecutor's
promise. Z wrote in reply: 'I've had your telegram of the 9th. I'm full of
hope and gratitude for your efforts. I firmly believe the review will be
favourable to me.' In a later letter he added: 'Dear Katya, some
prisoners' cases are going for review, some have been released. All that
encourages me and strengthens my permanent hope that my turn will
come. I've lived through a lot during this period, but that means it'll be
all the more joyful when I do meet you and the dear children again.'

From Z's statement his friends got the first concrete evidence of the
accusations against him. Insofar as these were based on an unsound and
tendentious reading of his poems, it had to be shown that this
interpretation was false. So as to support Z's declaration to the
Prosecutor, they decided to send the latter short statements about Z
written by authoritative people who knew his work well. Despite the
fact that any public utterance in favour of an 'enemy of the people'
might harm the official standing of the person who made it, the
requisite documents were quickly assembled. In Leningrad brief
favourable sketches of Z's work were written by Gitovich, Zoshchenko,
Kaverin and Tikhonov. Yekaterina and Gitovich took these documents
to Moscow, where Antokolsky and Aseyev added their pieces.
Chukovsky added his name to Zoshchenko's statement.

In Moscow the scholar Z. V. Yermolyeva, who was also making
efforts on behalf of her arrested husband, recommended an experienced
lawyer. With his help and the assistance of Chukovsky and Shklovsky a
deposition addressed to the chief of the Special Section of the Procuracy,
Osipenko, was compiled. Yekaterina's statement, the writers' contributions and other materials putting Z in a good light were handed by

Chukovsky to the chief of the Special Section personally, at the beginning of December 1939.

As a result the case was designated for review and sent for further investigation to the Leningrad district prosecutor's office, where it passed into the hands of an investigator called Ruchkin. As a senior member of the office, Ruchkin made an honest attempt to establish the truth. Nobody remembered a thing about any 'counter-revolutionary organization'. The basic question the investigator was trying to decide was about the character of Z's work – was it Soviet or anti-Soviet? At Ruchkin's request Yekaterina handed over copies of her husband's books and other publications, as well as favourable published articles about him (by Gitovich, Grinberg, Zoshchenko and Stepanov). The investigator explained that the case-file contained material treating Z's work as hostile to the Soviet system, and even read out to Yekaterina excerpts from Lesyuchevsky's statement, without concealing its authorship. Various writers who knew Z well, personally and through his work, were summoned to the office as witnesses: Zoshchenko, Kaverin, Gitovich, Tikhonov and also the widow of the poet Vaginov, the secretary of the Party organization of the Leningrad Writers' Union Miroshnichenko, the author of the denunciation Lesyuchevsky, and the superintendent of the house on Griboyedov Canal A. G. Kotov. Of course all Z's friends spoke very positively about him. Nothing bad was said by Miroshnichenko or even Kotov. Lesyuchevsky alone stood his ground stubbornly and spoke of the anti-Soviet character of Z's work.

At that time the war with Finland was in progress, and many Leningrad writers were serving in the army as war correspondents. Gitovich's wife recalled how her husband came back from the front at the prosecutor's behest:

Sanya* was serving on the Baltic and unexpectedly turned up at home all of a sudden – cheerful, in an unbuttoned naval greatcoat and with a hat pushed cheekily back on his head. As he came in the door he yelled excitedly: 'You'll never guess why I've turned up in Leningrad! Imagine it, I've just been at the prosecutor's office – I was called there about Zabolotsky's case. About time too!' . . . The investigator spoke quite confidingly with him 'no doubt because I was in uniform', he guessed. Thereupon the investigator informed him that the author of Zabolotsky's denunciation was a certain Lesyuchevsky; incidentally (he asked Gitovich) did he know this person? What could he say about him? 'I was once in the army with that scoundrel', said Sanya, upset. 'Well, anyhow, I tried to say everything I thought about him. I didn't hide a thing.'

* i.e. Aleksandr [Ed.].

Gitovich proudly told his friends that he had told the investigator that Lesyuchevsky could not be bothered to groom his own horse and kept getting ticked off by the commander. Since Gitovich adored animals, this fact was for him enough to remove all authority from Lesyuchevsky and the denunciation he had written.

By contrast Tikhonov, when he too arrived from the Finland front, simply cut off the investigator's question about Lesyuchevsky's criticism with the words: 'I don't know any such critic.' Of course Ruchkin realized that he was talking not about personal acquaintanceship, but about Lesyuchevsky's professional qualities.

A special commission to assess Z's work and public role, containing I. A. Gruzdev, F. S. Knyazev, M. L. Lozinsky, L. N. Rakhmanov and N. L. Stepanov, was set up in the Leningrad Writers' Union branch at the request of the Procuracy. The commission's conclusion ended with the words:

> Zabolotsky's work in Soviet literature as witnessed by the Leningrad reading public, his creative activity, his participation in Writers' Union activities, his image as a person and as a citizen give no grounds to doubt that he is a genuine Soviet writer, a straightforward and honest person who has earned the respect of all who know him.

Ruchkin was an honest and courageous investigator; the Union's report and all the individual testimony and documents convinced him that Z had been groundlessly convicted. In January 1940 the investigation was concluded and the case sent back again to Moscow – with (one assumes) the investigator's favourable conclusion. In Moscow, Chukovsky undertook to keep an eye on the further progress of the case. In February he wrote to Stepanov: 'Tell Zabolotsky's wife that yesterday I found out from reliable sources that her husband's case is close to a favourable conclusion. Yesterday I spoke with Yezerskaya, who showed me a bulging file. The case has been sent back to Leningrad and will shortly be reviewed again.' Early in March he wrote: 'Today I got very pleasant news, but it needs to be verified. On the 7th I'll go to the Prosecutor's again and shall no doubt learn the result – then I'll tell you at once.' However it was soon announced that the Procuracy's answer was held up by the review of 'parallel cases'.

But Lesyuchevsky too was not idle. He found Ruchkin's scepticism of his opinion intolerable, and refused to accept that his services as consultant to the NKVD organs were in doubt. In April 1940 there arrived at the Supreme Procuracy a letter from Lesyuchevsky in which he accused Ruchkin of lacking objectivity in his review of the case and of concealing the true nature of Z's work. This created a new situation that complicated and upset any favourable outcome to the case.

The Procuracy stayed silent, while the disquiet of Z's friends mounted. Yekaterina sent a telegram addressed to Beria requesting that the unnecessarily prolonged review of her husband's case should be speeded up. There was no answer. None the less in May it became known that the Procuracy had objected to the sentence, and Z's case was sent to the NKVD to confirm that it had been annulled. In response to this news Z wrote on 25 June:

> My dear Katya! I've recently had your letter of 31 May 1940 with the news that the Supreme Procuracy has transferred my case to the NKVD to confirm my sentence has been quashed. I've always firmly believed that this would happen and I'd be rehabilitated. All the same your letter has had such an effect on me that I'm still walking round overwhelmed by it. I've begun to live more easily. Every night I dream of you, my dear family, and of Leningrad. I believe I shan't need to wait very long for the NKVD's final resolution of the case.

Again months went by, but by now time was working against Z – the period when Beria, on coming to power, had permitted some liberalism, or slackening of the reins, was coming to an end.

In July 1940 the last hopes were destroyed. Yekaterina received a document from the USSR Procuracy reading: 'In response to your deposition the Procuracy informs you that the case of N. A. Zabolotsky has been re-examined. It has been established that he was properly convicted and that there are no grounds for review of his case.'

For a long time Yekaterina could not bring herself to let her husband know that the appeal had been refused, fearful that the news would deprive him of hope and break his will, without which living as a prisoner would be very difficult. But Z had already realized that his position was bad. Quite disillusioned, he wrote on 15 September:

> I feel that the resolution of my case has been held up for reasons of a general nature. At any rate I'm not the only person in the camps under a sentence that has been annulled by the Supreme Procuracy . . . In four days' time half my sentence will be up. Will the second half be easier than the first? One peasant here in prison said: 'When you carry a heavy load home, it's nothing till the half-way point, then it gets heavier and heavier the closer you get.'

To conceal the sad news for ever would have been impossible, and when she understood that Z was losing hope in any case Yekaterina plucked up courage, and on 25 October let him know the whole story. He received the news on 14 November and wrote back:

Yesterday I got your letter with the Procuracy's information. It astonished me, particularly taking into account the communication in May setting aside the sentence. Don't be scared on my behalf, dearest – I've read it perfectly calmly: only I'm endlessly sad for you and the children. We're going through troubled times now.

As for future appeals, I'll think about it and maybe write something in the future. You see it's impossible to clear yourself without knowing concretely what you're accused of. After all, if what I wrote about before and what I was concretely accused of then had been taken seriously, I'd be free now. It looks as if with my earlier statement I was pushing at an open door. There's no guessing what it's really about . . .

Soon I'll have done eight months of my third year. Time goes by. We'll keep on living and working and hoping that in a couple of years we'll be together again. That's the only thing for us, and common sense tells us so. My kisses and my thanks for everything; don't despair, look after yourself and the children.

In autumn 1940 Yekaterina was extremely surprised to hear a poem of her husband's – 'Sedov' – read out on radio. Could a poet's work be publicly broadcast if he was seriously considered an 'enemy of the people'? Again she composed a deposition, attached Z's *Second Book* to it and addressed it to Stalin in the Kremlin. On 30 November 1940 she was summoned to the Leningrad NKVD and informed that her request was granted – the case would be reviewed in Moscow. However, no further action on the part of the NKVD followed. Half a year later Russia entered the Second World War.

IV

The outbreak of war on 22 June 1941 instantly changed camp life at Komsomolsk. An instruction went out to transfer all prisoners including engineers and technicians to general duties deep in the taiga. A rumour went round the huts that in the event of a Japanese invasion of the Soviet Far East all prisoners would be killed. The camp inmates were alarmed anyhow at the prospect of abrupt changes in their way of life and their work.

A couple of days after the outbreak of war Z already knew that all the prisoners in the draughtsmen's office were to be sent to the heaviest jobs in the taiga. As a trained platoon commander he made a request to be sent to the front, but the officer in charge frowned at his application and muttered: 'Our Soviet land has enough defenders who are worthier than you are – we'll get along without you.'

The departure for their new location beyond the Amur was hurried and tense. Z wrote a hasty farewell note: '24 July 1941. Dear Katya and children! I'm going off with this column. I'm in good health. When we get to the new place I'll write with the address as soon as I can. Don't be too upset if the letter takes a long time. Love and kisses – look after yourself and the children as best you can. Your Kolya.'

The prisoners and their belongings were put in barges to cross to Pivan on the other side of the Amur. The head of the planning office was a free worker, Vorontsov, who was far from sympathetic towards the 'politicals' but understood that he could not do his job without convict specialists. Maybe he had some idea of the dark schemes of the authorities and suspected he might be left without a workforce. He charged down like a bull to the column of prisoners waiting at the riverside, swore wildly and began hauling off his own workers and shoving them into a separate group. Z was among them. The authorities and guards took no steps to oppose this hard and energetic man.

The prisoners were loaded onto barges, and despite the stormy weather – strong winds and big waves – the crossing of the Amur began. The barge containing the group out of which Vorontsov had extracted his own workers sank with all on board. Z was convinced that it had been sunk deliberately, and considered that he and the rest of the section owed their lives to Vorontsov. This cold-blooded, cruel destruction of lives haunted Z to the end of his days.

As a result of their boss's efforts all those in the Planning Section – twenty-five in all – remained in a single group. At Pivan they were put in a lorry and taken eastwards, to the forested foothills of the Sikhote-Alin range.

Around them stretched endless taiga, in which here and there former camp areas appeared, with their inevitable barbed wire and watch-towers. They finally arrived at a place called Lysaya Gora on the very beautiful taiga river Khungari, a tributary of the Amur. But the prisoners did not care to contemplate the beauties of nature. Once again they would be in a camp containing hardened criminals, long filthy huts with plank beds, a strict regime and hard physical work. They had grown out of all this while working at the planning office and particularly while living in Komsomolsk. The conditions were if possible even worse than the worst moments of general duties at the Start settlement.

At Lysaya Gora the prisoners were building a railway towards Sovetskaya Gavan. To lay the track along the side of a cliff, a so-called 'shelf' had to be hacked out. In addition chippings and ballast were needed. They worked in teams of four: two broke up stone with a pick and a crowbar, one loaded the wagon, one pulled the wagon full of stone to the cliff edge and tipped its load down the slope. The number of wagon-loads was checked by a controller. The foursome including Z and Tatosov occasionally managed to get extra wagon-loads noted and so to fulfil their norm.

In a letter to this author Tatosov recalled:

> Here is something that happened while we were working on the River Khungari. It was a tough time for us: bad food, work all the daylight hours. There was also a severe and senseless rule that those who hadn't fulfilled their norm should be detained till it was completed. Among us there were elderly people who had never held anything heavier than a pen, and naturally that rule was devastating for them. However long they were detained they couldn't reach the norm; and so we all agreed to stay with the old men and finish off their work for them. When I say 'all' I mean our group of about twelve. The guards went along quite happily with that, since they didn't want to spend all night hanging around in a quarry either, and used to knock a bit off the norm. Zabolotsky was the first to make this suggestion about helping these unfortunate people, and we accepted his proposal, since we couldn't abandon them to their fate. Later on, when circumstances changed, Sokolovsky and Zalkind (who were about sixty) were endlessly grateful to us, and when we were once again sitting in the Design Office we recollected those hard days ... Zabolotsky was incapable of looking on unconcernedly when people who had in any case been wronged were further wronged, and he always felt any injustices to others – and there were plenty such – sharply and painfully.

The taiga was full of bugs, mosquitoes and flies. On the way from camp to quarry the armed guards played practical jokes. They and their dogs accompanied the marching column. On the road there was a large puddle. When the whole column was going through the puddle a command would ring out: 'Halt! Lie down!' They would lie down in the cold, muddy water. 'Stand up! Lie down! Stand up!', and so on till the guards had enjoyed their power enough. Sometimes a shout would be heard from the column: 'The Gestapo taught you that!' 'Who said that?' – and a rifle-bolt would rattle threateningly.

The food was very bad at that time: 300 grams of bread and some chunks of boiled pumpkin. There were sometimes maggots in the soup. Those who overfulfilled their norm got 100 grams of bread extra and probably some porridge too.

Two hardened criminals once escaped from the Khungari camp. They dried bread for rusks, stored up some other food and kidnapped the

203

camp medical orderly as their baggage-carrier. When, after many days of blundering around in the taiga, their food ran out, they killed the orderly and ate him. Eventually the fugitives were captured and shot in front of the whole camp.

They worked on the Khungari for about two months and in that time became thin and emaciated. The camp regime was clearly intended for their physical destruction. Family letters ceased; all hope of release vanished. Z once again applied to be sent to the front and was refused. Fortunately someone up above decided to hasten the construction of the oil pipeline, and for this a design section was required. The engineering and technical workers were remembered and were ordered to be stationed closer to Komsomolsk. Z and his comrades were faced with 120 kilometres on foot through the taiga to the so-called 'Timber Centre'.

With the usual guards' shout, 'One step out of line and we open fire!', the column set off along the forest track. It was very hard going. It was impossible to move fast, and the prisoners began to abandon their possessions as too heavy to carry. Hard as it was, Z tried to commit what he saw around him to memory, and later wrote in *Pictures of the Far East*:

> Here there is still untouched nature, and dry land is not fully distin-guishable from swamp as happens in locations where mankind has gained control. Nature appears in all its solemn wildness and harshness. There are no nice strolls along convenient paths in which to admire mighty oaks or the picturesque disposition of groves and streams. You have to jump from tussock to tussock, sink into rust-coloured water, suffer from midges and gnats that come in great clouds and are a real menace to humans and animals alike. If you climb up a hill you'd be wrong to expect that at last you'll be treading on firm ground – no, even there you find the same swamp, the same tussocks.

They reached the Timber Centre, were put in a common hut and were all sent off to cut timber and load up logs. Autumnal chill, water up to the knees, hunger, nothing to smoke, no more strength . . .

At the Timber Centre a Design Office was again formed, and this made things easier. But they were still living with criminals, were fed very badly, and often in emergencies they went out on general duties, cutting down trees and loading up wagons. The hunger grew worse. The prisoners had already eaten any cats and dogs; there were cases of cannibalism. Many of them on returning from work threw themselves at the rubbish pits by the food hut in the hope of digging out something edible. Even among the Design Office workers there were sometimes quarrels about which morsel was best, about whose turn it was for a hunk of bread.

Once Z and Tatosov had a stroke of luck – they were sent to unload trucks full of cabbages. That sort of work was only given to 'politicals'; the criminals ate or pilfered too much. As a reward they were each given a cabbage-head, which they ate raw on the spot.

So another couple of months went by at the Timber Centre. Since the war began Z had not been able to correspond with his family, and only fragmentary news reached him about the situation at the front and the siege of Leningrad that had already started. Worry about the family aggravated his unhappy situation.

At the Timber Centre the chief of the Design Office was, as before, Vorontsov, whose efforts had managed to keep the staff of the office intact. Human sympathy was alien to him, but he understood that the fulfilment of his job depended on the physical condition of his people, and so he made efforts to improve their circumstances where possible: thus he tried to free them from general duties and wagon-loading in the taiga.

In November 1941 the Design Section was transferred from the Timber Centre to a familiar location, the settlement of Start. And by some miracle Z's postcard of 14 November got through the siege-ring into blockaded Leningrad: 'Dear Katya, I am well and back at my old job . . . I await your letter. The last was dated 5 July . . .' At the hardest, cruellest time, on Christmas Day (Old Style), 7 January 1942, Yekaterina, bloated and exhausted from starvation, saw this card in the postbox of her Leningrad flat. How such news of Z overjoyed her and the children! A month later they were evacuated from the besieged city over the ice of the 'Road of Life' across Lake Ladoga, and were placed in a special medical station at a textile mill in Kostroma. Over the course of a month the Leningrad evacuees, suffering from dystrophy, were gradually returned to normal food and human existence.

From Kostroma, Yekaterina sent her husband a telegram telling him that she and the children were alive and on their way to Urzhum. In answer Z described his life: 'All my time goes on work. But I'm fed, clothed, shod and live adequately.'

Of course at Start the living conditions for the Design Section were considerably better than at the Timber Centre, but far from what they were before the war. It was now basically a criminal camp in which a special hut was set aside with bunks and desks: the engineering and technical workers lived as if on an island. Although Z wrote that he was 'fed, clothed and shod', he still felt half-starved and frozen in his poor clothing.

Although in the winter of 1941–2 Z sometimes had to undertake logging and other work in the taiga, these emergencies were short-lived: the productivity of the Design Section was needed for building work. Seeing people who were on their last legs from physical labour he once again thanked fate for getting him into a 'warm place'. As Roy Medvedev wrote in his book *On Stalin and Stalinism*: 'As the war began, the working day was increased almost everywhere, while the skimpy rations were cut . . . The overall total of prisoners in 1941–2 is comparable, by my calculation, with the number of active soldiers. And the losses in east and west were roughly equal.'

Once when on general duties Z and his friends reached the spot in the taiga where dead prisoners were brought and then cremated. It was a frosty winter's day, and Z looked for some time at the heaps of corpses, powdered with snow. Here and there a contorted frozen arm or leg stuck out of the snow. Evidently this picture was deeply etched into his memory, since in the last year of his life he recalled it in writing about the Siberian travels of the French monk William of Rubruck:

> On the charred meadows
> Close to the valley streams
> Heaps of strange corpses could be seen
> Under the snows and drifts.
> Rubruck clambered off his horse
> And often gazed afar
> At how, from under the snow's crust
> A dead hand clenched its fingers.

Tatosov often recalled the following incident. Before the war he had been appointed legal consultant to the Directorate of Camps and had often appeared at legal hearings representing the construction industry's interests. So that the representative of the Directorate should look good he was told to order a suit, shoes, a tie and the rest of a respectable outfit from home. After the outbreak of war all parcels were held up, and Tatosov's city clothes, no longer needed, arrived for him at Start. He managed to swap these clothes with one of the bosses for twenty-five packets of coarse tobacco and some food supplies. The tobacco was a real treasure chest, since prisoners received three packets per month – hardly enough for a week. In this connection Z wrote a jocular missive to Tatosov called 'Prayer for Tobacco'. As Tatosov recalled,

> More than anything I regret that the bit of paper on which Zabolotsky made a drawing and wrote sixteen freshly minted lines of verse was stolen to roll cigarettes . . . I was owner of twenty-five packets of coarse

tobacco, which was worth its weight in gold. Once when I was going to bed and turned back my blanket I saw that a sheet of paper had been pinned to my pillow, with a picture of myself at full height with a halo, and below at my feet the tiny kneeling figure of Zabolotsky making an imploring gesture. Above was the title 'Prayer for Tobacco'. I was compared to all the misers of the world, of whom Harpagon was least bad, and was categorically ordered to hand out some tobacco. The poem was splendid, so was the drawing, and I can never stop regretting the loss.

Soon after being installed at Start Z began learning Armenian.* He relished all knowledge, and possibly even then realized that after his release he would have to earn his living by translation, and a knowledge of Armenian would enable him to translate its poetry without a crib. Z made a booklet from some bits of official paper, bound it and wrote neatly in ink: 'Armenian language. Vocabulary. 1942'. He copied out the Armenian alphabet and wrote down some Armenian words and their Russian equivalents in a special order. The various headings are characteristic: (1) people, (2) house, (3) nature, (4) country, (5) town, (6) feelings, senses, spirit, activity, (7) life and death, (8) time-space etc. On separate pages he copied out Armenian songs or poems, with Russian translations, that had pleased him or those close to him. Here is an example:

> The forest is my native land, the tree my house.
> I say to the wolf: lie down, Wolf, and down it lies
> Close to my feet. I say to the bird: Fly, Bird!
> And the bird flies up. I read the book of the earth.
> Why, dear one, do you not come near me?
> Already night has fallen, the stars shine.
> The beast is asleep in the forest, the river is quiet.
> I await you, May rose, come near to me.

Work in the Design Office finished late, but before going to sleep Z and Tatosov found time to hold a regular lesson. Z got on so well that soon he was able to exchange quite complicated sentences with two Armenian colleagues.

Remembering those days, Tatosov wrote:

There was always a striving for the life of the mind within Zabolotsky. It could be seen in everything – in his interest in other people's knowledge, in the wish to attain to this knowledge, in the study of surrounding nature. The chief thing was not to lose his identity, not to go downhill and

---

* Tatosov was a native speaker of Armenian [Ed.].

become an animal . . . Neither harsh language, nor vicious quarrels and fights over trifles, nor heavy labour nor the way we were neglected and despised – none of these changed him: he stayed just as pure-hearted, gentle and kind . . . He was an example to me, calmed me down and used to say: 'Don't demean yourself, don't lose your inner self.'

It was indeed the case that inside Z some sort of inner work was always going on unconnected with his surroundings. This spiritual independence helped him withstand all difficulties and humiliations – of which there were many. One of his prison comrades, the engineer I. S. Susanin, recounted how once, after emergency work, Z, Tatosov and another engineer, N. A. Derzhavin, were standing on a hill. Z picked a large red flower, looked at it and then said: 'After we die we shall all turn into flowers like this and we shall live quite different lives that we cannot now comprehend.' These words sounded profound, self-confident and convincing, so much so that the listeners took them as an important revelation and committed them to memory: Derzhavin told Susanin, who never forgot them. A few years after that conversation, Z was to write in his well-known poem 'Testament': 'I shall not die, my friend. In the respiration of flowers/I shall discover myself in this world.'*

The Project and Design Division stayed in the camp near Start all the winter of 1941–2 and summer of 1942. At the end of October 1942 it was again transferred to Komsomolsk. Thus the circle of wanderings, begun in the memorable days of June 1941, was closed: Komsomolsk – Lysaya Gora on the Khungari – Timber Centre – taiga near Start – Komsomolsk.

The winter of 1942–3 was spent in the town. Z worked as before as a draughtsman and lived tolerably, though in worse conditions than just before the war. Correspondence with the family was re-established with difficulty. Yekaterina's tribulations during the evacuation, delays on the journey, children's illnesses, the difficulties of finding accommodation and work at Urzhum – all these factors hindered regular correspondence, and anyhow letters often went astray at that time.

In March 1943 the five years since Z's arrest were up. He had never thought that he would have to drain this bitter cup to the dregs, but even less had he imagined that he would have an extra year and a half added to his sentence. By some general decree the release of prisoners whose term had expired was put off for the duration of the war (in fact Z was to be freed from close confinement a little earlier). On the anniversary of his arrest Z wrote sadly to his wife: 'So, dear friend, I'm entering into a new stage of my life that doesn't make me either joyful

* See translation on p.339.

or bitter, since my feelings are already blunted and the continuation of misfortune seems no more terrible than what happened five years ago.'

Z's time in the Far East ended in May 1943. The camp was wholly or partly transferred to the Altay region and renamed 'Altaylag'. For a prisoner, moving was always a torment, always a step in the dark, always a reason to worry about the future.

Z's new camp was close to the village of Mikhaylovskoye in the Kulunda steppe. For a time the prisoners were accommodated not in huts but in dugouts. The majority of them were put to work on constructing a railway line from Kulunda station to a soda works with the fine-sounding name Crimson Lake. Z was consigned to be a manual worker here.

Each day the group of escorted prisoners would make an eight-kilometre trek through steppe, pine wood and swamp to the soda works on the lake. Here, under the burning rays of the summer sun, squelching up to the knees in a thick solution of sodium carbonate, Z would scoop up the soda-rich liquid. He had already experienced much in the camps – quarrying, logging, soil-shifting, hunger, frosts – but until now his health had stood up to it all. Here it could no longer manage: his heart let him down. At the end of his life he wrote: 'I also have a long-standing heart complaint, since its strength was left behind in the soda mud of a certain Siberian lake.' Disinclined to complain of difficulties, he none the less wrote to his wife: 'At the beginning of summer things got really hard.'

The heavy labour at the soda lake lasted a couple of months, after which Z had to go to the sick-bay. Re-reading his old prison letters in 1956, he made a note: 'That was when, after the summer working at the soda lakes, the doctor diagnosed cardiac trouble. I was all swollen up and ill for a long time.' The sick-bay doctor, the wife of the engineer Arkhangelsky, later said that she had tried to detain the emaciated, exhausted and swollen-limbed Z as long as possible in the sick-bay, curing him basically through rest and hospital food. Her husband helped Z, who was still very weak, to be placed in a draughtsman's job in the Directorate of Altaylag. Again Z's ability to do technical drawings saved him from intolerable physical labour and perhaps death.

Work in the Directorate went on from morning till late at night, but could hardly be compared with soda-extraction. In any case the Altay climate was significantly milder than that in the Far East; in the autumn many fairly cheap vegetables, and even melons, appeared. The food became good, health gradually improved. Z's personality, conscientiousness and neatness in his draughtsman's work disposed his new colleagues – including his immediate boss, P. M. Tsishevsky – favourably towards him.

In the Altay Z began to receive letters from Stepanov, who had been evacuated from Leningrad and was living with his family at Molotov (Perm). In his first letter Stepanov told of the deaths of Daniil Kharms and Aleksandr Vvedensky; but Z did not then know of the reasons for these deaths. He was to learn only after his release that in August 1941 Kharms was arrested, and died in prison in February 1942. At the same time, at the beginning of the war, Vvedensky was arrested in Kharkov and shortly afterwards perished. In his hut in the camp Z mentally bade farewell to the literary friends of his youth. He was disturbed too about the fate of his brother Aleksey, who (as he heard from Yekaterina) was missing at the front. And again only on his release was he to learn that his brother had been a research student at the Peterhof Biological Institute, had joined the national militia on the outbreak of war and just after reaching the front had been surrounded, taken prisoner by the Germans and sent to do heavy work in the graphite mines.

At the end of 1943 Stepanov with his family moved from Molotov to Moscow, and here he again attempted to help his friend. In sketches for his memoirs he wrote:

> When I reached Moscow in 1943 I met Fadeyev at the Writers' Union and reminded him both of our meeting in 1939 and of his promise to help: he said that he had immediately looked into Z's 'case', that it was evident he was not guilty of anything, and again promised to begin agitating for his release. I got together a new application, which this time was signed by Ehrenburg, Marshak, Chukovsky and Shklovsky, and gave it to Fadeyev.

Perhaps as a result of this effort a meeting was arranged at the beginning of January 1944 between Z and some representatives of the Moscow authorities who had arrived at the settlement of Blagoveshchenka near Kulunda. In a cell at the transit prison there were four young people as well as Z: two students from Sverdlovsk who had been given ten years apiece for bringing out a handwritten journal, the nineteen-year-old Teddy Vitels and A. S. Sandler, who later wrote of his prison meeting with Z in a letter to this author and in his book *Knots for Memory*. Z was uncommunicative in the cell, did not reveal his full name and avoided answering their questions. When asked about his situation he said: 'Just now I don't even know anything myself.' About his work he said laconically, 'We draw on various bits of paper . . .' But in any case they did not press their questions on him – they knew that every prisoner rightly feared a stool-pigeon. Nevertheless Z at once

showed interest in the poems that Vitels and Sandler recited to one
another. He surprised them by instantly recognizing Khlebnikov's
authorship, asked for something of his own and listened to them
attentively.

One day the Sverdlovsk boys organized a spiritualist seance. Z was
lying down, but they invited him to join in, and after a bit he agreed and
sat at the board with letters of the alphabet on it and a glass. They
summoned up the spirit of Lev Tolstoy and the medium put various
questions to him. The last to put one was Z: 'When shall I get home,
Lev Nikolayevich?' He waited smilingly for an answer, and the glass
clearly and speedily indicated the letters that read out: 'After this
imperialist buffoonery.'

From time to time the warder took Z out for meetings with the
Moscow officials. There is no record of what they asked, but according
to Sandler he came back calmer. They called prisoners out by number,
so that his neighbours did not know the surname of their older
companion.

Once Sandler and Vitels, hungry after a skimpy supper, decided to
write a ballad about the thin soup (*balanda*) they were fed in their cell.
Z, normally silent, serious, plunged in his own thoughts, surprised
them by suddenly saying that he too would take part in its composition.
They just needed to make out a clear plan and decide in advance who
would write what. Teddy Vitels proposed the first line, and Z quickly
recited the first two stanzas he had composed:

> In Sherwood Forest the bonfire is burning
> The day is coming to its end
> The huntsman's knife is cruel and sharp –
> A noble stag has been slain!
> The bloody meat's juices are hissing,
> And it's browning evenly.
> And the flask goes the rounds, and the haunch crackles
> Our hunting has not been in vain.

Thus the whole of the ironic ballad was composed, its basic idea
contained in the couplet: 'Oh, all this bouquet of incomparable
foodstuffs/Is as nothing compared with you, *balanda*!'

Their time together at the transit prison came to an end. As Sandler
recalls (in a letter to the author):

The time came to part. The day before, the orderly at the evening roll-
call had said, instead of using a number, 'Zabolotsky! Get ready,
tomorrow you're going away!' That evening there was a long silence.
And suddenly Teddy Vitels called out: 'You should be ashamed, Nikolay

Alekseyevich. It turns out you're the poet Zabolotsky! Why didn't you tell us?'

'And what difference would that have made?'

'I consider myself a poet – totally young and inexperienced, but a poet none the less. What would I not have recited to you and learnt from you! It would have been a real academy.'

Z answered: 'We'll save our writing and poetry till after the "imperialist buffoonery" – wasn't that what Lev Tolstoy promised us? Work in your own way – take no notice of any authorities. Work all the time. You must send me your first book for review. Now, as for you' – he had turned to me – 'you're an excellent versifier, on the same level as many poets . . . But don't go on with it: you're a journalist by nature.' And off he went, leaving us all his tobacco.

By 11 January Z was again at Mikhaylovskoye and back at his draughtsman's work. It may be supposed that the meeting with the authorities moved him again to write an appeal for a review of his case and discharge from prison. On 18 February 1944 he wrote:

My dear Katya! Today I received your two January letters and before that your card. My dear, they are the first letters from which I've learnt what it was like for you in Leningrad before the evacuation. My heart trembles for you even though it's all in the past. Fate has kept you safe and I don't want to grumble at it, given such a miracle. My little heroes, what you've had to put up with and live through! Yes Katya, we've certainly been allotted an incredible life, and there's still something left ahead for us.

Don't even mention my books and my suits! You were entirely right to sell the books, and it's more than likely that the greatest service those books could perform was when they were sold by you: I mean that seriously – for the wisdom of books is all around us, while our lives and our children's are given us only once.

And why be silly enough to hang onto my black suit? What good is it to me? Am I going to be any the worse without it if I get out sometime? Sell it at the first opportunity and let the children have a bit more to eat. God knows you won't hear any kind of reproach from me – it looks as though in everyday life you behave more sensibly and better than me, and I'm certain that fate will reward you for all the deprivations and misfortunes that you have borne and still have to bear, dearest. I think I have become a bit different myself; at least I'm no longer attracted in life by suits or by money, and the living human soul remains for me now the one thing of value . . .

In reply Z received a letter from Yekaterina:

20 April 1944. Dear Kolya! Your birthday is coming close. Good God, a seventh year vanishing from life. Where's any trace of these years? Only

in our hearts – life has bypassed us just the same . . . For your birthday my wish for you is to live to a ripe and comfortable old age. Youth has disappeared and won't come back. Our mature years have been distorted and stifled. Our children are growing up. Maybe we'll see in them what we've missed in our own lives . . . Write to us as often as you can. I've not had any letters for a long time, about three weeks. We've sent off a present for your birthday. Only will it get there? And I've sent 300 roubles by post. As I wrote before, I've sold your light-coloured suit – and we've almost eaten the proceeds . . .

After getting this melancholy letter, Z tried to cheer up Yekaterina and sent her words of sympathy, optimism and hope for a better future:

24 May 1944. My dear Katya! I've had your letter of 20 April. It's so sad. Dearest, now just remember one thing: the heaviest burdens are already behind us, we've survived them. Now it's very important not to give in for these last difficult months. I very much hope (and have some reason to do so) that my fate may soon change and perhaps our moment of meeting is closer than we think.

You write 'life has bypassed us'. No, not true. For all our people these have been difficult years. Just look how many have lost those close to them, through no fault of their own . . . The time of my inner despair has long gone and I've come to understand a great deal about life that didn't occur to me before.

In the spring of 1944 Z's living conditions became noticeably better. The food became more varied. The authorities permitted him and Susanin to plant a small vegetable plot inside the camp, from which during the summer they harvested cucumbers, tomatoes, radishes and potatoes. They listened greedily to the radio – good news from the front encouraged hope of a quick end to the war and, with it, a new free life. They were allowed to go to work unescorted, and Z wrote: 'On the way to and from work I try to walk by myself, to look at nature, and it gives me the greatest delight. Now after all it's spring; how the natural world is changing!'

Once an event took place that Z described in a letter of 6 June 1944 to his son:

I was going to work, alone, past a cemetery. I was lost in thought and didn't notice much around me. Suddenly I heard someone calling me from behind. I looked round and saw an old woman coming out of the cemetery. I went up to her. She held out to me a couple of doughnuts and a hard-boiled egg. 'Don't say no, take them!' At first I didn't understand what was going on, but then it dawned on me: 'Have you just been burying somebody?' She explained that one son had been killed at the

213

front, a second had been buried here two weeks ago and now she was alone in the world. She wept and went off. I took her doughnuts, bowed to her, thanked her and walked on. You see how much grief there is in the world. And all the same people keep on living and can even help others. We can learn a lesson from this old woman who followed the ancient Russian custom and gave me, a writer and a prisoner, her memorial gift.*

As life got easier and the war was clearly coming to an end, thoughts of meeting the family, of life in the future and of writing became ever stronger. What else might fate promise the imprisoned poet? It was at that time that he wrote his memoir about nature in the Far East and sent it to Stepanov and Yekaterina. He wrote to the latter:

> I feel that everything is now different, and of course our life won't be a repetition of the old one but something else. Personally I don't need much from it, but I'd like the chance to help you and the children. Anyhow we'll see about that later. It's understandable you've been tormented. Just so long as you're well! I certainly hope that it'll be easier for you when I'm back and that you can relax a bit. The children are bigger; I've grown unused to them. Nikita has his own life, to some extent independent, and we'll have to get used to it. Natasha will be at school. We'll be alone together, make a garden, sow turnips, and play cards in our old age.

In the depths of his soul Z retained his dreams of taking up his writing again, of new poems which he still had it in him to write. Here in the camp there was no place for these dreams, still less for real hopes for the future. At times he wanted only a quiet, provincial life, since in all these years there had been an accumulation of inner weariness, of hidden incomprehension, of hurt that he concealed from outside eyes: could his work really be of no use to people, could he really be the only one to lose from his inability to write poetry? But at times of inner cheerfulness he reckoned that, despite the wounds he had suffered, he could still do much more as a writer, and maybe an interesting life filled with achievements awaited him. When he read a letter from Kaverin about the important place his translation of the *Igor Tale* would occupy in Russian literature, he again experienced the feelings he wrote about to his wife: 'At the end of work when you leave these smoke-filled rooms and a sweet spring breeze envelops your face, you so want to live, work, write and join in intellectual life. And nothing's frightening: happiness, calm and thought are at nature's feet.'

* This incident also inspired the fine poem 'It happened long ago...' ('Eto bylo davno...', 1957) [Ed.].

Susanin recounted how at this time Z, who normally hunched himself gloomily over his drawings, would sometimes become cheerful and open-hearted, would make jokes and turn into a pleasant, sociable and interesting person. Such flashes of inner uplift were connected with the fact that in the spring of 1944 he already knew that he had been put forward by the camp authorities to be released for good work before the end of the war.

V

Finally, on 18 August 1944 – six years and five months after his arrest – Z was released from imprisonment by a Special Commission in Moscow at the instance of the Altay camp directorate; but he had to remain within the camp system without the right to select his work or move around freely. After a few days of getting used to a free life and setting himself up in it he informed Yekaterina of his new situation.

25 August 1944. My dear Katya! Ten days have gone by since my release and only now can I write you a letter. So much to get done and fuss about that there was hardly time even to send you the telegram. Did you get it?

Anyhow, one thing at a time. The Special Commission decreed my release on 18 August with the provision that I must live here as a free worker till the end of the war (directive no. 185/2). It's not impossible that in the future I'll be called up into the army, but meanwhile I'm to stay here as a technical draughtsman, with a salary of 6–700 roubles a month and provisions to go with the job. They come to the following: 700 grams of bread, two meals a day in the canteen and maybe some other benefits which I haven't been told about yet. God knows, it won't be all that filling, but given the times we're in – particularly in comparison with what I was experiencing not long ago – it's very good. Life has changed a lot: I'm getting good food and enough of it. Two engineers have been let out at the same time and we're all three looking for somewhere to live, that is, a room in a peasant house. Despite a lot of time and bother we haven't yet found anything definite, but we hope soon to have a haven of our own. Meanwhile we are sheltering at the edge of the village in a filthy little hovel, but that's only temporarily . . .

Now for the details of everyday living. I came out dressed completely in my prison outfit, but I've been handed down one or two official things. I've got working boots – pretty rough ones but sound, old khaki trousers and a jacket, two changes of official-issue underwear, a mattress, two sheets, a pillowcase, my old green blanket (now full of holes), the fur-lined jacket you once sent me, a hat, worn-out felt boots. An iron pot

215

and a wooden spoon complete my lavish possessions. All the rest have been torn away from me and scattered all over the place by life's misfortunes.

The camp was soon due to move to a new location, and Z thought it would be better for the family to join him there. But Yekaterina could no longer stand the separation and, despite all her husband's sensible arguments, hurried to join him. So their long-awaited reunion took place on 17 November 1944. In a little station house lost in the Kulunda steppe Z, so recently behind barbed wire, set eyes on his wife and children at last. Nearly seven years of separation and hardships were behind them. This is what Yekaterina had to say about the meeting:

At Kulunda we again changed trains. On the new branch line we travelled to Mikhaylovskoye station. Here there was a little house, where the signalman worked, beside the rails. The branch-line had not yet been handed over and was still controlled by the camp. The duty officer had been warned that a former inmate's family was on the way to him. He had to warn the administration of our arrival so that a horse could be sent. Nikolay was unsure if he himself could come and meet us. There was no regular timetable: we didn't know quite when we would arrive – he might have been at work. There was not a single other house at the station: the village was three kilometres away.

The duty officer, only a young lad, was attentive and looked at us with interest. He began ringing the administration and then suddenly asked, 'Do you want me to ring him up now?' It was quite unexpected. All these years I'd been afraid of what he'd be like when I saw him . . . The only meeting (in Kresty Prison) had been on 5 November 1938, when I already knew we were off to exile to Urzhum on the 7th, and Nikolay was waiting to go to the camps any day. We had managed to get our sad news across to each other. I had told him to write poste restante to Urzhum. I've forgotten who had told me he'd spent eighteen days in a prison hospital for the mentally disturbed. When we met on that occasion I looked at him hard – no signs of his illness. But his face was crushed, unhealthy and he didn't seem to hear well. The prisoners stood on one side of the barrier behind wire netting, just like a chicken farm only with thicker wire – then a metre's gap, the barrier and more wire netting, then ourselves standing and waiting for our meetings. Down the gap a guard strolled. And everyone was shouting and trying to communicate, so it was hard to hear.

That face and the wire netting rose up before my eyes all through those years. What would he have turned into by now? And suddenly his voice was there on the telephone – happy and cheerful. No! Not that of a broken man.

Hard to believe that in a short time I'd be seeing him: not years, not even a day . . . unbelievable but true.

The orderly sat us on an oblong wooden divan to the right of the door. The room was tiny with a big stove. Darkness was falling; the children were dozing on the divan and I was continually going out to see if they were coming. No, not yet. By now it was quite dark; the sky was full of stars. Steppe; silence. I felt I couldn't have met him by daylight, I couldn't bear the emotion. Still nobody: I sat down again. Then at last I jumped up and we bumped against each other at the doors.

Their father, who couldn't stand any affectation, got down on his knees, looking and looking at the children . . .

Suddenly the driver who had brought Nikolay said in a muffled voice: 'It's the boss!' The coachman, Nikolay and the signalman all lined up with thumbs straight down their trouser-seams and greeted the boss in silence. The boss had come on his own business and paid no attention to us, but I felt terrified. We loaded ourselves into a horse-drawn sledge – grown-ups on seats, children on the baggage: so that they shouldn't catch cold after the warm house I wrapped them up from head to foot in a warm rug, where they crooned happily to themselves. The starry dome of the sky was above us, the sledge squeaked across the snowy plain and it would even have been nice for the journey to have been longer, but we soon arrived.

The Zabolotskys settled at the edge of the village in the house of the Mordovian woman who had given shelter to Z just after his release. She was quite pleased that a whole family should settle in. At her table she provided pies she had baked with wild herbs and salted melons: the children found them an unheard-of luxury. On freezing winter days she brought a calf, sheep and some poultry right into the house for shelter. It was cramped and stuffy.

Soon after their arrival the children got measles. They had to be nursed and fed carefully. Dr Arkhangelskaya, who eighteen months before had looked after Z in the camp sick-bay, came and brought the children semolina, then considered the most valuable of all medicines. The chief of the Design Department, Tsishevsky, gave them splendidly illustrated volumes of a children's encyclopaedia to read – they seemed a real marvel in those days.

On getting back from work Z would cut firewood, help Yekaterina fetch water, and on the long winter evenings they would recount to each other the many things that had befallen them in all those years. About the worst episodes of camp life Z would speak in a quiet voice, unwillingly and laconically. Yekaterina talked about the pre-war efforts to get a review of the case, about the good-hearted help of friends, about the hunger and the bombardment in Leningrad under siege, about the hard years of life as evacuees . . . How much they had undergone without each other! Z's heart was heavy when he discovered in detail how close his family had been to disaster. Yekaterina spoke of her incredible efforts to save the children in times of starvation, of the explosion of an enemy shell in the Shvartses' flat, close to the kitchen where she was staying with her sister and the children, of how they managed miraculously to leave the city across the ice of Lake Ladoga.

One evening in the semi-darkness of the peasant house Z started singing, 'I go out along the road alone . . .' – he sang well and with sadness, then fell silent. Yekaterina asked him to go on, and he continued: 'I do not expect anything from life / And I am not at all sorry for the past . . .'* In Lermontov's words he discerned a meaning that related to his personal fate.

New Year's Eve was to be celebrated in the Directorate, and Z was to recite at the party – not his own poetry (that was still quite unthinkable) but a translation of an English ballad by Alfred Noyes; at home he rehearsed it:

> The wind was a torrent of darkness among the gusty trees,
> The moon was a ghostly galleon tossed upon cloudy seas,
> The road was a ribbon of moonlight over the purple moor,
> And the highwayman came riding –
> Riding –
> The highwayman came riding, up to the old inn-door.

Yekaterina and Z saw in the new year of 1945 with the Arkhangelskys, to whom Z owed his deliverance from the intolerable work at the soda-lake. Good people were to be met with even in the hardest of circumstances. But other, malevolent people of whom there were many could not be forgotten. The caution bred in the camps, the fear of being watched and of denunciations would manifest themselves in Z quite unexpectedly.

The Zabolotskys lived in the Kulunda steppe for about four months. Yekaterina recalls:

> No difficulties got us down: after all we were together again. That hard winter at Mikhaylovskoye was perhaps the cosiest of any for our family. All that we had been through was still close and vivid and tangible to us. The miracle of our coming together filled life with joy, nourished tenderness and kindness in our relations.

The building of the railway line and the reconstruction of the soda-works had been completed, and in March 1945 the camp with all its

---

* Lines from a famous poem by Mikhail Lermontov (1814–41) [Ed.].

prisoners, semi-free and free workers was transferred to Karaganda. The Zabolotskys made the train journey with the free engineer G. M. Zotov. The hard frosts necessitated their taking turns to watch over the iron stove so as to keep it going round the clock. At one of the long halts the floor of the wagon was set on fire by the heat of the stove and the resulting inferno had to be doused with water. The cold in the wagon became insupportable. Zotov noted that even despite such events they all travelled in harmony. 'There were no complaints about the difficult conditions, and none of the bad feeling such events usually occasion.'

Some way from Karaganda the train halted on a loop-line, and since there was no other accommodation they were all left to live in the wagons. The workers were taken in to the administration in town by lorry, the children to school by sledge. Soon the foodstuffs issued before departure ran out, and the families were left without anything to eat. After a couple of days Z and Zotov got some provisions in the town, but a violent snowstorm blew up, covered the road, made it impossible for vehicles to get through and they had to make their way to the train on foot. Zotov writes:

> The storm was so strong that snow got into inner pockets despite the fact that our outer clothing was fastened tight. When he got to his wagon and slumped down on the planks, Z said: 'Yes – human beings are the most long-suffering of the beasts. What animal could possibly make a journey like that in such a storm?'

At last the Zabolotskys were given their own quarters in the village of Bolshaya Mikhaylovka about three kilometres from Karaganda New Town. In a mudbrick house (No. 10 Pervomaysky Lane) they took a small room with a kitchen-passage. The other room in the house was occupied by a pair of exiled Moscow Germans. After a thorough clean-up and a war against bedbugs they began to arrange their accommodation. They made a bed out of a couple of big limewood boards and planks, and the rest of the furniture out of boxes and other bits and pieces. They got coal for heating. Here they lived till autumn 1945, when they were given a room in a comfortable flat on Lenin Street, again in the New Town area of Karaganda.

Large-scale construction was going on around Karaganda. The Defence Committee had decreed that the Saran area of the Karaganda coal-basin should be exploited, and so the town of Saran, with its railway connections and whole infrastructure, was being planned. From 14 March 1945 Z worked as a senior technical draughtsman in the planning office, from 22 June as an engineer in the civilian construction division, and from 28 September as chief of the administrative housing section while simultaneously heading the Directorate office. He got on well with many of his colleagues – notably G. M. Zotov, I. S. Susanin, A. P. Shelius and P. M. Tsishevsky. The head of the Saran special construction administration, D. I. Chechelnitsky, was very well disposed towards him and was soon to play an important and positive role in Z's change of official status.

The family began to sense that life was becoming more human – they had their own front door, Z had an acceptable job and, finally, the long-awaited victory in the war, with which so many future hopes were bound up, came in May 1945. In the spring the family got a vegetable allotment somewhere near Saran: on Sundays they would travel there to plant and earth up potatoes, to hoe and to water them. Since autumn Z, as chief of the office, had been given an increased ration in a shop for sectional heads. The ration was far from top quality, but significantly improved the family nourishment.

Now in charge of the office, Z started getting its neglected papers into order. But of course he had no intention of devoting his life to office work and now, already in a position to make plans for the future, he started thinking how to get back to being a writer. However he still sensed all too strongly his external and internal lack of freedom. He could not allow himself to write original poetry, fearing (with reason) that it would again bring misfortune upon himself and his family. He said more than once that he would write no more poems of his own, and that all his hopes now rested on translation work. Deep down he might have had other hopes and plans, but for now he insisted on this harsh resolution for himself.

Forbidding himself thoughts of his own poetry, he strove with all his heart to take up translation work – the more so since Yekaterina had brought with her the manuscripts he was working on when arrested, including his unfinished work on the *Igor Tale*. This had survived at the Writers' House where Z had been working before his arrest, and had been taken by Yekaterina on her exile to Urzhum. It and other manuscripts remained among the objects left behind there when the family temporarily – as it had seemed – returned to Leningrad. Yekaterina got back to Urzhum only in 1942, this time as an evacuee, and found all the things she had left behind safely preserved. Thus she had a few objects that could be traded for food so as not to starve, and maybe could even help her husband. When setting out for the Altay she again left some of the manuscripts in safe keeping at Urzhum, but brought the beginning of the *Igor Tale* and the unfinished long poem 'The Siege of Kozelsk', thinking they might soon be needed by Z.

So here in the Altay Z tremulously re-read the pages that had miraculously come back to him, and, despite secret misgivings, decided to continue the translation at whatever cost. He remembered Kaverin's letter of May 1944: '. . . In literature the times have scarcely moved on – so little in fact that I can well imagine your coming back and continuing your translation of the *Igor Tale*; now I think this work would find an even more honourable place in our literature than when you first undertook it.'

In January 1945 Z sent a telegram to Stepanov asking him to send the text of the *Igor Tale*, since he wanted to get to know the Old Russian original as well as he could. He already understood, as he wrote to Stepanov, that the lines he had earlier composed were in need of large-scale revision and rewriting.

In the mudbrick house at Karaganda there were only minimal opportunities for getting down to work. It was hard: he lacked both time and reference books. After his three-kilometre journey back home and a quick meal Z would turn back the blankets from the edge of the 'bed' boards, put down his papers on them and begin to write. Not all went well at first: there was disappointment, but work on the *Tale* became Z's favourite occupation and his hope for a better future. The old manuscript served its purpose – it reminded him of his earlier conception, helped him to overcome the psychological barriers and return to writing.

In letters to Stepanov Z wrote of his work on the translation, his enthusiasm for the *Tale*, his plans and hopes for his renewed efforts. Here is one of them:

20 June 1945, Karaganda. Dear Kolya! A few days ago I finished my rough draft of the *Igor Tale*. Now, with the fair copy lying in front of me I understand that so far I've only just reached the entrance-way into this great and complex work. I know that I'm capable of carrying it through. The state of my manuscript has persuaded me of that. But I doubt if I'll have the strength to finish it off if my circumstances don't change for the better. Can a big task like this be done at odd moments and at night after a tiring day's work? Isn't it a shame to give only the last vestiges of your powers to this translation – to which a whole life could be devoted and all one's interests subordinated? But I don't even possess a table to put my papers on, not even a light that would burn all night.

You sit all day at work, copy drawings and passionately wait for the moment when you can get back home and pick up your pen. And then that moment escapes you. You trek three kilometres in a heatwave, eat with a book in your hands, take up the pen and feel yourself already weak and needing a rest, the head stuffy, the mind all sleepy, the pen won't work. And you know what sort of work it is. You can write a dozen variants of a single passage – not one of them is right. You can sometimes get quite delirious, curse the whole business and sink into sleep. Next day it's the same picture; it's only different on Sundays – but God knows how many Sundays you'd need!

Now that I've entered into the spirit of the work I'm totally awestruck, amazed and grateful to fate for preserving this miracle for us from the depths of the past. In the desert of our past centuries, where wars, fires and savage destruction have left not one stone standing upon another, this isolated temple of our ancient glory, resembling nothing else, still stands. It's alarming to approach it. The eye involuntarily wishes to find in it the usual proportions and golden sections of our familiar world masterpieces. A waste of effort! There's no such proportionality in it; everything about it is filled with a special tender savagery – the writer's measure is not ours. How moving it is to see it stand, this mysterious edifice, its corners battered, the haunt of ravens and wolves, for as long as Russian culture stands, knowing no equals.

In classical Latin there are lines that ring out like cast metal; but what are they in comparison with these passionate, unbelievably vivid and noble Old Russian formulae, which instantly enter the soul and stay there for ever? You read this tale and count your good fortune to be a Russian!

My translation is of course contentious – being rhymed and in tonic verse it cannot be exact – and of course introduces a certain modernization. Here sensitivity and restraint have to play their part. I'd reckon the problem solved if the features I've introduced don't contradict the overall style, and the contemporary verse sounds reasonably firm, without weak and pappy 'translationese'.

It's a hard task . . . Greetings from Katya to all – Yours, N.Z.

Despite all these difficulties the translation was finished very quickly: the work was begun in April–May and finished by the beginning of July, so the Karaganda period of translation lasted around three months. It remained of course for him to polish and edit it. On the 18 July Z was given leave, and spent about ten days at the rest-house at Akkul station, where he finally worked over the verse text. Out of 289 lines of the translation written before his arrest only 123 were kept unchanged, and an additional 54 lines were inserted – parts of the original that had been omitted in the Leningrad version. In all the Karaganda text consisted of 736 lines. Thus the translation had been practically done from scratch. In September a reading of the new translation took place in the Karaganda Party Educational Centre: about fifteen members of the local intelligentsia came. The paper *Socialist Karaganda* responded to the event with a brief notice by Nona Medelets, a teacher at Karaganda

College of Education – in essence a well-wishing review of the new translation. It ended with the words: 'It is a particular joy that the translation has appeared in 1945, the year of the Russian people's victory over its most stubborn foe, as a result of which the clear and resonant poetry of the translation, telling of a heroic struggle for the independence of the land of Russia, sounds particularly close and moving.'

This note in the paper was all the more pleasing to Z in that it was quite unexpected. He had already linked his hopes of a return to professional writing with this first literary task after his release. And any response to his work might influence the further fate not only of the translation, but of the translator, who had many obstacles still to face on the way to his goal.

It would appear that at the end of September Z sent the *Igor Tale* to Stepanov in Moscow with a request to try to have it published in the national press. Z thought that this would help to set him up again in the Writers' Union and get him permission to return to Russia proper.

Meanwhile his Moscow friends, particularly Stepanov, renewed their efforts on his behalf. In January 1945 Stepanov wrote to him:

> I devoutly believe you're going to come back into literature and write many good things; I often speak of you to all sorts of people (Fadeyev, Chagin, Shklovsky, Chukovsky) – all of them are equally convinced. I've already told you that Mariya Tikhonova sends a message that you should write to Nikolay Tikhonov about yourself and your position . . . Chagin also asks for precise news about you.

Tikhonova played an honourable part in these efforts; she reminded her husband several times of Z's cruel fate and of the need to re-establish his good name. In April 1945 Tikhonov, Ehrenburg and Marshak sent a collective letter to the Interior Ministry, evidently requesting that the legal restrictions on Z be lifted and that he be allowed to return to a writing career. P. I. Chagin, the influential Deputy Director of *Goslitizdat*, handed the letter in.

At the end of May 1945 Z received an encouraging postcard from Irakly Andronikov, his former colleague in Leningrad children's publishing and admirer of his work, who wrote:

> I talked a lot about you with Kolya Stepanov (we call him Styopa, he's gone quite grey) and outbid each other in our affection for you and in the abundance of our ideas about how to meet you again. We worked out a whole programme and tomorrow I shall try to see the people on whom our various possibilities depend. I am certain that our meeting is not in

the dim distance (literally speaking) but will take place here, in Moscow, very soon.

But time went by and his Moscow friends' efforts led to no actual results; judging by his letter to Stepanov of 4 July 1945, Z himself put little credence in them:

> So, dear Nikolay, June is already over and we're well into July. Your comforting information is just like what I had in 1940–1 that so disappointed me. I know from experience that if a business is long and drawn-out you can expect no good to come of it. It's clear no real heavyweights want to get seriously involved, and my evil destiny continues to weigh heavily upon me. There's one main regret: years go by, and one's creative possibilities trickle away.

But if friends were powerless to help Z out of his situation of half-freedom, it remained for him to take action himself. The wall separating him from the life of a writer could be breached from the Karaganda side as well as from that of Moscow. Z's attempts were helped by well-disposed people such as D. Chechelnitsky (head of the Saran Building Directorate), Tsishevsky and other engineering and technical employees, who well understood that someone of major poetic gifts was working alongside them. They were particularly aware of it after Z's readings of his translation both in the Building Directorate and the Party Educational Centre. The head of the Saran camp, of which Z had been an inmate not so long ago, also read it.

And so it happened that with Chechelnitsky's support Z managed to get the Directorate of the Saran construction unit of the NKVD to send a letter addressed to the President of the USSR Writers' Union, Nikolay Tikhonov, closing with the following appeal:

> 1. Since N. A. Zabolotsky through his good work in the camps has earned commendation as a citizen, he is worthy to return to his free employment – in view of his literary talents he should return to his work as a writer.
> 2. The Directorate of the Saranstroy NKVD requests the Administration of the Union of Soviet Writers to restore comrade Z to the rights of a member of the Union, and to accord him every assistance and support both in publishing his work and in affording him the right to reside in one of the central cities of the Soviet Union.

There followed the signatures of the administrative head and the chief of the political section of the Saran Corrective Labour Camp, and the date, 6 September 1945.

Reading his copy of this document, Z chuckled bitterly at the remarkable paradox of it: the camp bosses were recommending his literary work to the Union of Writers; the NKVD personnel were requesting that he – lately an inmate – should be given the proper conditions for literary work!

Days followed in tense anticipation of an answer from the capital. Moscow kept silent – Nikolay Tikhonov was dragging his feet. At the end of November it was decided to send one more letter, this time to the Special Commission of the Soviet NKVD. It is not known if there was an answer. And suddenly, when hope had already died in Z's heart, on the last day of 1945 there came the long-awaited official telegram, signed by Tikhonov, summoning him to the Union of Writers in Moscow. Z had never before received so welcome a New Year's present. The express telegram read: 'To the special Saran construction unit, copy to Zabolotsky. Beg dispatch Zabolotsky Nikolay Aleksandrovich city Moscow for two months. President Writers' Union USSR Tikhonov.'

Thanks to Chechelnitsky his departure, on 8 January 1946, was arranged without any hitch. Z speedily wound up all his business with the job, received 3,000 roubles (old money) for the journey, bade farewell to his family and set off towards his new tasks.

The Return

I

ON THE WAY back to Moscow Z thought hard about what his meetings in the capital boded for him, whom to turn to first, and how he should behave. He wanted to be clear in his own mind how to plan the rest of his life if he were allowed to live in Leningrad or Moscow, and if he were not, where he should settle with his family, in a big city or in somewhere old and small, like his home town of Urzhum. His work as a writer obviously demanded being near the cities in the centre, where there were publishing houses, libraries and literary friends, but it was still a question of whether he would be allowed to return to his chosen profession.

At the bottom of his trunk lay the neatly copied text of his translation of the *Igor Tale* which he was hoping to read to his friends and to try and get published in one or other of the journals. Then they would all realize that his talent had not been lost and that he was as much a master of words as he had been eight years earlier, before his arrest. For the moment he would not write poetry, but he would surely be able to get commissions for verse translations. And then he remembered how several months earlier he had sent a letter to the head office of the Union of Writers of Kazakhstan in Alma-Ata with a proposal to translate some Kazakh poetry – and he had received no answer. His future seemed to him uncertain, but he was ready to fight to get back to what he really wanted to do in life.

The train rumbled over a bridge, and Z looked out of the window. By the shapes of bushes and brown sedge through the curtain of falling snow he could just make out some little Russian river. He imagined this spot in summer, and thought of the words of his translation, and could not help applying them to himself:

> And as if becoming an ermine
> Igor the Prince bounded into the reeds,

And swam on the waves, like a golden-eye,
And flew like the wind on a horse.

The horse fell and the Prince left his horse behind,
And home he leapt, like a grey wolf.

He smiled at the sense of joy that welled up within him. Home! Was it really home he was going to? So much that lay behind him was absurd, unthinkably painful, terrifying. They were things he did not want to remember. Z lay on the carriage bench and thought about his strange destiny, which had given him great poetic talent, yet at the same time had done all it could to prevent this talent from being realized.

Z very much wanted to believe that a new and happier period of his life was about to begin, but he could not deceive himself. That freedom of thought that he had had when he was young would never be there again, just as there would never again be any feeling of complete physical safety. But after all he was only sharing honourably in the fate of his country.

Through the carriage window winter pictures of the countryside around Moscow were already flashing past and Z again began to think of what sort of greeting he would get from the capital. How much truth was there in what his friends had written to him? Did people remember him and what he had written? The life of the whole country and of every family had been turned upside down by a great and terrible war, and what an effort was now needed to return to normal life! And would this new life be normal? Did his own fate matter very much in the whirlpool of events that had engulfed the world in the previous decade?

But here he was already approaching Moscow, and in his ears sounded the joyful words of the ancient poem:

> But the sun rises up in the heavens,
> Prince Igor has appeared in Rus,
>
> The songs float from the distant Danube,
> Flying across the sea to Kiev.
>
> It rises up by bold Borichev
> To the Holy Mother of the Tower.
>
> And the lands are gladdened,
> The towns are joyous.

Z went out on the square in front of the station. He was carrying a small suitcase and certainly did not look in any way 'bold'. His long coat made from curtain material emphasized his thinness. A warm scarf was wound securely round his neck and his good-quality black trousers

227

underlined the rough appearance of his well-polished worker's boots. Each of these items of clothing had its own story. His suit had been bought in the old days, preserved by his wife with great difficulty, and was now much too big for him. The overcoat had been a great stroke of luck – in the department they had been issuing 'gifts from America', and Z had managed to get this almost unworn though rather old-fashioned item of clothing, sent from the other side of the ocean. The boots had been issued as part of his quota, and his hat was quite reasonable too. So in this grey, badly dressed post-war crowd Z looked completely respectable. But no one was paying any attention to him. They were all hurrying about their big-city business. The great capital had a multiform, complex, bustling life of its own. 'And the lands are gladdened, and the towns are joyous' – the poet thought ironically as he made his way to the metro to catch the train to the Lenin Library station.

When he came out of the metro he saw a city that was different from the one he had seen on the square in front of the station: the elegant, solemn walls and towers of the Kremlin, the deserted Mokhovaya Street, the new buildings of the Lenin Library, the building of the former Rumyantsev Museum on its hill. A quarter of a century had passed since, as a seventeen-year-old, he had worked in the library of this museum together with Misha Kasyanov – full of hope and prepared to overcome all obstacles on the path to his chosen goal. Fate had led him by its mysterious paths, and here he was again standing outside this building, once more full of hope, and his goal was still the same – to break through into literature.

Z crossed the street and went up to the small, old-style building which housed the Literary Museum. Here lived the Stepanovs – Nikolay, his wife, his mother and his son Alyosha. Their little apartment had a separate entrance from the courtyard, and consisted of the former nobleman's kitchen and the adjoining little room for the cook. There was no one in. Z sat down on a stack of firewood nearby and began to wait patiently. The meeting with the Stepanovs after all these years was on the surface restrained and even rather formal, yet each of these men, now no longer young, understood how much it meant to them. Later Stepanov recounted:

We put Zabolotsky in the big room where he had to sleep on the dining-table, because it was cold on the floor. Even we were sleeping on some sort of arrangement made out of boxes. With his usual sense of order, he folded his clothes neatly on going to bed, and in the morning was just as fresh and washed and glowing as normal. It was here that he had his first attacks of chest pains.

In the days that followed their meeting they talked a great deal about the past and their plans for the immediate future. Stepanov had most to say – about his life and work, about literary news and the situation in Moscow. Z spoke little. In his memoirs Stepanov wrote:

> He never complained about the extreme sufferings and deprivation he had suffered in innocence. He almost never spoke of them; even in his conversations with me he avoided mentioning what he had undergone while under arrest . . . He just told me on a couple of occasions that if he had gone on doing outdoor labouring in the taiga and not managed to get a job as a draughtsman in one of the offices he would undoubtedly have perished.

Stepanov told how in the closing stages of the war and the years that followed many Leningrad writers had come to Moscow, so that in the Union of Writers and in the publishing houses it was possible to meet many of the people Z had known earlier in Leningrad. The main centre of literary life was Moscow – here it was easier to get suitable work and easier to get published. They discussed Z's situation and how best to go about helping him.

Z said that he now had three basic tasks: to attempt to get his translation of the *Igor Tale* published, to get permission to live in one of the central cities of the country, preferably in Leningrad, and to get himself readmitted to the Writers' Union so that he could proceed unhindered with his poetry translations.

Soon after his arrival Z had meetings with Kaverin, Shvarts, Chikovani, Andronikov and Nikolay Chukovsky; he renewed old acquaintances and made new ones. He became convinced that he really had not been forgotten, that people remembered his poetry and believed there was much he could still write.

Several times he went with Stepanov across the Moscow River by the Kamenny Bridge to the famous grey 'house on the embankment', to see the Tikhonovs. He was given a warm welcome there, especially by Mariya Tikhonova who well understood his importance to poetry and was happy to take on the job of his defender and advocate. Stepanov recalled:

> There was always a crowd of people at the Tikhonovs. The evening meal would start late. There would be a lot of laughing and talking. Mariya – a kind and cheerful person who liked having guests – somehow imperceptibly knew how to make these evenings happy affairs and how to bring the most varied people together. They had everybody there: mountaineers, visiting Georgians, polar aviators . . .

At the Tikhonovs Z tried to be circumspect, but he would readily talk

229

about his translation of the *Igor Tale*, and listen attentively to the visitors' discussion. With people he did not know he was restrained, and by his looks and behaviour gave it to be understood that he would permit no questions about his past in the camps or conversations on political or other dangerous topics. At the same time those who spoke with him could see that he was worthy, courteous and interested. Stepanov used to recall how once at the Tikhonovs there turned up one particular poet, talkative, offensive and brimming over with undisguised self-importance. Z could not stand people like this. Evidently noticing Z's dislike and already having had a drink or two, the guest began to speak slightingly about him, garbling his surname. Z at once stood up from the table, put on his coat, and left. To Stepanov, who ran after him and caught him up, he complained bitterly of the man's senseless boorishness, and for some time he would not visit the house where he had been so insulted.

Z was given permission to take his midday meals in the Writers' Club restaurant, where his former Leningrad friends who were now settled in Moscow would also often go. One meeting there was extremely unusual. As he sat eating at a table in one corner of the half-empty hall, he was suddenly approached by a man who politely asked if he might sit at the same table. The man turned out to be that same Lesyuchevsky, whose efforts in the service of the NKVD had had such a destructive effect on Zabolotsky's fate. He had once been a casual acquaintance of Z who recognized him at once, but could do nothing about it; with a look of sombre hostility he finished his meal in order to get away from his unwelcome neighbour as quickly as he could. At that moment there came into the restaurant Aleksandr and Silva Gitovich, who had come from Leningrad specially to see Z. Gitovich knew of Lesyuchevsky's dishonourable part in his friend's affairs, and was now very surprised to see them sitting at the same table. In her memoirs his wife wrote: 'What a ridiculous sight! How absurd! At the other side of the table sat none other than Lesyuchevsky, stout, sleek and clean-shaven, enjoying his soup. The sight of the two of them together threw us completely. But we quickly came to our senses and rushed up to Z and greeted him warmly, then we had no time for anyone else.' In answer to the Gitoviches' questions about keeping such peculiar company Z said: 'Well, you can solve that psychological puzzle for yourselves. Why did he have to come and sit down next to me? Evidently he wanted to see for himself that I wasn't a ghost, and not only that, but real enough to be eating soup!'

The meeting with Lesyuchevsky had been an ominous and symbolic reminder of the fact that now the poet was back from the camps he would become the object of continuous surveillance, and his life would by no means be free, easy and untroubled. In fact, immediately after Z's arrival in Moscow, the organs of state security had at once begun to watch him, so that his caution in what he said and did was far from unwarranted.

In Moscow there were lots of other meetings – official, business, and friendly – but things were moving slowly. Only almost two months after his arrival, on 4 March, was there a reading of the translation of the *Igor Tale* in the Writers' Club, and on 14 March in the hall of the Literary Museum. Z and his friends had great hopes of this presentation of the new translation to leading figures in the Moscow literary and academic world. If the translation was a success its author's readmission to the Writers' Union would be made that much easier and other problems would be solved as well. The Club was visited by scholars of the ancient Russian verse epics, writers, lovers of poetry, friends – they would all be interested in this new work by a poet who had risen from the dead, and in seeing him in person. Z prefaced the reading with a brief talk in which he described what he was trying to achieve with his translation: 'I am a poet, not an academic,' he said, 'and I do not claim scholarly accuracy for my translation. I have tried to make it something that sticks in the memory, but at the same time I would not like it to be thought that it is a free adaptation.'

After the reading there was a discussion of this new version of the epic. The majority of those who spoke were warm in its praise and emphasized its undoubted worth. Those who said that the poet had coped well with the task he had set himself included a specialist on the period concerned, V. A. Dynnik, and the writers Antokolsky, Shklovsky, and Nikolay Chukovsky. A sharply negative critical reaction came from A. K. Yugov who pointed out what he thought were important omissions by the translator and incorrect interpretations of the original. True, he had recently published his own translation of the work containing a contentious version of some of the 'obscure passages' of the epic, so that what he said had a subjective and unconvincing ring to it. Yugov was answered by Professor G. A. Gukovsky who contrasted the slight omissions to the strengths of Z's version, and he proposed that the translation they had just heard should be published as soon as possible. Nevertheless Yugov's speech had an unfortunate effect on Z. He had expected too much from this evening and was nervous that some chance happening might spoil the generally favourable disposition of those present. The academician N. K. Gudziy spoke with restraint, but with great authority. The writer and literary historian Irina Tomashevskaya, a friend the Zabolotskys had acquired in their darkest hours, openly embraced and kissed when they met, congratulating him

231

not only on his translation, but on his return to normal life. Some official personage or other then remarked to her that such feelings, particularly expressed as they were in a public gathering, were out of place in relation to a recently imprisoned 'enemy of the people'. Characters like that were also present at the reading.

Literaturnaya Gazeta for 9 March contained a report of the reading and discussion of the translation at the Writers' Club. At the end of March the poet read the translation over the radio and there was a brief report of this in *Vechernyaya Moskva* (*Evening Moscow*). In general the public response was favourable.

In the mean time Z's situation in Moscow had become increasingly difficult and was even attended by a certain degree of risk. His official travel warrant had already expired, and his papers gave him no right to live in the capital. Z began to fear every policeman he met, and had already thought of leaving Moscow, but his friends succeeded in convincing him that if he left now, just when things were starting to get off the ground, his departure would considerably complicate and slow down their efforts. His friends believed that Z needed to live in no other city but Moscow, because it was precisely there that he had the chance of getting into the literary world. In any other place this would be much harder, if only because he would not have access to influential people, ready to give him support in moments of difficulty. In the attempts to obtain permission for him to remain in Moscow a part was played by the strong figure of A. A. Fadeyev, who had contacts at the very top.

At the end of March or the beginning of April the concierge at the Stepanovs' warned them of possible unpleasantness if the person living with them without permission did not leave at once. Their house, situated so near the Kremlin, was subject to especially strict surveillance. One evening several days after the warning a policeman turned up and asked to see Z's papers. The poet had already submitted all his documents with his application for permanent residence in Moscow — permission had been given in principle, but the documents had still not been drawn up. Fortunately the relevant offices were working late that day, and the situation of the documents could be checked by telephone. Thus Z was not arrested, but simply given twenty-four hours to leave the city, while the Stepanovs were fined 200 roubles.

Forced to change his place of refuge, Z took up an invitation from the Andronikovs and moved to their flat in Spasopeskovsky Lane. In his memoirs of those days Irakly Andronikov wrote:

At that period we were living in one room with our ten-year-old daughter and her nurse. Nikolay stayed with us, if my memory does not deceive me, from the middle of March 1946 until the May Day celebrations. Over the May period he was taken in by Mariya and Nikolay Tikhonov. From them he returned to us . . . We often had guests. And more often still we went out visiting ourselves, while Nikolay stayed behind, solving puzzles with our daughter. Only once do I remember us all going out together, to Boris Pasternak's.

It was probably in April that a meeting took place with Z's old friend from his Urzhum days and the time of his first visit to Moscow in 1920 – M. I. Kasyanov. The latter knew of the misfortune that had befallen his schoolfriend and had thought that he was long dead in the distant wastes of Siberia or the Far East. How great had been his surprise and delight when he had heard the poet's half-forgotten voice on the radio! The radio committee had helped them to find each other. A meeting was soon arranged between the resurrected poet and the military doctor who had gone through the sufferings of the Second World War. Their encounter was warm but tinged with sadness: in the quarter of a century that had elapsed both of them had suffered and changed a great deal. Kasyanov was struck by the impression produced on Z by his colonel's dress uniform with its many medals and decorations, hanging on the back of a chair ready for the May celebrations. Catching sight of it, Z suddenly became stern-faced, quiet and withdrawn. He had not, after all, been involved in the war, and had not yet forgotten other associations linked with military uniforms. Kasyanov told him how he had gone on to qualify at the medical faculty where they had once both studied together, how he had spent the whole war as an anatomical pathologist and was now working on a doctoral dissertation at a scientific institute. Z thawed a little, but as usual spoke little and unwillingly about his own adventures. He explained that the question of his residence in Moscow or Leningrad was at that very moment being decided. If he was not to be allowed to live in the centre, then he was going to have to give some thought as to how to arrange his life. Perhaps in Kirov,* nearer to his home district? As they parted he asked in some embarrassment whether Kasyanov could put him up for a couple of days. His old friend made a despairing gesture: the doctor's family lived in one little room, and there was no chance of fitting anyone else in there.

And then, on 28 April 1946, Z wrote to his wife in Karaganda:

My dear Katya, I was informed yesterday that the documents for our residence in Moscow have now been signed, and that a telegram has

* i.e. Vyatka [Ed.].

been sent to Karaganda authorizing an entry permit to Moscow for you and the children. As for me I shall set about getting my papers changed to Moscow ones and signed here. That's just a technical matter, the main business has been done. I have also been readmitted as a member of the union. It goes without saying that I am completely satisfied. I haven't spent the time here in vain . . .

And so the basic goals for which Z had hurried to Moscow had been achieved. He had received permission to live in the capital and had been readmitted to the Writers' Union. But now other questions came up – where to register and where to live, and how to earn a livelihood? Once again his friends came to his aid.

Nikolay and Marina Chukovsky found a kind, educated, middle-aged woman who agreed to register Z in her apartment in Babyegorodsky Lane. Irina Tomashevskaya introduced Z to the writer V. P. Ilyenkov who generously allowed the poet's family to live for the time being in his winter dacha in Peredelkino, the writers' settlement outside Moscow. Soon afterwards Ilyenkov, as a member of the editorial board of the journal *Oktyabr*, played an active part in the publishing of the translation of the *Igor Tale*.

II

One day in the spring of 1946 Z got into a suburban train at the Kiev Station and set off for Peredelkino to look at his new home. He had to walk some three kilometres from the station to the dachas. The path ran through beautiful country, beneath ancient fir trees, past a cemetery, past the little village of Lukino nestling under a hill, and over a bridge across the little River Setun. That spring Z found the unspoilt beauty of the Moscow countryside specially moving. What silence, solitude and peace! And he was again filled with those feelings for nature about which he had written to Stepanov in the spring of 1944: 'Nature produces such an effect on me that sometimes, when I am alone with her, I feel completely reborn. This great and wise force flows into me with such invigorating strength that at those moments I become another person. Fate certainly knows what it is doing!'

Once more fate knew what it was about – it had settled the poet in Peredelkino, it had once more surrounded him with mighty pine trees, little streams, fields and silence, it had reminded him once more of his unswerving commitment to poetry. In spite of everything he now believed that things would work out, that the grief and anxiety were behind him, and that he would once more be able to write verse. He wandered the empty paths through the spring mud and the cawing of the rooks, and the silent, abandoned-looking dachas and gave himself over completely to his exciting thoughts, forgetting all about the sufferings, the fears and the storms of his unsettled existence. It was as though all those terrible years had never been.

From the recent illegal life in Moscow, full of alarms, from the fuss and bother of everyday life, he had somehow been at once transported to a world of spiritual communion with nature. His mind worked easily and freely. He wanted to rethink his earlier conception of the universe, to ponder on what he had not thought through, and to come to understand what had remained unclear in his earlier years.

There are two great principles in the world, he thought. One of them is the mind of mankind, which offers a guarantee of the perfection of the unique and contradictory organism of Nature. The other principle is that high moral quality which is needed not only by man but by everything that exists in the world. This source of spiritual nobility is the very soul of nature. In the spirit of nature Z saw the aesthetic and moral expression of its wisdom, of the laws vested in it, aimed in the final analysis at the triumph of reason, justice and beauty. And now, when Z was finally able to breathe freely, his perception of the spirit of nature had become intermingled with the harsh experiences of his time under arrest. He repeated to himself the lines of the poem 'Woodland Lake', and was now able to see how the clear human soul was reflected in the purifying font of nature. But how terrifying it was when the evil that was part of nature manifested itself in human evil!

Z was overcome by an irresistible desire to write poetry again. And at that moment there was no stopping it – the everyday anxieties, caution and reason had retreated somewhere to the back of the mind in the face of this all-devouring feeling.

The date of the first poem known to have been written by the poet after a gap of many years is 16 April 1946. Its title is itself symbolic – 'Morning'. The morning of the year, the morning of a new life, the morning of new ideas.

> The cock is crowing, light dawns, it is time!
> In the wood beneath one's feet, a heap of silver.

If it was time, then one should not hold oneself back before the gates of creativity.

> And the birds in their shining plumage,
> Sit at the gates of a forgotten epic . . .

It is no accident that in the poems written after 'Morning' – 'The Blind Man' and 'The Storm' – we find the theme of creativity, inspiration and the poet's calling. In 'The Storm', written down on 3 May, we see a resolution of mental tensions through the excitement of poetic inspiration and self-expression, and at the same time the participation of nature in human creativity – their co-creativity. In the poem 'The Blind Man' there are the tragic doubts of the power to resurrect life, to find the poetic word to express the majesty of the surrounding world. 'The Blind Man' is striking in comparison with Z's earlier works because of its spiritual nakedness and its autobiographic qualities:

These songs of mine –
How often they have been sung in the world!
Where can I find words
For an exalted, living song?

And where are you leading me,
Dark threatening Muse,
Along the great highways
Of my unencompassable fatherland?
Never, never,
Did I seek a union with you,
Never did I want
To submit to your power, –

You chose me yourself,
And you pierced my soul,
You yourself showed me,
The great wonder of the Earth . . .
Sing then, blind old man!
The night is coming. Nocturnal luminaries,
Echoing you,
Coldly shine from afar.

The return to poetry was not merely joyful, it was difficult as well. There were happy moments of inspiration, there were doubts, there was also the feeling of being powerless to express all the enormous number of ideas that had built up and were looking for a way to poetic form. The poems of the year 1946 – 'The Storm', 'The Blind Man', 'Beethoven', 'Make a Little Space for Me, Starling', 'In This Birch Grove' – are undoubtedly among Z's major works. But who knows how many lines of verse were destroyed by him then, in those moments of disillusionment?

Later, in the summer of 1947, he was to write a poem about an old man with yellow bony fingers who, at night, when it was possible to escape from the fuss and bother of life, would go up into his attic full of lumber where there was a piano which he would begin to play. And at those times God himself would come down from the heaven and fill his music with his presence, and all that was worrying, fleeting and mundane would be forgotten. The theme of the act of creation was constantly being addressed in his verse. The poet could undoubtedly recall how, in the previous year, just like the old musician, he used to climb the wooden stairs to the second floor of the Ilyenkovs' dacha, where he had his little separate room with its bed and little table and there devote himself to his new poems. What exactly the poem about the musician and the piano in the attic was like, nobody knows – Z destroyed it very soon afterwards.

We know about its content from Yekaterina, and about its destruction from Nikolay Chukovsky, who had heard the author read it and been greatly moved by its long, musical lines. Z himself did not feel the same way about it, and when they next met and Chukovsky asked him to read the poem again, he replied with an air of indifference: 'I haven't got it any more. I've destroyed it.' And he refused to go into any further explanations.

Nevertheless he did not want to retreat from life to an old attic, even to create heavenly verse. For while still a youth he had written: 'There is a terrible temptation – the path to sweet loneliness, but it is a Cleopatra that kills.' From his 'attic' in the Ilyenkov dacha he sucked in the streams of spring life, and from his pen there flowed the lines:

> And there is such a jumble in the fields,
> And the streams are in such a mess,
> That just try not rushing from your attic,
> And dashing headlong into the wood!

He was turning his soul to face creation with all its contradictions, sorrows and joys. At the same time, however, he still held back, unable to believe completely in his new life of freedom. In this same poem 'Make a Little Space for Me, Starling', hinting with a sad irony at his earlier experiences, he wrote:

> I long to try my own skills,
> But my feathers are weak from the cold.
> If from childhood you are noisy,
> Then your breath will catch in your throat.

Subsequently he changed this verse, softening what he thought sounded too autobiographical:

> I long to try my own skills,
> But a wandering butterfly told me:
> He who is noisy in the spring,
> Will be voiceless when summer comes.

At that period, when Z had only just begun to live in Peredelkino, he was one day visited by Stepanov, and together they set off for the dacha of Boris Pasternak, whose poetry they both greatly admired. Z had no doubt recently read Pasternak's collections *Early Trains* (1943) and *Earth's Vastness* (1945), and had been struck by the change in this poet, in whom he had even before been greatly interested. Ten years later, in a letter to the young poet A.Ya. Sergeyev, Z was to write: 'I advise you to compare Pasternak's earlier writings with his wartime and post-war poems. These later poems are, of course, the best that he has written; the affectation has disappeared and Pasternak has remained. Just think about it – it's an instructive example.' Z was trying to find an overall pattern in Pasternak's development, which would, to a certain extent, have explained and justified his own development. He wanted to discuss all this with Pasternak personally.

In his writings Stepanov recalls their meeting:

> We went to see Pasternak. At his place we met Fedin and they dragged us off with them to N. F. Pogodin's dacha. When we arrived there the table was already laid for supper. The womenfolk were not there – they still had not come out to the dachas from Moscow. Unfortunately, I can't remember exactly what the discussion was about. I can recall only that it was about one or other of Pogodin's plays. I was just amazed at the sheer amount of drink on the table . . . and the capacity for drink of such exalted company. Fedin was stern and red-faced. Pasternak was happy, and his genial laughter was infectious. Pogodin was snuffling about with his duck-bill nose, a little reminiscent of a skilled artisan who had had a bit too much to drink. In general he was witty and wasn't lost for words. They were all knocking it back. Only Pogodin was a little bit on the morose side and gradually fell silent. Pasternak and Fedin kept up their lively and rather exaggerated behaviour. Z quickly got drunk, and his mood also gradually turned sombre. I sat there for an hour and a half, and after a bottle of *starka* had been emptied, I made my way rather uncertainly back to the Ilyenkovs' dacha. It was next morning before Z turned up, red in the face, and not quite steady on his legs.

This was probably a chance and isolated incident from Z's life at Peredelkino – he could not permit himself to spend time in this way, from the point of view of both cost and self-discipline – he was well aware just how important his renewed activity as a writer was for him. He was most likely annoyed that he had not been able to have a relaxed talk with Pasternak about mutual interests, whereas Fedin and Pogodin were not close to him, and he did not seek to keep up acquaintance with them subsequently.

In June Yekaterina arrived from Karaganda with their son and daughter. The whole family settled in on the first floor of the Ilyenkovs' dacha, in a room with a stove, while Z worked in the peaceful little upper room, the window of which looked out onto a grove of birches. Among the birches could be seen the trunks of isolated pines and firs, and all the trees were surrounded by forest fragrance and filled with birdsong. In front of the dacha opened out a broad clearing, only half jokingly known as 'Classics' Avenue'. Along it in the evenings would walk 'classic' writers, and on both sides lay their well-built dachas, with their flourishing families, their maids and their gate-keepers. It all exuded the half-forgotten feeling of well-being from times of peace. It was with obvious pleasure that Z entered into restrained conversations with these well-known writers, behaving politely with them, but somewhat at a distance, avoiding questions about his own past and present.

He was more open with the people close to him – with the Kaverins, who had rented a dacha not far from the writers' settlement, with the Stepanovs, who had arrived from Moscow, with Nikolay and Marina Chukovsky, who lived on the same 'Classics' Avenue', in Korney Chukovsky's dacha. But even to them Z did not bare his soul completely, usually presenting his deeper feelings in a jokingly ironic guise. All the same, he did have entirely serious conversations, and sometimes shared his plans and ideas for his translations. But about his own poems, while they were still unwritten, he kept silent.

He tried to trust in his future, but he nevertheless felt insecure, and to safeguard himself and his family from hunger, he obtained permission from the owners of the dacha to cultivate a part of the clearing in front of the house where he grew potatoes and other vegetables.

Thus his wife and children found a proper potato field in Peredelkino, with the green shoots already showing. They all knew about growing vegetables, and they soon set to, earthing up the potatoes and weeding the patch. Both husband and wife put their backs into setting up the new home, but Z spent the better part of the day over his work in his little room. There, early in the morning, he would throw open the window and gaze out onto the mass of white birch trunks, through which filtered the slanting rays of the morning sun. The trees seemed to him in some mysterious way connected with his destiny. As early as 1926, and perhaps even earlier, the image of a tree had come to occupy a central place in his perception of the world and in his poetry.

Birch groves had accompanied him all of his life. They had surrounded him at the dawn of his life, in the countryside near Kazan; he remembered the sacred old groves of Sernur, and recalled his youthful rendezvous in the Urzhum grove, near the Mitrofanyev church. Against his will he remembered how, after an agonizing two months of journeying across Siberia, he first saw the landscape of the Far Eastern region, and was struck by the sight of 'slim Far Eastern birches, rising to the very heavens'. Now birches rose up once more before him, and in them every now and then he could hear the melodious song of the oriole. As he recalled the time that had passed, he realized that perhaps his muse had not always been dark and threatening, but sometimes tender and defenceless just like this bird. And he turned to it – this oriole-muse:

> In this birch grove,
> Far from ills and sufferings,
> Where sways the pink,
> Unblinking morning light,
> Where in a transparent avalanche,
> The leaves flow down from the high branches, –
> Sing to me, oriole, your empty song:
> The song of my life.

Thus was created the poem 'In This Birch Grove'.* In a single glance the poet encompassed in it all his life, which had always been inextricably bound together with his poetic gift. Even in the darkest years his muse, though a 'silent wanderer', had been with him, and the poet was celebrating her loyalty, and her coming triumph.

In the mean time the discussions about the publication of the translation of the *Igor Tale* were still going on. Ilyenkov offered his help in this matter. He would occasionally come on a visit to his dacha, and then he would meet with Z and have long discussions with him. The chief editor of the poetry section of the journal *Oktyabr*, L. A. Ozerov, subsequently recalled meeting Z in the magazine's editorial offices:

Vasily Pavlovich Ilyenkov – a member of the editorial board, always an attentive and sensitive person – one day without a word placed on my desk a manuscript, neatly and tidily prepared. The title *The Tale of Igor's Expedition* caught my eye. It was not typewritten, it was a real manuscript. I leafed through it and looked at the last page.

'Zabolotsky?!', I cried in amazement.

'He's living here in my dacha in Peredelkino,' said Ilyenkov quietly, and gave a little cough.

* Full translation on pp.354–5 [Ed.].

A few days later Ilyenkov appeared in the office together with Zabolotsky, who immediately struck me as a man distinct and clear in manner, like his manuscript. He put his briefcase down on a chair, and offered me his hand. I could restrain myself no longer and burst out with:

> In Georgia there is an unusual town.
> There the buffaloes, poking their heads in the gates,
> Stand like gods of grey antiquity,
> Lowering their horns over the noisy waters.

After those lines from 'Gori Symphony' the editor of the poetry section began to recite by heart from the poet's early verses, one after another. Ozerov remembers how 'the poet's pale face was lit up by a smile and reflected quickly changing emotions: surprise, understanding, irony, gratitude'. It is likely there were other feelings – anxiety and mistrust. Ever since *Columns* and 'The Triumph of Agriculture' had served as a pretext for the ridiculous accusation that Z was involved in counter-revolutionary activity, he was always alarmed when someone he did not know very well quoted them to him. Into the poet's injured soul there had crept an unconscious doubt – what if they were testing him, deceiving him, what if it were a trap? When he got home that day he told his wife how one of the staff of the journal had quoted his poems, and how to begin with he had been surprised and alarmed, but then he had realized that this man really loved his poetry and wanted to show him his feelings. Despite all his sense of caution, Z valued meeting people who knew and understood what he wrote.

The translation of the *Igor Tale* was accepted by the journal and printed in the double issue 10–11, which came out in the middle of December 1946. This was an important event in Z's life – his translation had become accessible to readers, and after a gap of nearly ten years his name had again appeared in print. The long list of translations of the ancient Russian epic had been enriched by one more poetic version, about which the leading expert on Old Russian literature, D. S. Likhachov, was to write four years later in a letter to the poet: 'It is without doubt the best yet, the best for its poetic strength.' Many years later Kaverin was to exclaim: 'Just think that when the translation of the *Igor Tale* appeared in 1946, nowhere was there a line in response, not in the papers, not in the journals. You might have thought that great events in our poetry were an everyday occurrence!' At that period the critics indeed remained silent about the translation: they dared not praise it, and the obvious quality of the work prevented them from damning it.

Z wished his translation to be accepted as his patriotic response to the victory in the Second World War, and he wrote sadly in one of his letters: 'This work has cost me dearly, yet it seems to have come too late, not at the right moment.' Still, it was good enough that the translation had been published and the payment, which was somewhere in the region of 11,000 roubles (pre-currency reform) was not unwelcome: up to this point the poet's debts had simply gone on growing.

He had always considered it his first duty to provide for his family, and their precarious financial situation since coming to Moscow worried him very much, and forced him to seek any translation work he could cope with. Besides, he needed translations for other reasons – he needed to carve out a place for himself in post-war literature and for the time being he could not rely on his original poetry.

At the Tikhonovs' house Z got to know the Hungarian writer Antal Hidas (Gidash) and his wife, Agnessa Kun, who were living in Moscow at the time. Hidas suggested that Z make a verse translation of his long poem 'The Danube Groans' which depicted the tragic events in Hungary under Fascist rule. The poem was duly translated and published in the journal *Novy Mir*, and the couple remained the poet's firm friends.

One of the first to commission translations was the pianist and musicologist Mariya Yudina. She had heard a great deal about Z in his early years in Leningrad, had come to love his poetry, and knew his friends in the *Oberiu* movement. She had been on friendly terms with Daniil Kharms, and her cousin, L. A. Yudin, was the artist whom Z had commissioned to do the cover design for his first book.

Yudina proposed to the poet that he translate several poems for a collection of Schubert songs she was editing. At the beginning of September she arrived in Peredelkino to discuss the project, and she got to know the poet's family. In her memoirs she later recalled this meeting at the Ilyenkovs' dacha:

> Zabolotsky was in front of the house in the yard, or, to be more precise, at the edge of the wood. He was chopping wood, and standing next to him were a couple of nice children. 'This is Nikita, and this is Natasha', he introduced them to me . . . He told me that the school was some distance away, on the other side of the railway, and what a hard job of it they sometimes had getting there, whatever the weather; yet everyone knew that Z never complained about anything – what he had said was simply a statement of fact; I sat on a tree-stump while they collected up the firewood, and we then went upstairs to his study. I gave him more details of what I was proposing, and he readily agreed. Z loved music, symphonic and vocal . . . About its structure and theory he knew little, and for a while I had to adopt the role of teacher; we both enjoyed it, with me explaining and him learning.

Z was delighted to be translating poems by his favourite author Goethe, several by Schiller, and some other texts for the collection *Songs of Schubert*, but he was frustrated by the demands of the isometric translation which often prevented him from using the most appropriate word because the number of syllables did not coincide. In the course of this work he visited Yudina several times at her apartment on Begovaya Street, discussed ancient and contemporary music with her, read her his latest poems, and listened to her playing Beethoven's sonatas. The poem written at about this time, 'Beethoven', is to a certain extent linked to these meetings.

Yudina wanted to continue her work with Z, and suggested new translations, but the poet firmly refused. At the beginning of 1947 he sent her the last set of corrections and accompanied them with a somewhat dry note which put an end to his work on isometric translations and to his good relations with Yudina.

This was Z's nature – a mixture of the joys of inspiration and a fierce sense of shutting himself off, pleasure in communing with the 'live human soul' and a decisive rejection of any attempt by this soul to impinge on the inviolability of his inner world. Apparently, much as he respected Yudina, he was opposed to her desire to subject him to the force of her personality. In spite of the rift between these two unusual and complex personalities, Yudina remained a constant admirer and advocate of Z's work, and the poet valued highly the translations done in collaboration with her. When he was translating Schiller's 'The Knight of Toggenburg', and later 'The Cranes of Ibicus', he was boldly competing with earlier translations of these poems done by Zhukovsky, and in places his versions were superior to those of his great predecessor. The translation expert I. Kashkin wrote of the translation of 'The Cranes of Ibicus': 'Zabolotsky has conveyed to the reader what even Zhukovsky had missed.'

In August of the same year Zhdanov made his now notorious speech and the Central Committee issued its decree 'On the journals *Zvezda* and *Leningrad*', which gave everyone an unceremonious reminder of who it was who set the agenda for the country's literature. In the wake of the decree the presidium of the Writers' Union removed Tikhonov from his post as president of the Union and excluded Zoshchenko and Akhmatova who, according to the presidium, were writers who did not support Soviet power and were not participating in socialist construction. It also recommended that the Central Committee's decree should be discussed at a Moscow-wide assembly of writers. The assembly was to take place at the beginning of September, and Z had a difficult decision to make: to go and vote for the exclusion of

Zoshchenko and Akhmatova would mean acting against his conscience. This would be especially unthinkable with relation to Zoshchenko, whom Z respected highly as a writer and who had spoken out in his defence in 1939. Yet Z's own official position was so conditional and insecure that a vote in favour of Zoshchenko and Akhmatova would mean losing everything that he had built up with such difficulty over the past year. It would most likely mean arrest for a second time – and at the least being barred from literature. Even not to go to the assembly would be extremely risky. The outcome of this complex choice between the duty to his conscience and the necessity dictated by the harshness of the times is described in Kaverin's memoirs *Epilogue*:

> When the decision was taken to exclude Zoshchenko from the Writers' Union, Zabolotsky's friends (myself among them) persuaded him to go to the general assembly which was to confirm this decision. The question of whether to go or not affected me as well. But I could 'bravely hide' (as Shvarts wrote in 'The Red Bonnet'), whereas Zabolotsky could not . . . And so we talked him into going; this, of course, meant that he would have to vote for excluding Zoshchenko. Depressed, but relaxed, he put on his best clothes, had a good shave, and off he went, while we – Yekaterina, Stepanov and I – who had seen him off, remained behind (this was at Peredelkino, in the rented dacha) and spent a long time talking about how important it was that we had made him go. Not to go, not to vote, would have been more than risky and dangerous . . . Nowadays it would seem strange to say such things. In fact, Zabolotsky's wife and friends were pleased that we had persuaded him to act against his conscience, in other words had done something unworthy. But, as it turned out, we were too quick to rejoice. Two hours passed when I spotted, on the road leading from the station, a familiar figure wearing black trousers and a large white jacket. Staggering slightly, Zabolotsky was making his way home. Everyone groaned and exchanged glances. Yekaterina wrung her hands. He slowly approached us, smiling slightly, but with a hint of cunning, and the nearer he came, the clearer it was that he had not been to Moscow. He came into the room, sat down on a chair, and gave a sigh of relief. He had passed the whole of the two hours at the station, in the bar there, had a fair amount to drink, talked to the locals, and, in his own words, spent the time interestingly and profitably. For several days we waited anxiously to see what effect such an act of unheard-of daring would have on his fate. Luckily, nothing happened. His action had passed unpunished.

On 24 November Z had a visit from Yevgeny and Yekaterina Shvarts – they were old friends of the family who had done a great deal to make life better for Yekaterina and the children after Z's arrest. The Shvartses had brought with them what was at that time an unheard-of luxury – a huge goose. On that day there was real eating and drinking, to begin with at the Zabolotskys' and then at the Chukovskys'. They recalled times before the war, talked about current events, and enjoyed listening to Z's new poems.

The next day, at about eleven o'clock, as the hosts and their guests were still busy tidying up the room from the night before, there appeared outside the window the figure of A. A. Fadeyev, making his way to the front door of the dacha. The room was not in a fit state to receive such an exalted guest. The children were also sick in bed with a high temperature and there was nowhere else to put them. Z's room upstairs was unheated, because when the weather had turned colder he had moved downstairs into the big room. But there was nothing to be done. Someone went to get some vodka, and on the table appeared some potatoes and the remains of the goose. Fadeyev was imposing and smartly dressed, his manner was simple, yet at the same time he maintained a certain distance between himself and those to whom he spoke. They all soon realized that Fadeyev wished to talk with Z in private, and they left them alone. The conversation over the food lasted until the evening. They talked about the destiny of Russian literature, about nature and the people of the Far Eastern region, and about Z's situation. For the poet the meeting was of great significance. He was inwardly on guard, but behaved naturally and freely, for he could feel that he was talking to someone clever who understood him, although, perhaps, he did not always agree with him.

Fadeyev was interested in what Z was writing at that time. And so the latter began to read him his latest poems and translations. Fadeyev listened attentively, and he clearly liked the poems. When, at the end of the reading, he listened to 'The Blind Man', tears appeared on his tough, impassive face. For a long time he said nothing, as though struggling with something within himself, and then pronounced in a tone of voice which was out of keeping with the intimate nature of their previous conversation: 'We will not print poems like that now. Maybe at some time in the future – in many, many years' time.' After a pause he asked: 'And, really, why do you write "I am such a blind man with my face turned towards the sky?" How can you compare yourself to a blind man at a time like this, and in our society?'

Z did not even start to explain that we are all blind in the face of our own destiny and when we are penetrating the mighty secrets of nature. Instead, his face clouded, he did not answer Fadeyev's question and talked about something else.

That autumn and winter there were other meetings with the head of the Writers' Union, especially at the Chukovskys'. Some time later

Fadeyev happened to meet Nikolay Chukovsky near his dacha, and said about Z (these words are reproduced by Chukovsky in his memoirs):

'What a firm, clear-thinking man Zabolotsky is. He hasn't fallen apart or turned sour. You can depend on him.'

At one of their meetings Fadeyev suggested to Z that he gradually prepare a book of his poems for publication. And he promised his help in this matter.

Even before this proposal his friends, and in the first instance Stepanov, worried about his future, had begun to insist to the poet that he write something that could be published straight away, to strengthen his official position in literature and help with the publication of a book of poems. Simon Chikovani, the splendid Georgian poet, either at that time or at a later date, said with reference to his own experience that every poet must have 'locomotive verses': these can be used to haul his best poems into a book or selection in a journal.

The question of adapting his literary interests to official demands was an agonizing one for Z. He realized that in the conditions of the time his friends were right. Essentially he could, without any special effort, have written the sort of poems that any journal would have accepted. But if he were to write opportunistically, could he write a genuine work of poetry, and would it not be a betrayal of what was most valuable to him – his vocation as a poet? In his time in Leningrad he had written a few poems specially for publication in the papers and already then he had realized that those verses had turned out alien, weak, outside his usual creative channel. And why did people not want to understand that his personal interests in poetry, his ideas about mankind and nature in no way went against the ideals of society? Eventually the poet decided, without giving up his creative stance, to write about the large-scale confrontation of the mind and will of man with the chaos of nature, savage, lacking order, but powerful. To this end he decided to use material with which he had become familiar during his arduous work on the Far Eastern construction-sites. In the autumn of 1946 he wrote the long poem 'The Builders of Roads', and in 1947 two short poems on the same theme – 'The Beginning of Construction' and 'In the Taiga'.

Of course, those who had been prisoners could not write about the actual conditions, but that was not what he had in mind. Something else was far more important: even under the conditions of camp life, and against all logic, the poet had sensed something exalted and inspiring about the builders' work – after all, their labour was ordering primeval nature and opening up new possibilities to it of a reasoned coexistence with humanity. Surely, he thought, he could not be prohibited from

246

writing about a feeling like this? Moreover, the theme of the transformation of nature by inspired labour was just the thing for the kind of work his friends were urging him to write as a 'locomotive' for his future book.

'The Builders of Roads' was published in the first number of *Novy Mir* for 1947, and became the first original lines by Z to appear in print since 1937. The poet and his friends waited excitedly for a response to this publication: for at that period criticism served not only to evaluate the literary quality of a work, but was also a barometer of the writer's significance and standing in the eyes of officialdom. At last, in May, *Literaturnaya Gazeta* found room for a review of the first three numbers of *Novy Mir* for 1947, in which A. Makarov wrote:

> Zabolotsky's poem 'The Builder of Roads' is also devoted to the responsible theme of labour – the building of roads to the Pacific through the taiga and the mountains. But this theme has not found a true artistic expression in the poem. Here there is no trace of those passionate outbursts of feeling and imagination which make up the main charm of A. Nedogonov's poem ['The Flag over the Village Soviet' – N.Z.]. Zabolotsky's poem only pretends to depict the heroic achievements of the Soviet people.

He went on further to accuse the poet of being cold, mannered, literary and decadent; of indulging in high pathos and exaggerated melancholy. The critic could not allow the poet the right to interpret the workers' efforts against the scale of the whole of creation, the right to make a philosophical generalization on the basis of his own natural-philosophical conception. After all, it was precisely in the awareness of the exalted mission of man the constructor in his transformation of the savage chaos of the world that the main idea of the poet rested.

As he read further in the article Z caught sight of his name again, and, anticipating the worst, let his eyes run through a critique of P. Semynin's poem 'The Outskirts'. The critique, or to be more precise, the destruction, of the poem finished with the words: 'These are images similar to those of the early Zabolotsky, who once brought out a foolish little book in which, in his depictions of our new society, he took every opportunity to degrade it by mixing together the exalted and the base. Semynin's verses are a harmful imitation, a lampoon on our reality.'

In these words Z could sense a threat that was no joke, and an ominous portent that made his blood run cold. They reminded him vividly of the treatment he had had at the hands of the critics at the beginning of the thirties. Now he was well aware of what that could lead to.

A month later the original depressing effect of the article was somewhat softened by a mention of 'The Builders of Roads' in a report by Fadeyev to the eleventh plenum of the board of the Writers' Union – the reference was in a decidedly positive context. True, at the very end of the same year *Literaturnaya Gazeta* contained another negative mention of the poem. Quite justifiably maintaining that in 'The Builders of Roads' the living human characters of the construction workers were not revealed (what if the writer had tried to describe real prisoners!), D. Danin went on to write: 'In the solemn pictorialism and the cold, rhetorical emotion of "The Builders of Roads" Zabolotsky is unable to reveal even a shadow of live interest in mankind. Man is not a function, but a living soul, and in this bombastic poem, constructed with faultless accuracy and well thought-out effects, it is merely implied.' At least this critic was nearer to a concrete discussion of the poem – he had involuntarily guessed the drift of the poet's ideas: the movement from abstract man to the living human soul.

Such were the first critical responses to Z's return as a writer, responses that were in no way encouraging to the poet. He did not submit the poem 'The Beginning of Construction' for publication.

The line of creative thought begun in 'The Builders of Roads' had a twofold development in Z's later verses. His philosophical concept of creative labour for the good of nature was given more definite expression in the programmatic poem 'I do not seek harmony in nature', written in October 1947; while the workers, those prisoners with their heavy spiritual burden, appeared in his splendid poem 'Somewhere in the wilds of Magadan', not written till after the Twentieth Party Congress in 1956.

It has to be said that in the poet's conception humanity had become not only the abstract bearer of the thinking power of nature, but also to an ever-increasing degree had come to contain definite spiritual qualities. When the family met together to celebrate the New Year of 1947, Z made a short, solemn speech to his wife and children. 'Mankind's most splendid qualities', he said, 'are friendship, loyalty and love. There is nothing to fear from whatever fate does to us as long as these feelings are preserved.' Soon after this he was to write the poem 'On New Year's Eve', in which he expressed his feelings for Yekaterina, his admiration for her courageous behaviour in the days of the siege of Leningrad. The poem concluded with the words:

> As long as we do not lose each other,
> As long as we do not weaken along the way. . .

Happy New Year, my dear friend!
To live life is not the same as crossing a field.*

This poem, to a greater extent than 'The Blind Man', revealed a new direction in the poet's lyricism – a whole series of poems about the living soul of men and about its concrete manifestations.

Both the Zabolotskys had to travel reasonably often from Peredelkino into the city. Literary business, the acquisition of ration cards, even the purchase of kerosene and other trivial domestic items – all this was linked with Moscow. The journey by suburban steam train to the Kiev Station lasted about an hour. The passengers on the train were of all kinds, and often poorly dressed. More often than not one of the regular beggars would stand at the door to the carriage and sing some artless little song in a hoarse voice and then pass down the train, cap in hand: 'Dear brothers and sisters, please help a war veteran . . .' In the mornings at the Kiev Station a crowd of people would spill out onto the platform and hurry off into the city, and in the evenings, after the working day, all these people would come back again to their suburban homes. During the journey Z would observe his fellow passengers, mentally penetrating their consciousness, their interests and their ideas, comparing them with the people he had met in the camps, and about whom he had written to his wife: 'It may seem strange, but since we were parted, I have met almost no one who is seriously interested in literature. I have to admit that the world of literature is only a small island in the sea of those who are indifferent to art.' (23 January 1944). 'If that is the case,' he thought now, 'what primeval forces are at work, creating and forming the peoples' soul?' And he was once more brought to consider the enormous significance of nature in the development of the spiritual forces of humanity.

Sometimes, in the station buffet, or at the little booth in front of the station, he would drink a vodka and fall into a philosophical frame of mind. On one such occasion he said to his wife: 'These people have no time to think, they don't realize the greyness of their lives. I have to think for them. That is the true vocation of the writer.'

---

* By remarkable coincidence one of Pasternak's finest poems, 'Hamlet', ends with this same proverbial line; 'Hamlet' was probably written at the same period, and since both poets were then living in Peredelkino and admired each other, it is difficult not to conclude that these identical final lines represent either a borrowing by one from the other, or a shared memory of some conversation. 'On New Year's Eve' has never previously been published, nor has this coincidence been noticed in print [Ed.].

'Kolenka, aren't you getting a bit over the top?', answered Yekaterina, a little displeased that her husband was about to go up to the booth for a second time.

Meanwhile in the poet's mind there rose up thoughts of the fusion of people and nature, of the great role of reason in affirming the creative effort and goodness contained in this union. He recalled Tolstoy and Beethoven, and addressed his verse to human genius:

> The lyre sounds again in the horns of the bull,
> The bone of the eagle has become the shepherd's pipe,
> And you have understood the living charm of the world,
> And have separated its good from evil.

Human genius is called upon to create that harmony for which all of nature is striving. To do this it will have to unite its creative potential with the slumbering forces of nature, with its soul. A Beethoven symphony and the labour of the road builders were part of the same common effort, which was bringing the world nearer to harmony, freeing good from evil which still held the upper hand. Humankind was equivalent to nature. Its great strength and great soul had still not attained harmony. And who was it but the writer who had to aid it in its striving for a better existence?

Somewhere in the vicinity of the railway station Z had met an old blind beggar. He was walking slowly, looking straight ahead, and feeling his way along the path with a stick. Every now and then the old man would stop, sing the 'Lazarus', and people would drop a few coins into his old tin can. Z had noticed him on his first trips to Peredelkino, and reproduced the same image in the poem 'The Blind Man'. This was probably the first 'living human soul' to be celebrated in Z's verse. At this juncture he was also thinking about the role of the soul and of reason in confirming goodness, in its everyday and in its more exalted forms. He wanted to comprehend thoroughly the enormous significance of mankind's spiritual qualities and to give them faithful depiction in his verse.

At the end of the summer of 1946 Z was visited by his old Georgian friends, Simon Chikovani and Georgy Leonidze. They proposed to Z that he start some serious work on translating Georgian poetry, promising their help in organizing it and publishing the translations. The Georgians respected their fellow poet's talents highly and knew that, in his transposition, the poetry of Georgia would become accessible to the Russian reader in all its colour and majesty. Chikovani recalled how, even before his arrest, Z had made extremely successful translations of the long poem by Rustaveli, and a poem each by

Orbeliani and Vazha Pshavela, as well as several poems by modern Georgian poets. Now Z was in a position to carry on with this work. It would also be a way of improving his difficult financial situation, and at the same time it would improve the mutual awareness of the different cultures of the peoples of the USSR. This proposal seemed very attractive to Z, and he was already thinking how, in the long term, it would be possible to bring out an individual larger volume of Georgian translations.

On 11 December Simon Chikovani visited the Zabolotskys again with his wife Marika. Z read them his poems and new translations, and told them about his plans for making a book of Georgian classical poetry. He was interested in Simon's opinion about the proposed contents of this book. Chikovani thought the idea was interesting and completely feasible. He promised his support in Georgia, and invited Z and his family to spend the summer months in the Georgian House of Creativity. Naturally, a trip like this suited the Zabolotskys very well, because it temporarily solved the problem of somewhere to live and it offered the prospect of a needed holiday for the family. The main thing was that in Georgia it would be possible to come to a concrete agreement with a publishing house about the translations, and also to work well, without being side-tracked by the trivial problems of everyday living.

In the winter Z wrote in a letter to Simon Chikovani:

I continue to be attracted by the idea of making a large volume of Georgian translations. At this particular moment I am interested most of all in one of the basic sections of the book, the one devoted to the works of Orbeliani . . . I think I have generally got a good understanding of Orbeliani, and I have a very natural thought – to do the whole of Orbeliani, the more so since I have already translated most of his basic works, and his literary legacy is not all that great in scope . . . Then the Russian reader would have, together with Baratashvili in Pasternak's translation, yet another Romantic, translated not haphazardly, but in a consistent way, and lovingly.

By the spring of 1947 Z had translated about 2,500 lines of Orbeliani's poetry, and was very pleased that the Russian version had turned out so splendidly. 'I put all my heart into this work, and I made the translations in the same diligent way as I write my own verse', he wrote to Chikovani. Each newly translated poem would, as always, first be read to his wife, while he could get a chance himself of hearing how it sounded. On one occasion he read these lines, which the Georgian poet had once addressed to N. A. Griboyedova (widow of the playwright Griboyedov):

> At that blessed moment, when, my heavenly light,
> You looked at me with your smile,
> I forgot all life's heavy burdens
> As I lay at your feet.
> For the past I do not grieve at all,
> And my heart, newly filled with hope,
> Now so bitterly regrets
> That it once cursed its fate.

III

As he became more and more deeply involved in translation work, Z did not regard it as a burden or as merely a way of earning money. Translating poetry did not seem to him a mundane literary craft. On the contrary, he always felt that it was full of high social ideals. Familiarizing the Russian reader with poetry of the other peoples of the USSR and of other countries seemed to him to be an important educational endeavour, and a serious contribution to the strengthening of friendship and collaboration between nations, to their mutual cultural enrichment. He was a genuine internationalist. As he translated, and at the same time penetrated into the souls, not only of the poet, but also of the people that gave birth to the poet, he would try to reveal this soul to the reader and bring the reader to understand and to love what had previously been remote and alien.

In the spring of 1947 the chief editor of the almanac – later the journal – *Druzhba Narodov*, an old friend of Z's, V. V. Goltsev, organized a trip to Georgia by a group of Moscow writers. In addition to Goltsev and Z, the group consisted of the poets Nikolay Tikhonov, Pavel Antokolsky and A. P. Mezhirov. In the instructions from the Writers' Union it was stated that the poets were being sent to the republic 'to familiarize themselves with the latest industrial projects in Georgia'. For Z the trip had a fundamental significance in that he had been officially attached to a group of experts on Georgian poetry and this allowed him to decide more firmly on the spot about his translation plans for the near future. He wanted to be once more in this warm and hospitable country, to meet his Georgian friends, and to make new acquaintances among Georgian writers.

On the morning of 10 May the members of the delegation arrived at Vnukovo Airport in the capital and boarded a plane bound for Tbilisi.

Z had never been in an aeroplane before, and he waited for take-off with some trepidation. But once they were in the air he looked out of the window of the plane and was suddenly seized by a feeling of great spiritual uplift, by a joyful sensation of strength and self-assurance, and happiness from the fact that here he was, a repository of reason, dashing along in this miraculous little house, high above the unencompassable earth. The twin-engined propeller-driven plane was not flying as high or as fast as contemporary jet airliners, so that it was much easier for him to see the details of the countryside slowly floating past beneath him. Now and then great intricate cloud patterns rose up right next to them, and the sky seemed dense and unusually blue. 'There it is – the living organism of our Earth, which you can take in with a single glance from this height, and you can feel its unique majesty,' thought Z. Here for him everything was linked with normal life – the fields he could see below, the forests, rivers, roads, the heaped-up clouds, the mountain ranges, a ray of the sun, suddenly reflected off an ice-field. The complex pattern of intricate shapes, lines and colours concealed within it many of the secrets of existence. The compressed nature of space and time made him think about the past and the future of the mighty, mysterious organism of the planet.

As soon as he had got to the hotel in Tbilisi Z wrote down a rough version of the poem 'Air Travel', in which he gave form to his impressions of his first flight in an aeroplane.

Hospitable Georgia greeted the poets from Moscow with the scent of southern flowers, warm sun, and the cosy streets of old Tbilisi, and with a welcome from their old friends and a programme of trips around the republic. The guests spent some time at the citrus and tea farm at Shroma, saw the recently constructed hydro-electric power station on the mountain river Khrami, and travelled along the Kartali valley.

Pavel Antokolsky recalls how Georgy Leonidze invited him and Z to a collective farm some twenty kilometres from Gori on the birthday of one of the longest-lived inhabitants there:

> We arrived there on the third day of the celebrations, which were going on in the open air. Long tables were standing there, spread with all the produce of bountiful nature. Crowded at the table were just about all the old man's innumerable descendants: his sons, daughters, their wives and husbands, his grandchildren, great-grandchildren, and perhaps even some of the famous old fellow's great-great-grandchildren. All of this splendour was organized along highly patriarchal lines, in accordance with the age-old traditions of such assemblies. Naturally, the main ingredient of the festive proceedings was the local young wine. There was a lot of it, too much for us. Of course, Georgy Leonidze took charge

253

of affairs with a great deal of noise and gusto: he was a long-time friend of the family and the most honoured and respected guest. But the two Muscovites present were also, by the laws of hospitality, given their due attention.

Z liked this patriarchal loyalty to the customs of their forefathers, their oneness with nature, and the observance of the celebration ritual. He loved Georgian wine, the ritualistic quality of the toasts and the picturesqueness of this gathering. For him it was important to see all this in its elemental state, so that he could then sit down at his desk and give an accurate rendering of the spirit of Georgian poetry in his translations. Familiarization with the national way of life, and the sight of the surrounding mountains, gardens, vineyards, study of the history, art and literature of the country — all these were vital conditions for serious translating work.

Now, when he was once more able to write, he strove to subject everything to what he was doing. As he admired the mountain scenery, replied to toasts at the birthday celebrations, listened to the wonderful sounds of Georgian songs and poems, observed the people's way of life, he mentally related all this to the dry text of the word-for-word translation which he was going to have to turn into lines of verse. Later he was to write in 'A Translator's Notes': 'The word-for-word translation of a poem is like the ruins of the Colosseum. The original form of the building can only be reconstructed by someone who knows something about the history of Rome — about its life, its customs, its art, the development of its architecture. The casual observer is incapable of doing this.' Z tried his utmost not to be such a casual observer, for he tried to do any task he undertook, especially a literary one, as thoroughly as he possibly could.

In Tbilisi Z visited old friends and made new contacts. He concluded an agreement with the publishing house *Zarya Vostoka* to bring out an individual volume of translations of Orbeliani's poems. The book appeared in the same year, 1947. Its editors were Goltsev and Chikovani, and the introduction was written by the specialist Levan Asatiani, who had become a close friend, and with whom the poet had had several discussions about Georgian literature. This little book was the first separate publication of translations by Z in the post-war period, and significantly enhanced his standing as a translator. Two years later it was republished in Moscow.

Those who took part in the expedition to Georgia were expected to produce poetry about what they had seen. Z believed he could not dodge this responsibility, and he wrote two not very successful

254

'production' poems – 'Khramges' and 'The Feast at the Shroma Collective Farm'. The second of these was especially weak, and Z later rejected it and never included it in the canon of his work. The true poetic reflections of his impressions of the Georgia countryside were two other poems written in the same year – 'Night in Pasanauri' and 'I touched the leaves of the eucalyptus'.

At the beginning of June Z returned to Moscow, so that after the end of the children's school year he could return to Georgia with his family and set to work in the House of Creativity, as agreed with the Georgian Writers' Union.

And so, on 1 July, the Zabolotsky family arrived by plane in Georgia. The venerable Willys jeep from the Union turned up to collect them from the airport, the same jeep in which, a month before, the Moscow poets had travelled around the republic. The driver, Samebu, greeted Z like an old friend. In Tbilisi they handed in their ration cards and registered their warrants for the Saguramo House of Creativity. His wife and children were happy with their first 'peacetime' journey, with their new impressions, their forthcoming holiday and the long-forgotten carefree existence it promised. On the way to Saguramo, the jeep turned off the main road, crossed the racing Aragvi River, and began to climb a winding road which led to the former estate of the famous nineteenth-century Georgian writer and educator, Ilya Chavchavadze. Z asked Samebu to stop at a tall white obelisk which marked the spot where, in 1907, Ilya Chavchavadze had been killed. They stood for a while in silence at the monument and then drove on up into the foothills, overgrown with dogwood. By six in the evening the family were already accommodated in two rooms of the second floor of the old stone building.

From the window of the room in which he worked Z could see a stony grotto shaded by the branches of huge walnut trees: out of it flowed a stream of cool spring water, and round it stood ancient stone tables. Here the many residents in the House would gather in the evenings to talk and play games. On the other side of the building was an open terrace with a view across the wide valley of the Aragvi to the distant villages, gardens and fields, and to the mist-shrouded mountain ranges, in the midst of which, in clear weather, the twin white summits of Mount Kazbek could be seen.

In the House of Creativity Z was able to work on the translations undisturbed, and he devoted the best part of the day to them. After breakfast he would go straight off to his room, sit down at his desk, spread out the literal translations, the Georgian texts, his reference books, some paper, and set about writing. Sometimes he would pause for thought as he compared the possible variants and searched around for more accurate and expressive words to convey faithfully the idea and mood of the original. When he had finished the poem, or the number of words he had set himself to do, or when he had simply grown tired of working, he would read through what he had done, and alter those parts of the text that displeased him. He would recall the recent conversations he had had with neighbours in the House of Creativity about the problems of translating, and he would reflect on his own views on the matter:

> Translators are quite rightly criticized because many of them do not know the language from which they are translating. Yet it is also their first and vital duty to have a good knowledge of the language in which they are writing . . . If the translation from the foreign language does not read like a good piece of Russian, then this translation is either mediocre or unsuccessful . . . Smooth, facile writing is our special enemy. This sort of writing reflects an indifference of the heart and a disdain for the reader . . . The translator who tries to reproduce the precise measures of Georgian poetry is wasting time on trivia and losing sight of the main aim. The metres are just about possible to imitate, but reading the resulting verse is impossible, and it is hopeless trying to understand what it is about.

Both Georgian and Russian writers were living and working at Saguramo and Z was on good terms with a great many of them. He was specially attracted to the cheerful and happy-go-lucky Karlo Kaladze, whose poetry he had translated on several occasions, and to his wife, the talented artist Tamara Abaleliya. He was also very friendly with the young poet Aleksandr Mezhirov, and with Sergey Yermolinsky, who worked in the room next to his. Z's close friends, the writers Chikovani, Leonidze and L. Asatiani also came from Tbilisi to visit him. The most frequent visitor of these three was Georgy Leonidze – when he came they would have little banquets after supper in the open air. Sometimes they would even have roast lamb, goat's cheese and salad. They would drink wine, propose exotic toasts in honour of those present and exchange literary gossip.

Normally Z was unwilling to be torn away from his work, and seldom sought company. He would more often set off for a walk down to the River Aragvi or up to the ruins of an ancient monastery on the top of Mount Zedazeni. In the evenings he did not play cards or other games as many of the residents enjoyed doing. In the dining room, however, where all the writers gathered together two or three times a day with their families, he would chat for a while with those he knew, joke in a restrained way and smile at the ladies. He was a constant focus of attention. The uninitiated were loudly told, by those who knew, about the poet's harsh experiences, about the unusual poems in the collection *Columns*, about the critical attack on them, and, naturally, about the fact that Z had recently returned from the camps and was now trying to get his life back together again. People who looked at him were surprised that after all the suffering he seemed not only unbroken, unbowed, not ingratiating, but full of dignity and even a special kind of self-assurance.

Sergey Yermolinsky, who quickly got to know the poet well, said at the time and later wrote that:

> He is a powerful example. He could have been torn in two – between the sufferings of his time and his high ideals. He could have been crushed by the difficulties of life (and not only of his own). He could have become harsh and full of hatred. He could have become inward-looking and wrapped up in his own misfortunes. He could have become over-fearful, thinking that everyone was looking at him expectantly and searchingly. And finally he could have become tired, hopelessly tired. But this is not what happened. On the contrary! He did not get tired, disheartened or embittered, in spite of everything, he returned and discovered harmony!

Of course, not everything was as simple and clear for Z himself. The same Yermolinsky recalled a noteworthy conversation he had with the poet which went to the very heart of the latter's anxieties and doubts: it touched on the need for the creative writer to come to terms with the limitations and demands dictated by the Party ideological apparatus of the time, and of the possible limits there might be to this.

One day, when they had both finished the amount of work they had allotted themselves, they set off down the hillside into the valley of the Aragvi to the *dukhan*, or café, on the Georgian Military Highway near Mtskheta. There they had a leisurely drink of the sharp local wine, watched the few Georgian visitors who were there at the time, and had a good chat. About such escapes from their work, and there were only two or three such occasions, Yermolinsky related:

> Sometimes we had a fair bit to drink, and ate some goat's cheese which was none too fresh. The conversation would become animated, but I don't ever recall that we had one of those drunken 'heart-to-heart' talks with mutual outpourings that make you ashamed the next morning, both for yourself and for your companion. That sort of thing was not on. Anyhow we kept a certain distance between us, as though by silent agreement. With the companionable effects of the wine we became a little more talkative than usual, a bit more relaxed, that was all.

During one such talk down at the *dukhan* Yermolinsky spoke of Mikhail Bulgakov's novel *The Master and Margarita*, which was virtually unknown at the time. He said that Bulgakov considered the novel the main thing in his life and had doggedly gone on writing it up until his death, even though he had completely given up hope of ever getting it published. At the same time, because he was a man who had adapted himself to life he did not become estranged from other literary activity – he wrote librettos for operas, scenarios, stage adaptations, and edited plays by other writers. And this work which he needed to do to live in no way affected his talent and was not reflected in his main undertaking.

Z listened to all this with great interest – it was just what he had been thinking about for the past few months. Although he considered translations very important and necessary from a social point of view, although he worked at them with enjoyment and sometimes with inspiration, he was still troubled by doubts: in using this work to defend his position as a writer and to earn money for his family, was he not doing irreparable damage to his gifts, to his capacity to think independently, to his main work – a book of his own poems. After all, whatever the external obstacles, was he not committed to think first and foremost about such a book, even if he was fated never to see it published? And he said to Yermolinsky (who quotes these words in his memoirs):

> Nature always finds a defence mechanism for every kind of living growth. You notice that – living! Our character is formed before the age of five, of that I am convinced, and then, according to how we live, a defence mechanism develops. Do you see? Where there is something to defend then an adaptability grows up, and side by side with it an amazingly resilient sense of self-preservation. For each person it is different, but people like us need this more than anyone else. Don't you agree?

Then he thought for a moment, raised his finger and said with a smile: 'But even this adaptability has to have strict limits, otherwise everything goes to hell!'

One had, he thought, to keep a close watch on one's defence mechanism. It is one thing to translate masterpieces, like the works of Orbeliani, Chavchavadze and Vazha Pshavela, but quite another to translate second-rate poets, to undertake the business of improving someone else's weak verses. And one has to be particularly careful when it is suggested that one writes one's own time-serving, adaptable poems. As he thought about his defence mechanism, the poet considered not only his craft as a writer, but his whole behaviour under conditions where basic rights and freedoms were missing. To achieve his main aim he sometimes had to make a reasoned compromise. He firmly believed that he had what it took to defend himself against the whims of a savage time.

When his early poems were quoted to him, and Yermolinsky tried to read them at Saguramo, his face would darken, and he would cut short the reading with a frown: 'Stop it! Why on earth should that sort of thing stick in your memory!'

The defence mechanism about which he so often thought was also reflected in his decided unwillingness to talk about the *Columns* cycle of poems. And when, at the table in Georgia, a toast was proposed to the 'Great Leader and Teacher of All Ages and Peoples' he would stand up with all the others and empty his glass. This was also a form of defence. Only rarely would he do violence to his nature by writing verses which were supposed to convince the literary yes-men and bureaucrats around him of his reliability, and of the fact that he was following their rules. Such was the poem 'The Feast at the Shroma Collective Farm'. But he knew that in such cases he was sailing close to the edge beyond which there begins the degradation of the poet, the watering down of his talent in the face of mundane temptations. Rare were the poets at that time who had the courage not to cross that line and offer up the required praises to the exalted leader, the Party, the 'great achievements' of socialism. Z's whole being revolted against such a wholesale chorus of adulation. It was incredibly difficult in his position to avoid betraying his principles, and to do so in such a way as not to bring down fresh misfortunes on his head from the regime.

In the less than two months spent at Saguramo Z translated several long poems by Ilya Chavchavadze (in all he translated about 1,500 lines of this poet's works) and poems by contemporary Georgian poets such as Abashidze, Kaladze, Leonidze, R. Margiani, I. Noneshvili, I. Tarba and Chikovani.

On 7 August Simon and Marika Chikovani arrived in Saguramo. They invited the whole Zabolotsky family to stay with them in the mountain village of Tsikhi-Dzhvari, in one of the village houses which they had rented for the summer, where it was possible to live undisturbed, to enjoy the mountain air and the interesting countryside, and to talk freely about life and literary matters. Several days later, early in the morning, a small open truck sent by Chikovani drove up to the House of Creativity and the whole family set off across the Kartli Valley, through the Borzhomi Gorge and Bakuriani, and into the mountains.

In Tsikhi-Dzhvari they spent several days with the Chikovani family. On the day after their arrival they all went bathing together in the baths at the nearby curative hot sulphur springs. As they walked back Chikovani explained that the sulphur springs warmed up the earth and softened the local climate, so that even at this height, 1,600 metres above sea-level, there grew broad-leaf forests and luxuriant plants with amazingly large flowers. The clouds swam at ground level, at times concealing people and villages in an impenetrable gloom. At the time the village was inhabited mainly by Greeks and the Zabolotskys' Greek landlady would serve freshly churned buffalo butter for breakfast, snow-white and amazingly tasty.

Z and Chikovani would spend many hours talking together and reading to each other what they had just written. Z listened to the sounds of the Georgian verse with great interest, especially if it was something he had already translated or was about to translate into Russian. He also read aloud his own recently written 'Saguramo', a poem about the poet's surroundings, imbued with the spirit of his illustrious predecessors – the former owners of the Saguramo estate, David Guramishvili and Ilya Chavchavadze.

Simon Chikovani, a man of broad culture and a connoisseur of poetry, loved Z's work, considered him a most important contemporary poet, and valued highly his contribution of making Georgian literature accessible to the Russian reader. He wanted to help his Russian colleague to get back on his feet after the difficult years and to occupy the place in literature which he deserved. In Tsikhi-Dzhvari they once more discussed together the project of a Georgian publishing house bringing out a large volume of Z's translations, and what this might contain. As long ago as March Z had written in a letter to Chikovani that in this book he wanted to include Georgian folk poetry, works by Rustaveli, Orbeliani, Chavchavadze, and Vazha Pshavela. Of 8,000 lines of verse 6,000 had already been translated at that time. The remainder were to be done over the summer in Georgia.

In Saguramo the outstanding translations were finished off and presented to the Tbilisi publishing house *Zarya Vostoka*. A 'complete and significant' book, however, still did not emerge: it was accepted for publication at the end of the year and appeared in the following year, 1948, and it contained less than half of what the translator had proposed. This was, of course, not what Z had wanted.

Even before the book had appeared he had already been thinking about extending the basic volume, mainly by the inclusion of new translations of Vazha Pshavela. He consulted with Chikovani to discover whether it was worth his while to translate all the longer poems by this classic Georgian poet, even when some of them had been translated already by such outstanding figures as Tsvetayeva, Mandelshtam and Pasternak. Z thought that he had much in common with Vazha Pshavela's poetry because of its monumental nature, its picturesqueness, and, more than that, its folk spirit and its primordial fusion of man and nature. It was easier for him to feel sympathy with such poetry, and easier to reproduce it in Russian verse. Simon Chikovani approved of the inclusion of these translations.

Naturally, they both said that it was high time to publish a book of Z's own poetry. True, the situation in literature was not favourable for such a publication, and there was too much attached to the poet's name which gave cause for alarm: there were the earlier critical attacks on him still fresh in the memory, the unclear official attitude towards him, his conviction. Still, given that they could count on Fadeyev's support it was worth having a go.

Soon after the trip to Tsikhi-Dzhvari and the return to Saguramo, Z was summoned to Tbilisi on 4 September and was given the task of translating the verse text accompanying a gift from the Georgian Republic to the city of Moscow. That year the city was celebrating its eight-hundredth anniversary, and a Georgian delegation with a gift was flying by special plane to the festivities in the capital. Z went with the delegation, pleased that he had been entrusted with such an honour. A week later his family arrived back in Moscow.

IV

Over the course of the previous summer the Kaverins had built themselves a dacha at Peredelkino and they cordially offered the Zabolotskys the whole of the heated first floor – three rooms and a kitchen. The house was of a wooden Finnish design with a red-tiled roof and a large and (at that stage) open terrace. It was situated in the pinewoods, a little to one side of the older dachas of the writers' settlement.

Here the Zabolotskys were to spend the winter of 1947–8. Z was glad to have a heated room of his own to work in – he put a table in there and spread out his folders and books. From Saguramo the family brought back with them a grey and white puppy from one of the Caucasian sheepdogs used to guard the House of Creativity. They called the puppy Basar and gave him a kennel some twenty feet or so from the front step. Over the winter he turned into a strong, fierce dog who, when he got loose from his chain, inflicted several bites on friends who came visiting.

Basar became the favourite of the whole family, and Yekaterina called the ferocious dog her 'little darling', which was a constant source of jokes from her husband.

The end of 1947 was a time of spiritual uplift for Z, a time of heightened creative activity and of bright hopes for a settled life in front of him and for his establishment as a writer. A little of his poetry had begun to appear in print. The fifth issue of *Novy Mir* for that year had contained 'The City in the Steppes', a poem written about Karaganda and very similar in conception to 'The Builders of Roads'; in the tenth number of the same journal there had appeared the poems 'Air Travel' and 'Khramges'; in the almanac called *Year XXXI* 'The Feast at the Shroma Collective Farm' was included, while in the almanac which Goltsev edited they had promised to print 'Saguramo'. The poet was also pleased with his Georgian projects; his friendly relations with Georgian writers and with the publishing house had been strengthened, and he had the prospect of some interesting work on the poems of Vazha Pshavela. *Zarya Vostoka* had brought out two, albeit small, individual volumes of his translations (the Orbeliani poems and a small book of selected Georgian poetry). Z had begun to feel much more sure of himself than a year previously. The family's financial affairs were improving.

That autumn at the Kaverins' dacha Z devoted much deep and fruitful thought to what he wanted to write in his future poems. He was drawn to themes of natural philosophy. He had to reconstruct the whole course of his earlier thoughts on this and bring it into line with his new experience of life, to unite his previous conception of the universe with the actual people and events he saw around him.

Z had spent much of his time searching for a reason for the coexistence in nature of good and evil, ignorance and wisdom, stupidity and reason. It seemed to him that evil was redeemed by the generally positive progress of the world: from savage chaos – through the active participation of man's reason – to a single world-consciousness and harmony.

Humanity would reach perfection, but only on condition that it did not become detached from the whole of nature, and that it followed her wise laws. The poet was convinced that humanity must combine its striving for social justice and its own well-being with care for all nature. Only then would its achieve real progress and its own happiness. Z believed the future would be a world in which reason triumphed, a reason fired by the highest spiritual ideals, a world where all its elements would develop freely and in harmony.

In the mean time he wanted to be able to see signs in the world around him of a movement towards this orderly animate architecture of the future world. Real people with their individual souls and all their worries and sufferings, and with their labour of all kinds, could become the protagonists of Z's verse precisely in their roles as creators of the new, perfected nature. This is what should have happened in 'The Builders of Roads', but in this work there had been only a hint of the real interplay between the 'fabulous giants' and the spirit of nature. Now the time had come to give a firm definition to his attitude towards the activities of people in the world around him and to find a place for these activities in the general development of the universe.

In October 1947, at Peredelkino, Z wrote his programmatic poem 'I do not seek harmony in nature', which brought together both Lodeynikov's double vision of nature and the embodiment of its spiritual and moral principle – the sacred font of the forest lake, and the idea of the rebirth of nature in man's creation. In nature there is no harmony, but it is striving for it, and that is why:

> When the great world of contradictions
> Grows weary of its fruitless game, –
> It is as though the protoform of human pain
> Rises before me from the depths of the waters.
>
> And in that hour sorrowing nature
> Lies all around, deeply sighing
> And she does not like savage freedom,
> Where good and evil live together.
>
> And she dreams of the gleaming shafts of turbines,
> And the rhythmic sound of purposeful labour,
> And the song of chimneys, the glow of dams,
> And the current coursing through the wire.

At about the same time the decision was taken to write a longer poem in the same spirit which would describe people, their work on the construction of a large industrial centre, their complex mental and spiritual work, the life of nature and what seemed like its participation in human labour, the material and spiritual dependence of people on nature. To reconstruct the idea for this poem we can look at two works already written which were linked with it: a new version of the poem 'Lodeynikov', and 'The Urals', which had a subtitle 'Excerpt from a Longer Poem'. Yekaterina could still remember some beautiful lines about the life of the forest, which were to have formed part of the longer poem but were later destroyed. The project resurrected the poet's earlier intention of writing a poem-cycle or epic poem about Lodeynikov –

another indication of the continuity between the works written in the Leningrad period and the ideas of the years 1946–8.

The contents of this unwritten poem must have been along the following lines. The provincial thinker Lodeynikov tries to understand the meaning of the conflicting phenomena of nature, but he is not successful in his quest, just as he is unsuccessful in his feelings for Larisa. The frivolous young girl is not interested in what to Lodeynikov is the most important thing in his life: she is attracted by the handsome, empty-headed Sokolov, who is not burdened by any attempts to solve the complex mysteries of the universe. Driven by a maelstrom of feelings, Lodeynikov breaks with his former life and goes off to the Urals, where he finds an answer to the riddles of existence that have been tormenting him. He acquires a new vision of the world and begins to understand the meaning of its existence, and at the same time the meaning of his own life. He studies nature and comes to understand its soul and its striving for harmony. He realizes that his life is linked to that of the whole of the universe and through his thoughts and work he is taking part in its mighty purpose. It is possible that, in connection with Lodeynikov's quest, the poet wanted to give his interpretation of the life of the forest, to show the development in this complex co-existence of a special wisdom, a special perfection, aimed at meeting and helping the human mind (we may recall the last part of the long poem 'The Trees').

In the mean time, deprived of a contact with nature, and therefore of moral support, Sokolov deceives and abandons Larisa. Her spiritual crisis is also resolved through work and through creative contact with the surrounding world. She goes to the Urals and becomes a teacher. Filled with inspiration, she tells her pupils about the distant past of their native land, about the geological disasters that formed the Ural Mountains, about the people who breathed a living spirit into these dead mountains – and when she sees the light in the children's eyes she forgets all her own troubles and knows the happiness of creative work.

It was most likely the poet's intention to bring about a happy meeting between Lodeynikov and Larisa after their long separation. Made wise by their new understanding of life, they were to realize their genuine love for each other and for this existence which had been given a new and active interpretation.

In connection with this project Z intended to ask the Writers' Union to send him on a study visit to Magnitogorsk, so that he could get to know more about the metallurgical combine there, about the workers and the countryside of the Urals. At home he talked about his plans for the poem and the trip to the Urals, and he also sought Stepanov's advice. In a letter to Chikovani on 29 December he said: 'I have begun to write a long poem; I intend to go to Magnitogorsk and pick up some rhyme and reason there!'

The idea of the poem occupied Z a great deal. He had still not given up hope of feeling his way to an area where his own creative interests coincided with the demands of the official ideology. He knew that he could write more profoundly and more interestingly than people normally write about construction projects, and, against all logic, he hoped that his new poem would be appreciated on its merits by both the readers and the critics. Stepanov soon extinguished this rose-coloured hope. He was well acquainted with the internal affairs of the Writers' Union and the publishing houses, and with the situation that had arisen in literature after the Central Committee's decree on the journals *Zvezda* and *Leningrad*.

Z gave him a detailed account of his plans, and showed him some parts of the poem which he had already written. The conversation which took place between them must have gone something like this:

'You're writing for a journal? You want it to be published?' asked Stepanov.

'I'm writing for myself, and what happens after that, we'll see. Besides, it's the sort of thing that might be published. What do you think?'

'It's quite possible they would publish it. But if I were you I would be a bit careful. I don't think it's the kind of thing that's needed these days.'

'But I'm going to write a poem that's perfectly easy to read. It will touch on industry, working people and living nature.'

'Kolya! You write splendidly, but too individualistically. We're not allowed any sort of liberties now with a subject like that. They'll come down on you like a ton of bricks. Don't tempt fate!'

'But my ideas don't contradict the official line at all. Why should they single me out in any way?'

'Well, what can I say? You know very well what I'm talking about. They'll say that instead of the leading role of the Party and the building of socialism you have something about oneness with nature, and a concern with grasses and insects. Don't be in such a hurry, conserve yourself. We still need you as a writer.'

'But how long do I have to go on preserving myself! Years are going by, my whole life is slipping away, and my mind is not getting any more sharp . . . But I suppose you're right.'

Stepanov did everything he possibly could to protect his friend from harm. Both now and in the earlier period of the 'struggle against Formalism' he had tried to direct Z's work along safe channels, tried to restrain him in every way from extreme expressions of original natural-philosophical ideas, and was always alarmed when there was too much clear evidence of these ideas in the poetry that was published. At the same time he knew very well what Z's poetry was about, and was always pleased to hear a new poem; but he was divided between this pleasure at his friend's talent and great apprehension at his possible fate.

Stepanov dissuaded the poet from going to Magnitogorsk: given what was on Z's identity card, and his present situation, it would be incautious to appear in an industrial centre, and even more to visit the factories and to get to know the workers. In the hands of the state security organs his presence there could become an easy pretext for accusing him of espionage. He would have to wait – there would be a time for everything.

At the beginning of 1948 Z finally gave up all plans for the long poem. No integrated expression of his concept as he envisaged it in the 1940s was to enrich the corpus of his poetry. Nevertheless his views can be traced in a whole series of works from this time. In the poems from 1947 and 1948 – 'The Grasshopper', 'When, far off, the light of day is fading' and 'Through Levenhoek's magical apparatus' – his ideas acquired macrocosmic proportions, encompassing the infinite, mighty expanses of the universe, and the infinitely tiny, yet just as complex, particles of the microcosm.

In November 1947, at about the time when he was pondering ideas for the long poem 'Lodeynikov', Z wrote one of his best works – 'Testament' which parallels works from ten years earlier: 'Yesterday, Contemplating Death' and 'Metamorphosis'. There is significance in the original titles given to the poem: first, 'In declining years' and, later, 'Reminder'. The poet, now mature in years, looks back at his youthful perceptions and bears witness to his loyalty to them. But what had earlier been an abstract philosophical idea has now obviously taken on the form of a concrete personal experience. He affirms his lasting commitment to existence, the immortality of his materialized thoughts and deeds. As he greets the splendid future, 'when the millions of new generations will fill this world with the glitter of miracles and complete the building of nature', he sees himself in this perfect world as well:

> Ah, I did not live in this world in vain!
> And sweet it is to struggle out of darkness,
> For you to take me in your palm, distant descendant,
> And finish what I could not complete.*

* For full translation see p.339.

After 1948 Z moved away from the direct and pure expression of the natural-philosophical theme. He came increasingly to see the unity of humanity and nature as the mutual interaction of the human spirit and the moral impulse of nature. Mind and soul, the concrete historical path of civilization, man with his everyday doings and preoccupations – these were now the focus of the poet's thinking. The philosophical basis of the poet's ideas was developing, was being enriched, but was becoming more deeply integrated into the verse, making it less noticeable to the uninitiated gaze.

When he got back from Saguramo, Z decided that the time had come to make moves to get a book of his own verse published. He remembered his conversations of the previous autumn and winter with Fadeyev, and counted on his support in this difficult and responsible matter. To make the passage of the book easier he needed new poems which had been put to the test by first being published in one of the journals. Such poems now existed. In September or the beginning of October 1947 a fresh conversation with Fadeyev took place, after which the latter contacted the editor-in-chief of the *Soviet Writer* Publishing House, A. Tarasenkov, and told him that he thought it now expedient to publish a collection of Z's verse. He even promised to be the reviewer and the unofficial editor of the book, and this clinched the matter. It was Nikolay Chukovsky who conveyed the glad tidings to Z. He said that Tarasenkov had expressed himself in favour of the edition, and had asked for the manuscript to be submitted. He also said that this was the same Tarasenkov who was a famous collector of editions of twentieth-century Russian poets. For his part Z recalled that it was the same Tarasenkov who had one time written the articles 'In praise of Zabolotsky' (1933), 'Graphomanic incoherence' (1935), and 'N. Zabolotsky's new poems' (1938), thereby playing a part in the devastating attack on *Columns*, 'The Triumph of Agriculture' and later works.

'Well, now he's expiating his guilt before you,' said Chukovsky with a laugh, 'and at the same time he's adding your new book to his collection.'

'That's all very well', Z answered seriously, 'but I'd prefer the publishing house to deal with me formally.'

And then, on 16 or 17 October, a letter arrived from the publishing house on official paper with a courteous offer from Tarasenkov to publish the collection of poems.

A deal of careful thought had already gone into what the book should contain, and Z handed his manuscript in to the publishing house without delay. It was immediately sent to Fadeyev for a reader's report. When he had had a look at it he sent a note to the Kaverin dacha:

Dear Nikolay Alekseyevich, in general terms the book is very good, but I have serious objections to two or three of the poems. Anyhow, I think we should talk about it. If it is convenient, come to my dacha on Sunday at eleven in the morning. My warmest greetings to your family. All the very best. Al. Fadeyev.

The conversation between Z and Fadeyev apparently took place fairly soon afterwards: the poems to which there was objection were removed, and somewhat later the recently written 'Testament' was added. It was probably at that point that Z remembered about his difficulties with accommodation, and asked Fadeyev to bear him in mind when apartments for writers were being allocated.

Fadeyev wrote a brief report in positive terms and sent it off to *Soviet Writer*. A recommendation from the general secretary of the Writers' Union was enough, even for such ill-disposed figures as Tarasenkov. Z's book was allotted a place in the publishing schedule for the following year, and on 17 November a contract was signed with the author. Naturally, Z was well pleased with this course of events, and it was only his sad experiences in the past that told him that it was still too early to start celebrating.

That same autumn the poet received a letter from the organizers of the seventieth birthday celebrations of the literary scholar V. A. Desnitsky with a request to write a valedictory poem in the professor's honour for a special birthday edition of the *Academic Papers of the Herzen Pedagogical Institute*. Z did not like writing such verse, least of all for publication, and he almost never did so. With those who were close to him he generally had recourse to a jocular style, and would write what he called 'verselets' that were genially ironic and witty, and which were intended exclusively for domestic consumption. But Vasily Desnitsky occupied a special place in the poet's heart. His feelings of respect and gratitude were occasioned not only by Desnitsky's patronage during his student years, but also by his attempt to defend Z after his arrest. Yekaterina had naturally told her husband about Desnitsky's letter to Stalin, and Z felt particularly grateful to all those who had helped him and his family in those difficult years. At the same time he did not conceal his feeling of coolness if he came across those who had in one way or another contributed to his misfortunes. The poem, dedicated to Desnitsky and entitled 'The Gardener', was duly written and sent off to the *Academic Papers*.

On 14 December Yekaterina had to go to Leningrad to check on the condition of the dacha at Siverskaya, given to her as long ago as 1938 by her uncle Andrey Klykov, and also at the same time to meet her sisters and some of her old Leningrad friends. On the same day Z wrote a letter to Desnitsky which he gave to his wife to deliver. In it he said:

Dear Vasily Alekseyevich, Let me congratulate you with all my heart on your forthcoming birthday, and wish you health and many long years in your selfless work. I would like these congratulations to be a precursor, since I shall try to come to Leningrad for 30 January, so that I can embrace you and congratulate you properly. How many times over the years have Katya and I remembered you as if you were a father, and at the same time remembered our early years and the Herzen Institute, with which so much in our lives was linked.

A few words about myself. My life still hasn't got back to normal after all the troubles I have had. We are sheltering outside Moscow in someone else's property; I am very busy translating the Georgian classics; I have had some things published in *Novy Mir*; a book of my poetry has been accepted by *Soviet Writer*, and by all accounts it should be out by the spring. I write with difficulty, under tension, and there's a lot in my poems that I don't find very good; with the years I have lost my youthful self-assurance, but I've probably managed to learn how to look at people closely, and I have come to love them more than I did before.

In Leningrad Yekaterina went to the Desnitskys' apartment on the Kirovsky Prospect and delivered the letter to them. They gave her a meal and asked her all about the things that had been happening over the past few years. Over tea, when Desnitsky had gone off to his study, his wife Aleksandra said that they had read 'The Gardener' and that it was awkward for Desnitsky to praise a poem written in his honour, but that he had liked it very much and even wished to have it read over his grave when he died.

For the days that Yekaterina was in Leningrad their daughter Natasha was invited to stay with the Tikhonovs, while Z and his son stayed on their own, eating their main meals in the Peredelkino Writers' Club. After the summer break in the Caucasus the children were much fitter and did not fall ill so often. A currency reform had been introduced and rationing of foodstuffs had been abolished; life had noticeably improved, but plenty of difficulties still remained.

On one occasion Z succeeded in buying a copy of one of his favourite books, Tolstoy's *War and Peace*, and he presented it to his son with the edifying inscription: 'Dear Nikita, you will soon be sixteen. This book is equally useful for a sixteen-year-old, or for a sixty-year-old. Read it many times, and each time you will find something new in it – things that escaped your attention and understanding on a previous occasion. Love this book and love the people that gave birth to its author. Your father N. Zabolotsky. 23 December 1947. Peredelkino.'

Z followed his own advice – he would read and re-read all the books that he had selected from the mass of what he had read and made into his faithful companions for life. In them he sought confirmation of his own views, and he related them to his more recent observations and mental conclusions. The number of chosen books of this kind was not great, but he needed to have them within reach. The poet dreamt of a bookshelf with his favourite works, of his own study in his own house.

Two years had gone by since Z's arrival in Moscow, and in that time he had managed to achieve a considerable amount and had thereby shown that his dreadful experiences had not broken his spirit. Nevertheless, despite his spiritual resilience, despite his unswerving belief in the ultimate triumph of justice, the tragic events of 1938 and the years that followed had left an imprint on his character and on his behaviour in society after he was released. To the very end of his life he could not rid himself of the fear of once more losing his freedom, his family and the work he loved. He went in fear of being followed and informed upon. He knew that somehow his 'sentence' was marked in his identity card, and he was afraid to show it in official places. He was cautious with people he did not know very well, specially if they tried, as he put it, to get inside his soul. Among the people with whom he had to mix he tried to identify those who were taking too much interest in his way of thinking and reporting on it in the appropriate places.

Sometimes, but not often, these suspicions and fears would appear openly. The poet Semyon Lipkin, who was living in Peredelkino at that time, witnessed one such instance. Some time in February 1948 he met Z at the Kiev Station in Moscow so that they could travel back to Peredelkino together. Both carrying their briefcases and both in a mood where they were trading wisecracks all the time, they had a vodka at the station buffet, a bite to eat, and boarded their train home. During their journey Z suddenly broke off from their casual conversation and began to stare in some alarm at a man wearing a military-type jacket and breeches. With the experienced eye of a former camp inmate Z had identified the man as a member of the security service, and began to fear that he was going to be arrested. Indicating the man with a glance, he whispered to Lipkin: 'The second one on the seat over there. They're going to pick me up any minute now.' But they reached Peredelkino without incident. There, however, the man got out as well. Lipkin accompanied the frantic Z as far as the Kaverins' dacha and went into the house together with him. They sat in the warm room over a cup of tea, and it was a long while before Z could calm down. He was still awaiting the agent's arrival any moment. It was some two hours before he breathed a deep sigh and recovered himself.

Z was conscious of his fears and wanted to avoid taking the tragic events of those years too personally. He tried to rationalize them and see them on a global historical scale. It seemed to him that these social cataclysms played, perhaps, some special role in the development of civilization – in the same way as natural disasters played a part in the development of the whole of the earth's matter. He was striving to place his own destiny in the complex mosaic of the destiny of the whole nation, in the history of human society. He wanted to believe that his spiritual wounds would heal, and that the experience he had gained would prove useful in his future life and work. But the wounds were not healing. The past penetrated into his world in the form of memories, in the sharp tone of the reviews and in the muffled rumours of new repressions of innocent people at the end of the 1940s and the beginning of the 1950s. He did not want to think or speak about any of this. Only rarely did Z share his sombre thoughts with his wife or with his closest friends, and in such moments his eyes reflected a deep, concealed anguish.

One day, at the beginning of the 1950s, he copied out in his notebook some lines from Herzen's *My Past and Thoughts*:

Misfortune is the worst possible school! Naturally, a man who has suffered a lot can take more, but that, after all, is only because his spirit has been crushed and weakened. A man becomes worn out and more cowardly from all that he has had to put up with. He has lost that sense of assurance about the morrow, without which you cannot do anything; he becomes more indifferent because he has accustomed himself to terrible thoughts, and in the end he is afraid of misfortune in a selfish way, in other words he is afraid of once more undergoing a whole series of agonizing sufferings, a whole series of events which almost make his heart stop beating. The memory of this will not disperse with the clouds.

How little these were like the words Z had written in a letter to Yekaterina:

. . . these years have not gone by in vain: they have not only exhausted your strength, but at the same time they have enriched you, your soul, and – although it is wounded – it will now be full of more strength, peace and wisdom than it was before.

At the time he wrote these words in 1944, on the eve of being released, he believed, come what might, in his spiritual and creative rebirth; he was waiting to return to a normal life – and this lent him strength and resilience. That is why Z's previous literary interests and ideas began to come into their own again in his work after he was released, as though they had been preserved in the depths of his being.

In spite of all the poet's fears and anxieties, his hidden, preserved, creative potential began to burst through irresistibly in the years 1945–6. He immediately returned to what had been interrupted in 1938: in Karaganda he finished what he had begun before his arrest – the poetic transposition of the *Igor Tale* – and in Peredelkino he went on with his work of translating the Georgian classics which he had first come to know in 1935–6. The most essential thing was that he seemed to have constructed a poetic bridge between his earlier natural-philosophical ideas and works, from the long poems of the years 1929–33 – 'Metamorphosis', 'Immortality', 'The Woodland Lake' – to his new poems of 1946–8 – 'Trees, read the poems of Hesiod', 'I do not seek harmony in nature', 'Testament'; more than that, his poetry had become enriched with new ideas, motifs and attitudes. We can sense that given favourable social circumstances his poetry would not only have shown itself to be unbroken and not impoverished by the sufferings he had undergone, but to have emerged from all these trials even more perfect. The first poems he wrote in Peredelkino bear witness to this.

But unfortunately the atmosphere in literature and in society at the end of the 1940s and the beginning of the 1950s was not at all favourable to the realization of all the possibilities Z had retained within himself. Afraid that his ideas and poems would once more be used against him, he frequently held back and did not allow himself to put down on paper everything that had ripened in his consciousness and wanted to be expressed in verse. The creative outburst of 1946–8 was followed by a lull of two or three years when he almost completely transferred activity to the work of translating.

Growing difficulties with his book of poems also had an effect on Z. On 25 March 1948, the proofs of the collection arrived in the *Soviet Writer* offices and were passed straight on to Fadeyev for checking. The Central Committee's decree on Muradeli's opera *The Great Friendship* had only just been issued,* and in its sombre light the book appeared to be under threat. Fadeyev read closely through the proofs, and returned them to the publishing house with the following letter:

To: Comrade Tarasenkov

Dear Tolya! Some time ago I read this collection and approved it in its entirety. But now, when I subject it to more rigorous scrutiny, especially taking account of what has happened in the sphere of music, and the fact that Zabolotsky's book will be put under the microscope, I find that it should be changed in quite major ways.

---

* A decree identifying 'gross ideological errors' in the work of a number of Soviet composers and writers, particularly from the non-Russian republics [Ed.].

1. We should remove, or ask the author to rewrite, all instances where animals, insects, etc. occupy an equal place with mankind, mainly because it already no longer corresponds to reality: there are more people in the Arctic than there are walrus or polar bears. The book can't go forward looking like that, it detracts from the great things that are in it.

2. The following poems *must absolutely be removed*: 'Morning', 'The Beginning of Winter', 'Metamorphoses', 'Drought', 'Night Garden', 'Make a Little Space for Me, Starling', and 'Night in Pasanauri'.

Some of these poems could quite well exist in a book in other surroundings, but in the present context they lend the whole thing an undesirable tendency.

I hope Zabolotsky is not upset by the fact that without these poems the book will seem rather 'thin'. It will at least be all of a piece. Of course, we'll have to get rid of all the subdivisions and give the poems just as they come, followed by the *Igor Tale*.

Show this letter to Z and advise him to agree with me. I cannot speak to him personally since I am not very well. Also tell him that, as far as apartments are concerned, I have not forgotten.

Best wishes, A. Fadeyev. 5 April 1948.

The editor-in-chief sent the proofs of the book and a copy of Fadeyev's letter to Z, recommending him to agree with what the leader of the Writers' Union had said. Naturally, there was no arguing with Fadeyev's recommendations, the more so since they were dictated as part of a wider package of considerations and efforts to protect the poet from possible attacks by the critics. Of the twenty-six original poems in the book seventeen remained, with the addition of the translation of the *Igor Tale*. Of these seventeen remaining poems five had been written even before 1938. As it was the collection had been submitted with a strict editorial scrutiny in mind, and now, in its heavily pruned form, it was far from representative of Z's poetic personality. But he had to be grateful to fate that the book had not been withdrawn altogether, as had happened with his book in 1933. Fadeyev's bitter pill was somewhat sweetened by the encouraging words about the 'apartment business'. There were rumours going round about an imminent share-out of apartments for writers, and the Zabolotskys hoped to get a place of their own.

But if it was not possible to publish a book of poems in the form the poet wanted, then he could at least make another comprehensive collection of his works, even if only in one copy for himself and for any future publication. In this matter Z always strove to make absolutely clear and firmly defined how, in the case of his death or arrest, his descendants were to present his life's work in a published edition. The last such collection had been brought together in 1936. Two copies of this had been given to friends for safe-keeping (to Shvarts and Stepanov), and they had preserved them, despite all the ups and downs of the war years. A third copy, which was his own, and which had fortunately not been confiscated during the search of 1938, had been handed by his wife, after her husband's arrest, to the Tomashevskys, and this copy had now come back to Z. In January 1948 Irina Tomashevskaya had brought it from Leningrad, together with a large one-volume edition of Pushkin, once presented to Z by Boris Tomashevsky, its academic editor.

Both books – the typed collection of his poetry and the Pushkin edition – filled Z with joy. He would read and re-read the Pushkin constantly, and always find something new and meaningful for himself. In his own collection, meanwhile, he carried out an editorial polishing, taking out some earlier poems altogether. He replaced them with what he had written recently. In the newly collated collection there were 101 lyric poems and three narrative verse works.

Z realized sadly that only a very small number of the poems he had gathered together had found their way into the book that had been accepted for publication. Overall in his forty-five years of life he seemed to have achieved far too little. On the other hand who was to say that writing a lot was what mattered? What was needed was to write well. At the end of the book he added the following:

> From the author. This book contains my lyric and narrative poems written in the period 1926–1948. Some of them have already been published elsewhere, others have remained in manuscript form. Almost all my previously published poems are presented here in their original form, and a very small number have been reworked. The text of this book should be considered definitive and the only correct one for publication. N. Zabolotsky. March 1948. Moscow.

In spite of the categorical nature of this statement the make-up of the book was not, of course, definitive. As new poems were written they were stuck in or attached to the end of the book, and some of the earlier ones were destroyed or removed. From time to time similar changes were made to the copies given to Stepanov and Shvarts: nevertheless these books also retained older variants and poems which the author had scrapped. Thus, for example, Shvarts's copy still contained the earlier variants of *Columns*, while in Stepanov's there was 'The Beginning of Construction', a poem removed from other copies.

Works not included in the basic collection, drafts and sketches, Z as a rule destroyed, although he kept certain works of this nature among his papers. In Peredelkino he burnt almost all his old Leningrad manuscripts which had somehow not been removed during the searches and which Yekaterina had kept. Some of them she had taken to her husband when he was in the Altay region, the remainder had been left with her former landlady in Urzhum. Yekaterina asked for them to be sent to Peredelkino. Thus it was that a large basket of venerable age arrived and was brought into the Kaverins' dacha. It contained some old clothes, a Singer sewing machine and a folder of papers.

Anticipating a possible imminent move of house, Z decided to sort through all his papers. In the room where he was working there was an opening into the heating stove and this was very convenient for him to burn everything he decided to destroy. He went through his old manuscripts and as he did so pictures from his Leningrad past rose up in front of him. It took an effort of will to rid himself of a deep longing for his youth and all the bold hopes and illusions that had disappeared. It had all gone, as life itself passes, never to return. Now there was no time to think about it and no time for regrets. He had to work!

There was an early version of the translation of two sections of the *Igor Tale* copied out in Yelizavetino; it had played its part and was not needed any more – the manuscript flew in at the open door of the stove. There was an exercise book with the unfinished long poem 'The Siege of Kozelsk' which was hardly worth going on with now. He recalled how they had asked about it at his interrogation – and into the fire it went. There was another exercise book with the long poem 'Shaman' and the neatly written-out lines of a poem not included in the 1936 collection. Z began to read:

> The house of Time is tall;
> Statues of sciences stand.
> A piece of eternity is seen,
> Unmoving, like a trunk.

When he had read it he thought for a moment. No, this had all gone now and was not needed any more. Why keep all that? He must not burden his uneasy, wandering life with an archive. Who knows, someone might become interested in why these papers had not been destroyed at the time: had he not been hiding them on purpose? And then, after his death, they would start to grub around in his 'laundry basket', they would find all these poems and include them in his collected works. They would ruin the book of his life. No, what he had to keep was the important part – the basic corpus of work, and what he was currently working on, and all the rest must be consigned to the fire!

Z was not sentimental; he was strict with himself, and with his past, and also at times with those near to him.

That day he spared only a few of his old manuscripts. Yekaterina was bitterly upset to discover that her husband's papers, which she had preserved with such love and care, had been destroyed. In 1938 both she and the poet's friends had considered it so important to collect and hide and preserve everything written by Z that had survived the searches and his arrest. In the difficult years of exile and then evacuation she used to show these manuscripts to the children as though they were holy relics, which still contained the memory of their father. She herself used to feel happy as she looked at them, imagining how she would be reunited with her husband and he would take his old papers in his hands again, and thinking what pleasure they would give him. The handwriting, the layout of the text – everything was such a vivid reminder of him, of his wisdom, neatness and devotion to poetry. She also believed in the historical value of everything in her husband's work, and she was secretly proud that she had managed to preserve them. And he had destroyed them. It made Yekaterina bitter that her husband had not been able to understand or had not taken into account that these papers contained a whole chunk of her own life too.

The spring of 1948 arrived. Increasingly Z would break off from his work to get some fresh air in the pinewoods surrounding the dacha. He would have a game with the dog Basar, saw some wood with his wife or son, then split some logs. Sometimes he would take a walk as far as the Peredelkino pond, drop in at the popular little eating-house (half buffet, half bar) and meet some of the writers he knew there for a social chat, but he never stayed long – work was waiting at home. On his way he would admire the fantastic trunks of the old willows at the edge of the pond, watch the icicles melting and dripping in the spring sun, and the water noisily pouring over the wooden race of the weir.

The poem 'The Thaw' was written about the spring of that year, as were 'It was approaching the middle of April' and 'Late Spring'. They contain the observations he made during his walks around Peredelkino, or simply what he saw from the window of his room. One day, in the vicinity of the pond, he noticed a strange man, who would now look into a book, and then look around himself, then back at the book, as though checking what he was reading with the real world outside. The image of this middle-aged man with an uneaten loaf of bread and an open book in his hands, his solemn and wondering gaze at the spring awakening of nature, are all described in the poem 'It was approaching the middle of April'. In it the poet creates a symbolic picture of the mutual interaction of the man, the book and the natural surroundings, as a result of which human knowledge is born. It is as though, in creating the poem, the poet is recalling the distant sensations of childhood, the figure of his agronomist father, and even his own attempts to reconcile book knowledge and reality (for example in the poem from 1936, 'All that was in my soul').

It is likely that the splendid poem 'The Passer-by' was written at about the same time. In it the autobiographical details serve as the basis for a truly rich store of poetic associations. The poet's soul rejects the noise and bustle of life, and becomes part of the spirit of nature, and of the spirits of those who have lived before, and at the same time:

> Meanwhile his body strays along the road,
> Stepping through a thousand ills,
> And his grief and his alarms
> Run, like dogs, behind it.

In Z's later verse there is an even closer and more organic inter-weaving of actual human psychological features with pictures of nature which seem to reflect and echo them. His philosophical concept now appears in the very depth of the verse, at times becoming an aesthetic method of depicting the unity of mankind and nature.

On 26 April Yekaterina went on one of her regular shopping trips to Moscow. In order to get everything that she needed she had to go to several shops and stand in the queues. At that time Nikolay and Marina Chukovsky already had an apartment on the Arbat, and it was convenient to take her bags of shopping to them, so that she did not have to carry them all round the city. Then Yekaterina would come back there and collect all her shopping before going off to catch her suburban train at the Kiev Station. That was what she had done this day when she suddenly discovered the joyful news – the family had been allocated their own flat in Moscow.

Getting their own place to live, and more than that a flat with two rooms, really was a major event in the life of the family. For Z the flat was a place where he could work, represented a fixed base in Moscow, and indirectly showed that his services to literature had been recognized. In the past he had only had an apartment of his own for four years in Leningrad. All the rest of the time, beginning with his student years, he had had either to live in a hostel or to rent rooms. For so many years he had found it impossible to have an hour of solitude; whether in his prison cell or in the hut in the camp there had always been other people around. A flat of his own was sheer bliss. At forty-five Z wanted stability, security for the morrow, his own writing desk, a shelf with the books he needed, the sort of conditions that would enable him to work in peace. His wife would also welcome the chance to rest after her wandering existence, to build a home of her own, and the children would benefit from schooling in Moscow.

In May Yekaterina sold the house at Siverskaya and the family found themselves with 15,000 roubles at the old currency rate. This was also a providential gift – the house had for a long time been on German-occupied territory, had suffered all the privations of the war years, and might not have survived at all. But it had survived, and now, just as they were about to move into their own flat, the Zabolotskys found themselves with the money needed to buy furniture, some clothes, crockery and other household items.

On 26 June 1948, a truck arrived at the house in Peredelkino with the Kaverins' possessions, in preparation for their move from the city to their dacha. The same vehicle took the Zabolotskys back to Moscow to their own apartment on the corner of Begovaya Street and the Khoroshevsky Highway. The years of homeless wandering had come to an end.

The Last Decade

I

AT THE END of the 1940s and in the 1950s Begovaya Street had a provincial tranquillity; many of its houses were small, nestling among fruit orchards. Down the middle of the road ran a tramway, which continued across a narrow wooden bridge over noisy railway-tracks, then past the Vagankovskoye Cemetery towards Krasnaya Presnya. Soon after the end of the war, opposite this bridge where Begovaya Street turned into Khoroshevsky Highway, it was decided to build a small housing estate of two- and three-storey buildings in an old-fashioned style. Similar 'cottages' stretched along the highway towards Serebryanny Bor. Space around the buildings was generously allocated: the blocks were well separated, with broad gardens and open spaces around them, separated off by low ornamented fences. Narrow asphalt paths led between the buildings. The housing estate was marked off by an iron railing with several gateways in it.

The Zabolotskys were given a flat in a grey-brick two-storey block of four apartments, in the middle of the estate. Behind their block was an open space, all overgrown and smelling pleasantly of wormwood. The flat occupied half of the upper floor, and consisted of a large room which served simultaneously as a study for Z, a dining room and a bedroom, and then there was a smaller room which was used by the children. The kitchen was tiny – and apart from the gas stove there was hardly any room in it for the little table at which they normally ate and a couch for the maid whom they quickly engaged.

Even before they moved in to the self-contained and permanent accommodation which they had at long last acquired, the Zabolotskys had set about furnishing it to their taste: they bought the furniture they needed, hung curtains at the windows, and installed simple lighting. As the years passed, and as they could afford it, they replaced the original light, cheap furniture with more expensive mahogany. Z liked to go to the second-hand furniture shops himself and choose solid, old-fashioned pieces. Once the purchase had been made, he would put the article in place, admire it, and joke and boast about it as he showed it to his friends. Thus, sitting on a capacious ottoman opposite a sideboard which he had just bought, he exclaimed, not without a touch of irony: 'Look at that sideboard! It's not just a sideboard, it's a whole university!' At the time the tower block of the university on the Lenin Hills was being built, and there were frequent enthusiastic reports about it in the press. Z and his wife had been to see the new building on an excursion organized by the Writers' Union.

Apart from the sideboard, over this period they acquired no more than a new bookcase, a desk, and two or three other items.

After ten years of unsettled living, Z again had a chance to gather together a domestic library. He began to drop in regularly to the Writers' Bookshop and buy what he wanted for his work: the collected works of his favourite writers and reference books. He did not try to re-create exactly his library of the 1930s. His aim was to limit his collection to just one bookcase, but as the years went by the target number of books was exceeded – bookshelves had to be put up in the living room and in the passageway. An old carpenter was engaged to make them. When he was young he had been a boatswain on the famous cruiser, the *Viking*. Z loved to chat with him, valued his skilled workmanship, and paid him handsomely for it.

Z's library contained the collected works of Pushkin, Lermontov, Zhukovsky, Boratynsky, Tyutchev, Fet, Khlebnikov, Blok, Gogol, Dostoevsky, Lev Tolstoy, Bunin, Kuprin, Chekhov, Leonid Andreyev, Melnikov-Pechersky, Dickens, Hamsun, Maeterlinck, Dante, Goethe, Schiller, Byron and many other writers. On the shelves there were also some epic poems which Z set great store by: a couple of dozen volumes of Russian *byliny*, the works of Homer, the Karelo-Finnish *Kalevala*, the Latvian *Lachplesis*, the Kirghizian *Manas*, the French *Chanson de Roland*, and Macpherson's Ossianic poems. Among the philosophical works were collections of Lucretius, Plato, Skovoroda, Tsiolkovsky and Engels. Poets of the Soviet period included Bryusov, Klyuyev, Yesenin, Pasternak, Mandelshtam, Martynov, Slutsky and a few other writers. But he deliberately made no attempt to acquire volumes by Mayakovsky, Isakovsky, Tvardovsky, Selvinsky and a whole host of other Soviet figures. When Stepanov gave Z's son a collection of Mayakovsky for his school work, Z took offence, and almost came to blows with his old friend.

Z tried not to let odd books which came his way into his little library. If he had to keep them, he banished them to the shelves in the passage-way. Boris Slutsky, who was a frequent visitor at Z's in the period

1956–8, recalls how he would on occasion take him an edition of this or that, only to have Z glance at it and more often than not return it with a kindly smile, pointing to his overcrowded bookshelves as he did so. At these times he would say, with slight exaggeration: 'What do you want me to do – chuck out Tyutchev or Boratynsky and put this in its place?'

Until 1956 a prominent position at the top of the bookcase was occupied by the complete works of Lenin and Stalin. Z never read them; their role was to be a symbol of his loyalty to the official ideology. It was assumed that either the maid or one of the visitors to the house would be reporting to the appropriate authorities on what he was reading and whom he was meeting. When times changed a new bookcase was bought, and Stalin and Lenin were consigned to the space in the lobby which had previously housed the donkey-jacket and sturdy boots that were now no longer needed.

Under the windows of the apartment, on either side of the block, small gardens had been laid out. Top soil had been put down, some lilac bushes, poplar and chestnut saplings had been planted, and a flowerbed made. The small garden under the window of the big room was the object of constant care and attention, especially on the part of Yekaterina. On summer evenings Z used to like to water the flowers from the window of his room, using a hose run through from the kitchen. Sometimes he would go out and sit on a bench beneath the window and talk with one of his friends who lived nearby.

The inhabitants of 'Begovaya Village', as the newly constructed estate was sometimes called, included a great many writers and composers, amongst them old and new acquaintances of Z's, the Stepanovs, Kaverins, Goltsevs, Andronikovs, Kazakeviches, Libedinskys, Grossmans and Peykos. The apartment opposite was occupied for two years by Kazakevich, who had become well known at about this time, thanks to his story 'The Star'. Z and Kazakevich often crossed the landing to see each other , to share a bottle of wine, to chat and to read each other mock 'entries in the encyclopaedia' devoted to mutual acquaintances (at the time the second edition of the *Great Soviet Encyclopaedia* was in preparation), as well as poetry and *byliny*. Z respected Kazakevich's innate sense of tact, his mind and intelligence, his sober irony in his evaluation of people and events – and also a particular kind of almost military sense of daring. Kazakevich liked Z's poetry and was capable of commenting on it wisely and unobtrusively.

Initially good relations also existed with their neighbours, the Grossmans. But Grossman's maliciously ironic sense of humour, and his unwillingness in conversation to keep within the limits that Z thought necessary at the time, soon led to disagreements between these two powerful but all too different personalities. Grossman was always trying to uncover the authentic motives of the person he was talking to and find out what was going on inside them, without taking into account the pain he might be causing in so doing. It was as though the generally accepted official clichés did not exist for him. Thus, without mincing his words, he would make a direct comparison between certain traits of German fascism and the system that had come into being under Stalin. Z well remembered what such outspokenness had led to little over a decade before in the cases of Matveyev and Oleynikov. He would refuse to go on with conversations like this, not wishing to jeopardize his work or the well-being of his family. His system of values included humanity, viewed on the biospheric and cosmic plane (even in his personal affairs), and was on a different level from that of Grossman, who, by contrast, perceived events in a socio-historical context. In 1956 the magnetism of Grossman's personality was the chief cause of the sad breakdown in relations between Z and Yekaterina.

After 1948 there was renewed persecution of 'enemies of the people' who had already undergone punishment. At the time these newly arrested innocent people were known as 'repeaters'. Z was afraid that he too might be affected by this campaign. During a visit by one of his erstwhile fellow sufferers in the camps – I. S. Susanin – Z reached a reluctant agreement with him to break off their relationship so as not to attract the suspicions of those who, as Kazakevich put it, wrote 'le dono'. This comic French-sounding word was a transparent reference to *donos* – the Russian for informing.

Z valued his acquaintance with two writers who were Party members, his neighbours Goltsev and Libedinsky, who genuinely admired his poetry. Goltsev, like Z, had close links with Georgian literature. Not only were they well-disposed and interesting people, but both, so Z thought, could if need be vouch for his reliability.

During the first period of Z's Moscow life there was a series of friendly meetings with the Andronikovs, but these fairly quickly came to a stop, and their previous friendship dried up. Something in Irakly Andronikov's character had become alien to Z.

There were chance visitors from time to time, poets more often than not. Sometimes Z received them with interest (P. A. Semynin came, and there were the younger poets Yevtushenko, Sergeyev and others*), but

---

* Yevtushenko once told the present Editor of a dinner-party to which he and two others were invited by Z. They sat down at a well-laden table with, disconcertingly, only a single bottle of red wine. When this was finished, however, Z leant back and reached out behind him: a hand appeared through a door and gave him another full bottle. This process was repeated fifteen times [Ed.].

normally he made himself unavailable. On one occasion he caught sight through the window of Ksenya Nekrasova coming up to the door of the block. She had been agitating to see him for some time, so he ordered one of the other people in the house to say that he was not at home, then he grabbed his cigarettes and went off to smoke, as usual, in the bathroom, where there was a good draught. He had long disliked her work. According to the testimony of Slutsky, Z 'told him twice with a grin that women could not write poetry. And he made no exceptions to this rule'. On the other hand this view did not prevent him from liking, respecting and approving of the translation work of women such as Zvyagintseva, Petrovykh and Potapova.

Generally speaking Z enjoyed other people's company, but fate and the age in which he lived had seldom provided him with like-minded friends. In his Moscow flat those who were close to him began to meet together. There was a particular air about the household which made unspoken demands on guests. They had to show respect, but without being effusive; they had also to be sincere without being familiar; and they certainly could not force their company, their intellect or their opinions on anyone else. There were limits to what was permitted in conversation, and some subjects were unacceptable. They could not broach politically dangerous topics, or ask about Z's youth, about his time in the camps, or read or praise his early verse. Z was jealous of the privacy of his inner world, and saw no point in prodding emotional wounds which had hardly healed.

For his own part he was impeccably polite and cordial in a restrained way. The basic trustworthiness and integrity of his character attracted people to him, whether they were poets, professors, taxi-drivers or plumbers. He was never crude or hail-fellow-well-met in the way he spoke, and only occasionally ironic or joking in his attitude to those close to him. He liked the Georgian way of behaving with a certain amount of formality and ceremony, long conversations at the dinner table and friendly toasts which expressed love and respect indirectly, often using ritual metaphors.

When the Zabolotskys entertained, the guests included those who lived nearby – the Stepanovs, Kaverins, Goltsevs, Grossmans and Libedinskys – visitors from Georgia, like the Chikovanis, Leonidzes, Zhgentis and the Kaladzes – friends from Leningrad – the Shvartses and the Gitoviches – and from Kiev the Bazhans. There were other acquaintances too, but never more than ten people at one time in the cramped apartment. Z would ring up beforehand, and ask them to come at a specific time. Then he would discuss the menu with Yekaterina and give her some more money in addition to the normal family budget. Z would usually go and get the wine himself, or else send Polya the maid, or his son. They would go to the Georgian shop on Gorky Street and buy some Teliani – this was the best dry red wine at the time; if there was no Teliani they would get some Mukuzani. Stronger drinks would be served as well – good brandy and vodka. Z derived real pleasure from being able to have a lot to offer, and entertaining well; it was, after all, something he had for so long only been able to dream about.

The table would be laid in advance, before the guests arrived. At the appointed time they would arrive by transport or walk over from the neighbouring blocks. Their host would meet them with great ceremony in the little entrance hall, and help them with their coats. After a few brief words the guests would take their places at the table, their glasses would be raised in the first toasts, and delighted appreciation expressed at Yekaterina's well-baked pies. In the interval between the courses one of those present would ask Z to read some of his poems. Sometimes he himself would suggest that they listen to a piece he had just written, either comic or serious. He would take out a slim file with his new or not so new poems, and in the ensuing silence he would begin to read. He never recited by heart when he was at home. When the guests had listened closely to the poem, they would express their approval and ask him to read some more. Z would read another poem, or sometimes a translation which had been particularly successful, or he might simply close the file and put it away.

Z had a special way of reading poetry. He had a characteristic way of emphasizing certain sounds, often consonants, and sound repetitions. The end of the line would be read without drawing out the vowels, firmly, even abruptly. Each word would be pronounced deliberately and completely, and at the same time there was a certain unique musicality of meaning in the reading.

His friends praised his poetry, and told him that he had acquired new poetic strength, and that along with Pasternak he was undoubtedly the best living Russian poet. There would come a time when he would be widely published, and readers would become properly familiar with his works. They also valued his poetic sense of honour and his unwilling-ness to take part in the chorus in praise of Stalin, the Party and the Five-Year Plan. This approval from his friends meant a lot to Z. He had hardly been printed at all in literary journals before 1956, and he had remained practically unknown as a poet. For a long time the reading of his poetry in private gatherings had been the sole opportunity of assessing his effect on an audience.

And so he would read poems from the slim file to his friends, and watch carefully to see what reaction they produced. After the reading a general discussion would start up, more often than not on literary topics, and then there would be more toasts. When the guests began to depart Z would accompany them and help them on with their coats. Each time he did so he would repeat without fail the dictum: 'In the guest's battle with his coat the host must always be on the side of the guest.' Then he would help to clear the table. They never left the dirty dishes until the next morning. Just a little the worse for drink, Z would help to carry the remains of the food and the washing up into the kitchen, raising one shoulder slightly and giving a sly grin as he remembered episodes from the course of the evening. The last thing they would do was to air the room. The next day the host would, as a matter of course, ring all the guests, thank them for coming and enquire whether they had got home safely.

In the first years of life in Moscow Z found it difficult to write original poetry, and there was really very little of it in the slim file. When he read out 'Swan in the Zoo', written in 1948, everyone easily recognized places in the vicinity of the flat on Begovaya Street. Z often had to get on the No.6 bus or a tram and go on business to the Writers' Union on Vorovsky Street or into the centre of the city. The route ran by way of the old wooden Vagankovsky Bridge and then along Krasnaya Presnya past the zoo, which Z used to visit in the period just after the move to Moscow. And now he read to his friends the transparently descriptive lines:

> Above the park the trams go grinding by,
> The bridge squeaks beneath the traffic,
> The parrots call out mournfully,
> Their pearly tails drooping.
>
> The animals squat some distance off,
> Attached to the entrance of their dens,
> And the figures of the deer
> Look at the water through the slender fence.

In the accumulation of vivid images, in the strange interweaving of the city and the animals, could be divined echoes of his earlier attraction to the paintings of Filonov and the eye and hand of the author of *Columns*. It is not surprising that lines from 'Swan in the Zoo' evoked special hostility on the part of such figures as Akhmatova and Tvardovsky, who, although major poets, were remote from the spirit of modernism. Lines like these seemed particularly strange:

> The snow-white wonder floats,
> An animal full of reveries,

> Stirring on the bosom of the inlet
> The lilac shadows of the birches.

There is a curious story associated with these lines. In 1953 Z was approached by *Novy Mir* with a request for some poems. In the six years since 1947 only two or three poems had been published in the journals, and because of this Z hopefully sent off several pieces, among them 'Swan in the Zoo'. What happened subsequently is recorded in Lipkin's memoirs:

> It turned out that Tvardovsky didn't like the poem, but because he respected Zabolotsky, he decided to discuss the matter with him. In their conversation he apparently tried to get Zabolotsky to be candid and look at things from his, the editor's, sensible point of view. I well remember Zabolotsky's version of a phrase of Tvardovsky's, pronounced with a certain air of kindly reproach: 'You're not young any more, yet here you are still clowning.' You can imagine what Zabolotsky felt at that moment. As often happens with great poets who are contemporaries, both of them, Tvardovsky and Zabolotsky, regarded each other's work with a degree of coolness. Later, after they had made a trip to Italy together, I believe their relationship became decidedly warmer, but on that earlier occasion, seeing that the author was listening politely to his opinions, but not showing the slightest interest in them, even inwardly resisting them, Tvardovsky turned to one of his colleagues on the journal, and said, as though seeking support: 'He says that a swan is an animal filled with reveries.' His colleagues laughed at this. Zabolotsky felt hurt and embittered.

It was not only Tvardovsky who objected to this 'animal filled with reveries'. Actually, according to biological classification, the swan is, of course, an animal (there are four recognized kingdoms – animals, plants, fungi and bacteria) and the attribution to the swan of the capacity to daydream corresponds to Z's long-held desire to humanize everything living. The image of the dreaming bird thus fits well into the general make-up of his poetry.

At the end of the summer of 1948 Z's book of poems, which had been cut about by Fadeyev, came out in an edition of 7,000 copies. In a letter to the Shvartses written on 12 September of that year Z said:

> Dear Yekaterina Ivanovna and Yevgeny Lvovich, I am sending you and Kaverin my book – read it, don't go over the top, don't say bad words about it, or think ill of the author. I would have written better, but oats are dear, my innards aren't too good, and I get dizzy spells. Dear friends, do me a favour, hand the book on to my few friends in Leningrad; don't take offence that I am burdening you. You know yourselves that it is difficult for me to get to Leningrad, and it's not good to forget your

friends . . . You can pass the book on to Desnitsky and Lozinsky via the Tomashevskys.

In October 1948, after settling in to their new flat, the Zabolotskys went to Tbilisi for a month. There an agreement was reached on the translation of Vazha Pshavela's long poems, and on a visit by the whole family the following summer to the Saguramo House of Creativity. It was at this time that the poem 'Tbilisi Nights' appeared – in its way a declaration of love by the Northern poet for the composite figure of a beautiful Georgian woman, and through her, for the whole of Georgia.

On the evening of 1 July 1949, the Zabolotskys set off for the south, for Simferopol. From there they went in a taxi by the old, winding road to the Tomashevskys' house in Gurzuf. Their house was situated right on the sea-shore, among the rocky cliffs, next to the cottage which had once belonged to Olga Knipper, Chekhov's widow. The Zabolotskys were met by Irina Tomashevskaya and the family of her son, Nikolay. Boris Tomashevsky was still in Leningrad. On the following day Z went swimming with them all on the little 'Chekhov beach', tucked away between the cliffs. Then they made their way to the Nikitsky Botanical Garden, where Z took an interest in the young plants, and chatted with the old gardener. Later on the evening of 8 July he stood on the quayside in Yalta and watched the MV *Molotov* docking, ablaze with lights, to the sound of music. In the wild open space of the sea and the darkness of the night the huge vessel seemed like the outcome of the human organizing principle which was destined to bring order and spirit into this savage world. 'It was a phenomenon of meaning on the sea', wrote Z in his poem 'On the Roadstead'.

He also wrote a poem about Gurzuf, at that period still uncluttered with tourists and not built up with modern houses. In it the picture of the Bay of Gurzuf is linked with a sense of certain profound processes of creation, uniting the culture and peoples of different generations and epochs.

Early on the morning of 10 July the ship on which the Zabolotskys made a short journey from Yalta dropped anchor off Sochi (the quay had not yet been constructed), and the passengers were taken ashore by boat. Yekaterina's sister Olga lived in Sochi, together with her son and her surgeon husband. The Zabolotskys spent three days with them. One evening they organized an outing to the open-air cinema belonging to one of the sanatoria on the coast, where they were showing a film version of 'The Gypsy Baron'. On the way home, Z, fed up with having wasted an evening on an indifferent film, stopped to rest on the craggy sea-shore. He had begun to put on weight that year, and his heart was having difficulty coping with the extra burden. While the children chased fireflies in and out of the oleander and box trees, he stood a little way off, at the cliff-top, with the noisy sea below. Suddenly he became agitated, and begun to urge them all to hurry home because there was a storm coming off the sea. He seemed to be finding the walk an effort, and to be burdened down with thoughts of his own, but firmly imprinted on his consciousness was the swarm of fireflies, the roar of the sea and the rumble of distant thunder. In the fiery points of light of the insects he 'could sense the breathing of the stars', and by dint of some analogy of his own he recalled the *Oberiu* ideas about the multi-layered meaning of words, ideas reflected in two manuscript lines of poetry which he wrote in the 1950s: 'Beneath the surface of every word/there stirs a bottomless darkness.' In both cases, whether observing the insect, or thinking about the meaning of words, the artist should overcome his normal impressions, and see the great behind the small.

Several days passed, and then he read out to the others the poem 'Fireflies', in which he described both the place on the shore, where he had stopped to give his heart a rest, and his ideas about how the word-insect, transformed by the artist, can acquire awesome power.

> Words are like glow-worms with great lights.
> When you peer distractedly into the gloom,
> Their modest flame seems insignificant and dim
> . And their animated glow remains unnoticed. . .
>
> The breath of strange fanfares and bells
> Slowly resounds on high,
> What are pitiful words? A kind of insect!
> And yet these creatures were obedient to me.

The poet glorifies his power over the word and is proud of the fact that his momentary inspiration has found its way into words and become art. But by no means all impressions from life were poetically fruitful. After 'Fireflies' Z's muse was silent for three years.

On 14 July the Zabolotskys arrived in Tbilisi, and soon afterwards Z went on a visit with a group of Georgian writers to Chargali, the native region of the poet Vazha Pshavela. Along their route all kinds of receptions had been arranged with a multitude of wines and toasts, folk-dancing and singing, and meetings with local poets. The glasses were filled with splendid wine, and toasts followed to Stalin, to Georgia, to the leadership, to friendship amongst peoples. Z occupied a seat of honour, together with Leonidze, and manfully tossed back the requisite number of glasses.

The village of Chargali lay in a wooded gorge high in the mountains below Mount Charglis-tsveri, next to the rushing River Charguli. It was a wild spot, completely untouched by civilization. Mankind here existed on a par with the mountains, the ravines, the tangled forest and the mountain streams. Vazha's house looked like a hermit's hut. Z had to see these places so that he could understand the spirit of the poet he was translating and the sources of his inspiration. It was not for nothing that the son of the village priest Luka Razikashvili had adopted the proud pseudonym Vazha Pshavela – 'Man of the Pshava'. Z had a long talk with an old man of ninety who had been a friend of the young Vazha, and he was even presented with a memento – a simple bull's horn, from which, according to legend, the great Georgian poet had drunk. Z brought the horn back with him to Moscow, and whenever his Georgian friends were gathered together he would drink from the Chargali horn to the honour of Georgian poetry, saying respectfully as he did so that from this very horn had drunk Vazha Pshavela, his favourite Georgian poet.

In Saguramo the Zabolotskys rented the same two rooms on the first floor as they had stayed in two years previously. And in fact they spent their time in just the same way. Z worked away at the Pshavela translations for whole days on end, deriving great pleasure from discovering in the poetry themes with which he had an affinity. It took a great deal of effort on Yekaterina's part to persuade her husband to leave his study and come for a walk. Wearing striped pyjamas, and leaning on a stick, he would climb, in the company of the other residents of the house, a little way up into the foothills, overgrown with mountain-cherry and ash. Every now and then he would stop and admire the landscape. Sometimes he would go as far as the half-ruined walls of the ancient church of Zedazeni, and chat with one of the monks who lived nearby.

In August Simon Chikovani sent his car to Saguramo with his driver Sameboi to take the Zabolotskys along the Georgian Military Highway and show them the Daryal Gorge. On their way there they were to be joined by the poet Gomiashvili in his car. Gomiashvili was a native of the village of Kazbegi, and knew the whole area very well. When they arrived in Kazbegi it was already dark. Gomiashvili had not arrived yet, and the Zabolotskys only just managed to get into the house reserved for visitors. Later Yekaterina recalled:

It was pitch dark – even in the house. There was no electricity. The house was not in the main part of the village, and right beside us was the roaring River Terek. One false step and you might plummet into its depths. We had already settled down for the night when Gomiashvili

289

turned up. Then there was uproar! People came running to find us, and they took us to the poet's parents' house, where an all-night feast had already been prepared. It was very exhausting. Z occupied the place of honour, and the drinking of toasts began. Even though the children and I managed to get away to have some sleep, their father had to sit through till the end of the festivities, propose the toasts in reply, and drink as much as was required. At such feasts you had to drink both from glasses and from horns. Although the tables were spread with all kinds of Georgian delicacies, Z ate very little.

In the early morning cold of the following day they prepared to travel further along the gorge. When he came out of the house and took a breath of the fresh mountain air Z looked around him. The village clung to the foothills of the Shat mountains, and on the opposite side there opened up a view of craggy peaks, beyond which Mount Kazbek rose up like an enormous icy white tooth, the morning sun lit up its pure crystal summit, and the ring of white cloud which clung to it. During his visit the previous autumn Z had already been to the hundredth anniversary celebrations of the writer A. Kazbegi, and had admired then the lifeless face of Kazbek. Eight years later he was to write the poem 'Kazbek', based on the impressions of these two visits. The poem is directed against the soulless 'superior' will, which is so hostile to the living spirit of humanity. In it there was to be an exact description of what he had seen on that cold August morning.

When he returned to Moscow Z went on with his translations of Vazha Pshavela and other poets. He wrote virtually every day. He looked upon going to the publisher's or the doctor as irritating interruptions to his work. He would get up towards nine, when the children had already gone to school, and after a light breakfast he would sit down at his desk. He would write until lunch,* and sometimes afterwards as well. Even when he went to the bathroom for a smoke, he would take with him the sheets of paper with the lines he had just written. Towards the end of his working day he would count up how many lines he had translated, and check whether he had done the amount he had set himself. There were days when the work went particularly well, and he would tell his family that he had written around a hundred lines of verse. This was a record performance. If he did not reach his target by lunchtime Z would quickly gulp down what he was served for a meal, and go back to his room again to finish what he was doing. Yekaterina's pleas of 'Kolya, dear, do sit down and eat

---

* This, the main meal of the day in Russia (*obed*), is normally taken later in the afternoon than in Western countries [Ed.].

with us' would simply be dismissed with a wave of the hand. The party walls were far from soundproof, but Z had a knack of being able to shut himself off from what was going on in the house around him, and the normal conversations of the others did not disturb him. When he had finished writing he would read, or meet and chat with one of his friends who lived nearby. He also enjoyed listening to serious music or playing a simple game of patience.

From the summer of 1949 until 1952 Z wrote practically no poetry of his own. He deliberately immersed himself completely in translation work, so that he could expend all his creative energy on it. He subsequently remarked on a number of occasions that the Georgians ought to put up a statue to him: what he had in mind was not only the high quality of his translations of the Georgian classics, but also the time and effort he had spent at the expense of his own work. But the situation in the country was such that he could not, or did not want to, write verse of his own.

It was a difficult time. In the papers and at meetings there were thundering denunciations of 'rootless cosmopolitans', 'ideological deviationists', and 'lackeys of world imperialism'. Priority was given to everything Russian, however twisted or absurdly inappropriate the outcome. Lysenko's theories were at their height, wreaking untold damage on genuine science. The waves of persecution were growing stronger. An article in *Pravda* or *Kultura i zhizn* could almost physically destroy any writer, however worthy or famous. Every morning Z would take the daily paper out of the post box and hurriedly open it while he was still standing in the middle of the room. He would glance through the bottom-of-the-page article devoted to the next victim, and say to his wife in a low voice, 'Here we go again!', and he would read out the name of a writer accused of 'cosmopolitanism' or some other 'sin'. After that he would put the paper aside, and sit down at his desk, trying not to think about what he had just read.

II

In 1950 Z returned once more to his translation of the *Igor Tale*. On 2 February he received a letter from the leading specialist on Old Russian literature, D. S. Likhachov. The latter was proposing to publish the translation in the 'School Library' series, and also in the Academy series 'Literaturnye Pamyatniki' ('Monuments of Literature'). Z was pleased to be offered the chance of republishing his work, and was also glad that an academic specialist sympathized with his approach to transposing the ancient Russian epic. In Likhachov's letter he read: 'I place great value on your translation as a contemporary poetic reaction to the poetry of the past. In such circumstances there can be only one aim for a translation: to render the poetic system of the past into the poetic system of the present.' Further on in the letter Likhachov listed twenty-six points where he deemed it necessary to make alterations in the text. The poet used these as a starting-point for a re-editing of his version. In answer to Likhachov he wrote:

> I have looked at your comments on my translation, and I am convinced of your enlightened appreciation of the specifically poetic tasks that I faced. I have to say that not all experts show such an understanding of the poet's work. For that reason I shall find collaborating with you a double pleasure, and I only regret that I have not had the benefit of your advice before.

There were also some corrections which were made on the advice of the academic editor of the 'Literaturnye Pamyatniki' series, V. P. Adrianova-Peretts. Naturally, in relation to the overall size of the text, this work was comparatively minor, but it required getting into the spirit of the epic again and re-experiencing it. Only after the corrections carried out in 1950 did Z consider his work on translating the *Tale* complete. But he did not want to part with Old Russian literature altogether. As a result of his studies of the background materials to the *Tale* and to the culture of Old Russia, there appeared in 1951 an article by Z entitled 'On the rhythmic structure of the *Igor Tale*'. He concluded that the epic had come into being as a musical and oral work, and in that respect was related to the *byliny*.* He then began to study the *byliny*, and became so interested in them that he conceived a project of reworking them into modern verse.

Z considered that 'the *byliny* had once formed part of a whole series of artistically self-contained works' and that 'the *byliny* were written down by compilers at various stages of the decline of the old folk tradition'. He saw his task as the re-creation, from the fragments of the epic which 'had been preserved in a multitude of often contradictory interpretations of their subjects', of an integral work (or series of works) of folk literature. We can assume that Z was thinking of two basic possibilities: either the bringing together of many *byliny* into a work unified in composition and, if possible, in theme, or a compilation from different sources of variants of those *byliny* that had similar subjects, so as to create for each subject an artistically unified *bylina*, by

* Russian oral epic folk-poems (singular *bylina*) [Ed.].

using all that was most valuable from the variants. In the first instance the outcome would be one large epic poem; in the second a cycle of re-worked *byliny*.

There is evidence to show that Z was trying to create a stylistically and compositionally integral Russian epic. 'He envisaged a collection of *byliny* on the pattern of the *Kalevala*',* recalled Stepanov, with whom Z often discussed his idea. In his memoirs L. A. Ozerov remembers that Z shared one such project with him:

> I want to make a compilation of *byliny* as a sort of heroic song, homo-geneous and coherent. I have seen what Professor Vodovozov had done, and I am familiar with other attempts. We do not yet possess our own national epos: it existed, but, as with many peoples, it has not survived intact. Others have their *Iliad*, their *Niebelungen*, their *Kalevala*. And what have we got?. . . The ruins of a temple. We absolutely must restore the whole temple.

So as to set about the restoration of the 'temple of the Russian epic' Z gathered together the basic editions of the *byliny* in his library. The many inserted pieces of paper with pencilled notes, and the marks in the pages of the introductory articles, bear witness to the fact that the preparatory work had begun. The *bylina* 'The Healing of Ilya Muromets' was written as a trial project, and this gives us some idea of how he intended to realize his plans.

In his letter to Z, Likhachov expressed keen support for the poet's idea of reworking the *byliny* for children. He wrote:

> Irina Tomashevskaya has told me about your new project: to do a reworking of the *byliny* for children. I wish you success in this from the bottom of my heart. I have a genuine love for the *byliny*, and for folk songs and laments. They contain exceptionally beautiful passages, but these are interspersed with passages of prolixity and dullness. A choice needs to be made, and what is superfluous should be rejected, and sometimes pieces from various sources should be joined together . . . So I wish you every success in your great and patriotic project. Let us hope your *byliny* will be thoroughly Russian, thoroughly popular, and will preserve all the freshness of the fields and meadows of Old Russia, and let them be loved by both children and adults. I am convinced that you will be successful with your book.

Z had still not abandoned his intentions in the spring of 1953. He wrote in a letter to Tomashevsky: 'As far as work is concerned, I'm

---

* Finnish epic poem, created on the basis of folk material in the nineteenth century by E. Lönnrot [Ed.].

going to rest for the moment, and then in the autumn I shall get down to the *byliny*.' But he did not get down to the *byliny*, either that autumn or later. Folklore specialists reacted hesitantly to the poet's plans. Essentially their reaction to his proposals to the publishing house amounted to a rejection of his basic aim – to retell the *byliny* in modern literary Russian, while at the same time preserving the spirit of the popular epic. Breaking off work he had begun was, generally speaking, not in Z's nature, but the conditions imposed by the publishers seemed unacceptable, and he put off his work on the *byliny* indefinitely. He never returned to the Russian national epos, although the tendency towards epic poetry was discernible throughout the last years of his life in both his translation work and his sketches of unwritten poems.

In May 1950, Z's friends gathered in his flat to celebrate his birthday. After the traditional glasses of Teliani, he made the important announcement that he had been given a pair of pyjamas as a present, and with a sense of sly irony he read out the following poem:

> My wife has given me pyjamas:
> Since which auspicious time, dear friends,
> I've been a complex panorama
> Of various sartorial trends.
> Striped like a tiger in the zoo,
> Tense as a leopard – only stronger –
> I stand, mid little children, who
> Graze safely, wish to linger longer,
> Round one huge leg; while round the other
> Bustles my goodly spouse, their mother.
> Friends, I have just turned forty-seven:
> My life's a veritable heaven!

In his comic verse Z gave full expression to some of his feelings, allowing himself hyperbole, grotesquerie, irony and a sense of the absurd – all things which had been left far behind in the 1920s and 1930s, but which still excited his poetic feelings and needed an outlet. On one occasion when the Tomashevskys paid a visit to Begovaya Street Z entertained them by reading out a mock tragedy set in the royal court of medieval England. The tragedy, entitled 'Prince Henry', and subsequently destroyed, was an immediate success. Tomashevsky, a famous scholar, a man of great seriousness, with high literary standards, collapsed in tears of laughter as he listened to this tale of lords and archbishops, discussing the situation of the state and the intrigues of the court. As each lord discovered that Prince Henry had fled to France he would let out a long drawn-out noise, and the next important person to enter the stage would sniff the air and ask reproachfully and airily at such a critical moment for the realm (all this in the highest of styles) 'who has delivered himself of a smell in the chamber, my lords?'

In July 1950, in a letter to the Shvartses in Leningrad, Z wrote:

> My family has marked the advent of summer with a series of important achievements: a) Natalya got a top mark (five) in her exams, and has moved up to the seventh class, b) Nikita, in his exams, has got a matriculation certificate with five fours and the rest fives, c) my lawful wife has completed with credits the universally recognized Courses in Knitting and Sewing and has received the appropriate diploma, which fact has caused amazement in the whole district. As far as I am concerned, I have finished my labour (Vazha Pshavela – a volume of long poems), and on 15th I shall add the finishing touches on the spot, and hand it in to the publishers in Tbilisi.

When Nikita finished school he decided to enrol at the Timiryazev Agricultural Academy. It was a choice that pleased Z: in his eyes the profession of agronomist was in the family tradition. A drawing by Z has been preserved which shows a bandy-legged cow watching 'the learned agronomist Nikita' as he ponders the scientific transformation of agriculture. Several years later, when his daughter Natalya entered a pharmaceutical institute, Z said, half in jest, half seriously: 'That's splendid! Now I shan't go short in my old age – an agronomist won't leave me without a crust of bread, and there'll be someone to cure my illnesses as well . . .' And then he added, in all seriousness: 'Fame and money will sooner or later come of themselves. That's not the main thing – the main thing in life is to choose your path and to follow it with love and skill.'

On one occasion, while he was still a student, Nikita told the rest of the family how, during a lab session, he had isolated vitamin C in pickled cucumbers. Shortly afterwards the eccentric hero of Z's comic poetic cycle 'Notes of an old chemist' was thoughtfully announcing to the world: 'It's possible that the gherkins we have for tea/Contain an awful lot of vitamin C.'

When he was doing his agricultural practice on a collective farm Nikita received a letter from home consisting of three sheets, one each from his sister, his mother and his father. From his sister's letter he learnt:

> One day I went to Khimki with father and Georgy Tsagareli. We went boating on the Moscow river and ended up in an unattractive little place called Chiverevo. Nevertheless I managed to catch a bee carrying some

pollen. We're very much into bees at the moment, all of us – me, mother, and even father. At the moment he's reading that book by Khalifman . . . I have been nagging father to write a few words to you, and at last he's done so.

On a separate sheet, written in Z's own hand was a frivolous poem:

> A botanist, as I have heard,
> Happened one day to drop a turd
> So monstrous, that the very sight
> Of it caused universal fright.
> The cows implored the shepherd, saying
> 'Shepherd, what has this man been laying?
> It makes us ill to see this heap –
> Disturbs us so we cannot sleep.'
> 'You idiots!' the shepherd shouted,
> 'That it's a turd I never doubted:
> But just you think who dropped it here –
> A botanist who graduated with first-class honours from the
>> Timiryazev Agricultural Academy last year!'

Naturally, Z did not consider these comic poems a serious matter. In addition to the immediate intention of amusing his friends and acquaintances, they had to a certain extent served the unadmitted function of fixing and working through specific images and situations. Because he had to rein in his desire to write serious poetry, Z slaked at least a little of his thirst to create, not only by translating, but also by writing these comic impromptu pieces.

The impressions and images that captured his interest remained fresh and alive in his consciousness until the right moment came along to use them in a poem. As we have already seen, the image of Kazbek remained in his memory for eight years until, in 1957, he wrote the poem of the same name. The same thing happened with the poem 'Gombori Forest'.

In the autumn of 1950 Z travelled to Georgia with his wife. To begin with they stayed in Sukhumi at the Hotel Abkhazia, then later in Tbilisi, where he had to supervise the preparation of the book of Vazha Pshavela poems for publication. Z finally completed his revision of the translation together with the book's editor, Professor P. N. Ingorokva. He had spent more than two years working on Pshavela, and considered it the most successful of all his translations from Georgian.

It was at this period that the Zabolotskys made a trip to Kakhetia through the Gombori Pass. Yekaterina recorded her impressions of this wonderful place:

In the autumn of 1950 Chikovani decided to show us Kakhetia. We travelled through the Gombori Pass. All of us, Chikovani, Leonidze's wife Yefimya, my husband and myself, got out of the car near the pass in a forest of plane trees. Against the clear blue sky were etched the passing lilac clouds and the tall grey trunks and lemon-yellow foliage of the plane trees, and below all this was a mass of shrubs, ablaze with every shade of red and yellow. We walked for hardly more than half an hour, possibly less. Nikolay did not seem to find this walk irksome as usual. His face simply shone with a clear expression of ecstasy, and he shared his impressions without a trace of his normal reticence.

And just as they had done all that time ago in Gori, here in the luxuriant Gombori Forest Z and Chikovani promised each other that they would write a poem about this wonder of nature. But then was not the time for poetry, and Z wrote his 'Gombori Forest' some seven years later, carefully preserving the emotional reaction and the clarity of the visual image until then. It was even later when Chikovani wrote his version; his splendid poem appeared only in 1958.

When he had finished his work on Pshavela and handed it in to the publishers, first in Tbilisi, then in Moscow, Z began work on another important classic of Georgian literature, the eighteenth-century poet David Guramishvili. He immersed himself once more in a study of the history of Georgia, in Guramishvili's biography and works. In May 1951, he went to Saguramo – which happened to be the estate that had once belonged to Guramishvili, and had later been in the possession of Ilya Chavchavadze – in order to take part in the opening there of a historical and literary museum. At the same time he concluded an agreement with the Georgian publishing house for an edition of Guramishvili's 'Davitiani'.

Z wanted to spend the following summer in the Ukraine – in the area where Guramishvili had lived for more than thirty years in exile and written some of his best works. In addition, as early as 1948 and 1949 Z had translated some poems by Lesya Ukrainka and Mikola Bazhan. The latter, who knew of his old friend's interest in the Ukraine and its poetry, had invited the Zabolotskys to come and stay there with him.

Thus Z, his daughter, his wife and her niece Kira travelled to Kiev. There they met Bazhan and set off again for the picturesque old town of Boguslav, where they proposed to spend the months of July and August. They rented part of a house on the outskirts of the town near the little River Ros, the bed of which was strewn with huge granite boulders. Z spent his days working on Guramishvili's poetry, only occasionally emerging from the house to look at the maize fields, scorched by the drought, the little white houses and the neighbouring plots and gardens.

On these hot days of high summer they all went bathing in the river, and on Sundays they would go to the market to buy provisions for the week.

Soon after their arrival in Boguslav Z was disturbed by the visit of a policeman who came to check his identity card. He was particularly apprehensive about this procedure, since he assumed that the serial number of his card had encoded in it the fact that he had served a sentence, and he was afraid that any check might give rise to new unpleasantness. Yekaterina testifies:

> This serial number preyed on his mind. He had decided not to travel about the country independently. In any hotel where he was due to stay he would get the Writers' Union to reserve the room in advance, mainly because he was afraid of exposing his identity card to chance inspection. When we were living in Boguslav a policeman called in the first week to check whether we were registered. Nikolay was extremely alarmed, but tried not to show it. He invited the man to sit down, had a chat, and drank half a bottle of vodka with him. When he had gone I was cross, but Nikolay explained that here the policeman represented authority, and it was possible that he had been told to keep an eye on him.

July passed, and part of August. Then a telegram arrived from Moscow: a message had been received there instructing Z to present himself immediately at police headquarters. What was to be done? Z sensed that the clouds were gathering over his head again, and he prepared himself for the worst. He decided to travel alone. He left his family in Boguslav and flew straight to Moscow; fortunately Bazhan was in Kiev and was instrumental in getting him a ticket on the next flight.

At the police station in Moscow Z had his passport taken away, and, as a person sentenced under Article 58, was told to leave the city within ten days. Did this mean exile again? It is not hard to imagine what the world-weary poet was going through in those days. He knew only too well what the consequences of exile from the capital would be. He sent an urgent telegram summoning his wife, so that they could set about arranging the move straight away. At the same time his friends tried to see if they could at least delay the repressive measures adopted by the authorities. At Goltsev's insistence Tikhonov got in touch with the Secretary-General of the Writers' Union, Fadeyev, and asked him to intervene. On this occasion too Fadeyev was able to help. He approached the relevant authorities with a proposal to cancel Z's exile from Moscow, and to remove the stigma of the sentence from him, so that there should be no such unpleasant occurrences in future.

Z had no idea how seriously the 'relevant authorities' regarded this procedure. The check on his reliability did not reveal anything untoward. He knew he was under constant surveillance and so behaved with sufficient caution in his actions and utterances. A remarkable document was placed in his file at that time:

TOP SECRET
Report on ZABOLOTSKY Nikolay Alekseyevich.
No materials compromising ZABOLOTSKY N.A. have been received since his release; agents' reports describe him positively.
(Signed) Head of 1st division of 5th Directorate of the MGB of USSR.
Colonel Agayants
21 September 1951.

For confirmation it was decided to interrogate once again the former 'witness' in Z's case, Yelena Tager, who was then living either in prison-camp or at a settlement in the Altay. A document issued by the local Altay Ministry of the Interior (MGB) office on 14 September 1951 states: 'At interrogation she now denies the given testimony.'

As the result of an Extraordinary Commission decision Z's sentence was rescinded; in November he received a precious official document to that effect – which, however, did not imply his rehabilitation. There was a long way to go before that took place.

On 26 November 1951, he addressed a letter to Fadeyev in which he said:

I am writing to let you know that my sentence has been rescinded, and that I have an official statement which says so. I must thank you yet again for intervening to such effect in this matter. This is a great and important event in my life. Yours sincerely, N. Zabolotsky.

Living and working became more peaceful. All the same, in the drawer of Z's desk were several neatly rolled-up trouser belts, and in the lobby were objects which were completely unnecessary in town life – felt boots, a pair of unusually stout heavy-duty leather boots and a donkey-jacket. In the bookcase was a good-quality case of drawing instruments, acquired in a second-hand shop. It was good to have all these things ready to hand in case of a sudden change in his way of life.

At the end of 1951 and the beginning of 1952 Z had trouble with his eyes. The doctors identified it as tuberculosis of the retina; he was placed in a clinic, and when he emerged he began to consume large quantities of phtivasite and other medicines. From time to time he was aware of a dark spot on his vision when looking at a sheet of white paper. Eye-trouble had to be taken seriously.

For the summer of 1952 the family took a dacha on the outskirts of the village of Aprelevka. Z, however, did not want to go there, and, under the pretext of taking care of his eyes, he stayed behind in the city. At the beginning of August he flew to the Ukraine for a few days with a delegation of writers to celebrate the 160th anniversary of the death of Guramishvili; on his return Z went together with his wife to the dacha in Aprelevka, but he did not spend long there. The tabby cat which they had brought with them from the city had given birth, and the squealing of the kittens kept everyone awake. This made Z cross, and he went back to the apartment. There in the city he found life difficult because of the heat, so he got a travel warrant and went off to a study centre at Dubulti on the coast near Riga.

In the autumn of that year Z broke his self-imposed silence and wrote four poems of his own: 'An Old Tale', 'The last poppies are dropping their petals', 'Remembrance', and one of his most heartfelt poems 'Goodbye to Friends'. They are all redolent with sad thoughts about the passing of life, all that had been irretrievably lost, and friends who had perished before their time.

One gloomy autumn day, as he stood at the window of his room, he watched Stepanov making his way over from the neighbouring block. The poplar trees were nearly bare, and Stepanov was shuffling his feet as he walked through the damp, brown, fallen leaves. He was looking mournful, his head down, the cold wind stirring the grey hairs on his bare head. Z thought how his friend, who had shown such promise when he was younger, now seemed crushed by life, and his writing had become somehow wordy, opportunistic and uninteresting. Even when he wrote about Gogol, whom both of them considered second only to Tolstoy, he always followed the official line. He felt anguish for him, for himself, and for the whole of modern Russian literature. The lines of a poem rose up in Z's mind (only the concluding stanza is given here):

> Though the walls of the home be unstable,
> And the road lead into gloom, –
> In the world there is no sadder betrayal,
> Than the betrayal of oneself.

The second line of the final stanza had originally been: 'Let the road lead off to prison', but this was too dangerous, and too direct. It was replaced by 'into gloom'. It was presumably in those days that 'An Old Tale' was written as well. Here the poet gave an accurate definition of how honourable people had lived under Stalin's rule, 'patiently' and 'in silence':

Burns down with a patient light
Our life in this sequestered place,
And here in silence we meet
The fate we cannot outrun.*

At the beginning of the 1950s Z acquired a copy of Delacroix's *Diary*. When he had finished work at his desk he would bury himself in reading it, underlining and even copying out passages where the ideas seemed particularly in line with his own thoughts. Among the places marked it is possible to find sentences which echo the poems he wrote in 1952:

You have to possess great bravery in order to decide to be yourself; this quality is especially rare in periods of decline such as ours.

. . . Faith in yourself is a very rare gift, nevertheless it alone can give rise to masterpieces.

In the hope that he had still managed to preserve the capacity to be himself, Z also recognized the distorting effect of living under the extreme stress of fear and ideological pressure. It was then that he copied out the sentences already quoted from Herzen's *My Life and Thoughts*: 'misfortune is the worst possible school . . .' and the remarkable words by Walford:

Every person is what they consider themselves to be. And they are equally what other people consider them to be. And a person is also what he was, what he will be, and, to a certain extent what he might be . . . One of the greatest tragedies of our modern, distorted world lies precisely in the fact that these two beings – what a man is, and what he has been made to be – exist within him at one and the same time.

These notes made by the poet from the books he had read are an essential commentary on his poetry.

Sometimes ideas suppressed since his youth broke through to the surface. Such was the case, for example, on the occasion of a visit to the workshop of the sculptor Konyonkov organized by the Writers' Union. Z was interested in the work of this outstanding artist who had returned from America a few years previously, and he and his wife had gone on the excursion for this reason. Konyonkov himself conducted the party round the studio. Z told him that he admired the highly spiritual nature of the sculptures, and pointed out in particular a portrait of Surikov that struck him specially because it had the hands of a worker which were as though enveloped in creative thought. Konyonkov took him to a bust of Peshkova, and demonstrated in gestures how the thoughts

* Full translation on p.355.

swirled around her head. 'Reason should be given life and a material form', he said. The poet and the sculptor chatted together for quite some time. Z was greatly interested in plans to make a sculpture of the world of the stars, the Cosmos, not a dead world, but one permeated by reason and the music of the spheres. The artist, who had fashioned portraits of Einstein and Tsiolkovsky, had a highly original way of looking at the universe, and Z sensed that it had much in common with his own previous ideas.

Recognizing in the poet someone who was interested in him and who understood him, Konyonkov willingly shared with him his ideas about the cosmic programme of mankind's development, about the fourth and other dimensions of space, and about the depiction of the cosmos in art. That same evening Z went to see Stepanov and told him enthusiastically about his conversation with the sculptor and about what an enormous impression the latter's works, views and ideas had made on him: 'You know, it was just like taking a refreshing bath, that's the feeling it's left me with.' As he listened to his friend, Stepanov became more and more depressed. By the standards of the official ideology all these notions were simply 'bourgeois idealism', and if they started to influence the poet's work, which God forbid, then the outcome could be disastrous. Stepanov now regretted that Konyonkov's wife had not been in the studio. She would certainly not have allowed such outspoken discussions, since she fully understood that an artist who had lived abroad for twenty-two years and put so much free thought into his work could not be too careful. It was not for nothing that very 'correct' articles signed by Konyonkov appeared from time to time in the press, faithfully following the line of the paper's leader columns. This was an insurance and a kind of fee that had to be paid for the opportunity to go on working relatively freely. So it was that Stepanov feared that Z might let his imagination run away with him, and this fear was certainly well founded.

Z was fond of reading the little volume of Tsiolkovsky's pamphlets that he had bound together long ago, and of discussing over a bottle of Teliani the transformation of matter, immortality and the perfection of reasoning beings and the whole of nature on Earth. Was it not perhaps his visit to Konyonkov that had turned his thoughts once more to his earlier discussions with his *Oberiu* colleagues, with Lipavsky and Oleynikov, and that in turn inspired the writing of 'Goodbye to Friends'?*

It was rare for the memory of a far distant period of his life to provide

---

* Translation on p.356.

the subject for one of his works, but on this occasion the poem reflected both pain at the untimely death of his friends, regret at the loss for ever of those 'immortal illusions of the spirit' that had so moved him, and faith in the all-embracing nature of existence.

III

On 5 March 1953, Stalin, who had seemed immortal to everyone, died. The whole country shuddered from an almost fanatical sense of grief and a sudden boundless hope for change in the future. No one doubted that life without Stalin would change, but nobody knew what it might become, and this created fear. Intellectuals had been horrified by the affair of the 'doctors' plot' and the officially inspired wave of anti-Semitism which was then at its peak. Everyone anticipated fresh persecution and show trials. Now, in the first days after Stalin, they were afraid of something even worse – chaos, internecine strife and a bloody orgy of terror. It was as though everyone had taken cover and was waiting to see what would happen. Z had never had any illusions about Stalin, but he feared 'walls which had ears', or being informed on by the maid, so he did not give expression to his hopes and fears.

At home the Zabolotskys had recently acquired a record-player for the LPs that had just begun to appear, and the children were dying to try it out. But Z would only allow them to put on Tchaikovsky's slow 'Meditation', and even then made sure that the music was not too loud. There were no other appropriate records in the house.

His son told him how, on the day following the death of the 'leader and teacher', his professor broke down and wept at the morning lecture in the Timiryazev Academy, and how the whole audience followed suit, and how there were crowds of people making their way to the House of the Unions where Stalin's body had been placed. It seemed strange to see, on Pushkin Square, a black car with a loudspeaker telling people to return to their homes. On Trubnaya Square the dense throng making its way to the Hall of Columns* was pressed tightly against the walls of the houses by a line of military trucks. People were so crushed that those who fell could not get up again, and those who were forced against the posts of the street lights clung there while they had the strength, not daring to tread on the heads and shoulders of the others. The entire square was filled to overflowing with crowds trying to join the queue.

* Ceremonial hall in the House of the Unions, dating from the eighteenth century, where Stalin's body lay in state [Ed.].

Whenever a gap appeared between the blockading lorries a stream of people would burst through it, but the trucks would immediately close up again. From the queue there came groans, shrieks and cries for help. Where possible those who had been crushed were dragged from the crowd and placed on the benches in the boulevard, or laid out on the dirty snow. Sightseers had climbed up into the trees. There were also groups of soldiers standing around, and nearby were some field kitchens. With the onset of evening special canvas-covered vehicles drove up and removed the bodies of these last of Stalin's victims.

Yekaterina recalls those days of mourning:

> It was very frightening: what would happen next? Z and I would often stand together looking out of the window. Our little estate was deserted. Then we were summoned to a memorial meeting at the Writers' Union. It was impossible not to go, and Z went. When he returned he said that he had noticed a certain hesitancy about the proceedings. Then they began to ask people to write poems on Stalin's death. Nikolay was luckily able to get out of it by arguing that he was busy working on a poetic translation of a poem Bazhan had sent him in a literal version. Bazhan's poem was quite proper and acceptable. It was not however published in Moscow, where the breeze already seemed somehow to be blowing in a different direction. Then there arrived the literal version of a poem by Noneshvili. It was full of out-and-out flattery. Stalin had not only been the sun, but, so it would seem, the entire cosmos. Z refused to translate this. And in fact after a few days Noneshvili had no need of it either.

It gradually became evident that the terrible years were receding into the past, though very few understood the true nature of the abyss into which the country had fallen and out of which it had to extract itself. It was a mystery how and when the process of renewal was to begin, because everything – people, the power structure, the way of life, the ideology – had remained the same.

At the beginning of April Z and Yekaterina went to Miskhor, to the Pinewood Sanatorium. Living there were some of their neighbours from Begovaya Street, Yury and Lidiya Libedinsky. They had not been particularly close acquaintances of the Zabolotskys, but after the move to Begovaya they had all got on well together. At the time Z was officially attached to Libedinsky, who was a Party member, with whom he was supposed to study the history of the Bolshevik Party and the fundamentals of Marxism. Largely against his will he would prepare the work that he had been allotted, read the odd book and even make notes, since he felt uncomfortable about turning up at the meetings unprepared. Libedinsky was fully aware that all this history, a compound of demagogy and formalism, held no interest at all for Z, and fulfilling his task as mentor he would not so much listen to what Z had done as do most of it himself.

Lidiya describes life at the sanatorium in her memoirs:

We drove around the Crimea a lot, went up the mountain Ai-petri, and wandered along the narrow streets of Gurzuf and Alupka and down the shady avenues of the Nikitsky Gardens. Zabolotsky was keen to come along on our walks and trips. But then, suddenly, in the middle of the most animated and cheerful conversation, he would become serious and begin talking emotionally about what excited us all the time, the fact that a new page was opening in Russia's history, and consequently in Soviet literature. 'I am convinced', he said on one occasion, 'that every genuine poet has poems in the drawer of his desk which he has been writing over the years. Now it will be possible to publish them, and then it will become clear that our poetry has always been rich and varied.'

One day the Libedinskys suddenly noticed that the normally affable Z had begun to avoid their company, and when he did meet them he was morose and irritable. After two or three days Lidiya tried to find out the reason for this change, and she approached Yekaterina.

'Is Nikolay ill? Perhaps something has happened?'

'He wants to get on with writing his poems, but he can't allow himself to do it,' Yekaterina answered after a slight hesitation. Some time passed, Z overcame his bad humour, and became quite friendly again. 'Choosing a moment when he seemed in a good mood,' writes Libedinskaya, 'I plucked up courage and asked: "Nikolay, is it true that you are not allowing yourself to write poetry?" '

Z's answer was restrained – I had begun to probe an area which outsiders were not normally permitted to probe.

'Lidiya Borisovna,' he said politely (a bit too politely, in fact, even with a slight patronizing tone), 'poems should be written when you can't not write them. Then the reader can't not read them. But if you just write about everything that comes before your eyes, in other words put into rhyme and rhythm every idea that comes into your head, then you'll get the kind of poems I make up when we are out for our walks . . . But they don't have anything in common with real poetry.'

This incident, and the words that were spoken, are very characteristic of Z, yet the real reason for his sudden coolness had nothing to do with the fact that he was gestating poems. Yekaterina knew very well what the problem was, but she could not bring herself to explain it to the Libedinskys: what she said was true, though not in all respects. This is in fact what had happened. The Zabolotskys and the Libedinskys sat at the same table in the sanatorium. They were surrounded by people, possibly employees of the Ministry of Foreign Affairs – the sanatorium belonged to that particular ministry. It happened one day that Libedinsky started to recite aloud and with great expression some verses from *Columns*. He liked Z's early poetry, and wanted to show that he knew it by heart. Z, on the other hand, as always in such circumstances, was afraid of a trick, or some involuntary provocation. A subconsciously developed reaction on his part put him on his guard and made him withdraw into himself. Naturally, Yekaterina could not explain all this, because Z entrusted his wife with his inner secrets on the basis that he could rely on her.

Immediately after their return from Miskhor Z celebrated his fiftieth birthday. A party was arranged and the Stepanovs and Kaverins came, together with the Goltsevs, the Libedinskys, both the Chukovskys and Antokolsky. On 3 June, in one of the smaller rooms of the Writers' House, the friends gathered together for an evening devoted to Z's work, to mark the birthday. There were not many present, though all were genuine lovers of Z's poetry. Stepanov gave an opening address, and the Georgian writers sent flowers by plane. Despite the fact that all present offered their warmest congratulations to him, Z was sad: this was not at all how he had imagined his fiftieth birthday. It was with bitterness that he remarked afterwards: 'Virtually none of the other poets came.' In a letter to Simon Chikovani Z wrote:

> They put on an evening of my work, linked to my fiftieth birthday; it went off well. I read my poetry, quite a lot of it, in fact, and it was very well received – true, there weren't many there, say forty or fifty people. At the moment I'm busy with the Russian *byliny*. What will come of this pastime is still difficult to say. Life in the family goes on as normal, Nikita is going off on his practical, and Natasha is finishing her exams. We're planning a holiday on the coast near Riga.

The Zabolotskys spent July 1953 in the House of Creativity at Dubulti. They rented rooms on the fourth floor of a detached house in the heart of the leafy park, not far from the sandy beach.

On their return to Moscow they spent some time at the Kaverins' dacha in Peredelkino. On 12 August Boris Pasternak sent a note inviting them to dinner at his dacha, and asking Z to do what he had long promised to do – read his unpublished poem 'The Crazy Wolf'. Apparently, at some previous meeting, the two poets had talked about the poem, and Z was pleased to be reminded of it again now. He was also looking forward to meeting Pasternak again. Against his normal habit, he did not destroy the note, but tucked it between the pages of a copy of *Earth's Vastness* which the author had given him, and which he had already had bound and placed in a position of honour on his bookshelves.

It is not difficult to imagine that the conversations between Z, Pasternak, and the third person present, Simon Chikovani, were confiding, frank and deep. In addition to 'The Crazy Wolf' Z read some of his other poems. Pasternak liked the poem, and his authoritative opinion was important to Z, since he himself viewed this work as one of his most serious achievements, in a way his 'Faust'. On hearing these philosophical verses his host remarked with friendly irony: 'By comparison with you, I reckon that I am just a member of the rank and file!' Z was hardly in a position to agree with such an appraisal of the socio-political significance of his poem. Four years later he was to write 'The Solitary Oak', in which he was to refer possibly to himself, possibly to Pasternak, or just simply to the lonely struggle of the artist in general:

> The ground is poor: this oak
> Is too gnarled, and there is no majesty
> In its branches. Some kind of ragged growth
> Rises above it and rustles dully.
>
> But its tightly twisted members
> Have developed so much, that it seems if struck
> It would resound like a bell of glory,
> And amber would drip from its trunk.
>
> Look closely at it: calm and imposing
> Among its lifeless gullies.
> Who can say that it is not a warrior in the field?
> It is a warrior there, even if alone.

This poem was to be written in 1957, but at the time, in 1953, with the impressions from his meeting with Pasternak still fresh in his mind, Z wrote 'Poet', in which he described the dacha where the meeting took place, Pasternak himself, and the feelings he experienced on meeting him.

> Black are the pines behind this old house,
> In front of it, a field of oats.
> A cloud unimaginably beautiful
> Hangs in the tender sky, like a ball of silver.
> On either side, mistily lilac,
> In the middle, bright and menacing –
> The wing of an injured swan,
> Slowly floating away.

> Below, on the rickety verandah,
> Sits a grey-haired youth,
> Like a portrait in an antique medallion
> Made of camomile flowers from the fields.
> He screws up his slanting eyes,
> Warmed by the sun of the Moscow countryside, –
> Forged by the storms of Russia,
> Companion of my heart and poet.
> And the trees, like night, stand behind the house,
> And the oats push up crazily . . .
> That which before was unfamiliar
> Is here made close to the heart.

When he talked of contemporary poets, Z referred warmly to Martynov, Semynin, Tarkovsky and several others. But in the last years of his life he was specially enthusiastic about Pasternak. In his own ambitious estimation it was only to Pasternak that he was prepared to yield first place in modern poetry. Z had copied out or retyped into a special notebook the latter's unpublished poems, basically those which were to be included in the novel *Doctor Zhivago*. He was moved most of all by the simple wisdom and power of penetration of 'Christmas Star', which he considered one of the supreme achievements of world poetry.

Judging by the diary entries of Zoya Maslenikova, who sculpted a bust of Pasternak, the latter also valued Z's poetry highly. Maslenikova recalls Pasternak as saying:

> He (Zabolotsky) has one very rare quality – thematic unity, a complete correspondence between content and title . . . as though a picture had been given its label strictly in accordance with its purpose. You also find this with some French writers, Baudelaire for example, but you do not come across it very much in Russian poetry, which is more of a constant live outpouring of self-expression . . . People I don't really like have become friends of the family – it's a matter of having got used to them – but there are some people who are very close to me, and whom I meet regularly, but not very often. Zabolotsky was one such. We met three or four times, with long intervals in between. I place a great value on his reactions to my poems. He rejected everything I had written before *On Early Trains*. When he read his own poems here it was as though he had hung lots of framed pictures round the walls, and they have not disappeared, they are still hanging there . . .

This, that might be called a painterly reaction to Z's poetry, exactly reflects the special nature of his poetic talent.

In the same year of 1953 Z's interest in painting re-emerged with renewed vigour. He visited galleries, artists' exhibitions and studios. He made a study of the works of Rerikh, Pirosmani, Gudiashvili and the sculptor Erzi. Two years later he visited an exhibition of pictures from the Dresden Gallery (on 12 May 1955, he wrote on a sheet of his tear-off calendar: 'We saw the Madonna by Raphael, and the Dresden Gallery').

It was not that Z had a liking for painting in general. He always saw it in relation to his own aesthetic and philosophical views. His relationship to this or that artist was always based on how closely their works corresponded to these views. Z became particularly interested in portraiture. He gave a great deal of attention to one Russian artist, the eighteenth-century portrait painter Rokotov. He would go to the Tretyakov Gallery and spend a long time looking at his pictures, and he would also read books about him. Then he acquired a portrait of a woman by Rokotov or one of his pupils, hung it in a prominent place in his room, and would discuss it with any of his friends who dropped in. In A. V. Lebedev's book *F. S. Rokotov (Studies for a Monograph)* Z marked one characterization of the artist that alerted his interest: '. . . that quivering of the life force, that inspiration which is unique to Rokotov, and which none of his copiers have ever been able to achieve'. This elusive quivering, this duality of expression, the mysterious quality of the look and smile in combination with the classical form of the eighteenth-century portrait: all this attracted Z.

An expression of this interest in painting is the poem 'Portrait', written in 1953. In it are concentrated the poet's impressions of Rokotov's painting of Mme Struyskaya. What attracted him in this painting was the way that the artist had been able to express the inner spiritual essence of a person through her external traits. Z himself liked to look at people's faces and relate them to their character and their personal destiny. Evidence of this is provided by the poems 'In the Cinema', 'The Plain Little Girl', 'Childhood', 'On the Beauty of Human Faces'.

An edition of translations and a publication containing his own poetry that appeared in 1953 served to cheer Z up somewhat. The *Moskva* publishing house issued the *Longer Poems* of Vazha Pshavela and Guramishvili's *Davitiani* in Z's translation, and after a long wait two of Z's poems appeared in No.10 of *Novy Mir* for that year – 'The Thaw' and 'The Wife'. An anthology put together by Goltsev, *In the Hills of Georgia*, included several more of Z's poems, among them two which now appeared in print for the first time ('Night in Pasanauri' and 'The Tower of Gremi'). With S. P. Shchipachov as intermediary, discussions began with the *Soviet Writer* publishing house about the publication of a volume of poems. In a letter dated 7 December 1953, Z reported: 'Recently I handed in a small book of verse to the publishing house.' Unfortunately the discussions led to nothing. Communicating with the director, N. V. Lesyuchevsky, was both difficult and unpleasant, and it was also obvious that the man was deliberately dragging the matter out. Publication in magazines was also for the moment going slowly and awkwardly: people were still afraid to publish Z's poetry. There was only one thing left for it – to get on with his translations.

In 1953 Z spent two periods in Tbilisi. In September he had concluded an agreement there for a new large-scale work – a complete translation of Rustaveli's *The Knight in the Panther Skin*. The various translations of the poem that existed at the time (by Konstantin Balmont, P. Petrenko, G. Tsagareli, and S. Nutzubidze) had not satisfied the experts, while Z had shown by his previous work that he was admirably suited to translate it. In addition he had made an in-depth study of the epic poem in 1937, when he had been engaged in reworking it for young readership.

Work began on 22 November. In the process Z made a closer study of a literal translation, discussed passages of the text that were unclear with the editor of the translation, Chikovani, and read to his close friends and family bits of the Russian version where he thought he had been particularly successful. His declining health proved to be a serious obstacle: the pains in his heart were giving cause for concern, and his sight was getting worse. Z spent the period from 5 April to 26 May 1954 being treated in an eye clinic. At the end of June he travelled to Tbilisi to attend the congress of the Georgian Writers' Union.

On 14 September 1954, Z was laid low for a lengthy period by a serious heart attack. His condition was critical, and he was only saved by injections administered by a doctor from the emergency services who arrived speedily on the scene. He spent two months at home in bed, to begin with motionless, and then he gradually became accustomed to moving again. Both he and Yekaterina followed the doctors' instructions strictly, and kept a careful watch on the course of the illness. Throughout the whole time the sick man was not allowed to do any work, or have any visitors – he was seen only by the doctor and the nurse. Z lay there, and at times strange fantasies and visions took over his thoughts. Later he wrote about this time:

> An angel, guardian of my days,
> Sat in my room with a lamp.
> It was guarding my abode,
> Where I was lying ill.

Worn out by sickness,
Far from my friends,
I slumbered. And one after another
Visions passed before my eyes . . .

One of the first to visit the patient was Shvarts, who arrived from Leningrad. The old friends spent a long time talking together, recalling the days when they had first met, their work on the children's magazines, and their life in Leningrad. A year later Shvarts wrote in his diary:

> I turned up at the Zabolotskys several months after the attack had happened. Z was still bedridden. I began to talk to him as though nothing had happened. I didn't want to upset him by asking about his health, but he got angry with me for not taking things seriously. A middle-aged man going to visit another middle-aged man who was sick shouldn't behave like that. But I managed to smooth over my mistake. Then we got to talking about the latest literary news, and Z suddenly said: 'That's as may be, but our life is already over.' It didn't make me afraid or bitter, but it was as though I had heard the tolling of a bell. I had been reminded that apart from life with its literary gossip there was something else, something else that might be sad, but was also solemn . . . Z decided to get up for dinner. And then something happened that touched me more deeply than any reminder of death. Yekaterina Vasilevna suddenly knelt down in one movement at her husband's feet. She went down on her knees and put on his shoes. And she did it with such ease and such readiness to help him. I was struck by the beauty and softness of this feminine movement. And that was all. I am not saying all this to defend Yekaterina from her husband. He loves her more than any of us, her friends and champions. He wrote the poem 'The Wife', and his strength is in what he writes and not in whatever he says when he's had a little to drink. And he respects his wife well enough. The fact that he would read his poems to her first of all is no joke. Who am I to judge him? They have lived all those years together and brought up their children. There is no one who is nearer to him than her, and no one nearer to her than him.

After seeing in the New Year of 1955 quietly and modestly at home, the Zabolotskys went off to the Bolshevo Sanatorium in the countryside near Moscow. There Z would take regular walks at fixed times along the paths which had been swept clear of snow. He would have unhurried conversations with Kaverin's brother who was following a rest cure at the same sanatorium. The brother was L. A. Zilber, internationally known as the founder of the viral-genetic theory of cancer. Z would also talk to the Jewish poet S. Z. Galkin. He subsequently recalled: 'I

311

heard the kindest words about my poetry from Galkin. He said there was something mysterious in it.'

On his return from the rest home Z took up work again on the translation of *The Knight in the Panther Skin*, only breaking off now and then to write some verse of his own, an article to celebrate the birth of Guramishvili, and an autobiographical sketch 'Early Years'. He finished *The Knight* in the summer in a dacha at Zhavoronki, outside Moscow. In sum total he had translated 6,664 lines of poetry. Despite his illness, and the difficulties of the rhyme scheme – all four lines of a stanza were linked by a single rhyme – this colossal work had been completed in a very short time. The translation still had to be checked and edited in collaboration with Simon Chikovani.

The work with Chikovani was finished by 15 January 1956, and in February the edited translation of *The Knight in the Panther Skin* was finally handed to the publishers at *Goslitizdat*. It came out in a sumptuous edition with illustrations by S. S. Kolubadze in 1957, and was reprinted many times in the years that followed.

This translation of Rustaveli completed a whole series of versions of the Georgian classics by Z, including the works of Orbeliani, Chavchavadze, A. Tsereteli, Vazha Pshavela, D. Guramishvili and now Rustaveli.

IV

In the last three years that fate granted Z there appeared signs of the onset of a fresh period in his life and works. In those years the whole country had become much more politically aware, and had begun to throw off the deadening shackles and blind worship of the dead dictator. Khrushchov's 'Thaw' had begun, stirring spiritual life and hinting at hitherto unthought-of possibilities. Of course, these were only the first faltering steps on the path to democracy, but they created optimism and hope. From 14 to 25 February 1956, the Twentieth Party Congress took place, which condemned the cult of absolute power. In institutions up and down the country, in crowded halls and auditoriums, the semi-secret letter of the Central Committee was read out, horrifying everyone with the facts it revealed about Stalin's cult of personality. Z too heard this letter at a general meeting of writers.

He arrived home excited, with the feeling of having participated in a turning-point of history. Now the time had come to write about the things he had only dared to tell his wife, and occasionally Stepanov. He sat down and wrote 'The Story of My Imprisonment': he wrote with documentary accuracy and concision, simply because he did not want to resurrect the events of those years in more detail. He recalled his 'strange belief', like many of the prisoners then, in 1938, that he was in the hands of the fascists. In 'The Story' he wrote: 'Only now, eighteen years later, has life at last shown me how far we were right, and how far we were mistaken.' He wanted to continue his sombre story with memories of life in the camps, but he did not do so, and merely made excerpts from his camp letters. Then he copied what he had written into a single manuscript, and tucked it away somewhere safe: he still did not feel completely free.

Nevertheless, he decided that it was finally time to apply to be rehabilitated. He wrote to the Committee of State Security:

> After the unmasking of Beria I did not petition the KGB for the reason that I considered it improper to trouble the KGB with my case at a time when there were thousands of cases in need of urgent re-examination, and while those still alive in the camps who had been unjustly sentenced had still to be set free. More than two years have passed since then. Now the time has come for my case too to be re-examined, because, although my sentence has been revoked, I have still so far not been politically rehabilitated, and I am still considered an ex-prisoner who has served his sentence under the law.

This document was never sent off, however, and the poet remained unrehabilitated for the rest of his life. He continued to hope that the KGB would pluck up courage to apologize to the innocent people who had suffered, and rehabilitate them systematically, without anyone having to apply.

Z was interested to see how free he would be to publish his poems now. During the ten years which had passed since his arrival from Karaganda, of the approximately seventy poems which he had written, only twenty-one had appeared either in journals, anthologies, or in his own small volume. And how many had he conceived, but never written down? In 1956 the situation changed markedly. In that year alone thirty of his poems were published, and nine were composed. But there was still a long way to go to complete freedom of publication.

First *Novy Mir* and then the other journals began to telephone Z with requests for poems. Ask they might, but they still only wanted to publish what suited them. What the poet offered did not suit them. Strict official limits still existed. The great temptation arose to give in to the editors' conditions, and to write what they were asking for. After yet another call from a journal or a newspaper Z wrote the poem 'Odysseus and the Sirens', in which he told how the sea-nymphs (the editors) enticed the ancient Greek traveller (the poet) with promises of love and riches. 'If they want to publish it – let them,' said Z, and sent the poem to *Literaturnaya Gazeta*. It was not published. And that was in 1957.

The story of Z's part in the socio-literary anthology *Literaturnaya Moskva* is typical of that time. The miscellany had been arranged at the initiative of Kazakevich, Aliger and Kaverin, with the active support of many of the progressive writers, and was now being published in a new way – without unnecessary bureaucratic interference, but of course not outside the control of the Writers' Union, the publishing house, and the censorship. The first issue was being prepared on the eve of the Twentieth Party Congress. Aliger, who was in charge of the poetry side of the anthology, visited Z and took away several of his poems. Z was considered a 'difficult' poet, and to get his poems through the various 'stages' an ideologically sound 'locomotive' was needed which could pull the other poems behind it. In this case one was found in 'The Petitioners', a poem about some peasants who had come to Lenin seeking the truth. Z once said about it: 'I needed to write a poem about Lenin. I had a long think about what I could say about him without compromising my beliefs. And then I found a subject which had always been close to me – I wrote about the peasants.' The peasants are in fact the same peasants as those in 'The Triumph of Agriculture', but depicted in a real historical situation. In a poem written after the Twentieth Party Congress and entitled 'Somewhere in a Field near Magadan' they are shown in a camp in the savage frosts of Kolyma, where they are freezing to death as they try to escape 'the soldiers, their metallic throats, and the marauding bands of thieves'. The theme of the peasantry is reflected in only a few of Z's works, but it had been active in his consciousness ever since childhood.

Among the poems intended for the anthology were 'Make a little space for me, starling' and 'In the Cinema', and these soon caused some difficulties. The following lines in the first one caused objections:

> He who shouts in the spring,
> Will be deprived of his voice by summer.

This was, of course, an indirect reference to the poet's own fate, and an affirmation (impermissible at that time) that the free expression of his own ideas was not something that should be punished, in other words a direct reference to the absence of freedom of speech. Such lines could not get past without being noticed, if only by the director of the publishing house, Kotov, who was in overall charge of the anthology. When he was approached by the editors Z began to ask himself how he could save the poem. On a torn-off sheet from a calendar he rapidly jotted down:

> He who gave no voice when he was young,
> Will remain without a voice to this day.

This version was worse than the first one in all respects, and in the end the editorial team succeeded in preserving the original lines.

Matters were worse still in the case of 'In the Cinema'.

On one particular occasion, as long ago as 1954, Z, Yekaterina, and Vasily Grossman had gone for a break to the park near the Dynamo Stadium, and after their walk they went to the cinema under the stands around the edge of the football pitch. Before the programme began there was a performance in the foyer by a comic wearing a loud brown suit. But neither this crude joker, nor the film (it was apparently called 'The Robot') interested Z. His attention was caught by a sad, tired-looking woman in the crowd, and he pointed her out to his companions. After just a few days he wrote the poem 'In the Cinema'. What was bad about it from the point of view of the 'authorities' was the sceptical attitude towards mass art, the image of the woman worn out by her hard life, and especially the reference to the fate of her husband, presumably a prisoner.

> Why is he not with you?
> Can it be that he fell in battle,
> Or can it be that, torn from his home by fate,
> He is perishing in a distant place?

The assumption that her husband was 'perishing in a distant place' was not acceptable, and, on his way to a meeting with the editors, Z tried to think of what else he could write: 'he had left his family for ever', 'he had not come back to his family', 'he forgets his woman', or 'he was wandering somewhere far away'. None of these worked, the original line was the only authentic one. As a result this poem did not appear in either the first or the second volume of *Literaturnaya Moskva*. About the second collection Kaverin writes: 'At an all-night session at *Goslitizdat* we managed to get agreement to four poems. For the fifth – 'In the Cinema' – we could do nothing.'

This story demonstrates how difficult it was at the time to publish poetry, and how laughably absurd, by today's standards, were the nit-picking objections raised to writers. All the same, in the two volumes of *Literaturnaya Moskva* eleven of Z's poems were published, alongside other daring publications: this was no mean achievement by the editorial team. The powers that be did not hesitate long – on instructions from the highest level the third volume did not appear. In the mean time the Khrushchov 'Thaw' was continuing, and the poem 'In the Cinema' was published without the slightest hitch in Issue No. 7 of *Oktyabr* in 1956, while for the poem 'Somewhere in a Field near Magadan' the thaw was still apparently not warm enough – it never appeared during the author's lifetime.

Z went on thinking about his new book, but it had got stuck in *Soviet Writer*, and Z did not feel like taking up the matter with the director of the publishing house, Lesyuchevsky. And so, in March 1956, when the general situation had improved, a typed version of the book was submitted to the *Khudozhestvennaya literatura* publishing house, where everything progressed without any particular difficulty. The book appeared in May 1957. This fourth collection to appear in Z's lifetime contained sixty-four poems from the 1930s to 1950s, selected translations of Old German and modern Georgian poets, and the *Igor Tale*. There had never before been a book of Z's works which was so comprehensive in scope. It was a genuine achievement and brought great joy to the writer. Letters began to arrive from friends and from unknown readers, lovers of poetry.

Marina Chukovskaya recalls:

> I remember him coming to see Korney Chukovsky in Peredelkino in 1957. He was reserved and inscrutable and dressed in black. With great ceremony he handed Korney his newly published little book of poems. He sat there very stiffly, for as long as was decent, and then departed. Then we began to read it . . . and we could not tear ourselves away. When we read 'The Cranes' Korney wept.

Z was well aware of all the good that Chukovsky had done him by having his case re-examined in 1939–40, and by looking after his wife during the difficult years that followed. It was as though he was reaffirming with his book that all the effort had been worth while, not only as far as he was concerned, but for Russian literature as a whole. In response to being presented with the book Chukovsky wrote enthusiastically to this poet who had not been broken by all the criticism levelled at him:

> I am writing to you with the sort of humble respect with which I would have written to Tyutchev or Derzhavin. I myself have no doubt that the author of 'The Cranes', 'The Swan', 'Make a Little Space for Me, Starling', 'The Unlucky One', 'The Actress', 'Human Faces', 'Morning', 'The Plain Little Girl' and 'I do not seek harmony in nature' is a truly great poet whose work will sooner or later cause Soviet literature (perhaps against its will) to be proud of it as one of the greatest of its

achievements. There may be those among us now who will consider my words rash or simply mistaken, but I will vouch for them with all my seventy years' experience as a reader.

From 1956 on Z's name began to appear more and more often in critical literature. *Literaturnaya Gazeta* for 20 September 1956 contained an article by A. Marchenko entitled 'A Demanding Craftsman' – this was the first serious work of criticism about his work for many years. The 1957 book was also discussed in articles by A. Urban, D. Maksimov, and A. Makedonov. An interesting evaluation of these reviews was supplied by one of the poet's readers, a long-time admirer of his work, the metal-worker A. K. Krutetsky. He had been corresponding with Z since 1954. On 20 September, having just read *Literaturnaya Gazeta*, he reached for his pen:

> Greetings, dear and respected Nikolay Alekseyevich!
> I rejoice at the publication of the article 'A Demanding Craftsman'. This article will make many readers who love good poetry look more closely at your work, and think about the similes and the images. That in itself is good . . . But now that I have read Marchenko's article I am very dissatisfied. He calls you a demanding craftsman. But wasn't that crystal clear twenty-five years ago? In the past critics knew how to say strong words about strong people and how to draw them to the attention of the crowd. Marchenko concludes the article by saying: 'Z's poetry, which is difficult to characterize by a single motif or a single melody, is a clear example of the living richness and multi-faceted nature of a genuine talent.' That's good. Correct. Clear to all. But this 'difficult to characterize' in itself requires definition and exploration by today's critics. That's what today's reader of your poems wants to hear from the critics, and he's not hearing it. A large, comprehensive, up-to-date monograph is needed. It's you who in however many years will come to represent our times, even if you don't write anything more. Don't throw my letter away, put it somewhere safe. What I am saying is true, and it will be interesting to look at it in, say, a few years' time.

And that is just what Z did – he placed this letter, and all the subsequent ones from Krutetsky, in an ornamental box made of Karelian birch which he kept specially for the more interesting correspondence from readers and friends. He never once met Krutetsky, but the letters were redolent with sympathy and trust. He was pleased to know that there was someone who understood him properly and who felt poetry deeply.

A year later Krutetsky again read a critic's article about Z, and on 3 March 1958 wrote to him:

I did not like Maksimov's article about your work, despite the fact that there is a lot in it which is true. When you read the article you felt all the while that the critic would like to praise you as you deserve . . . but somehow he's scared, and he keeps looking over his shoulder all the time in case he gets told off for doing so . . .

Z recalled how Maksimov had once visited him in his humble room on Konnaya Street in Leningrad, and he wrote back giving his opinion of the worker-writer's observation:

As far as the article about me is concerned, I liked it up to certain point. The scissors have certainly been at work on it. The result is to make it seem as though two people had written the thing. The first wrote the main section, and when you read that I come over as a fool, and the other wrote the supplementary bits, and according to them I'm virtually a genius. It's a most peculiar article!

I would say two things to the writer of the first section. First – about the 'coldness'. A poem is like a human being; it has a face, a mind and a heart. If the human being is not a savage or a fool, his face is more or less always in repose. The face of a poem should likewise be reposeful. The intelligent reader is perfectly capable of seeing the interplay of mind and heart behind the cover of external calm. I am banking on the intelligent reader. I don't want to be over-familiar with him: I respect him too much.

Second – on the subject of poems like 'The Old Actress'. Here undoubtedly, some of what the writer says is true. But I realized this as early as last year, and I've done something about it.

In September 1956 Z visited Leningrad for the only time after his arrest. Yekaterina and he were met at the station by the Gitoviches and taken off to the Hotel Yevropeyskaya. From there they all set off on foot across Mikhaylovsky Square and along Rakov Street as far as the little bridge over the Griboyedov Canal. How many bitter-sweet memories and how many unfulfilled hopes were linked with these places! Z went in through the main door of house No. 9 and up the same staircase down which he had been led eighteen years before by the investigator and his assistant. Then he went along the corridor to the door of his old apartment. There he was struck by the specially designed mailbox that he had once bought, still hanging there, for all the world as though nothing had happened. It was different from all the other boxes, and he recognized it at once. Turning to Silva Gitovich who was with him, he exclaimed: 'Look! How many years is it? God knows what has happened in all that time – wars, the deaths of millions, changes of government, and there's my old mailbox, still hanging on the door! You see how things manage to survive . . .'

Then the Zabolotskys and the Gitoviches took a taxi and spent a long time driving round the city. Z was miserable, and to drown the anguish he was feeling he and Gitovich went and bought several bottles of wine. They dropped Yekaterina at her sister's house on Kirov Prospect, and drove off in the car. Silva Gitovich writes:

> Passing from hand to hand, gradually the bottle emptied, and Z grew more and more thoughtful and sad. The car drove round and round the embankments and streets of Leningrad, while he sat there with unseeing eyes, carefully nursing the opened bottle on his lap. Past him floated houses, embankments, bridges, and all the while he was talking, in a muffled voice, as though speaking to himself, saying that the general laws of creativity are the same for the different forms of art, whether it be poetry, painting or music; that the testing of human hearts by harmony is not a peaceful activity, that happiness and love are always a trial, always a mystery.

Next day Z read to his friends a poem which he had written that summer at Peredelkino entitled 'Mars in Opposition', in which the problem of Stalin's personality cult was developed to become a general denial of reason without emotion. Subsequently, after the appearance of the tenth number of *Novy Mir* for that year which contained the poem, Z received a number of telegrams expressing gratitude from Leningrad writers – from Gitovich and those who shared his views. After 'Mars in Opposition' he read 'The Thistle' – a poem describing the growing difficulties he was having at the time in his relationship with his wife. It ends with the following lines:

> I dreamt of a prison tower
> And a grating, black as night,
> Behind it sat a fabulous bird,
> One that could not be helped by anyone.
> But it must be that I too live badly,
> For I have not the power to help it.
> And a wall of thistles
> Rises up between me and my joy.
> A thorn, like a wedge, has pierced
> My heart, and now for the last time
> I see the sad and beautiful light
> From its inextinguishable eyes.

Later a further nine poems were joined to this one, and together they formed the cycle 'Last Love'.*

---

* For full translations of 'The Thistle' and 'Meeting' from this cycle, see pp.356–8. The title 'Last Love' comes from Fyodor Tyutchev [Ed.].

After the distressing days they had spent in Leningrad the Zabolotskys went to Gurzuf to visit the Tomashevskys. Irina Tomashevskaya and her two small grandchildren, Masha and Nastya, were no longer living in the house where the Zabolotskys had stayed in 1949, but had moved to one on the hillside facing the sea, looking out over Artek. Despite the fact that it was October the weather was warm. The sheltered garden, going down in terraces from the house to the road, the view of the sea and the cliffs of Aladara, the mountain slopes in their autumn colours, all this miraculously calmed and soothed their troubled minds and bodies. Influenced by the Crimea in the autumn, and by the expanse of sea stretching away in front of the Tomashevskys' house, Z wrote 'Gurzuf by Night' and 'Over the Sea'.

Z spent virtually the whole time on the verandah, drinking wine, looking at the sea through binoculars, and listening to music, putting his favourite records on the gramophone one after the other. The neighbourhood resounded to the strains of Ravel's *Bolero*, its rapidly quickening tempo creating an atmosphere of uncontrollable alarm and doom. Z was particularly fond of this piece in his last years, normally listening to it through several times in succession. But then he would put on some of Yves Montand's songs, and everything would become calm again.

On one occasion, when their son arrived in Gurzuf, Z and Yekaterina set off on a walk with him along a path high above the sea, which led by way of the Nikitsky Garden to Yalta. In his dark hat, with his coat thrown over his arm, leaning on a stick, Z walked slowly along, unhappy about something. He soon got tired and announced that he did not want to walk any further. All three sat down to rest amongst the Crimean pines and the thickly growing juniper bushes. These shapely junipers with their dark violet-blue, sappy berries stuck in Z's mind, and much later, in Moscow, living for a while apart from his wife, he was to write:

> In a dream I saw a juniper bush,
> From afar I heard the metallic crunch,
> I caught the resonant sound of the amethyst berries,
> And in my dream, in the silence, it pleased me . . .
>
> In the golden heavens beyond my window
> One after another the clouds floated by,
> Flying past my little garden, lifeless and empty.
> May God forgive you, juniper bush!

Another trip which the three of them took, by speedboat along the shore of the Crimea to where the Pushkin Grotto gaped among the cliffs, provided the background for the poem 'A Sea Voyage'.

Husband and wife returned separately to Moscow on 18 and 19 October. A sad time of discord had come upon their relationship. It was a strange falling-out: both were unhappy apart from each other, but stubbornly attempted to create some other kind of life with other people. Soon both understood that no good could come of it: too much bound them together, their love had undergone too many difficult tests in the past, they were too old not to go on loving each other.

But at that time – the end of October 1956 – relations between them reached a critical point. Z could not reconcile himself with the deep mutual attraction that had existed for some time already between Grossman and Yekaterina. Living in adjoining blocks on Begovaya Street, the Zabolotskys and the Grossmans had quickly become close enough to be in and out of each others' homes all the time: the wives and children made friends, while Z and Grossman found it most interesting to get to know each other. In truth, though, their relationship was always complicated. Conversations with Grossman used to head towards the very topic that exacerbated Z's old inner wounds and disrupted the hard-won balance he needed in life and in his poetic work: he used to refuse to continue conversations of such a nature. Yekaterina, though she well understood her husband's state and the reasons for his behaviour, could still not remain indifferent to Grossman's strength of mind, talent and charm as a man. His nature demanded social action, and in the circumstances of unceasing ideological control and officially inspired anti-Semitism of the late 1940s and early 1950s he often found himself in awkward situations. At such moments he was particularly touched by Yekaterina's innate sensitivity and sympathy, her readiness to come to his help every time he needed moral support. Their relations were for a long time limited to family gatherings, but then they sometimes started to take walks together in the Neskuchny Park or on the city streets. Z saw that Grossman's friendship with his wife was growing into a deeper feeling. At first, sure of her devotion to him, he was not much worried, but evidently began to realize in the first months of 1956 that danger was threatening him from the very quarter he least expected. His wife admitted that she was in love with Grossman. Z demanded that she should stop meeting him, but this proved not to be easy. Normally obedient to his will, Yekaterina showed firmness and said that there was nothing reprehensible in her relations with Grossman, and she could not break them off.

The sort of ambiguous, ill-defined situation that had arisen was intolerable for Z. Finally, after some tough talking in the Crimea, he announced on their return to Moscow that he could not live in that way and that they must get divorced. Yekaterina could go off to Grossman, and he would find another wife. Stubbornly, deadening his inner pain with wine, he began to put his plan for straightening out family life into effect. On 28 October he rang up a young, beautiful woman, Natalya Roskina, who moved in literary circles but whom he hardly knew, and asked for a meeting. As yet he knew nothing about her except that she liked his poems. The second time they met, in a restaurant, he made her the proposal to become his wife. Roskina, who was inclined to make bold decisions, agreed without much pondering, and this saved Z from full-scale despair and possibly fatal actions.

Z lived for two or three weeks with Roskina in her small room in a communal flat. Yekaterina and the children remained on Begovaya Street; however, soon afterwards she and Grossman, who had left his family, took a room together in the suburb of Maryina Roshcha. A few months later they moved to a room Grossman obtained on Lomonosov Prospect, where he continued to write his major novel *Life and Fate*.

On 19 November Z and Roskina, declaring themselves man and wife (there was no official divorce or wedding), left to stay at the Artists' House at Maleyevka. At first this beautiful and interesting woman captivated Z and to some extent diverted him from sombre thoughts. But he wanted to exchange his beloved wife not for a lover but for another wife, with a view to organizing his life and work in his previous pattern. It soon became obvious that such a simple resolution of his family troubles was impossible. To begin with, his inner commitment to his new wife was hindered by his continual yearning for Yekaterina. Roskina once told Z's son: 'I'm sorry for Nikolay, but can't do much for him, since he spends all his time thinking about Yekaterina.'

Apart from that Z was wary of excessive openness, sociability and, above all, sharp anti-Soviet utterances not just among friends but in the presence of outsiders. With youthful enthusiasm Roskina tried to explain to him things he very well knew but preferred not to talk about. Later Z confessed to Yekaterina that at one time he had even speculated that Roskina was a Security Service informer, but subsequently realized he was mistaken. All these misunderstandings did not exclude heart-to-heart, confiding talks between the poet and the clearly sympathetic young woman. At such moments of frankness Z talked about his past, his literary enthusiasms and his attitude towards his own work. Recollecting such conversations, Roskina wrote these significant words about him:

322

It would have been hard, in my view, to hurt Z more than by either reproaching him or praising him for abandoning the poetic strivings of his youth. It was precisely those strivings and those years when he first proclaimed his poetic personality that remained the best years in his memory. He treasured them boundlessly; refraining from judgements about 'political matters', distancing himself from them in every way, he consciously constructed his spiritual world on the reliability and firmness of his poetic ideals. His strength, his constancy, his very self resided in this. His boldness (he was daring and fearfully proud), his efforts to do everything he did in a big way, naturally enthused him, and he invested much of his soul in his poetic work – including his translations – after his return from camp. Once he told me he realized that he could express everything that he had earlier expressed in sharply individualistic manner through the classical forms to which he had recourse in those later years.

Further on Roskina expressed doubt as to the spontaneity and naturalness of Z's creative evolution: 'I feel that all this was merely self-consolation in that epoch, unprecedented in the world of history of poetry, when the Party and government dictated all forms of the poet's existence, including poetic ones.'

All the same Z could not last out the entire stay that he and Roskina had arranged at Maleyevka. Their disagreements and 'dissimilarity of character' led to a complete break. On 8 December Z returned home alone, attempted to drown his sorrows in wine and after a couple of days went off again, probably to the Artists' House at Golitsyno, forbidding his children to tell Roskina where he was. Subsequently, after 15 December, there were one or two more attempts to patch up relations with her. She even lived with her little daughter in the flat on Begovaya Street for a short time. But in early February 1957 they finally parted. To his young not-quite-wife Z dedicated the tender-tragic poem 'Recognition', ending thus:

> What is augmented will not be diminished,
> What won't be realized will be forgotten . . .
> Why are you in tears, my beauty?
> Or do I just imagine it?

As he parted with the illusory hope of founding a new family, Z immersed himself in work, began to drink less, and after talking with Yekaterina became convinced that after a time she would return to him and everything would be forgiven.

To restore their fractured life together was not easy, but four months after their break, in March 1957, the slow and gradual process of reconciliation began. At the end of May their son Nikita wrote in a letter to Tomashevskaya: 'No changes at home. Mummy often comes and visits us, everything has now settled down and is calm.' Meanwhile Z wrote at about the same time in his poem 'Meeting':*

> As a rusty door-hinge opens,
> With difficulty and an effort – forgetting about the past,
> She, my unawaited one, now
> Opened her face towards me.
> And light poured – not light, but a whole sheaf
> Of living rays, – not a sheaf, but a whole conglomeration
> Of spring and joy, and, eternal misanthrope,
> I was confused . . .

At the end of June Z went off with his daughter for just over two months to Tarusa. His son, by now a postgraduate student, was working in the city.

In 1957 Z's creative activity reached its highest pitch – his file of finished work contained thirty-three new poems, twenty-four of which he included in his new volume. The following, final year of the poet's life was also reasonably productive; it brought fifteen more poems, and also 5,000 lines of translation of Serbian epic poetry. The themes of Z's last poems were marked by a great deal of variety: they reflected personal experiences, a psychologically rich landscape, portraits of people, social motifs and an intertwining of history and contemporary life.

V

In 1957 it so happened that some Italian poets invited a group of Soviet poets to visit them in Italy, and Z was among their number. The Writers' Union had tried to include someone else in the delegation, someone 'more deserving of a trip abroad', but the Italians had been insistent: they knew and esteemed Z, principally for his early poetry, and it was he whom they wanted to take part in the discussions. Surkov, the head of the Writers' Union, talked over the situation with Z and even suggested that he take *Columns* with him. He said that with a little editing it might even be possible to republish these early poems. Z interpreted this conversation as a kind of political rehabilitation – after all, he had been allowed a trip abroad, the other side of the Iron Curtain, for a first meeting with Italian poets, and he was being promised publication of *Columns*! Both were beyond his wildest dreams.

* Full translation on pp.357–8.

Z had previously made some minor alterations to the poems of the period 1926–8, but now he considered a more fundamental revision of the text was needed. This he proceeded to undertake, and it was not always in line with his original intentions. As a result, some of the unity of the composition was lost, which distorted the thought of the poem, and in some cases the second variant was clearly inferior to the original. A number of poems from the 1930s were also subjected to reworking by the author: these included 'The Crowning with Fruits', 'Morning Song', and 'Night Garden'. It is hard to determine when the alterations were made on genuine literary-aesthetic grounds, when they were made because the writer's taste had changed, and when they were made under the influence of a conscious or unconscious 'internal editor', that is for reasons of a non-literary nature. Z dearly wanted to see these poems published together in a single volume with his later works. He valued his early verse highly, a fact he now spoke about openly. He even found pleasure in reading poems from the twenties and thirties to his friends.

Yet, overjoyed as he was by the bold imagery of his early poems, he felt at the same time that if they were pruned of some of their unnecessary mannerisms and extreme 'novelty' it would help them to survive and to be successful with future generations. In this respect the ideas that he had underlined in Delacroix's *Diary* were specially important to him:

> . . . What is needed is a real rejection of vanity so as to dare to be simple, if, of course, we have the strength to be so: the proof of this, even with the greatest of masters, is that they nearly always begin with over-indulgence! . . . In their youth, when there are almost too many opportunities in front of them, they give themselves up to floweriness and witticisms . . . They want to shine, rather than move people, so that the artist should get the praise, rather than those he depicts; they think they are insubstantial when they are in fact touching and transparent. . . A mannered style pleases a public that is sated, and consequently hungry for more novelties; but such a style means that the works of these artists, inspired, but yet deceived by a false novelty, which they think they have introduced into art, *become out-of-date unusually quickly.*

These words correspond fairly closely with Z's own views, not only on his own creative destiny, but on that of a large number of other writers and poets. He was fond of discovering examples in the history of literature of the short-lived nature of works by writers who could not or would not overcome the misuse of experimentations in form.

He also focused his attention on some of Delacroix's thoughts in another direction:

The man who sits down and reads through a manuscript with a pen in his hand, making corrections in it, has become to a certain extent a different person from the one who first put it all down fresh on the page.

Experience teaches us two things: *first – we have to do a lot of correcting; second – we should not correct too much . . .*

To show bravery when we risk compromising our past is a sign of great strength.

It can well be imagined that as he went back to his poems of the twenties and thirties and made significant changes to them, Z was aware what a risk and what a sacrifice he had undertaken. True, not all the works of the Leningrad period were subject to such revision. From the collection which he had made in 1932 ('Poems 1926–1932') no more than a third of the poems and the long work 'The Triumph of Agriculture' were subjected to any significant revision.

The group of poets that set off for Italy included, in addition to Z, Surkov as group leader, Mikola Bazhan, Vera Inber, Mikhail Isakovsky, Leonid Martynov, Aleksandr Prokofyev, Boris Slutsky, Sergey Smirnov and Aleksandr Tvardovsky. The delegation was accompanied by a specialist in Italian literature, G. S. Breitburd. All of them, with the exception of Z and Slutsky, flew to Rome. Because of the bad state of Z's heart the doctor had recommended him to go by train, and Slutsky, who was a genuine admirer of his work, had volunteered to travel with him so that he should not be alone on his first trip abroad. The two poets had become close friends in 1956 when they had both appeared on television as contributors to the miscellany *Literaturnaya Moskva*.

In his memoir sketch Slutsky described how he and Z sat in the Writers' Union and waited for the car that was to take them to the station. Z wanted to smoke, but in his rush and excitement he had left his cigarettes at home. 'A little ape-like man came into the room,' Slutsky writes:

> He didn't come, so much as slink, into the room, as though he was looking for someone. Z rushed up to him and asked him for a cigarette, at which the newcomer said cheerfully: 'But of course, Nikolay Alekseyevich', and then left the room. Z sat down, took one or two draws on the cigarette and, as he savoured them, asked: 'Who was that then, the fellow with the cigarettes?'
> I answered: 'Yermilov.'
> Z threw the cigarette to the ground, trod it out, and grimaced in anger.

Right to the end of his life he never forgave those who had been directly or indirectly responsible for what happened to him. He remembered the malicious article by Yermilov in *Pravda* in 1933 that had seriously jeopardized his standing in literature and in life.

They arrived in Rome on 11 October, after the other members of the delegation, when the meetings with the Italian writers there were already over. They all left for Florence on the same day. There Z spoke at a meeting discussing optimism and pessimism in poetry.* He genuinely considered himself an optimist, and said so in his speech, but the Italian writers interpreted this as a gesture in the direction of official Soviet propaganda, and suspected him of being partisan and insincere. This was what A. M. Ripellino wrote later, though in general he admired Z greatly, both as a poet and a person. It was hard for the Italian writers to understand that his optimism was not on a social level, had nothing in common with officially-manufactured optimism, and was based on his own natural-philosophical views. In the social field he was certainly not an optimist, and in those years he did not always keep his inner thoughts concealed, and spoke openly about Stalin's socialism as a police state. Natalya Roskina recalls that in a moment of 'mental relaxation' he once said to her: 'I am only a poet, and I can judge only by poetry. I don't know, maybe socialism really is useful for techno-logical things – but as far as art is concerned, it's the kiss of death.'

Naturally, when he was in the company of officials, and especially when he was in Italy, he would not allow himself to say anything of the kind. He was well aware that other members of the delegation were not being completely frank either. Consequently Z did not find the discussions themselves particularly interesting, though, of course, he was interested to meet such important writers as Ripellino, Strada, Levi, Ungaretti and Quasimodo, to find out about Western poetry, and to realize that in Italy, as Slutsky put it, of all the Soviet poets in the delegation he was the least unknown.

Among the Italians he had more to do with the professor and poet Ripellino than with the others. He even made him a present of the copy of *Columns* he had brought with him, containing the manuscript revisions he had made recently. Later Ripellino was to write that Z looked more like a clerk or a chemist than a poet. This upset Z, and he said to Slutsky: 'Well, he looks like a hairdresser.' But he said it without malice, in his characteristic joking and ironic way. Soon afterwards, when Ripellino visited the Soviet Union, Z entertained him in Moscow, and gave him Teliani to drink. The meeting was an interesting one, happy and convivial. One of the themes they discussed was the question

---

* Extracts from the notes probably intended for lectures in Italy constitute the Epigraph to this volume on pp.xix–xx [Ed.].

of translating poetry between Italian and Russian. Z promised to translate some poems that appealed to him by Ripellino. In fact soon after Z's death a splendid edition of his own poetry appeared in Italy, translated by the specialist in Russian literature Vittorio Strada.

What affected Z most in Italy was a visit to the Uffizi Gallery. He spent several hours looking at the Botticellis, which particularly attracted him because of the way the faces had been painted. In the poet's notebook, among his other notes, is a short *aide-mémoire* of the details that struck him as particularly characteristic of the artist:

> The faces of Botticelli are like grapes . . . [there follows a list of five of the artist's paintings]. The secret is in the corners of the lips. They are deeply drawn, soft and indistinct. The eyebrows are thinly drawn and placed high on the face. The eyes have a wonderful purity and are either wide open or lowered. The locks of golden curls are brushed back. The hands and fingers are long and white. A diamond crown. The face of the Madonna has a thoughtful tenderness and a slightly suffering submissiveness to fate. The background is a Tuscan scene.

As we can see, what attracted the poet in Botticelli's works was a similarity (not in the manner of execution, but in essence) with the portraits of Rokotov. Here were the same 'portents of the inconstant soul', 'mystery in the corners of the lips', 'thoughtful softness', and 'suffering submissiveness to fate' that were so important to him in the external appearance of the people he observed.

When he got back to Moscow Z was full of his enthusiastic reactions to the paintings by the great Italian artist. It was destined to be his last artistic enthusiasm. He brought back from Italy several volumes of his favourite painters: Botticelli, Brueghel, Matisse, Cézanne, Monet and Chagall.

After Florence Z visited some of the cities and smaller towns of Italy, Bologna, Ravenna, Trieste, Venice and Modena. In Venice, when there was only an hour or two left before their departure, both he and Slutsky had to go to the police to have their passports stamped. The Russian guests had already been shown the main waterway of the Grand Canal and the view of the city from the Lagoon, but Z wanted to have another trip along the narrow side-streets, so that he could feel the atmosphere of Venice. He stopped Slutsky, and held out his passport: 'Boris, you go to the police on your own. You'll come to Italy again and go on a gondola. But this is the last chance for me.' He climbed into the gondola with surprising agility, and as they floated away he turned and gave a happy and slightly crafty smile. He thought he had cheated fate.

Unfortunately the two of his poems that are actually set in Venice ('Incident on the Grand Canal' and 'Venice') contain passages which pay lip-service to the official line – they mention the city's slums, the poverty, the revolt of the poor against the rich and the power of the foreign bosses. Z thought he had to write about Italy in this way, as though to justify his inclusion in a representative delegation abroad. After both poems had appeared in *Literaturnaya Gazeta* of 18 January 1958, they were rejected by the author, and he never included them in the main body of his work. This contained only one Italian poem – 'At the tomb of Dante' – about a visit Z made to the grave of the writer of the *Divina Commedia*, of which he was very fond.

The trip abroad did much for Z. He reacted powerfully to the free air of the beautiful countryside of Italy, and it was as though his own spirit became charged with it. His friends and relatives were struck by the change that took place in him as a result of the visit. He forgot all his adversities, physical and mental. He was energetic and cheerful, moved around quickly, fussed about giving the porter orders on the station in Moscow, carried his own case, and was bright and jocular when he introduced his son to Tvardovsky, who had arrived on the same train. Everything in life seemed to him to be about to fall into place – normal family life would be resumed, his health would get better, and above all he would now be able to write his poems freely, without being afraid of persecution and without shackling himself with any sense of caution. His book had come out, his poetry was beginning to appear in the journals, and an appreciative readership had grown up. If only his heart did not let him down and allowed him to go on for perhaps another five years. How much he would be able to achieve if he went on working like he was now! To Krutetsky he wrote: 'We understand each other, my heart and I. It knows that I won't spare it, and I hope that its peasant origins will help it to survive a little longer.'

There was now a very real hope that in two or three years' time a book could be published containing the poems from the 1920s. In the safety of his home Z would say about those in power at the time: 'They are fools not to recognize me, they would get a lot out of publishing my poetry.' To his son he said one day: 'I shall not be here, but you wait and see, in eight or so years' time they'll start to publish me widely.'

In March 1958 there was a ten-day festival of Georgian literature and art which effectively seemed to sum up Z's translations of Georgian classical poetry. To Krutetsky he confided:

> I am absolutely snowed under with work – that's why I haven't written to you for some time. To mark the festival of Georgian art the *Iskusstvo* publishing house here is issuing under the *Zarya Vostoka* imprint a two-volume edition of my translations of Georgian classics. There's a great pile of proof-correcting, work that I can't entrust to anyone else.

Z was agitated in case the edition would not be ready in time. In the event there *was* something to show the Georgians: the proof copy of the first of the two volumes of *Georgian Classical Poetry, translated by N. Zabolotsky* appeared on 19 March, just before the literary evenings called to celebrate the festival, and by 30 March Z was signing author's complimentary copies of the first print run.

Z was very happy to have finished this arduous project, begun as long ago as the years before his arrest: he considered it worthy of his vocation. As early as February 1957 he had drawn up a plan for a three- or four-volume edition of his collected works, which he hoped would some time or other see the light of day: the first volume contained *Columns*, the long poems, and the shorter verse; the second and third, translations of the Georgian classics; and the fourth, miscellaneous works. From this it can be seen how highly he rated his Georgian translations, placing them immediately after his own poems.

While the festival celebrations were on, Z went to a Georgian opera, visited an exhibition of Georgian paintings, took part in discussions of poetry, and entertained Georgian guests. On 22 March, in the Hall of Columns, he gave a formal reading of part of his translation of Rustaveli:

Is there anyone more despicable than the coward, worn out by the fight,
Who is flustered and hesitates, faced with death?
How is he any better than the weak spider – this doughty warrior?
Better to be proud of fame, than of any other gain.

Through ravines and through mountains Death can fly in a moment.
Cowards and heroes – all are swept off in an instant.
Only the grave awaits children and dotards alike.
Better a glorious end, than a shameful escape!

Not many of the audience that day realized that in these lines the poet was proclaiming his own attitude to the philistine way of looking at death, and his belief in a life that was lived honourably and crowned with fame. It is worth noting that these lines of verse are the only recording of Z's voice to have survived.

During the course of the celebrations Z received the Order of Red Labour for his translation work. He was pleased at this rare token of official recognition, realizing that every such sign bolstered his social defences. He thanked the Georgians who had recommended him for the award, and, as was the time-honoured custom, he marked the event at a little celebration with his friends in his flat on Begovaya Street. But he was far from thinking that the award could in any way compensate for all the misfortunes and injustices he had suffered in his life. While he was in bed, when his heart troubles were at their worst, he asked

Yekaterina for the photograph of himself wearing his medal. He cut out the bit containing the medal, and asked for the scraps of paper to be thrown away. By an irony of fate the main window at the photographer's was decorated with the same photograph for some time after the poet's death. That was just what he had feared. He wanted his image for posterity to be as it really was: without all the vanities of life and petty ambition.

As we have already mentioned, Z spent the summer of 1957 at Tarusa on the Oka, a hundred kilometres from Moscow. He lived there during the summer of 1958 as well. He loved this tiny little town with its grass-grown streets and its rustic way of life. The high banks of the full-flowing river, the stands of birch all around, the herds of cows on the water-meadows of the Oka – all these features of life in central Russia had been near and dear to him since childhood. He had come to Tarusa on the advice of Antal and Agnessa Hidas. He had first met them in 1946, and he had now got to know them more closely in the House of Creativity in Dubulti. It was there on the coast near Riga, as he walked along the beach in the evening with Hidas, that he had seen a happy sign – an emerald-green ray of the setting sun suddenly burst through the clouds. In Tarusa they both remembered this vision, and Z thought that there would hardly be enough of his life left to benefit from this portent of happiness. His poem 'The Green Ray' ends with the lines:

> A ray, like emerald,
> A key to golden happiness –
> I shall reach it yet,
> My pale green ray.
>
> But the bastions grow pale
> The towers fall far off,
> The green ray fades,
> Far from the earth.
>
> Only he who is young in spirit,
> Hungry in body and powerful,
> Will reach the cloud-clapped city
> And grasp the green ray!

The Hidases rented a house for Z on Karl Liebknecht Street, at no. 36. The accommodation consisted of two rooms and a verandah overlooking a courtyard crowded with chickens and geese. Above the fence, beyond the gardens and the green roofs, could be seen the Oka. Under the porch lived a wise old dog with a rough, wiry coat and a little beard.

All this pleased Z, and he paid twice the sum asked, on condition that the place was not let to any of the other holiday-makers. As a result, when Chekmazov and Favorskaya, two artists who had rented the rooms previously, turned up, there was nowhere for them to stay. The problem was solved to everyone's satisfaction. The Chekmazovs were helped to find another house, and in them Z acquired two new and well-disposed acquaintances. Chekmazov later painted a portrait of Z's daughter Natasha, and it is he who is referred to in the poem 'September': ' In rich red and gold like fire, paint this girl for me.' Discarding his earlier sense of caution, Z willingly read the Chekmazovs poems from *Columns* (he was possibly even then thinking of reworking them).

Z lived in Tarusa together with his daughter, and almost every day when he had finished work he would meet the Hidases and the Chekmazovs. He also visited Paustovsky a couple of times and met other writers who were there. The friendship with the Hidases was the closest. They would meet and go for a walk in the afternoon, around five. The Hidases had hired a boat, and in the early days they invited Z and his daughter to go out on the Oka with them. One day, when they had all got in and the boat was cast off from the shore it was found to have a leak, and the bottom started to fill with water. The leak was not a serious one, but they were all surprised by Z's strange reaction to it; he went deathly white and, hardly able to suppress his panic, begged them to row back to the shore. He could not begin to explain that out on the wide river he had suddenly been reminded of the stormy waters of the Amur and the barge overcrowded with prisoners. And he recalled his terror in the face of the senseless cruelty of the camp administration, which had caused one of these barges to sink. He took no further part in their trips on the river, and simply sat on a bench on the high bank of the Oka and gazed after the boat as it went off into the distance. Afterwards he would play dominoes with the Hidases, joking and acting the fool, or he would stroll, deep in conversation with them, through the neighbouring countryside. Hidas told Z how, after the events of 1956, he had returned home to Hungary, and how the liberation movement there had been savagely crushed with the aid of the Soviet Army, and what a dreadful thing it had been for him to have to sign a collective letter condemning that movement. Z sympathized with him.

At the beginning of 1958 Z set about translating Serbian epic poetry. The work went quickly and easily, and gave him obvious pleasure. He would laugh as he told how boldly the heroes of the epics fought and slew each other. The elemental nature of the Middle Ages, the historical distance, the interrelationship of the past and the present, all occupied his attention and gave him food for new ideas. Work on the epics, in all about five thousand lines, was completed that summer in Tarusa.

Just before his departure for the Oka, in other words before 29 June 1958, he concluded an agreement with a publishing house for his next large-scale translation project, which was to be a poetic version of the famous German epic, the *Nibelungenlied*. This work had been next on the author's mental list for some time. He wanted to get first-hand experience of the ancient folk sagas of Germany, to be in contact once again with the Middle Ages, where heroism was cheek by jowl with brutality, high ideals with treachery, hatred for the enemy with exalted courtly love. Now when he undertook large-scale translation work it was not the financial but the literary side of things that was important. What attracted him was the prospect of once more being able to apply his experience and his principles of poetic transposition to a foreign-language text. In addition the translation of a large and substantial piece of work enabled him to organize his time with precision, blending this work into a strictly ordered way of life, and this helped him to continue his long-established practice of self-discipline.

As usual, Z made very careful preparations for the execution of his project – he studied the text, the history of the country, previous translations, and thought out the principles on which he was going to operate. In his talks with all those who visited him that summer – Aliger, Libedinsky, Semynin, Slutsky and Stepanov – he was full of his plans for forthcoming work on the *Nibelungenlied*. When Margarita Aliger asked him whether he was not afraid that there would be unavoidable associations between the ancient warrior epics and the terrible years of Germany's recent past, he said:

> That's what will have to be resolved in the translation. It'll have to be overcome. It'll definitely have to be overcome. The great folk epic of Germany must not be given up to Nazism. That's the last thing we want.

The translation of the *Nibelungenlied* was never realized. Among the poet's papers there were found only fifteen or so pages of the original manuscript text, containing multiple variants of the same first stanza of the epic. The translator was searching for a key to the Russian equivalent of the German verse.

The preoccupation with the epic and its historical background is reflected in Z's own work. During the course of that summer the observation of provincial life and of surrounding nature became more and more linked to thoughts about time, and about the events of long ago. The historical perspective allowed the poet to see the surrounding world in a new light. In his Tarusa poems an ordinary village cockerel

333

became a kind of optical lens in which were concentrated infinite space and historical time. The cockerel was for the poet an 'astrologer', 'an ancient time-piece', a 'fiery prophet', 'extinct verses', the 'reason of the universe'; it caused him to remember the journeys of Magellan and Columbus, Tsar Peter the Great, the heroic St George, and the campaigns of the warrior-horsemen ('The Cocks are Crowing'). The oaks and birchwoods of the Moscow countryside blended together with the men of Peter's time, with the poet's youth, with memories of churches on the old country estates and the Pioneer bugles of the modern age ('Moscow Country Woods'). It was as though at this point Z's natural-philosophical concept received a new dimension – that of time. An overall view of the events of the past and the present allowed them to be brought together in a single system, thus giving the poet a sense of power over time.

The poet was drawn deep into past centuries. At one time he had begun to write a long poem called 'The Siege of Kozelsk', about the siege and capture of the town by the Tatars in 1238. The poem had remained unfinished and been destroyed by the author. Now Z turned once more to the broad panorama of those historical events, but on a completely different level: he wrote the remarkable cycle 'Rubruck in Mongolia'. The basis of this cycle (or narrative poem) is the journey of the French monk William of Rubruck (Rubrucius) at the time of Ghengis Khan to the country of the Mongols across the then still unexplored Siberian wastes. The work begins with the words: 'I can remember even now how, with a small team of servants, wandering in the northern wastes, William of Rubruck entered Mongolia.' These very first words bring us at once to the poet's own participation in those far-off adventures which befell the French monk. The whole, totally modern, intonation of the poem and its language confirm this impression of involvement. Naturally, in the creation of the work Z was guided not only by his meticulous study of William of Rubruck's papers but by his own memories of his enforced travels and life in the Far Eastern Region, in the Altay and in Kazakhstan. The poet's ability to feel himself simultaneously in two different historical epochs is the most remarkable feature of this cycle of poems.

In Z's last poems we find the culmination of his thinking about the mutual links between humanity's inner, spiritual world and the surrounding natural world. On his evening walks he looked closely at the piled-up banks of cloud, at isolated trees, at flowering meadows or the quickly flowing waters of the little River Taruska. He reproduced these observations and his thoughts on them in the poem 'At Sunset'. In this poem we find what is for Z a very unusual opposition of two worlds –

the inner mental and spiritual world of humanity and that of external nature, his domicile, so to speak. True, the opposition is not absolute: we, together with our inner world, are a product of the creation of nature. Nevertheless, man's soul is full of his own stories and wonders – of all those products of the activity of reason and spirit that are the stuff of the poet's creative work. The words about uncompleted work sound tragic, as though the poet, sensing the approach of death, is grieving for the irretrievable loss of those fruits of his mental work which have failed to find expression in verse. In the final quatrain a parallel is introduced that rounds off Z's natural-philosophical thought: man is to nature what thought is to the spirit. At a specific point in its development thought is, as it were, torn away from the poet's mental and spiritual essence ('as it grows faint in itself'). In the same way mankind at some point in its development is torn away from nature, and this situation is tragic, it is unstable, and seeks to resolve itself in the flowing together of mankind and nature, of thought and spiritual essence. The opposite can happen, and the unstable situation can lead to an explosion. Thus it was on a completely new level that the poet approached the tragic split between mankind and nature – that same problem, essentially, with which his creative work had started back in 1926.

It is not surprising that the common people, who are constantly in contact with nature, are characterized by a union of thought and spirit: 'There's mind and heart in them,/Freely speaking one tongue.' Living amid nature, human beings pick up its spiritual and moral impulses. These feed and nurture their souls, and through this process they seek a link with everyday existence. Such a link enables them to give reason to existence – human reason. This was apparently the way in which Z thought. It was for that reason that he cautioned in his last poem: 'Don't let the soul be idle!' For without a soul, without high moral attitudes and a firm ethical base, reason is not capable of fulfilling its exalted purpose, that of leading nature into a world of harmony.

Z felt so good in Tarusa, and his work was going so well, that he decided to buy a cottage and live there all year round. He soon found a wooden house in construction on Nekrasov Street. It was a quiet road, grass-grown and petering out into allotments and a wooded ravine. Z and the children had watched over the building carefully, taking care to see that none of the wood was infected with woodworm, discussing with the owner the price and the possibility of adding a covered porch. The building plan which they drew up still exists.

In his last year Z spent some time in the second-hand bookshops buying up year sets of *Russkaya Starina* (*Russian Antiquity*), the pre-revolutionary issues of which contained many historical memoirs and documents. His plan was to transport them to the house in Tarusa, and then to read them through carefully at his leisure. His notebook contains a list of all the years of publication of this old journal with the years for which he had complete sets marked in red. He already had nineteen of them when he announced with some pleasure: 'By the time I've read all this lot I shall really have a bit of education.'

During his time in Tarusa Z frequently rang Moscow, so that he could keep up to date with what was happening there, and he would spend two or three days there whenever necessary. The Hidases had a car with a driver which they generously allowed him to use on such occasions. Thus it was that Z was in Moscow at the end of August. He had brought with him the by now complete 'Rubruck in Mongolia', and read it to his son and Nikolay Chukovsky with special pleasure and satisfaction.

It was at about this time that his relations with Nikolay Chukovsky grew noticeably cooler. He did not share some of Nikolay's tastes in literature, nor did he like the latter's desire to obtain an official post in the Writers' Union. He had been particularly offended by one letter of Chukovsky's in which he was brutally sarcastic about Z's dearly-held beliefs concerning the metamorphosis of matter and the immortality of all that exists.

When they next met, Chukovsky asked whether Z had received his letter, and why he had not answered. Z fell silent, frowned and quickly left the room. Chukovsky still did not know what the matter was: he thought that Z was simply afraid of death and that all this philosophical structure was designed to be a protection against such a fear. In fact, nothing could be further from the truth: Z lived for poetry, and at the base of his poetry were his natural-philosophical beliefs, the most important component of which was his concept of the eternal nature of life. Death he did not fear, and on one of his last days he said calmly to Yekaterina: 'No people like myself have really died. Nature produces no one in vain, and won't allow its best creations just to disappear. It's not as simple as that. . .'

In the intervening period husband and wife had agreed to forget the difficult period in their life and to live together from then on. On 4 September 1958, when Z again arrived from Tarusa, Yekaterina was once more installed in Begovaya Street. Between 6 and 16 September she was in Tarusa, caring for their sick son, and hoping that her husband would come there too, but he was unable to do so.

On 11 September Z took part in a meeting with the Italian poets who had arrived in Moscow on a return visit. That day the well-known Italian poet Salvatore Quasimodo suffered a heart attack in his hotel, and Z and Margarita Aliger were asked to go and visit him to convey the best wishes of all the assembled Soviet and Italian writers. By the time the two poets reached the right floor of the Hotel Moskva, they were met by Quasimodo being carried out on a stretcher. The doctors had diagnosed a serious heart condition. This encounter with a man who was dangerously ill upset Z so much that he immediately felt a sharp pain around his own heart. He took no further part in the discussions with the Italians. His doctors recommended that he should stay in bed and have complete rest.

He lay at home on his couch, thinking and reading. At the end of September he wrote on his calendar three quotations from the letters of Van Gogh which seemed to reflect what he was turning over in his own mind:

> I maintain that a person's thought is healthier when it arises from a direct contact with things than when people look at things with the preconceived notion of finding this or that in them.
>
> You begin with fruitless musings, attempting to follow nature, and everything goes against the grain; but you end by calmly taking colours from your palette and nature agrees with you, and follows you.
>
> We (artists) are like old nags pulling cartloads of people who are enjoying the springtime.

On 30 September, when there was a temporary improvement in his health, Z went with his wife to the stationers to buy some paper. All his poems would have to be copied out to form a final corpus.

In the night of 2–3 October he began to feel worse. On 6 October Z wrote his literary testament, lying on the couch. He knew that he himself would no longer be able to copy out and rebind into a single volume his last, summary, complete collection of lyric poems and longer verse. At the top of the page he wrote 'Attention', underlined it, and put an exclamation mark. When he was no longer there, and his papers were being sorted out, this sheet would naturally be noticed at once. He was convinced that his wife, children and friends would carry out his wishes to the letter.

The whole family was together for the evening of 13 October. They watched *The Cranes are Flying* on the television – a daring and excellent film for those times. Z was lying on the couch. He felt good and was in a good mood. He asked his son to do some errand for him, and as he was going (he lived separately at the time), and was already standing with his coat on in the doorway, followed him with the long look of farewell of a dying man. He had once written:

> And if you know
> How people look at you the day they die,

> You will understand the look of
> The river. Already halfway
> The mortally blackened water
> Was twitching with scales of ice.
> (from 'Beginning of Winter', 1935)

The son did not know and did not understand, but Z knew himself that his last hours were beginning. When just he and Yekaterina remained alone he went on talking to her for a long time about what he would have liked to write. Yekaterina related afterwards:

He said that he needed two more years to write a trilogy of long poems, 'The Death of Socrates', 'The Adoration of the Magi' and 'Stalin'. The third subject astounded me. Z explained to me that Stalin was a complex figure, on the borderline between two epochs. It was hard for him to escape from the old system of ethics and morals and the old culture, because he had been brought up on them himself, he had been educated in a religious seminary, and this had left its mark on him. He had grown up in Georgia, where the rulers were hypocritical, deceitful and often bloodthirsty. Z said that it was easier for Khrushchov to deal with the old culture because it was not within him. Years would go past and so little would remain of the old aristocratic culture, in whose shadow we still lived, that it would be difficult to imagine it. 'It's as though', he said, 'all that was left of *our* life together was a pair of scissors and a piece of cloth.'

The long poems Z was envisaging would have been a cross-section of civilization at its most tragic turning-points. The language of the verse would undoubtedly have contained all that was best of the daring grotesquerie of *Columns* and of the classically clear and harmonious poems of the last years. 'Rubruck in Mongolia' had been a prelude to this grandiose project.

On the morning of 14 October 1958, Nikolay Alekseyevich Zabolotsky died of a second heart attack.

There remained lying on his desk a clean sheet of paper with the neatly written words:

1. Shepherds, animals, angels.
2.

The second point remained uncompleted. And it would be good to think that providence stopped his hand on the final peace-bearing word – 'angels'.

Now, when we look back on Z's difficult life, on his 'majestic constructions of thought' and his living human soul, we can hear his wise, courageous, and still living voice:

Testament

When the years tilt and my life drains away,
when I blow out the candle and set off
into the unmeasured universe of mist and metamorphosis,
when million on million generations
fill this whole world with miracles of light,
when they complete this half-constructed work that nature is,
let my ashes be in these waters,
let me be in this wood.

O friend, I will not die but be made known
to this world in the musk breath of flowers,
and many-centuried the oak will knot my soul alive
into its root, sadly and austerely;
I will be the mind's shelter in its leaves,
and in those big branches my own thoughts be cherished and live,
above you in the dark wood
a common consciousness.

And I shall be a slow bird through the sky
above your head, distant descendant,
the pale sheet-lightning bursting above you,
the pouring rain of summers glistening in grass.
There is no light as bright as existence.
The wordless grave is an empty languor.
I have lived out my life and not seen peace.
There is no peace.
My presence. Life's presence.

I was not born when I looked first
from the cradle to the world,
I thought first when the hard crystal sensed,
because the raindrop fell on it,
disintegrating rays of light.

I have not lived on earth without meaning,
and it is sweet to strive out of darkness
for you to hold me, distant descendant,
on the palm of your hand and to finish
what I did not finish.

(1947)   (tr. Robin Milner-Gulland and Peter Levi)

Appendix I: Lesyuchevsky's Denunciation (from NKVD Archives)

On N. Zabolotsky's Poetry

1. N. Zabolotsky emerged from the grouplet (*gruppka*) of the so-called *Oberiuty*, a reactionary little group, openly propagating lack of ideological content (*bezydeynost*) and meaninglessness in art, invariably transforming its performances into socio-political scandals. (The group included N. Zabolotsky, A. Vvedensky, K. Vaginov, D. Kharms etc.) The clowning and hooliganism of the *Oberiuty* on the stage had only one meaning – a reactionary protest against ideological content, simplicity and comprehensibility in art, and against the norms of public behaviour established in our country.

The *Oberiuty* declared Zabolotsky a 'great poet' who will be 'valued by posterity' and who will occupy in history the place of begetter of the new poetry.

2. In 1929 a small book of Zabolotsky's poems, *Columns*, appeared from the Writers' Publishing House in Leningrad. In this little book Zabolotsky gives a 'representation' of Soviet life and people distorted in a crooked mirror. This is a fearful, deformed way of life, these are disgusting, deformed people. Only Zabolotsky manages to see them like this. The attempt to put forward this 'representation' as satire of the old way of life has been a cheap deception. For Zabolotsky, as he himself asserted, was writing about 'the new way of life'. And with equal deformation, with equal mockery, he depicts Soviet officials, and 'little ladies', and a Red Army barracks, and Red Army soldiers, and our young people. Here, for instance is a 'characterization' of our youth:

> Then he feasts to satiety
> In the full swing of working life.
> Look! look! He has drunk some kvas,
> He touches girls with his hand,

340

And suddenly, stepping over the table,
Seats himself straight into the Komsomol.

Zabolotsky plays the fool and puts on poses, thus trying to cover up his true position. But this position is clear: it is that of someone hostile to the Soviet way of life, to Soviet people, hating them – that is, hating the Soviet order and actively struggling against it by means of poetry.

3. In 1929 (*Zvezda* no. 2) and 1933 (*Zvezda* nos. 2–3) there were published fragments from Zabolotsky's long poem 'The Triumph of Agriculture'. It is an undisguised, nakedly counter-revolutionary 'work'. It is a disgusting lampoon on Socialism and the development of collective farming. If one takes into account the fact that the first extract from 'The Triumph of Agriculture' was published in the year of the great breakthrough, the subjective, consciously counter-revolutionary position of its author and his actively hostile statement against Socialism at one of the most delicate of political moments will become clear.

There is basically no sense in copying out quotations from 'The Triumph of Agriculture', since the whole poem from first line to last is a dirty lampoon splattering forth the spittle of an enemy's hatred. All the same I shall quote two passages as examples.

Here is a 'picture' of the collectivized village, a 'picture' of the 'triumph of agriculture':

> Everywhere there are varied occupations:
> people sit in clumps,
> these ones sew great dresses,
> those ones puff smoke out of pipes.
> One old man, sitting in a ravine,
> explains philosophy to a dog;
> another, also tsar and god
> of the agricultural weaponry,
> has been pinching the cows' udders
> and thin legs.
> Then he quietly puts together
> the idea of precise threshing machines
> and explains it to the cows,
> joyous and ardent in his heart.

And here is the 'sum total', according to Zabolotsky, of the achievements of Socialism: 'in its byre the donkey sang of freedom,/having achieved full intelligence'. Only a sworn enemy of Socialism, who furiously loathes Soviet reality and the Soviet people, could write this slanderous, counter-revolutionary, rotten lampoon.

4. In subsequent years Zabolotsky declared his abandonment of his old positions and his 'reconstruction' (*perestroyka*). It cannot be doubted that this is merely the disguise of an enemy in concealment. Could one indeed imagine in 1937 the publication of such openly militant counter-revolutionary verse as 'The Triumph of Agriculture'? Now Zabolotsky writes 'different' poems. He even publishes odes in honour of the leaders. But how much indifference, artificiality, false 'fire' – that is, hypocrisy – is essentially to be found in these 'odes'! Meanwhile the fundamental thing for Zabolotsky in these years has been his 'pantheistic' verse, in which in the guise of a 'scientific experimenter' observing Nature, the author paints a full picture of the Soviet land:

> The animals have no names –
> who ordered them to name themselves?
> An equal measure of suffering
> Is their invisible lot.

It is not hard to decipher 'animals' as people involved in collectivism, the people of Socialism. Or there are the even more candid lines:

'All nature grinned,/like a tall prison'; 'On the abyss of torments sparkle our waters,/On the abyss of grief there rise our forests!' (From a poem published in *Literary Contemporary* in 1937, and subsequently appearing in a separate little volume from Leningrad State Publishing House.)

In 1937, with the full and active support of Gorelov, Zabolotsky attempted to publish the poem 'The Birds'. This is without doubt an allegorical work. It depicts (in grim physiological detail) a disgusting bloody feast of birds devouring an innocent dove.

Thus Zabolotsky's 'work' is an active counter-revolutionary struggle against the Soviet order, against the Soviet people, against Socialism.

(Signed) N. Lesyuchevsky, literary critic (Candidate of the Union of Soviet Writers), deputy editor of the journal *Zvezda* – 3 July 1938.

Appendix II: A Select Anthology of Zabolotsky's Poetry in Translation

In contrast to the verse quotations in the main text, which in general have been rendered 'prosaically' so as to give their literal sense (save for the free rendering of 'Testament' that concludes the biography), these are poetic versions by various hands that treat the forms and wording of the originals with a greater or lesser degree of creative freedom. Though they date from all periods of Zabolotsky's career, it will be understood that they provide only a small and not necessarily representative sample of his very diverse work. One of his longer poems ends the selection.

The Face of the Horse

Animals do not sleep. At night
They stand over the world like a stone wall.

The cow's retreating head
Rustles the straw with its smooth horns,
The rocky brow a wedge
Between age-old cheek bones,
And the mute eyes
Turning sluggishly.

There's more intelligence and beauty in the horse's face.
He hears the talk of leaves and stones.
Intent, he knows the animal's cry
And the nightingale's murmur in the copse.

And knowing all, to whom may he recount
His wonderful visions?
The night is hushed. In the dark sky
Constellations rise.
The horse stands like a knight keeping watch,
The wind plays in his light hair,

343

His eyes burn like two huge worlds,
And his mane lifts like the imperial purple.

And if a man should see
The horse's magical face,
He would tear out his own impotent tongue
And give it to the horse. For
This magical creature is surely worthy of it.

Then we should hear words.
Words large as apples. Thick
As honey or butter-milk.
Words which penetrate like flame
And, once within the soul, like fire in some hut,
Illuminate its wretched trappings,
Words which do not die
And which we celebrate in song.

But now the stable is empty,
The trees have dispersed,
Pinch-faced morning has swaddled the hills,
Unlocked the fields for work.
And the horse, caged within its shafts,
Dragging a covered wagon,
Gazes out of its meek eyes
Upon the enigmatic, stationary world.

(1926)   (tr. D. Weissbort)

The Sentry

On guard the night grows denser,
the sentry stands like a puppet,
his expressionless eyes reflect
the tetrahedral bayonet.
Before him, ponderous as icon-lamps,
the glorious regimental banners,
with their crumpled hammers and sickles,
hang suspended from the ceiling.
A mounted proletarian
larks thunderously in the moonlight;
the regimental cuckoo's howl
gloomily sinks behind the wall;
while a small white house appears,

with a square turret topping it,
and there's a maiden on the wall,
who plays on a transparent flute;
already cows have gathered to her,
with a pale smile upon their lips.
The guard is standing in the darkness
draped in his conical great-coat,
above him the red flame of the star
and the sacred sickle at the head of the bed.
Look! Mice are peeking through
cracks in the flagstones,
faces like triangles of chalk,
with sorrowful eyes on either side.
One of them sits at the window
with a floweret of music in its hand,
and the day extends its fingers through the grille,
but cannot reach the banners.
Straining, it sees the sentry,
standing like a puppet,
and the mounted proletarian
protecting him, straightening the lances.
Banners form his bed-head,
and the fixed bayonet is a call to battle . . .
And the day's well satisfied with him.

(February 1927)   (tr. D. Weissbort)

At the Market

Garlanded and strung with pots
the market opened wide its gates.

Here are women fat as barrels
in shawls of matchless beauty,
and cucumbers like giants
diligently tread the water.
Herrings flash like sabres,
their little eyes are meek,
but once split with the knife,
they coil up like snakes;
flesh, by the power of the axe,
lies like a red hole,
and a sausage like a gory entrail
floats in a crude brazier;

345

and after it a curly mongrel
points his lean muzzle in the air,
and his mouth hangs open like a door,
and his head is like a dish,
and his sure legs are busy,
bending slowly in the middle.
But what is this?
With a look of regret
he's stopped dead in his tracks,
and like grapes his tears
are flying through the air.

Cripples have lined up in a row,
one of them's playing the guitar,
bends back as far as he can go,
his stump comes to his aid
and on that stump his crutch,
like a flagon made of wood.

His embryonic hand another
brags about and flourishes.
He draws a finger through his mouth
and the finger squeals like a mole,
and the crossed bones crack
and his face contracts into a thimble.

The third one, twirling his moustache,
glares like a military hero.
His squinting tartar eyes
are neither troubled nor untroubled:
a thwart on wheels makes up his mount,
the stout helm's held between his teeth,
his arms are withering under ground,
his legs are slumbering in a stream.
All that this brave lad has left
is a belly and a head
and a big mouth to grip
the merry tiller with.

And there's a woman with eyes filmed over
sitting alone on a chair,
and a little book with magic holes
(sister of mercy to her fingers)
sings the praises of officials,
and the woman's fingers are swift . . .

She dreams of a dog.
And, by fate's hand
promptly supplied,
one stands before her, crushed
by his lovely sou!!
Around her, scales tip like Magellan's ships,
scraps of butter, fat of love,
freaks like graven images
with rich, calculating blood,
and the wail of the suppliant guitar
and headgear gleaming with copper
like tiaras . . . The moment's not far off
when, retired to their shaky den
together, he – drunk, crimson
with cold and singing and wine,
armless, obese – and she –
a blind hag – will sweetly dance
the lovely goat-trot,
till the rafters start to crack
and sparks spurt under heel.
And the lamp howls like a marmot.

(December 1927)   (tr. D. Weissbort)

At the Fishmonger's

And here, forgetting human wisdom,
We enter quite another kingdom . . .
A rosy sturgeon's corpse suspended
(Loveliest of all the sturgeons he)
Hangs from a hook, his fins extended,
Pierced through the tail – a sight to see!
Below him salmon smoke in butter
And eels, like links of sausage, sputter,
In smoking gravy twist and bend
And join each other end to end,
And midmost, like a yellowed bone,
Sits the smoked sturgeon on his throne.

O sumptuous ruler of the belly,
O God and master of my guts,

347

The secret leader of my spirit
And formulator of my thoughts, –
O give yourself to my desire,
And let my throat absorb your savour!
My lips are trembling – all on fire,
Like hottentots my innards quaver.
My guts are all inflamed with greed
And tortured by the juice of hunger,
Now seeming to contract at need,
Now like a dragon growing longer;
The spittle in my mouth tastes stronger,
My jaws are double-locked with wire –
O give yourself to my desire!

On each side jars of spices clatter,
While gang-fish bellow all around
And butcher knives, with blood bespattered,
Quiver and twist within the wound.
Here glows a small sub-aqueous garden,
Where, past a green translucent wall,
Bream swim in sad hallucination,
Oppressed by frenzy, filled with gall,
With doubt and – can it be, with panic?
Above, the hawker, death, prevails
And threatens with his spear titanic.

'Our Father,' read the brazen scales;
Two quiet weights, in saucer standing,
Define the road of life and death;
The portal creaks, the fish responding
With waving gills draw in their breath.

(1928)   (tr. Alec Merivale)

The Ivanovs

The trees stand clerically straight,
So close their branches almost poke
Into each house, nomads of late,
Now behind bars and under lock.
The boulevard's narrowness protests,
By houses hemmed in till it hurts.

But then all doors are opened wide
And the word is going round:

348

The Ivanov boys are off to work,
Rigged out in boots and pants.
The tramcar standing sleek and empty
Offers them its vacant seats;
Our heroes climb aboard and buy
Brittle pasteboard tickets, sit
Holding them out in front of them,
Unmoved by the quickness of the tram.

And where there are walls of stone,
Honking horns, the swish of wheels,
Bewitching sirens stand alone,
Adrift in clouds of orange hair.
Others dressed up like country gawks
Don't sit around at home and fidget.
Rattling castanets, they walk.
Where are they going? Who is it
They're bringing their blood red mouths to?
By whose beds will they kick off their shoes
And their blouse buttons undo?
Is there really nowhere to go?!

Oh world of mine, my leaden idol,
Let your vast waves pound the shore,
Bring them repose, these damsels,
Upended at the crossroads!
The stern world sleeps today,
In the houses peace and quiet hold sway.

And will they really find a place
For me beside a bride who waits,
Where chairs are set out in a row,
Where the cabinet, like Ararat,
Puts on a most important air,
Where a table stands foursquare
And a three-tiered samovar, iron clad,
Huffs like a household general?

Oh world, roll yourself into a city block,
Into a pitted stretch of road,
A single barn, besmirched with muck,
A solitary mouse hole,
But be prepared to take up arms:
Ivanov's wench is in his arms!

(1928)   (tr. D. Weissbort)

349

A Walk

Animals have no names –
Who said they should be given them?
Their unseen lot
Is uniform suffering.
The bull, conversing with nature,
Moves off into the meadow,
White horns planted
Over lovely eyes.
The stream like a plain girl
Lies gently amidst pastures,
Laughing, moaning,
Thrusting its limbs into the earth.
Why does it weep? Why is it sad?
For what reason does it ail?
The whole of nature smiles,
Like a looming prison.
Each little flower
Diminutively waves.
The bull sheds grey tears,
Stands in its splendour, scarcely stirring.
A weightless bird circles
In the deserted sky,
Its throat labouring
Over an ancient song.
Before its eyes the waters sparkle.
The great forest sways,
And the whole of nature laughs,
Dying with every instant of the day.

(1929)   (tr. D. Weissbort)

Dinner

We'll straighten out our weary bodies.
Beyond the window fades a splendid evening.
It is so pleasant to prepare our meal –
The bloodstained art of living!

Little potatoes skid around the pan,
Wagging their childish heads;
A purple slug of meat hangs down,
So heavy and so gluey,

The pallid water scarcely can ingest it –
It simmers slowly, turning gently pink,
While the meat lengthens out,
Nakedly sinking to the saucepan's bottom.
Out now run onion-heads,
Translucent skins asqueak,
Then suddenly divest them –
Shining in splendid nudity.
Here the fat carrot stirs about,
Falls on its dish in rings;
There hides the crafty celery
In delicate ringlet-curls,
A turnip with its well-smoothed breast,
Weightier than Atlas, sways.

Beyond the window fades a splendid evening,
But sunlight bathes the shining vegetables.
We'll gather them in placid hands,
Wash them in pallid water:
They will be warmed between our palms,
Then slowly go down to the bottom.
Our stumpy household dwarf, the primus-stove,
Will flare forth in a tinkling halo.

And this is death. If only we might see
Instead of city squares and walls
Into the tepid bowels of the earth,
Still heated with the languor of the spring;
If in the shining of their rays, we might
Discern the blessed infancy of plants –
We surely would descend upon our knees
Before the seething pan of vegetables.

(1929)   (tr. Robin Milner-Gulland)

The Battle of the Elephants

Warrior of the word, it is time
For your sword to sing out at night.

The horses of adjectives throw themselves
Upon the impotent figures of nouns,
Shaggy horsemen
Chase after the cavalry of verbs,
And shells of interjections

Tear overhead
Like signal rockets.

A battle of elephants! Clash of meanings!
The tower of Syntax plundered.
The Europe of consciousness
In the flames of revolt.
Ignoring the enemies' bullets
That scud like fragmented letters,
The warlike elephants of the subconscious
Make their stamping entry,
Like gigantic babes.

But now, having eaten nothing since birth,
They hurl themselves into the secret breaches
And, with human figures in their teeth,
Rear happily on their hind legs.
Elephants of the subconscious!
Warlike beasts of the nether world!
They stand saluting with merry thunder
Everything that they have plundered.

The elephants' little eyes
Brim with laughter and joy.
What a lot of playthings, pop-guns!
The bloodied cannons fall silent,
Syntax is not building the right houses,
The world stands in all its clumsy beauty.
The old code of the trees is cast aside,
The battle has shown them a new land.
They discuss, write pieces of prose,
The whole world is packed with clumsy meaning!
The wolf, who has fitted a human face
Over his own scarred head,
Digs out a flute, plays wordlessly thereon
The warlike elephants' first song.

Poetry, having lost the fight,
Stands in its tattered crown.
Mont Blancs of age-old towers have fallen,
Where figures gleamed like centaurs,
Where the sword of syllogism flashed and blazed,
Tried in the light of pure reason.
And to what end? It lost the battle
To the glory of other turns of phrase.

Poetry, in great distress,
Wrings its hands,

Curses the whole world,
Feels like cutting its throat,
Starts laughing crazily,
Then rushes into the field, and as suddenly
Lies down in the dust, beset with woes.
Indeed, how did it come to pass
That the ancient capital fell?

The whole world was used to poetry.
Everything was so comprehensible.
The cavalry stood drawn up,
Each gun was numbered,
While on the standards the word 'Mind'
Nodded to all like a kind god-parent.
And suddenly a few elephants –
And everything was overturned!
Poetry begins to get the idea,
Studying the new configurations,
It begins to understand the beauty of clumsiness,
The beauty of the elephant cast out by the nether world.

The battle is over. In the dust
Blossom the plants of the earth,
And the elephant, tamed by reason,
Eats pies and washes them down with tea.

(1933)   (tr. D. Weissbort)

Night Garden

Night garden, mysterious instrument,
Forest of long organ pipes, refuge of cellos!
Night garden, sad train
Of silent oaks and still firs!

All day long it roared and tossed.
Oak battled, poplar clashed.
Countless leaves like countless bodies
Wove endlessly the autumn air.

Iron August in jackboots
Stood at a distance with a platter of game.
Shots rang out over the meadows,
And birds' bodies flashed in the air.

353

The garden fell silent and the moon came out,
Below, dozens of long shadows lay down,
And the souls of lime trees raised clustered arms,
Voicing their indignation at the crime.

Night garden, oh poor night garden,
Presence fallen into a long sleep!
Mysterious Volga risen
Over the very head of the obscure stars!

(1936)   (tr. D. Weissbort)

In This Birch Grove

Oriole sing an empty song
in this birch grove
far from trouble,
where the pink stare of daybreak trembles
and the transparent avalanches
of leaves cascade from the high branches:
the song of my life.

Fly over us, spy glade out
take a too tiny to be seen
wooden flute
and visit my morning –
in the fresh hours of the morning –
and at my human door
sing matins virtuous and poor.

But still we are soldiers and men;
and an atomic explosion
flings up houses, a white whirlwind
on the boundary of mind
the war flaps its banners round
like a mad windmill in the wind.
Why are you silent my friend?
Hermit in the forest, O bird.

Flying through bombardment
where black rushes line the stream
and high over ravines
or death and his ruins

354

silently wandering
into battle my friend –
there is a fatal cloud
low and loud
over your head.

The sun will rise beyond the great rivers,
sunken-templed I shall drop with the killed
in the morning's dark moment.
Machine-guns cry out like the wild
raven, shake and grow quiet;
in my torn heart
your note will start.

Above the birch grove
above my birches
where rosy avalanches
of leaves drop from high branches
where the fragments of a flower
grow cold under the rainshower
century beyond century
will solemnize eternal victory.

(1946)   (tr. Peter Levi and Robin Milner-Gulland)

An Old Tale

In this world where our person plays an unclear role
you and I shall grow old like the old king in the tale;
our life is burning down, the glimmer of patience
in protected places; inevitable fate
encountered in silence.
One day ropes of silver will overshadow your temples and then
I will tear up these notebooks and abandon my poems;
let my soul be lapping as if it were a lake
at the underground gates, where purple foliage
clear of the surface shakes.

(1952)   (tr. Peter Levi and Robin Milner-Gulland)

Goodbye to Friends*

In broadbrimmed hats and long overcoats
    with whole notebooks full of your poems
long, long ago you crumbled to ashes,
    like leafless lilac branches.

In that country no shape is ready-made
    all is mingled, dislocated, broken,
    the only sky is the heap of the grave
    and the moon's orbit does not move.

And the noiseless insect assembly sings
    in another and indistinct language,
    and the man-beetle welcomes his friends
    with a small lantern in his hand.

    Is it peaceful for you, old comrades?
Are you easy? Do you forget everything?
    Now your brothers are ants and grasses
and roots and heaps of dust and sighs.

Your sisters are the pinks and lilac-nipples,
the chickens in the woodshavings, you cannot
remember the language of your brother,
who has no place yet in the country where

light you disappeared like shadows
in broadbrimmed hats and long overcoats
with whole notebooks full of your poems.

(1952)   (tr. Peter Levi and Robin Milner-Gulland)

From LAST LOVE

Thistle

They brought a bouquet of thistles
And set it on the table,
And at once there was ferment and fire
And a crimson roundelay of flames.
These bristling stars,
These splashes of a northern dawn,

---

* Probably written in memory of Kharms, Vvedensky and Oleynikov [Ed.].

Jingle and moan like bells,
Blazing like lamps from within.
Here too is an image of the universe,
An organism woven out of rays,
The raging of undecided battle,
The flashing of uplifted blades.
Here is a tower of fury and of glory,
Where lance is laid on lance,
Where bunches of bloody-headed flowers
Are graven on my heart.
I dreamt of a vast dungeon
And barred windows black as night,
Behind the bars the legendary bird
Whose plight no man can help.
But clearly I too am poor in spirit
For I have not the strength to help,
And the wall of thistles rises
Between me and my happiness.
And the thorn blade has pierced my breast,
And already the sad, lovely gaze
Of its undimmed eyes
Shines on me for the last time.

(1956)   (tr. D. Weissbort)

From LAST LOVE

Meeting

> *And the face, with its watchful eyes,*
> *smiled with difficulty, painfully, like*
> *a rusted door opening.*
> (L. Tolstoy, *War and Peace*.)

Like a rusted door opening,
With difficulty, painfully, forgetting what had happened,
My unexpected visitor now
Opened her face on seeing me.
And light poured forth – not just light, a living
Shaft of it – and not just that, a veritable flood
Of spring and happiness; and I, the eternal misanthrope,
Grew confused . . . And in our conversations,
In our smiles, our exclamations – and yet, no,

Not exactly in them, but somewhere, somewhere behind them –
There now shone an inextinguishable light
That took possession of my thoughts.
And we opened the window and looked out into the garden,
And innumerable moths senselessly cascaded
In a multicoloured stream
About the brilliant lampshade.
One of them settled on my shoulder,
Transparent, palpitating, pink.
I had no questions yet,
And, indeed, there was no need for questions.

(1957)   (tr. D. Weissbort)

In Much Wisdom Is Much Grief . . .

In much wisdom is much grief:
Thus said the writer of Ecclesiastes.
I am no sage, yet why do I
So often pity all the world and man?

Nature wants to live, and for that reason
Feeds countless seeds to the birds.
Yet of a million birds scarce one
Will ever soar towards the lightning and the spheres.

The universe is clamouring for beauty,
The seas are crying out, spattered with foam,
Yet on the hills of this earth, in the graveyards
Of the universe, only the chosen flowers shine.

Am I only myself? I am but a brief moment
Among other existences. Righteous God,
Why did you create the world both cruel and good
And give me intellect that I might understand it!

(1957)   (tr. D. Weissbort)

The Birds

If you would learn how the dove is made, how constructed –

                                                                            what veins

are within it, its wings how arranged, how its legs,
how its organs disposed and, marvellously suspended

form a threefold shape in the frame of its bones –
first you must seek out a board; then with a keen plane
smooth down the surface completely, rub it with oil,
put it to hang in the wind, so that into the pores of the wood
the oil should thoroughly soak and remove any roughness.
After that, pupil, your instruments must be made ready:
wax-bottomed bath, cup full of transparent water,
bag of sharp pins, whipcord, balance with weights;
wash your hands well and report to me when you are ready.

Birds, heaven's populace, hermits of air!
Singing passerines, thrushes, nightingales, linnets!
Put down your flutes, that's enough of your whistling and clicking.
Yes, and you come away from your organ-pipes, woodpecker.
You're an old organist, I know your tricks,
how with your bill you drum upon dry boughs:
the instrument throbs and vibrates, and the shattering notes
carry on wind through the whole of the neighbouring woodland.
Then, as I know, you select a bough somewhat longer;
a thinner sound is produced; a third thunders like a simandron.
O, wooden music of old untouched forests!
Creation's first converse, cradle of man's own speech.

Woodpecker, be you my witness, and you, musicians,
I've no quarrel with birds, nor am guilty of bloodshed,
unlike you, splendid birds, who can sweep through the air.
A hawk I'd gladly have been – but my hands are too feeble;
a falcon I'd gladly have been – but I cannot fly;
an eagle – but where the beak of an eagle should be
only my soft mouth stirs in a tousled beard.
Birds – open my eyes! Birds – tell me whence
you appeared? What riddle you carry within you?
How to decipher the time of the secretive cuckoo,
raven's alphabet, dove's arithmetic and heraldry?

Pupil, do as I say. Get your board ready.
Turn the dove onto its back with one hand. Its flight-feathers
must be pulled upwards, fastened with screws to the board,
so that the tips of wings reach up to the corners.
Then take two bits of cord, knot running loops in them,
put the loops over the feet and tie the ends to the free
lower corners – only make sure that the cord
is stretched as tight as can be, and the body is stable.

Here, then, before us it lies: a dove, a bird of the heavens,
haunter of steeples, inhabitant of wooden rafters;
having, at either side, wings of pure blue,

and a subtly-gleaming halo crowning its head.
Don't be afraid, but (plunging your hand in the vessel)
pluck off the feathers and down from its breast and its belly;
when you've done that, with your scalpel make an incision
right in the middle, where the long breastbone rises.
Splendid the keel of a ship, powerfully-sharp through the water,
strongly constructed by man to serve his own purpose!
How should we even begin to praise that marvel of lightness
the small breastbone of the dove, model for human endeavour?

All right lad, bring me your board. But what's going on?
You've gone pale, you've rushed to the window. Whose cries
do I hear in the wind? Louder and louder they grow.
Birds! birds flying this way! the sky is almost exploding,
cleft with hundreds of wings. The sun itself is eclipsed;
the roof's beginning to dance: the birds are on it – while others
are getting into the chimney. Yet others beat at the glass,
show me their bills, crush at the pane, clamber
onto each other, thrashing, calling, breaking the latch.
Birds! that's enough! Keep off I tell you! just wait!

Magpie, go to the devil! – you're always trying
to push to the front. Stop banging your beak for a moment!
Stop all that noise on the glass. You'll break it, and find
it hard to replace. Come on, bird, get out of the way,
no more playing the fool. You, long-billed herons,
you move away. That's better. Just take your hands off me, crow!
You'll get such a dusting-down you'll be cawing like crazy
for weeks. That's the window open at last.

Well then, come along quick! Here are your seats and your benches.
Smaller ones, warblers, jays, robin-redbreasts,
you sit in front, to see what's going on. Crows and woodpeckers,
owls, hawks, sit behind them. Capercailzie can sit
on the backs of the chairs. Bluetit, you on the candlestick;
chaffinch, you on the clock (but don't touch the hands!). We shall have to
move the screen forward a bit, or the cuckoo and nightingale
won't have a place to sit. Magpie, quiet with the lamp!
Glitter it may, but you won't drag it off to your nest.
Quiet now, everyone. Time to get on with our work.

Strange is the huddle of organs which we now glimpse:
pipes, branches, sacks; some reddish, while some
are deep blue, some translucent. Among them, most delicate membranes
are everywhere stretched. Search out, pupil, a piece
of glass tube, thrust it into the opening of the trachea,

carefully blow. You see how the transparent membranes
swell like balloons. Very well now, birds, tell me
how do you breathe when in flight? whence comes the air you inhale?
If you had no such air-bags within you, surely
would you not gasp for breath in the wind up aloft?

We must divide ourselves now into three smaller groups.
The woodpecker will be the first group's leader. The mocking-bird
will be the second's, the heron the third's. Look, woodpecker:
the pale-blue thing in this bag is the heart. Take some scissors
in your black claws, and snip through the bag. Now you see –
there is the heart! Mocking-bird, you must remove
the red liver, and after – the spleen. Now from the belly
the crop must be drawn out, with gullet, intestines and stomach,
and, when dissected and washed, in the wax-bottomed bath
be secured firmly with pins. Where's the long-billed heron?
You, heron, busy yourself with the brain. Go on – hold the head tighter;
Turn back the skin, and then take it off like a glove. Now look:
the bone has been bared. So it shouldn't get in the way,
it must be filed through. Easy enough. Well, begin.

So our work is now over. In front of us lie
the delicate bones, veins, organs and nerves of the dove
in a heap. Dissected with a sharp knife,
the dove is no longer a bird, and never again will it fly
onto the roof with its mate. Even were we to wish
once again to suspend organs from bones, and the veins
so to extend that the blood coursed along them again,
connect up the muscles as previously they were connected,
so that the body resumed its entire former shape – even then
the dove would not come back to life. Puny, man's hand:
that which once has been killed he cannot resurrect.

Could I assimilate this will of mine to the will
of Nature, my word to the visionary word,
could I envisage how all that I see – birds, animals, trees,
stones, rivers and lakes – were homogeneous limbs
of a single marvellous body, then, without doubt,
should I be the better creator, my reason not blunder –
striding the highroad of truth. Benighted my science;
yet even now something speaks of the mighty chain
of creation, where all metamorphoses are directed
to a single wise end: that old, worn-out forms
should be recast into vessels of more perfect aspect.

Sit down at table now, birds. We're going to have supper. Eat up
the remains of the dove, crows! what once cooed up above

can be put to good use. You, yellow-hammers and quails,
can peck at some meal – here you are. For the others
here's a trug full of worms and a bowl of caterpillars.
See how they wriggle? These ones with a furry back –
they're very tasty. As for those sausage-shaped ones,
threads are strung though them in various places. And these
put out long horns in front; while some describe a tall arc
standing quite firm on their heads and their tails.
Splendid creatures they are! Peck at them, chop them and rip them!

But for us, pupil, bring the fat meat of the cow:
boiled to perfection, and giving an excellent soup.
Cut me some bread, grate some onion onto the plate,
put out pepper, to warm my insides in an instant.
I nearly forgot! Would you look on the shelf by my mortar:
there's a grey bag, and in it should still be
an old bunch of garlic. There is? bring it out, lad.
That head for you, this for me . . . let's begin.

A quiet sunset hangs over the earth. Reddish patches
stretch from window to floor. Nature's mysterious rest
is near. Would you open the door, lad, and give me
my evening hat from the peg? Greetings, bright evening,
evening of life, my old age! Very soon shall I too
lie down and rest, and above my permanent bed
may clouds swim, and birds fly, and the planets
follow their course. Birds, the closer my hour draws
the more do I love you. Small sons of the Universe,
scraps, aerial fauna, fragments of animal life,
drawn into the sky – why do you keep such a troubled
gaze fixed upon me? No answer? Let's go outside
together and watch the sun go down to its rest.

Off with you, children. Beyond the great darkening forest
the bright sun has set. From over the rim of the world
its rays just reach to the clouds. The tops of the evening trees
stand against their red glow. Golden figures of clouds
undulate gently, and changing from shape to shape
slowly move through the sky. There's the head of a giant,
there – an aerial horse. Beyond it, three clouds fused together
take up the form of Laocoon. There by the forest
rides a cloud-horseman; the wind is removing
head from right arm, and bearing it off to the West.

Evening, I welcome you. Ponderous herons and woodpeckers
stride along next to me, full of importance. The quail,
warblers and yellow-hammers dart by in flocks, now descending,

now rising again, and in the air over my head
twitter gaily. The robin, abandoning the flock,
suddenly sits on my shoulder and leans his soft head
on my cheek. Funny fellow, what is it? Maybe
you've something to tell me? No? Look at the sky:
see how the clouds hurry past? You and I, lad,
are also perhaps two clouds, only one has a beard,
and one a light wing – growing into eternity, both.

Here's the end of our path. We have climbed a green hillock
and shall not go further. The narrow edge of the sun
can from here still be seen. Well, children, goodbye.
Time to sleep, time to sleep. Tomorrow a marvellous morning
will rise on the earth, and the sun, washed with dew,
will look into your nests, and, with a delicate ray,
open your clear eyes. And there one flock rises,
with a rustle of wings and a cry it departs for the forest,
saying farewell to me. Thereupon rises another
up from under my feet. Farewell! And a third
leaps from the earth, detaches itself into air. Further,
further the birds fly, and the sun's angled rays
inundate flock after flock, paint them rosy.

Only the robin-redbreast remains. Silly bird!
What have you lingered behind for? Hop into my hands!
Don't you see night is approaching? Humans too
are going to sleep – some on beds, some in haylofts.
Animals go to their lairs, cows slumber in stalls.
Past the houses walks Sleep, glances into the windows, keeps looking:
'Who's still awake? He'll be for it!' The watchman
bangs on his sounding-board. How about this? –
I'll stretch out my hand, you take off from my palm, and you'll quickly
catch up the flock. All right? Fly away! And he's flown.

Sleep walks past the houses. Earth, mother mine, I shall lie –
soon shall I too lie down in your depths. Then, as if to a child,
tell me this tale. Sleep walks past the houses . . . still walks,
looks: 'Who's still awake? I'll give him what for!'. . . Only these,
only these words are needed, not another word more.*

(1933)   (tr. Robin Milner-Gulland)

---

* For 1936 revision of final lines, see p.127.

Notes on Persons Mentioned in the Text

Brief notes on main persons mentioned in the text (excluding world-famous figures on whom comment would be superfluous, and minor figures explained in context).

AKHMATOVA Anna (1889–1966). One of the outstanding woman poets of twentieth-century Russia; a central figure in the 1910s–20s of the Acmeist movement (which supported precision and 'this-worldliness' in opposition to Symbolist vagueness).

ALIGER Margarita (1915–92). Poet, whose popular war poetry was unremarkable but whose subsequent lyric verse had a role in the literary 'Thaw'.

ANDRONIKOV Irakly (b. 1908). Literary figure (of Georgian origin); he worked with Z and colleagues in children's publishing in about 1930, when he played an ambiguous role (a partly hostile report on his colleagues survives in KGB archives): generally helpful towards Z in his later difficulties.

ANTOKOLSKY Pavel (1896–1978). Poet; best known for his rather 'classicizing' verse on historical themes.

AZHAYEV Vasily (1915–68). Prose writer, whose popular novel *Far from Moscow* derived from experiences as a convict in eastern Siberia.

BAKHTEREV Igor (b. 1908). The youngest and longest-lived of the *Oberiu* writers; he has written notable memoirs about them, but most of his own early work has been lost.

BALMONT Konstantin (1867–1942). Poet who was one of the early stars of Russian Symbolism; his melodious, sentimental poetry enjoyed great transient fame in its day. Lived in France from 1920.

BAZHAN Mykola (1904–83). Notable modernist Ukrainian poet, severely criticized in the 1930s.

BELY Andrey (1880–1934). Leading poet, novelist and theorist of the Symbolist movement, now most generally remembered for his phantasmagoric novel *Petersburg*.

BERDYAYEV Nikolay (1874–1948). Famous turn-of-the-century religious philosopher, forced into exile from the Soviet Union in the 1920s.

BERGGOLTS Olga (1910–75). Poet and journalist, who (after losing her husband, the poet Boris Kornilov, to Stalin's Terror in 1936) lived through the siege of Leningrad and gave notable voice to its sufferings and resistance.

BEZYMENSKY Aleksandr (1898–1973). Poet and literary activist on behalf of far-left 'proletarian' groups in the 1920s: his agitational poetry, once thought of as seriously rivalling Mayakovsky, is now little read.

BORATYNSKY (or Baratynsky) Yevgeny (1800–44). Philosophic poet: one of the brightest stars of the 'Pushkin Pleiad'. His knotty verbal textures and paradoxical thought-processes have always made him a writer for connoisseurs rather than to the general taste: Z valued him, with Tyutchev and Pushkin, higher than any other nineteenth-century poets.

BRAUN Nikolay (1902–75). Leningrad poet, friend of the young Z.

BRYUSOV Valery (1873–1924). Poet and important early proponent of the Russian Symbolist movement.

BULGAKOV Mikhail (1891–1940). Prose writer (originally a doctor): his *The Master and Margarita* is one of the thematically richest and most unusual novels of modern Russian literature.

CHAGALL (= Shagal) Mark (1887–1985). Leading twentieth-century painter, of Russian-Jewish origin. Chagall, in whose work Russian and Jewish motifs remained strong throughout his life, worked mostly in Paris from before the Revolution, but was an important figure in the arts (as head of the Vitebsk Art School) in the first years of the Soviet Union.

CHIKOVANI Simon (1902–66). Notable modern Georgian poet and colleague of Z, who translated his work.

CHUKOVSKY Korney (originally Korneychuk; 1882–1969). Critic, writer about and for children, memoirist and translator.

CHUKOVSKY Nikolay (1904–65). Prose writer; adoptive son of Korney Chukovsky and brother of Lidiya Chukovskaya (children's editor, subsequently 'dissident' activist); friend of Z, about whom he wrote a not wholly accurate memoir.

DESNITSKY Vasily (1878–1958). Old Bolshevik, pre-Revolutionary colleague of Gorky; subsequently literary scholar and teacher of Z.

DRUSKIN Yakov (1909–70). Philosopher, friend of Kharms and Vvedensky, whose manuscripts he was largely instrumental in saving for posterity.

ERENBURG (Ehrenburg) Ilya (1891–1967). Novelist, poet and journalist. A much-travelled figure of considerable culture, who managed both to be an able publicist for Stalin's USSR and to support disgraced writers and artists. The title of his novel *The Thaw* was taken over to apply to the post-Stalin period of cultural relaxation, in which his memoirs *People, Years, Life* were a notable landmark.

EYKHENBAUM Boris (1886–1959). Literary critic and teacher in Petersburg/Leningrad, particularly known for his work on Tolstoy: close to the Formalist group.

FADEYEV Aleksandr (1901–56). Novelist, head of the Writers' Union 1946–54: thus a figure of immense power when, after Z's return from exile, they met at Peredelkino and talked at length. Fadeyev was sufficiently impressed to allow Z to publish a slim book in 1948 and to re-establish himself as a writer in Moscow. After Khrushchov's denunciation of Stalin, Fadeyev shot himself.

FILONOV Pavel (1883–1941). Painter. The least-known (until recently) of the major artists of Russian modernism, Filonov was also a notable theoretician and teacher, renowned for his dedicated and ascetic life. His minutely fragmented pictorial textures were underpinned by an organic concept of 'Universal Flowering'. Z took informal lessons with Filonov, whose example and method (known as 'Analytic Art') affected him deeply.

GASTEV Aleksey (1882–1941). Probably the best of the 'proletarian' poets, visionary celebrator of labour; arrested in 1938.

GERASIMOV Mikhail (1889–1939). 'Proletarian' poet and old Bolshevik, whose verse exalts labour; arrested in 1937.

GINZBURG Lidiya (1902–1990). Notable literary theorist; colleague of Z and the *Oberiu* writers in children's literature.

GITOVICH Aleksandr (1909–66). Poet; friend and staunch public defender of Z.

GORKY Maksim (1868–1936). Prose writer who enjoyed international fame in the early twentieth century: he was probably best remembered for his early play *Lower Depths*, and for his role in the 1930s in establishing the direction official Soviet literature would take under 'Socialist Realism'. An old revolutionary, he was at first ambivalent towards Bolshevism and lived abroad 1921–31; subsequently however he was 'canonized' as a Soviet classic writer.

GROSSMAN Vasily (1905–64). Novelist: popular in the Second World War, his subsequent work deviated ever more strikingly from Soviet norms, and was unpublishable in the USSR. He was a neighbour and friend of the Zabolotskys in the 1950s, but his liaison with Yekaterina Vasilyevna caused her temporary breach with Z.

GUMILYOV Nikolay (1886–1921). Distinguished poet, leader of the post-Symbolist Acmeist movement, for a time husband of Anna

Akhmatova; shot for involvement in the anti-Bolshevik Tagantsev plot.

HERZEN (= Gertsen) Aleksandr (1812–70). Writer, publicist, memoirist; one of the most substantial liberal intellectuals of nineteenth-century Europe, who left Russia in 1847 and settled in England; author of classic memoirs *My Past and Thoughts*.

HIDAS (in Russian, Gidash) Antal (1899–1980). Hungarian poet who to escape Fascism lived in the USSR: neighbour and friend of Z in his last years; he returned to Hungary in 1959.

KAMENSKY Vasily (1884–1961). Poet; the oldest of the founders of literary Futurism, publishing from 1908; also well-known as a pioneer airman.

KANDINSKY Vasily (1866–1944). Painter, who worked in Munich (and subsequently in France) from the 1900s, but kept close links with Russia; pioneer of abstract art from about 1910; author of the influential book *On the Spiritual in Art*.

KAVERIN Venyamin (originally Zilber; 1902–89). Prose-writer; his most original novels, of the late 1920s, reflect the intellectual milieu that gave rise to *Oberiu*. Family friend of Z (whose daughter married Kaverin's son).

KAZAKEVICH Emmanuil (1913–62). Prose-writer and publicist, in both Yiddish and Russian; his most popular works deal with the Second World War.

KEDRIN Dmitry (1907–45). Poet, strong on themes of gratuitous suffering; little known in his lifetime (he was murdered in unclear circumstances).

KHARMS Daniil (pseudonym of Daniil Ivanovich Yuvachov; 1905–1942). Poet, story-writer, dramatist, writer for children; one of the most important figures in Z's creative biography. A figure of great originality, indeed eccentricity (in his life as in his work), he organized literary-theatrical events in Leningrad from the mid 1920s and was the moving spirit behind the *Oberiu* group, whose manifesto Z mostly drafted. After the collapse of *Oberiu* in 1930 Z and Kharms remained friends and colleagues till Z's arrest. Kharms too was later arrested and died in prison hospital in the siege of Leningrad. Almost unpublished in his lifetime, his stories and poems have lately become widely read and influential.

KHLEBNIKOV Velimir (previously Viktor; 1885–1922). Poet and visionary thinker. Regarded in his lifetime largely as an eccentric and naïve experimenter with language, he has come to be seen as the most truly original Russian Futurist (he preferred the Slavonic term *budetlyanin*) – a 'King of Time' who subjected not just poetry, but all human existence to startling reappraisal. He represents the major influence from the immediately preceding generation on Z and his close colleagues.

KHODASEVICH Vladislav (1886–1939). Poet, first close to Symbolism, then Acmeism; emigrated in 1922 and became an influential non-Soviet literary commentator. Hostile to Futuristic modernism, and hence a severe critic of the young Z.

KIRILLOV Vladimir (1890–1943). Revolutionary-minded 'proletarian' poet; arrested in 1937.

KIROV Sergey (1886–1934). Bolshevik political leader; native, like Z, of Urzhum near Vyatka (which was named after him until recently). A relatively popular figure, he was secretly mooted in the Party as a possible alternative leader to Stalin in the 1930s; Stalin probably instigated his assassination in Leningrad, where he was Party chief (Dec. 1934), setting the scene for subsequent trials and the 'Great Terror'.

KLYUYEV Nikolay (1887–1937). Senior so-called 'peasant poet', but also a modernist writer of considerable distinction, whose self-conscious peasant pose and mannerisms made him a flamboyant figure in 1920s Petrograd; hostile to all authority, he was arrested in the 1930s.

KONYONKOV Sergey (1874–1971). Sculptor, originally close to Symbolist and primitive aesthetics, later known as a portraitist; he lived in the USA from 1924 to 1945, thereafter in Moscow.

KORNILOV Boris (1907–38) Poet; former husband of Olga Berggolts (q.v.). A writer of considerable verve and reflective power, he fell victim like Z to a denunciation by Lesyuchevsky during the 'Terror'.

LESYUCHEVSKY Nikolay (1895–1978). Minor literary figure, assistant editor of journal *Zvezda*, writer of 'literary assessments' for the KGB and chief denouncer of Z.

LEVIN Doyvber (previously Boris; 1904–42). Experimental prose-writer who joined *Oberiu*; he was killed in the war and nearly all his work has been lost.

LIBEDINSKY Yury (1898–1959). Novelist: one of the earliest successful writers of the 'Proletarian' movement, and a stalwart of the Russian Association of Proletarian Writers (RAPP).

LIFSHITS Vladimir (1913–78). Poet and friend of Z.

LIKHACHOV Dmitry (b. 1906). Literary scholar, medievalist, cultural historian. Since *glasnost* he has belatedly become a major figure in many areas of Russian cultural life; when Z corresponded with him, and took his advice on points of translation of the *Igor Tale* (in the late 1940s) he was known as a specialist on the Old Russian chronicles and oral epics.

LIPAVSKY Leonid (pseudonym Savelyev; 1904–41). Children's writer, philosopher and friend of Z, Kharms and their colleagues, who met at his house for regular discussions in the early 1930s.

LIPKIN Semyon (b. 1911). Poet; a copious writer and translator, whose most interesting work dealt with political themes that rendered it unpublishable in the old USSR.

LIVSHITS Benedikt (1887–1938). Futurist poet and well-known memoirist; arrested shortly before Z, he was forced to sign a document incriminating him, then shot.

MAKSIMOV Dmitry (1905–87). Critic and acquaintance of Z; one of the first to write seriously about him (and so help to establish his reputation) after his return from prison-camp.

MALEVICH Kazimir (1878–1935). Restless and innovative pioneer of modernist painting in Russia, known above all for the 'hard-edged' abstractionism he developed in about 1915 and called Suprematism. He put forward his theories in many writings (notably *The Non-Objective World*) and was a leading figure in art education. In the Leningrad of the late 1920s he was close to the much younger Z and his colleagues, and considered joining their organization *Oberiu*.

MANDELSHTAM Osip (1891–1938). Leading Russian poet of the 'Silver Age', central figure of the post-Symbolist 'Acmeist' movement; much respected by Z. A poem against Stalin led to his arrest and exile; he died in prison. His widow Nadezhda wrote two notable volumes of memoirs in the 1960s–70s.

MANSUROV Pavel (1896–1984). Artist; leading member of *Ginkhuk* (Institute of Artistic Culture); left Russia in 1928.

MARSHAK Samuil (1887–1964). Poet and editor; he travelled to Great Britain before the Revolution, and is probably best known for translations of Robert Burns. As head of the Children's Literature section of the State Publishing House in the 1920s–30s he encouraged fantasy and originality, recruiting Z, Kharms, Vvedensky, Oleynikov and other young experimentally-minded writers to work as writers for children – their only reliable source of income. This policy came under official attack in the later 1930s.

MAYAKOVSKY Vladimir (1893–1930). One of the great innovatory poets of twentieth-century Europe – a revolutionary both in politics and literary practice; prime mover of the anti-Symbolist 'Futurist' movement in literature and art. In the 1920s he edited *LEF* and associated journals, retaining a commitment to experiment in the arts through personal and political vicissitudes until his suicide in 1930.

MEDVEDEV Pavel (1891–1938). Critic and theorist, collaborator with the cultural thinker Mikhail Bakhtin; he was arrested at about the same time as Z.

MEYERHOLD (= Meyerkhold) Vsevolod (1874–1940). The most important Russian theatrical director after Stanislavsky (from whom he broke free in the 1900s); close colleague of Mayakovsky and the Futurists, chief creator of the non-realistic innovative theatre of the early Soviet Union. In the late 1930s his theatre was suppressed and he died in prison.

MIRSKY Dmitry (1890–1939). Literary historian. An aristocrat, he emigrated after the Revolution and became the leading specialist in Russian literature at London University; in 1932 he took up Soviet citizenship, and on his return played a polemic role on the 'far left' of literary life until his arrest.

NADSON Semyon (1862–87). Poet, whose short (consumptive) life and extremely melancholy, mellifluous verse made him something of a romantic legend; a poet at the opposite extreme from Z, on whom he none the less seems to have exercised a certain fascination.

OLEYNIKOV Nikolay (1898–1937). Children's writer and parodistic poet. Of Cossack origin, he came to Leningrad with his friend Yevgeny Shvarts (q.v.) and became a colleague of Z and others in children's literature; he remained a close friend of Z and Kharms till his arrest, and often makes appearances in their poetry. A small number of poems from the early 1930s are among the funniest and most creative of Russian parodies. A bold and unconventional figure (and old Party member) he was arrested and shot early in the purges.

ORBELIANI Grigol (1800–1883). Georgian Romantic poet and political figure, translated by Z.

PASTERNAK Boris (1890–1960). Poet and novelist: one of the best-known Russian writers of the twentieth century, whose literary progress – from demanding modernism to an individual poetic 'classicism' – parallels that of Z. They lived near each other at Peredelkino after Z's return from exile in the later 1940s: their friendship, and the growing admiration of each for the other's work, is a significant chapter of Russian literary history little explored by scholars to date.

PAUSTOVSKY Konstantin (1892–1968). Story-writer and memoirist, whose multi-volume *Tale of My Life* was a notable contribution to 'Thaw' literature.

PIROSMANISHVILI (or Pirosmani) Niko (1848–1918). Georgian artist. A self-taught signwriter and 'primitive' painter, he was taken up by Russian and Georgian modernists in much the same way as 'Douanier' Rousseau in France.

POGODIN Nikolay (1900–62). Writer of popular Soviet plays dealing with the problems of the individual.

PROKOFYEV Aleksandr (1900–71). Well-known 'official' Soviet poet.

PSHAVELA, see VAZHA PSHAVELA

PUGACHOV Yemilian (d. 1775). Cossack leader of the greatest peasant uprising of imperial Russia; he gave himself out to be the late Tsar Peter III.

RAZIN Stepan (popularly, Stenka) (d. 1671). Cossack freebooter who led a great rebellion centred on the lower Volga against the Tsar's government; after his execution, he became a figure of legend and folklore.

ROKOTOV Fyodor (1735–1808). One of the finest eighteenth-century Russian portrait painters, whose undemonstrative but subtle work was almost forgotten till the early twentieth century.

RUSTAVELI Shota (lived *c.* 1200). Writer of the great Georgian epic romance *The Knight in the Panther Skin*.

SELVINSKY Ilya (1899–1968). Poet and adventurer; an experimental modernist in the 1920s, he was the leading literary 'Constructivist', aiming to use the verbal materials of everyday life as poetry. He later wrote more conventionally.

SEVERYANIN Igor (pseudonym of I. Lotaryov; 1887–1941). Poet who founded his own brand of modernism, 'Ego-Futurism', in 1911: his achievement, striking but shallow, never matched his considerable skills as a self-publicist.

SHCHERBA Lev (1880–1944). Linguist and lexicographer.

SHERSHENEVICH Vadim (1893–1942). Poet, first associated with Futurism (founded a Futurist group 'Mezzanine of Poetry'), and from 1919 with Imaginism, which he helped to create; a committed experimentalist, he saw true poetry as a continuous chain of fresh images.

SHKLOVSKY Viktor (1893–1984). Literary theorist, writer of novels and film-scripts; the most dazzling and accessible proponent of the Formalist critical method.

SHVARTS Yevgeny (1896–1958). Dramatist, whom Z met when both worked in children's literature: his most notable plays are satires in fairy-tale guise, and he had much difficulty getting his works on to the Soviet stage. Shvarts and his family looked after the Zabolotsky family after Z's arrest, and his diaries give interesting biographical testimony. Not to be confused with the radio announcer Anton Shvarts (mentioned in Chapter 3).

SKOVORODA Grigory (1722–94). Philosopher and religious poet, who gave up an academic career to become an itinerant teacher in the Ukraine, preaching the virtues of the simple life and of meditation. His philosophical dialogues were imitated by Z.

SLUTSKY Boris (1919–86). One of the most distinctive modern Russian poets: laconic and prosaic in manner, criticizing Stalin's regime in a cycle first published anonymously. He knew Z well in his last years and wrote a memoir of their visit to Italy.

SOLOGUB Fyodor (1863–1927). Symbolist writer, considered to belong to the 'Decadent' tendency in the movement, best known for his satirical novel *The Petty Demon*.

STEPANOV Nikolay (1902–72). Literary critic and scholar, who introduced himself to the *Oberiu* writers in the late 1920s and remained a lifelong friend of Z. His major achievement was the edition of Khlebnikov's difficult manuscript legacy (1928–33); thereafter he generally 'played safe' from the point of view of literary officialdom.

SURKOV Aleksey (1899–1983). Poet and literary official; simultaneously a voice of Soviet propaganda and an appreciator of good poetry (he edited Akhmatova).

TABIDZE Titsian (1895–1937). Notable modernist Georgian poet, shot in the Stalin Terror.

TARKOVSKY Arseny (1907–89). Poet, whose style and philosophic concerns are close to, and maybe influenced by, those of Z; father of film-maker Andrey Tarkovsky.

TAGER Yelena (1895–1964). Writer; arrested shortly before Z (whom she scarcely knew), she was, like Livshits, forced to denounce him: she survived the camps and withdrew her testimony.

TARASENKOV Anatoly (1909–56). Literary critic, subsequently editor, well-known as a poetry book-collector and bibliographer; he attacked Z damagingly in the 1930s, and played a more congenial role in his life later.

TATLIN Vladimir (1885–1953). Artist and designer; close colleague of Khlebnikov, rival of Malevich. Known chiefly for his 'culture of materials', first developed in abstract sculptural reliefs from 1914 on, then for his project for the 'Monument to the Third International', intended as a giant (400-metre) skew spiral of glass and steel. He put on an influential dramatic performance of Khlebnikov's 'supertale' *Zangezi* (1923).

TERENTYEV Igor (1892–1937). Minor Futurist poet who became a notable modernistic theatre producer in the 1920s: his notorious production of Gogol's *Inspector General* was designed by members of the School of Filonov.

TIKHONOV Nikolay (1896–1979). Writer; he made his name with a small number of finely crafted short poems from the period of the Civil War (1918–21). His subsequent poems and short stories are largely concerned with Central Asia, though some reflect the Finnish campaign and the siege of Leningrad. An early enthusiast for Z's poetry, he played an important and ambiguous role in his life, as chapter 4 of this biography recounts. From the late 1930s he found favour with the Soviet authorities and rose to be Secretary of the Writer's Union in the mid 1940s when Z returned from exile. His wife Mariya played a significant and positive role in Z's fate.

TOLSTOY Aleksey Konstantinovich (1817–75; not to be confused with Aleksey Nikolayevich, the Soviet novelist). One of the most remarkable nineteenth-century Russian poets, if only for his versatility; he wrote romantic lyrics, historical pastiche, and some of the best Russian humorous verse, part of it in the quasi-serious person of 'Kozma Prutkov'. A forerunner of Z and his colleagues in their more parodistic vein.

TOMASHEVSKY Boris (1890–1957). Scholar, editor and teacher of literature in Leningrad, whose principles were close to those of the Formalists. Family friend of the Zabolotskys.

TSIOLKOVSKY Konstantin (1857–1935). Scientist and thinker; generally credited with being the father of Russian rocket technology. Lived ascetically in Kaluga and published a stream of booklets about the future of humanity and of the cosmos during the 1920s–30s; Z corresponded with him.

TSVETAYEVA Marina (1892–1941). One of the most dynamic, original and unclassifiable of twentieth-century poets. Strongly anti-Bolshevik, she lived in exile 1922–39, but returned to Soviet Russia, where she committed suicide after losing most of her family and being evacuated to a remote provincial town.

TUFANOV Aleksandr (1877–?1941). Futurist poet who propagated *zaum* ('transrationality') in the mid 1920s, and influenced the creative development of Vvedensky, Kharms and the *Oberiu* group generally.

TVARDOVSKY Aleksandr (1910–71). Poet, and editor of the liberal Soviet journal *Novy Mir*; he visited Italy with Z and others in 1957.

TYNYANOV Yury (1894–1943). Novelist, teacher and literary theorist; one of the most original of the Formalist scholars.

TYUTCHEV Fyodor (1803–73). Poet, whose work constitutes an essential link between Russian (and European) Romanticism and the Symbolism of the end of the century; a handful of philosophical lyrics (contrasting chaos and cosmos) are among the most original and 'modern' works of the nineteenth century. His 'Last Love' provided the title for Z's cycle of the 1950s; Z admired him greatly.

VAGINOV Konstantin (1899–1934). Poet and novelist. An adherent of Acmeism in the early 1920s, he became progressively more experimental and original; he joined *Oberiu* (as its oldest member) and wrote three remarkable, rather surrealistic novels, the movement's most substantial achievement in prose.

VASILYEV Pavel (1910–37). Poet: precociously brilliant, energetic and indisciplined, he was a youthful victim of the Terror.

VAZHA PSHAVELA (pseudonym of Luka Razikashvili, lit. 'Man of Pshava', 1861–1915), notable Georgian poet.

VERNADSKY Vladimir (1863–1945). Notable natural scientist, active in several fields, particularly biochemistry and geology.

VINOGRADOV Viktor (1895–1969). Leading modern Russian historian of language and teacher.

VOLOSHIN Maksmilian (1877–1932). Russian Symbolist poet whose best-known work evokes and deplores the brutality of the post-Revolution period; from 1917 he lived in the Crimea where he became a much-visited (if little-published) literary celebrity.

VVEDENSKY Aleksandr (1904–41). Poet and dramatist; like his friend Kharms he remained almost unpublished on an 'adult' level till long after his death – he earned his living through children's literature. His remarkable poetry, taking off from Futurism, develops transcendental themes in a manner that often seems absurdist and deeply obscure though impressive. Temperamental differences between him and Z – founder members of *Oberiu* – soon became apparent, though even in the 1930s when they were no longer in contact their poetic interests to some extent developed in parallel. He was shot in unclear circumstances at the beginning of the war. He and Kharms inspired Z's poem 'Goodbye to Friends' (1952).

YESENIN Sergey (1895–1925). One of the best-loved Russian poets of the twentieth century; first lionized as a 'peasant poet', he joined the modernist Imaginist group in 1919. He married the dancer Isadora Duncan in 1923; his disorderly and alcoholic life ended in suicide.

YEVTUSHENKO Yevgeny (b. 1933). Poet and public figure: acquainted with Z as a young (but already well-known) writer in the 1950s.

YUDINA Mariya (1899–1970). Pianist, who lived a bold and eccentric life; friend of Kharms, Z and their colleagues.

ZHIRMUNSKY Viktor (1881–1971). Literary scholar and notable teacher in Petersburg/Leningrad; probably the most traditionally minded of the Formalist group.

ZHUKOVSKY Vasily (1783–1852). Finest Russian poet of early Romanticism, who made classic translations of Western European poets.

ZOSHCHENKO Mikhail (1895–1958). Writer of hugely popular short stories (generally satirical or humorous) and a serious work of psychological autobiography, *Before Sunrise*: he was attacked, with Akhmatova, by Stalin's henchman Zhdanov in 1946. Admirer and defender of Z's poetry.

Author's Bibliography

Azadovsky K. M., *Nikolay Klyuyev: put' poeta* (Leningrad 1990)

Bakhterev I. and Razumovsky A., 'O Nikolaye Oleynikove', in *Den' poezii* (Leningrad 1964)

'Donos. Obrazets literaturnykh iskaniy neizvestnogo sovetskogo kritika N. Lesyuchevskogo', ed. Ye. Lunin, *Nevsky prospekt*, 1:2 (1990)

'Donos. K istorii dvykh dokumentov minuvshey epokhi', ed. S. Lesnevsky, *Literaturnaya Rossiya*, 10 March 1989

Druskin Ya., 'Chinari', Lipavsky L. 'Iz razgovorov chinarey', ed. L. Druskina, *Avrora*, 6(1989)

D'yakonov L., 'Vyatskiye gody Nikolaya Zabolotskogo', *Kirovskaya pravda*, 8 May 1978

Filippov B., 'Put' poeta', in *Nikolay Zabolotsky: stikhotvoreniya* (New York, 1965)

Filippov G. V., 'Filosofsko-esteticheskiye iskaniya N. Zabolotskogo', in *Russkaya sovetskaya filosofskaya poeziya* (Leningrad 1984)

Ginzburg L. Ya., 'Vybor temy', *Neva*, 12(1988)

Gor G., 'Zamedleniye vremeni', *Zvezda*, 4(1968)

Grushinsky K. and Filippov G., 'Tak oni nachinali . . . O studen-cheskom zhurnale *Mysl'*, o N. Braune i N. Zabolotskom', *Zvezda*, 11(1978)

Gruzdev I., 'Pismo A. M. Gor'komu ot 2 iyunya 1929 g.', in *Arkhiv A.M. Gor'kogo*, vol. II (Moscow 1966)

'Iz istorii russkogo avangarda (P. N. Filonov)', ed. Ye. Kovtun, in *Yezhegodnik rukopisnogo otdela Pushkinskogo doma 1977* (Leningrad 1979)

Kaverin V. A., *Epilog: memuary* (Moscow 1989)

Kharms D., *Polyot v nebesa*, ed. A. Aleksandrov (Leningrad 1988)

Khodasevich V. F., 'Nekropol'', in *Serebryanniy vek* (Moscow 1980); ibid., 'Dom iskusstv', *Ogonyok*, 13(1989)

Kovtun Ye. F., 'Ochevidets nezrimego i dr.', in *Pavel Nikolayevich Filonov: Katolog vystavki* (Leningrad 1988)

Krasovsky Yu. A., Introd. to 'Bol'shoy chelovek' (article by Paustovsky on Gorky), in *Vstrechi s proshlym* 1 (Moscow 1983)

Levin I., 'The Fifth Meaning of the Motor-Car: Malevich and the Oberiuty', *Soviet Union*, 5:2(1978)

Likhachov D. S., 'Chem "nesamostoyatel'neye" lyubaya kul'tura, tem ona samostoyatel'neye', *Vosprosy literatury*, 12(1986)

Lunin Ye., 'Velikaya dusha', *Leningradskaya panorama*, 5(1989); ibid., 'Ne dayte pogibnut' poetu', *Leningradskaya panorama*, 8(1989)

Makedonov A. V., *Nikolay Zabolotsky* (Leningrad 1987)

Maslenikova Z. A., *Portret Borisa Pasternaka* (Moscow 1990)

Pavlovsky A. I., 'Iz perepiski N. A. Zabolotskogo c Tsiolkovskim', *Russkaya literatura*, 3(1964)

Ibid., 'Poeticheskaya "naturfilosofiya" Nikolaya Zabolotskogo', in *Sovetskaya filosofskaya poeziya* (Leningrad 1984)

Popov Ya., 'Nikolay Zabolotsky v Karagande', in *Prostor*, 4(1984)

'Rabota N. Zabolotskogo nad perevodom "Slova o polku Igoreve"', ed. D. Likhachov and N. Stepanov, in *Voprosy literatury*, 1(1969)

Roskina N. A., *Chetyre glavy* (Paris, 1980)

Rostovtseva I. I., *Nikolay Zabolotsky* (Moscow 1984)

Russkiye sovetskiye pisateli. Poety. Bibliog. ukazatel', vol. 9 (Moscow 1986)

Saakyants A. A., *Marina Tsvetayeva* (Moscow 1986)

Sandler A. S., *Uzelki na pamyat': Zapiski reabilitirovannogo* (Magadan, 1988)

Shvarts Ye. L., 'Prevratnosti kharaktera', ed. K. N. Kirilenko, *Voprosy literatury*, 2(1987)

Slutsky B. A., 'O drugikh i o sebe', ed. Yu. Boldyrev, *Voprosy literatury*, 10(1989)

Turkov A. M., *Nikolay Zabolotsky* (Moscow 1981)

Vasin K., 'Zhar-ptitsa', in Vasin K., *Kuznets pesen* (Yoshkar-Ola 1976)

Vasin K., *Na zemle Onara* (Yoshkar-Ola 1983)

Vospominaniya o N. Zabolotskom (Moscow 1977; 2nd edn., 1984)

Zabolotsky N. A., 'Pis'ma k S. I. Chikovani', in *Druzhba* (Tbilisi 1979)

Ibid., *Sobraniye sochineniy v 3-kh tomakh* (Moscow 1983–4)

Ibid., *Veshnikh dney laboratoriya* (Moscow 1987)

Ibid., 'Istoriya moyego zaklyucheniya', *Chistye prudy*, 2(1988)

Ibid., 'Pis'ma 1938-49 godov', *Znamya*, 1(1989)

Ibid., 'Ya nashol sebe silu ostat'sya v zhivykh', ed. Ye. Lunin, *Avrora*, 8(1990)

The author has also made use of unpublished materials from the TsGALI archive, from the Manuscript Section of Pushkin House (IRLI), from the Zabolotsky family archive, as well as verbal information and suggestions from Yekaterina Vasilyevna Zabolotskaya and others who knew Zabolotsky. To all who helped in the preparation of this book the author expresses his profound gratitude.

N.Z.

There are of course many Russian-language editions of Zabolotsky's works: the fullest is *Sobraniye sochineniy* (3 vols., 1983–4) [Ed.].

Bibliography of Material in English
(Compiled by the Editor)

The chief English-language critical studies and translations of Zabolotsky's work [with annotations in square brackets]:

F. Björling, *'Stolbcy' by Nikolai Zabolotsky. Analyses* (Stockholm 1973) [A detailed analysis of 3 early poems]

Ibid., *'Ofort* by Nikolaj Zabolockij. The Poem and the Title', *Scando-Slavica*, 23(1975)

G. Gibian, *Russia's Lost Literature of the Absurd* (Ithaca and London 1971) [Contains translation of *Oberiu* declaration, largely composed by Z]

J. Glad and D. Weissbort (eds.), *Russian Poetry: The Modern Period* (Iowa 1978) [11 poems in translation]

D. Goldstein, *Nikolai Zabolotsky: Play for Mortal Stakes* (Cambridge 1993) [A book-length study, centred on Z's long poems of the early 1930s]

S. Karlinsky, 'Surrealism in twentieth-century Russian poetry: Churilin, Zabolotskii, Poplavsky', *Slavic Review*, 26(1967).

V. Markov and M. Sparks (eds.), *Modern Russian Poetry* (London 1962) [5 poems with translations]

I. Masing-Delic, 'Some themes and motifs in N. Zabolockij's *Stolbcy*', *Scando-Slavica*, 20(1974)

Ibid., 'Zabolockij's occult poem "Carica Much"', *Svantevit. Dansk Tidesskrift for Slavistik*, 3:2(1977)

Ibid., 'Zabolotsky's "The Triumph of Agriculture": Satire or Utopia?', *Russian Review*, 42(1983)

Ibid., '"The Chickens also Want to Live": a motif in Zabolockij's *Columns*', *Slavic and East European Journal*, 31:3(1987).

R. Milner-Gulland, 'Two Russian rediscoveries', *Times Literary Supplement*, 11 May 1967 [review article on Z and Mandelshtam]

Ibid., 'Left Art in Leningrad: the *Oberiu* Declaration', *Oxford Slavonic Papers* (1970).

Ibid., 'Zabolotsky and the Birds' [article], with 'The Birds' [translation of long poem], *London Magazine*, 10:12(1971).

Ibid., 'Zabolotsky: philosopher-poet', *Soviet Studies*, April 1971 [on Z's 'world of ideas']

Ibid., 'The Birds', and (with P. Levi) 7 shorter poems by Z [of 1940s–50s] translated in *Russian Literature Triquarterly*, 8(1974)

Ibid., 'Zabolotsky and the reader: problems of approach', *Russian Literature Triquarterly*, 8(1974).

Ibid., with M. Dewhirst (eds.), *Russian Writing Today* (Harmondsworth, 1976) [translations of poems of 1940s–50s]

Ibid., 'Grandsons of Kozma Prutkov', in R. Freeborn, C. Wood and R. Milner-Gulland (eds.), *Russian and Slavic Literatures* (Slavica, Indiana, 1976) [on Z, Oleynikov and the parodistic tradition]

Ibid., 'Zabolotsky's *Vremya*', *Essays in Poetics*, 6:1(1981) [analysis of a key poem of the 1930s]

D. Obolensky (ed.), *Penguin Book of Russian Verse* (Harmondsworth 1962), republished as *Heritage of Russian Verse* [four poems in Russian with English prose translations]

S. Pratt, 'Antithesis and completion: Zabolockij responds to Tiutcev', *Slavic and East European Journal*, 27:2(1983).

A. Rannit, 'Zabolotskii – a visionary at the crossroads of Expressionism and Classicism', in G. Struve and B. Filippov (eds.), *Nikolay Zabolotsky: Stikhotvoreniya* (New York 1965) [the first of three introductions to a Russian-language edition of the poems]

V. Sandomirsky, 'N. A. Zabolockij 1903–1958', *Russian Review* (1960) [the first article on Z in English, with two poems]

D. Weissbort (ed.), *Post-War Russian Poetry* (Harmondsworth 1974) [11 poems in translation]

N. A. Zabolotsky, *Scrolls*, tr. and ed. D. Weissbort (Cape edns., London

1971) [the only volume of Z's poetry in English – 20 poems, mostly of the 1920s–30s]

N. Zabolotsky, 'The story of my imprisonment', tr. and ed. R. Milner-Gulland, *Times Literary Supplement*, 9 October 1981 [Z's account of his arrest]